THE TUNISIAN CAMPAIGN

This book is dedicated to the combined forces of the Allied countries – United Kingdom, United States of America, Canada, France, Australia, South Africa, New Zealand, Netherlands, Poland, India, Countries of the British Commonwealth – which were formed during the Second World War, and the men and women who sacrificed so much and fought so bravely and valiantly to remove the constant threat of the Axis Force of Germany and Italy during the battles for North Africa, Sicily, Crete, Greece, the Balkan States and Italy.

This book concentrates on the Tunisian campaign from 8–16 November 1942 to 13 May 1943, the precursor to the battles yet to be fought in Sicily under Operation Husky, and in Italy under Operation Avalanche.

My heartfelt gratitude to you all that were called to serve and fight against the aggressors, and my deepest condolences to the families who lost their loved ones, who gave of their tomorrow so that we could have our todays. May the Grace of God see you all sat at His right hand in Heaven.

Philip Lamb, Author

THE TUNISIAN CAMPAIGN

NORTH AFRICA 1942–1943

PHILIP LAMB

Pen & Sword
MILITARY
AN IMPRINT OF PEN & SWORD BOOKS LTD.
YORKSHIRE – PHILADELPHIA

First published in Great Britain in 2026 by
PEN AND SWORD MILITARY
An imprint of
Pen & Sword Books Limited
Yorkshire – Philadelphia

Print ISBN 978 1 03619 723 0
ePUB ISBN 978 1 03619 725 4
ePDF ISBN 978 1 03619 726 1

A CIP catalogue record for this book is available from the British Library.

Front & Back Cover Original Artwork Design by Jim Erskine Art
*Front & Back Cover Final Artwork by Mark Lamb
[*Refer to the accreditations on pages 283, 284 & 285]

Typeset in Times New Roman 10/12 by
SJmagic DESIGN SERVICES, India.
Printed in the UK by CPI Group (UK) Ltd, Croydon, CR0 4YY.

The Publisher's authorised representative in the EU for product safety is
Authorised Rep Compliance Ltd., Ground Floor, 71 Lower Baggot Street,
Dublin D02 P593, Ireland.
www.arccompliance.com

For a complete list of Pen & Sword titles please contact
PEN & SWORD BOOKS LIMITED
George House, Units 12 & 13, Beevor Street, Off Pontefract Road,
Barnsley, South Yorkshire, S71 1HN, England
E-mail: enquiries@pen-and-sword.co.uk
Website: www.pen-and-sword.co.uk

or

PEN AND SWORD BOOKS
1950 Lawrence Rd, Havertown, PA 19083, USA
E-mail: uspen-and-sword@casematepublishers.com
Website: www.penandswordbooks.com

FSC www.fsc.org
MIX
Paper | Supporting responsible forestry
FSC® C013604

Contents

Preface

Following on from the publication of my book *The Second World War North Africa & Italy 1940 to 1945 'One Man's Story'*, a biography about my father's Royal Air Force (RAF) service during the Second World War, and as my research developed I quickly established that RAF 73 Squadron he was attached to, were present in the Tunisian campaign during November 1942 to May 1943, which saw the final battles of the North Africa campaign being fought to remove the Axis forces of Germany and Italy out of North Africa, and it is fitting that the exploits and courage of the Allied forces are brought together to give full credit for their incredible achievements during the battles and those still to be fought.

During the research work carried out in preparing the groundwork for the writing of this book, I came across many books by eminent historians and authors, who in their own way took the necessary time to compile and pull together their research material which outlines the Allied forces' specific achievements during late 1942 to mid-1943. All are great books and make compelling reading that set down the courage and bravery of the combined Allied forces to remove the Axis force aggressors (Germany and Italy) throughout the region of North Africa, and particularly the Western Desert, including Tunisia.

This book endeavours to pull together the documents and records which detail the events of the forthcoming operations and battles to which the Allied command had committed their military might and sets out to lay bare the operations and the battles yet to be fought in the Western Desert during 1942 and 1943.

With the Allied victory at El Alamein in 1942, the Allied command pressed forwards with their attacks to push the Axis forces further and further westwards across North Africa. During the Allies' advancement, their next goal would be to recapture Tobruk, previously taken by the Axis forces in June 1941. *(The defeat inflicted on the Allied forces by the Axis forces in June 1941 with them capturing Tobruk was to be their last major victory. The Allied decision to stop Rommel in his tracks from capturing Egypt at El Alamein in 1942 was to be a **defining moment** and one that saw the start of the demise of the German/Italian Axis force throughout the whole of North Africa.)*

The book makes great use of the operational records that cover the Tunisian campaign of the Joint Allied Command and RAF Records held at National Archives. RAF 73 Squadrons - Operational Record Reports (AIRs) from late 1942 to 1943, daily records of events as they took place, all covered and detailed in Chapter 14. Notwithstanding the efforts by RAF 73 Squadron, they were one of many squadrons used during this period of the war and this book recognizes the work that all forces made in removing the Axis force from North Africa and preventing in excess of 267,000 troops and equipment from reaching the island of Sicily and then mainland Europe. Had this been achieved, then the battles to take place in Normandy – Operation Overlord on 6 June 1944 – may well have been considerably different, certainly protracted over a longer period than what took place.

The Tunisian campaign: 17 November 1942 to 13 May 1943: *The Tunisian campaign began with an Allied amphibious landing near Sfax in eastern Tunisia on 5 January 1943, and an attack on German positions at Gafsa in west-central Tunisia on 17 March 1943. On 4 February 1943, the British Eighth Army crossed the border from Libya into Tunisia. Squeezed between US and British Commonwealth forces and cut off from his supply bases, German General Erwin Rommel attempted to stall the Allies with defensive operations. German and Italian troops managed to rout the US II Corps at the Kasserine Pass on 18 February, but the Axis forces were vastly outnumbered and outgunned. The Allies made slow but steady progress in forcing the Axis troops into a pocket along the north-central Tunisian coast.*

Casualties: *During the North African campaign, the Germans and Italians suffered 620,000 casualties, whilst the British Commonwealth lost 220,000 men. American casualties in Tunisia alone totalled more than 18,500. The Allied victory in North Africa destroyed or neutralized 900,000 German and Italian troops, opened a second front against the Axis, permitted the invasion of Sicily and the Italian mainland in summer of 1943, and removed the Axis threat to the oilfields of the Middle East and to British supply lines to Asia and Africa.*

Footnote: Why did Germany, especially Adolf Hitler, want to capture Egypt and beyond?

Germany under Adolf Hitler had started the Second World War by invading Poland, which caused Great Britain and its Allies to mobilize their forces to prevent the Germans from overrunning Europe with little or no success. As the German Army extended the fronts on which they were fighting on, they needed greater supply levels of oil and fuel to be supplied to the German war machine. The German forces were constantly running short of oil and fuel as their lines of supply were ever extended, and they struggled to maintain operational capability. During the conflict, German scientists were experimenting with the production of oil and fuel from fossil fuel and were successful to a degree. However, oil and fuel production could not be maintained and hence the need to invade Africa, with plans to invade Egypt and beyond to capture the rich oil fields of the Middle East. **The Allied forces were determined to stop this at all costs.**

Introduction

To continue the theme of what war meant in the Middle East, it was necessary for me to look at and understand the joint Allied operations that took place after the recapture of Tobruk in early November 1942. The joint Allied forces were planning how best they could drive out the Axis forces from North Africa, plans that would take place prior to the planned taking of Sicily (Operation Husky) and then Italy (Operation Avalanche). The joint Allied command's next major objective was to drive the joint Axis forces (Germany and Italy) out of Tunisia, which required the taking of Morocco and Algeria in the west, and then, after El Alamein, the taking of Cyrenaica and Tripolitania in the east, with Tunisia being the final goal.

After Pearl Harbor (7 December 1941), during which the United States were dealt a very bloody nose by the Japanese, which only hastened their entry into the Second World War. The United States declared war on Japan on 8 December 1941. The British government declared war on Japan immediately after learning that their territory had also been attacked.

The co-ordination carried out by the Allies, which now included the United States, left no stone unturned, and as you will read in the chapters of the book how they went about their task in finally defeating and removing the aggressors from their foothold in the Western Desert.

The battles to take place in the Western Desert were eagerly being planned and co-ordinated and for the first time will see American forces taking part in the planned operations. Operation Torch became the US military's first step towards the defeat of Nazi Germany in Europe.

To try and imagine what the men went through during the Second World War is hard to comprehend or contemplate. It is only during the last eighty-plus years where other conflicts have taken place, which required the British military to embark on new battles across the world that the measure of conflict can now be established and today is known as post-traumatic stress disorder (PTSD).

Whilst every effort has been made to provide a true and factual account of the next phases of the battles to remove the Axis forces from North Africa, I apologize in advance for any misrepresentation of any facts.

This book is dedicated to the men who fought for **King and country** and thus provide a world in which we could all live together as one, and in peace.

Footnote

On a personal note, this book would not have been possible had it not been for the continued support and encouragement of my wife Jane, my son Mark, my daughter Emma-Jane, granddaughters Chloe and Emily, plus all family members and enthusiastic friends.

A huge thank you to Jim Erskine (Wing Commander Retired) for the initial sketch design of the front and back covers, and my son Mark for producing the final artwork for the front and back cover of the book.

I would like to pass on my gratitude and thanks to Damien Lewis, author, for his endless encouragement and support, along with his endorsement of my book.

A very special thank-you goes out to Lieutenant Colonel Roger S. Metcalfe, formerly of Headquarters Allied Rapid Reaction Corps, Imjin Barracks, Innsworth, Gloucester, Gloucestershire for his book foreword, which encapsulates all that to which the book portrays.

To all those fighting men of all nationalities who fought so bravely on all fronts to ensure that our freedom was maintained, and the aggressor was stopped. To those who died in the conflict and those who survived and have since departed this world, my heartfelt thanks and prayers go out to you all in allowing me to have 'My Todays', and to tell your story. **May you all rest in peace.**

Book Endorsement

As an author myself I am fully aware of the time, work, effort, and research that goes into producing a manuscript on any given subject in preparing the work for publishing. The Tunisian Campaign - North Africa Western Desert is one such manuscript that uses Second World War memorabilia, which had been collected through 1940 to 1945 by Leo Bernard Lamb–RAF SR:1012281, along with official military records from that time, many of which are now archived at the National Archives, Kew.

This book sets out to follow the Allied forces through the many battles across North Africa, including Tobruk in 1941 and 1942, the crucial battle at El Alamein 1942 and then on to the Western Desert Tunisian campaign from November 1942 to May 1943, the prelude to Operation Husky (Sicily) and Operation Avalanche (Italy).

As an author, I'm always intrigued to witness new authors coming forwards with stories that relate to their families; stories which otherwise would be lost in time. I am very happy to endorse the book as I have witnessed the book's development. It is undoubtedly a story which should be told and read.

Endorsement by
Damien Lewis – Author

Foreword

Philip Lamb first honoured his father's memory and service in the Second World War with the book ***The Second World War North Africa and Italy 1940-1945 'One Man's Story'.*** The book tracked the wartime career and experiences of Leading Aircraftman (LAC) Leo Bernard Lamb from his training through the campaigns in North Africa and Italy, to being returned wounded to Wales - RAF St. Athan, 32-MU (Maintenance Unit) and finally to his demobilization on 1 February 1946, effective date of release, Class 'A'.

This book focuses on a most notable phase of LAC Lamb's actions on operational service with the Royal Air Force in Tunisia; from November 1942 to the final surrender of Axis forces by General von Arnim in May 1943, and the complete victory of Allied forces in North Africa. Lamb relates the importance of the rearming of the Eighth Army, and provision of heavy bombers as well as Spitfires and Hurricanes, as well as new tanks and 6-pounder guns for the Eighth Army, which were such important contributions to the multiple victories throughout the campaign.

The personal account has been told in the first book; this is an account of the campaign itself, although LAC Lamb does make a cameo appearance. The importance of the campaign in which LAC Lamb took part cannot be underestimated, because it was the essential prelude to the Allied invasion of Europe, and of the eventual Allied victory over the Nazis. The campaign was also the prototype for most of the military techniques of all-arms co-operation which were to prove so indispensable in Italy, and later in Normandy and the Allied drive to the Rhineland and the Baltic.

The daily and nightly slog of support to air forces by the RAF ground crews was vital, to protect our bombers, to prevent enemy air action, to keep up the demoralizing of the enemy ground forces in depth, and to conduct photographic reconnaissance of enemy positions and movements. This campaign was a truly mobile one for the Allied forces, not least the RAF; to achieve this agility, the Desert Air Force became adept at rapidly bringing airfields into operational condition close behind the Army divisions at the front; this was the continual duty of all ground crew, men such as LAC Lamb, and their efforts directly contributed to the improved tempo of, and to the eventual complete victory of, General Montgomery's Eighth Army in North Africa.

FOREWORD

As veterans with firsthand knowledge of the Second World War campaigns and battles have all contributed, the importance of meticulously researched records cannot be underestimated. There is no place for re-imagining in such an important work, and Philip Lamb's second book is as true to the record as his first. This is essential reading for all students of military tactics and strategy and will appeal equally to the interested reader of military history.

Lieutenant Colonel Roger S. Metcalfe, formerly of Headquarters Allied Rapid Reaction Corps, Imjin Barracks, Innsworth, Gloucester. Gloucestershire

Chapter 1

Operation Torch

November 1942

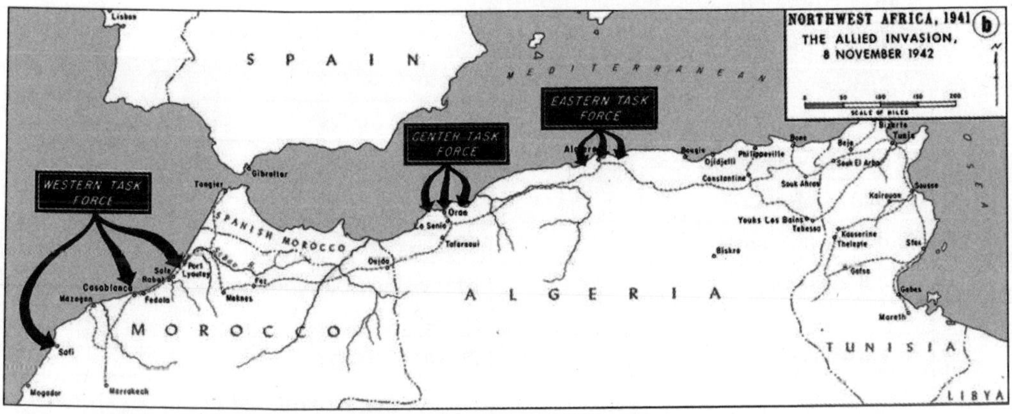

Casablanca (Western), Oran (Centre) and Algiers (Eastern).
(*This file is a work of a US Army soldier or employee, taken or made as part of that person's official duties. As a work of the US Federal Government, it is in the Public Domain in the United States.–NO Copyright in the USA. Source: www.dean.usma.edu.* Email dated 20/09/2023: "Map(s) courtesy of the United States Military Academy Department of History.")

Landings During the Operation	
Date: 8–16 November 1942 **Location:** French Morocco, French Algeria **Result:** Allied Victory **Territorial changes:** • Anglo-American occupation of Morocco and Algeria • Free French control of French West Africa • Case Anton (Axis occupation of southern France)	
Belligerents	
United States	**Vichy France**
United Kingdom **• India** **Free France**	**• Algeria** **• Morocco**

Naval only: ***Canada*** ***Netherlands*** ***Australia***	**Germany** **Italy**
Commanders	
United States: Dwight D Eisenhower	**Vichy France**: François Darlan
United States: George S Patton	**Vichy France**: Alphonse Juin
United States: Henry Kent Hewitt	**Vichy France**: Charles Noguès
United States: Lloyd Fredendall	**Germany**: Ernst Kals
United Kingdom: Andrew Cunningham	
United Kingdom: Kenneth Anderson	
Strength	
Ground forces:	**Ground forces:**
107,000 troops	125,000 troops
35,000 in Morocco	210 tanks
39,000 near Algiers	500 aircraft
33,000 near Oran	Many shore batteries and artillery pieces
Naval activity:	**Naval activity:**
350 warships	1 battleship partially armed
500 transports	10 other warships
Total: 850	11 submarines
	Germany: 14 submarines
	Italy: 14 submarines
Casualties and Losses	
United States:	**Vichy France:**
526 dead	1,346+ dead
United Kingdom:	1,997 wounded
574 dead	Several shore batteries destroyed
All other Allies:	All artillery pieces captured
756 total wounded	1 light cruiser lost
1 escort carrier (HMS *Avenger*) sunk	5 destroyers lost
With a loss of 506 men	6 submarines lost
4 destroyers lost	2 flotilla leaders lost
2 sloops lost	**Germany:** 8 submarines lost by 17 November

6 troopships lost	
1 minesweeper lost	**Italy:** 2 submarines lost by 17 November
1 auxiliary anti-aircraft ship lost	

Operation Torch (8 November 1942–16 November 1942) was an Allied invasion of French North Africa during the Second World War. Torch was a compromise operation that met the British objective of securing victory in North Africa whilst allowing American armed forces the opportunity to engage in the fight against Nazi Germany on a limited scale. It was the first mass involvement of US troops in the European-North African Theatre and saw the first major airborne assault carried out by the United States.

Whilst the French colonies were formally aligned with Germany via Vichy France, the loyalties of the population were mixed. Reports indicated that they might support the Allies.

American General Dwight D. Eisenhower, supreme commander of the Allied forces in Mediterranean Theatre of operations, planned a three-pronged attack on Casablanca (Western), Oran (Centre) and Algiers (Eastern), then a rapid move on Tunis to catch Axis forces (Afrika Korps) in North Africa from the west in conjunction with the Allied Eighth Army advance from Egypt to the east.

Operation Torch's Western Task Force encountered unexpected resistance and bad weather, but Casablanca, the principal French Atlantic naval base, was captured after a short siege. The Centre Task Force suffered some damage to its ships when trying to land in shallow water, but the French ships were sunk or driven off; Oran surrendered after bombardment by British battleships. The French Resistance had successfully attempted a coup in Algiers and, even though the late alert raised in the Vichy forces, the Eastern Task Force met less opposition and were able to push inland and compel surrender on the first day.

The success of Torch caused Admiral François Darlan, commander of the Vichy French forces, who was in Algiers, to order co-operation with the Allies, in return for being installed as high commissioner, with many other Vichy officials keeping their jobs. Darlan was assassinated soon afterwards, and the Free French gradually came to dominate the government.

Background

The Allies planned an Anglo-American invasion of French North Africa/Maghred–Morocco, Algeria and Tunisia, territory normally in the hands of the Vichy French government. With British forces advancing from Egypt, this would eventually allow the Allies to carry out a pincer operation against Axis forces in North Africa. The Vichy French had around 125,000 soldiers in the territories as well as coastal artillery, 210 operational but out-of-date tanks and about 500 aircraft, half of which were Dewoitine D.520 fighters–equal to many British and US fighters. These forces included 60,000 troops in Morocco, 15,000 in Tunisia, and 50,000 in Algeria, with coastal artillery, and a small number of tanks and aircraft. In addition, there were ten or so warships and eleven submarines at Casablanca.

Political Situation on the Ground

The Allies believed that the Vichy French Armistice Army would not fight, partly because of information supplied by the American Consul Robert Daniel Murphy in Algiers. The French were former members of the Allies, and the American troops were instructed not to fire unless they were fired upon. However, they harboured suspicions that the Vichy French Navy would bear a grudge over the actions of the British in June 1940 to prevent French ships being taken by the Germans; the attack on the French Navy in harbour at Mers-el-Kébir, near Oran, killed almost 1,300 French sailors.

An assessment of the sympathies of the French forces in North Africa was essential, and plans were made to secure their co-operation, rather than resistance. German support for the Vichy French came in the shape of air support. Several Luftwaffe bomber wings undertook anti-shipping strikes against Allied ports in Algiers and along the north African coast.

Operational Command

The operation was originally scheduled to be led by General Joseph Stilwell, but he was reassigned after the Arcadia Conference revealed his vitriolic Anglophobia and scepticism over the operation. Lt. General Dwight D. Eisenhower was given command of the operation, and he set up his headquarters in Gibraltar. The Allied Naval commander of the expeditionary force was Admiral Sir Andrew Cunningham; his deputy was Vice Admiral Sir Bertram Ramsay, who planned the amphibious landings.

Strategic Debate Among the Allies

Senior US commanders remained strongly opposed to the landings and after the western Allied Combined Chiefs of Staff (CCS) met in London on 30 July 1942, General George Marshall and Admiral Ernest King declined to approve the plan. Marshall and other US generals advocated the invasion of Northern Europe later that year, which the British rejected. After Prime Minister Winston Churchill pressed for a landing in French North Africa in 1942, Marshall suggested instead to President Franklin D. Roosevelt that the United States abandon the Germany first strategy and take the offensive in the Pacific. Roosevelt said 'it would do nothing to help the Russians'. With Marshall unable to persuade the British to change their minds, President Roosevelt gave a direct order that Torch was to have precedence over other operations and was to take place at the earliest possible date: one of only two direct orders he gave to military commanders during the war.

In conducting their planning, Allied military strategists needed to consider the political situation on the ground in North Africa, which was complex, as well as external diplomatic political aspects.

The Americans had recognized Pétain and the Vichy government in 1940, whereas the British did not and had recognized General Charles de Gaulle's French National Committee as a government-in-exile instead and agreed to fund them. North Africa was part of France's colonial empire and nominally in support of Vichy, but that support was far from universal among the population.

Political events on the ground contributed to, and in some cases were even primary over, military aspects. The French population in North Africa were divided into three groups:

1. Gaullists: De Gaulle was the rallying point for the French National Committee. This comprised French refugees who escaped metropolitan France rather than succumb to the German occupation, or those who stayed and joined the French Resistance. One acolyte, General Philippe Leclerc de Hauteclocque, organized a fighting force and conducted raids in 1943 along a 1,600-mile (2.575 km) path from Lake Chad to Tripoli and joined with General Bernard Montgomery's British Eight Army on 25 January 1943.
2. French Liberation Movement: Some Frenchmen living in North Africa and operating in secret under German surveillance organized an underground 'French Liberation Movement', whose aim was to liberate France. General Henri Giraud, recently escaped from Germany, later became its leader. The personal clash between de Gaulle and Giraud prevented the Free French Forces and the French Liberation Movement groups from unifying during the North African campaign (Torch).
3. Loyal pro-Vichy French: There were those who remained loyal to Marshal Phillippe Pétain and believed collaboration with the Axis powers was the best method of ensuring the future of France. François Darlan was Pétain's designated successor.

American strategy in planning the attack had to take into account these complexities on the ground. The planners assumed that if the leaders were given Allied military support, they would take steps to liberate themselves, and the United States embarked on detailed negotiations under American Consul General Robert Murphy in Rabat with the French Liberation Movement. Since Britain was already diplomatically and financially committed to de Gaulle, it was clear that negotiations with the French Liberation Movement would have to be conducted by the Americans, and the invasion as well. Because of divided loyalties among the groups on the ground their support was uncertain, and due to the need to maintain secrecy, detailed plans could not be shared with the French.

Allied Plans

Planners had identified Oran, Algiers, and Casablanca as key targets. Ideally there would also be a landing at Tunis to secure Tunisia and facilitate the rapid interdiction of supplies travelling via Tripoli to Erwin Rommel's Afrika Korps forces in Italian Libya. However, Tunis was much too close to the Axis airfields in Sicily and Sardinia

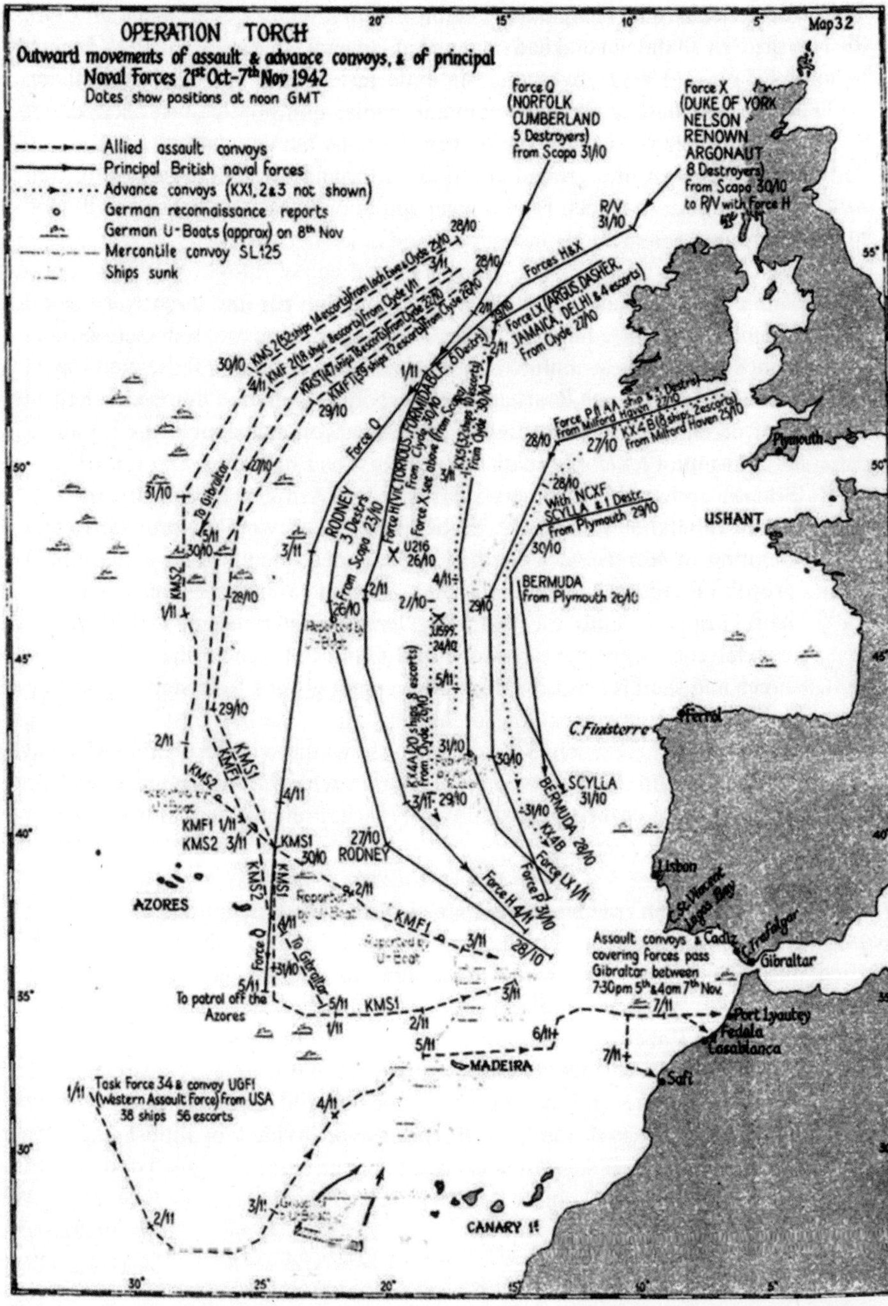

Allied Convoys Map–Operation Torch.
(*This work created by the United Kingdom Government is in the Public Domain. HMSP has declared that the expiry of Crown Copyrights applies worldwide (Ref: HMSO Email Reply) Source: 'The War at Sea 1939-1945', Chapter XII by S. W. Roskill - Author*)

for any hope of success. A compromise would be to land at Bône in eastern Algeria, some 300 miles (483 km) closer to Tunis than Algiers. Limited resources dictated that the Allies could only make three landings and Eisenhower – who believed that any plan must include landings at Oran and Algiers – had two main options. The options were either the western option, to land at Casablanca, Oran and Algiers and then make as rapid a move as possible to Tunis some 500 miles (805 km) east of Algiers once the Vichy opposition was suppressed; or the eastern option, to land at Oran, Algiers and Bône and then advance overland to Casablanca some 500 miles (805 km) west of Oran. He favoured the eastern option because of the advantages it gave to an early capture of Tunis and also because the Atlantic swells off Casablanca presented considerably greater risks to an amphibious landing there than would be encountered in the Mediterranean.

The CCS, however, were concerned that should Operation Torch cause Spain to abandon neutrality and join the Axis, the Straits of Gibraltar could be closed cutting off the entire Allied force's lines of communication. They therefore chose the Casablanca option as the less risky since the forces in Algeria and Tunisia could be supplied overland from Casablanca (albeit with considerable difficulty) in the event of closure of the straits.

Marshall's opposition to Operation Torch delayed the landings by almost a month, and his opposition to landings in Algeria led British military leaders to question his strategic ability; the Royal Navy controlled the Strait of Gibraltar, and Spain was unlikely to intervene, as Francisco Franco was hedging his bets. The Morocco landings ruled out the early occupation of Tunisia, Marshall did convince the Allies to abandon the planned invasions of Madeira and Tangier in preparation for the landings, which he maintained would lose the element of surprise and draw large Spanish military contingents in Spanish Morocco and the Canary Islands into the war. However, Harry Hopkins convinced President Franklin D. Roosevelt to agree to the general plan. Eisenhower told Patton that *the past six weeks were the most trying of his life.* In Eisenhower's acceptance of landings in Algeria and Morocco, he pointed out that the decision removed the early capture of Tunis from the probable to only the remotely possible because of the extra time it would afford the Axis to move forces into Tunisia.

Intelligence Gathering

In July 1941, Mieczyslaw Slowikowski (using the codename *Rygor* – Polish for 'Rigour') set up 'Agency Africa', one of the Second World War's most successful intelligence organizations. His Polish allies in these endeavours included Lieutenant Colonel Gwido Langer and Major Maksymilian Cieki. The information gathered by the agency was used by the Americans and British in planning the amphibious November 1942 Operation Torch landings in North Africa.

Preliminary Contact with Vichy French

To gauge the feeling of the Vichy French forces, Murphy was appointed to the American consulate in Algeria. His covert mission was to determine the mood of the French forces and to make contact with elements that might support an Allied invasion. He succeeded in contacting several French officers, including General Charles Mast, the French commander-in-chief in Algeria.

These officers were willing to support the Allies but asked for a clandestine conference with senior Allied General in Algeria. Major General Mark W. Clark – one of Eisenhower's senior commanders – was dispatched to Cherchell in Algeria aboard the British submarine HMS *Seraph* and met with these Vichy French officers on 21 October 1942.

With help from the Resistance, the Allies also succeeded in slipping French General Henri Giraud out of Vichy France on HMS *Seraph* – passing itself off as an American submarine – to Gibraltar, where Eisenhower had his headquarters, intending to offer him the post of commander-in-chief of French forces in North Africa after the invasion. However, Giraud would take no position lower than commander-in-chief of all the invading forces, a job already given to Eisenhower. When he was refused, he decided to remain 'a spectator in this affair'.

Battle

The Allies organized three amphibious task forces to simultaneously seize the key ports and airports in Morocco and Algeria, targeting Casablanca, Oran, and Algiers. Successful completion of these operations was to be followed by an eastward's advance into Tunisia.

The Western Task Force (aimed at Casablanca) was composed of American units, with Major General George S. Patton in command and Rear Admiral Henry Kent Hewitt heading the naval operations. This Western Task Force consisted of the

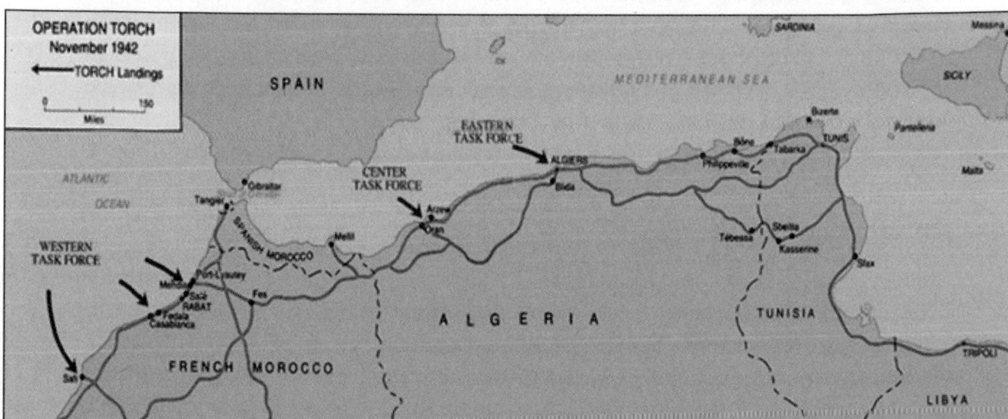

Operation Torch Battle Map: November 1942–Torch Landing.
(The above image is in the Public Domain because it contains materials that originally came from the US Army Center of Military History. Source: US Army Center of Military History Online Bookshelves. Email dated 20/09/2023: "Map(s) courtesy of the United States Military Academy Department of History.")

US 3rd and 9th Infantry divisions, and two battalions from the US 2nd Armoured Division – 35,000 troops in a convoy of over 100 ships. They were transported directly from the United States in the first of a new series of US convoys providing logistic support for the North African campaign.

The Centre Task Force, aimed at Oran, included the US 2nd Battalion 59 Parachute Infantry Regiment, the US 1st Infantry Division, and the US 1st Armoured Division–a total of 18,500 troops. They sailed from the United Kingdom and were commanded by Major General Lloyd Fredenall, the naval forces being commanded by Commodore Thomas Troubridge.

Operation Torch was, for propaganda purposes, a landing by US forces, supported by British warships and aircraft, under the belief that this would be more palatable to the French public opinion, than an Anglo-American invasion. For the same reason, Churchill suggested that British soldiers might wear US Army uniforms, and No. 6 Commando did so. (Fleet Air Arm aircraft did carry US 'star' roundels during the operation, and two British destroyers flew the Stars and Stripes.)

The Eastern Task Force – aimed at Algiers – was commanded by Lieutenant General Kenneth Anderson and consisted of a brigade from the British 78th and the US 34th Infantry divisions, along with two British commando units (No. 1 and No. 6 Commandos) together with the RAF Regiment providing five squadrons of infantry and five light anti-aircraft flights, totalling 20,000 troops. During the landing phase, ground forces were to be commanded by US Major General Charles W Ryder, commanding general (CG) of the 34th Division, and naval forces were commanded by Royal Navy Vice Admiral Sir Harold Burrough.

U-boats operating in the eastern Atlantic area crossed by the invasion convoys had been drawn away to attack trade convoy SL 125. Aerial operations were split into two commands, with Royal Air Force aircraft under Air Marshal Sir William Welsh operating east of Cape Tenez in Algeria, and all United States Army Air Force aircraft under Major General Jimmy Doolittle, who was under the direct command of Major General George S. Patton, operating west of Cape Tenez. P-40s of the 33rd Fighter Group were launched from US Navy escort carriers and landed at Port Lyautey on 10 November. Additional air support was provided by carrier USS *Ranger*, whose squadrons intercepted Vichy aircraft and bombed hostile ships.

Casablanca

The Western Task Force landed before daybreak on 8 November 1942, at three points in Morocco: Safi (Operation Blackstone), Fédala (Operation Brushwood, the largest landing with 19,000 men) and the Mehdita-Port Lyautey (Operation Goalpost). Because it was hoped that the French would not resist, there were no preliminary bombardments. This proved to be a costly error as French defences took a toll on American landing forces. On the night of 7 November, pro-Allied General Antoine Béthouart attempted a *coup d'etat* against the French command in Morocco, so that he could surrender to the Allies the next day. His forces surrounded the villa of General Charles Noguès, the Vichy-loyal high commissioner. However,

Noguès telephoned loyal forces, who stopped the coup. In addition, the coup attempt alerted Noguès to the impending Allied invasion, and he immediately bolstered French coastal defences.

During the battles around Casablanca and the streets, the Allied forces distributed flyers in both French and Arabic calling on the citizens to co-operate with the Allied forces.

At Fédala, a small port with a large beach close to Casablanca, weather disrupted the landings. The landing beaches again came under French fire after daybreak. Patton landed at 08:00 hours and the beachheads were secured later in the day. The Americans surrounded the port of Casablanca by 10 November, and the city surrendered an hour before the final assault was due to take place. Casablanca was the principal French Atlantic naval base after German occupation of the European coast. The Naval Battle of Casablanca resulted from a sortie of French cruisers, destroyers, and submarines opposing the landings. A cruiser, six destroyers and six submarines were destroyed by American gunfire and aircraft. The incomplete French battleship *Jean Bart* – which was docked and immobile – fired on the landing force with her one working gun turret until disabled by the 41cm (16-inch) calibre American naval gunfire of USS *Massachusetts*, the first such heavy-calibre shells fired by the US Navy anywhere in the Second World War. Many of her 1-ton shells didn't explode, linked to poor detonators, and aircraft bombers sank the *Jean Bart*. Two US destroyers were damaged.

At Safi, the objective being capturing the port facilities to land Western Task Force's medium tanks, the landings being mostly successful.

The landings were begun without covering fire, in the same hope that the French would not rest at all. However, once French coastal batteries opened fire, Allied warships returned fire. By the time the 3rd Battalion, 67th Armoured Regiment arrived, French snipers had pinned the assault troops (most of whom were in combat for the first time) on Safi's beaches. Most of the landings occurred behind schedule. Carrier aircraft destroyed a French truck convoy bringing reinforcements to the beach defences.

Safi surrendered on then 8 November, by 10 November, the remaining defenders were pinned down, and the bulk of Harmon's forces raced to join the siege of Casablanca.

At Port Lyautey, the landing troops were uncertain of their position, and the second wave was delayed. This gave the French defenders time to organize resistance, and the remaining landings were conducted under artillery bombardment. A former French pilot of the port on board a US destroyer led her up the shallow river to take over the artillery battery, clearing the way to the airbase. With the assistance of carrier air support, the troops pushed ahead, and the objectives were captured.

Oran

The Centre Task Force was split between three beaches: two west of Oran and one east. Landings at the westernmost beach were delayed because of a French convoy which appeared whilst the minesweepers were clearing a path. Some delay and confusion, and damage to landing ships, was caused by the unexpected shallowness of water and sandbars; although periscope observations had been carried out, no reconnaissance parties had landed on the beaches to determine the local maritime conditions. This helped inform subsequent amphibious assaults – such as Operation Overlord – in which considerable weight was given to pre-invasion reconnaissance.

The US 1st Ranger Battalion landed east of Oran and quickly captured the shore battery at Arzew. An attempt was made to land US infantry at the harbour directly, in order to quickly prevent destruction of the port facilities and scuttling of ships. The operation known as Operation Reservist failed as the two Banff-class sloops were destroyed by crossfire from the French vessels there. The Vichy French naval fleet broke from the harbour and attacked the Allied invasion fleet, but its ships were all sunk or driven ashore. The commander of Operation Reservist, Captain Frederick Thornton Peters, was awarded the Victoria Cross for valour in pushing the attack through Oran harbour in the face of point-blank fire. French batteries and the invasion fleet exchanged fire throughout 8–9 November, with French troops defending Oran and the surrounding area stubbornly; bombardment by the British battleships brought about Oran's surrender on 10 November.

Airborne Landings

Operation Torch was the first major airborne assault carried out by the United States. The 2nd Battalion, 509th Parachute Infantry Regiment, aboard 39 C-47 Dakotas, flew all the way from Cornwall in England, over Spain, to drop near Oran and capture airfields at Tafraoui and La Sénia, respectively 15 miles (24 km) and 5 miles (8 km) south of Oran. The operation was marked by communicational and navigational problem's owing to the anti-aircraft and beacon ship HMS *Alynbank* broadcasting on the wrong frequency. Poor weather over Spain and the extreme range caused the formation to scatter and forced thirty of the thirty-seven air transports to land in the city Salt Lake to the west of the objective. Of the other aircraft, one pilot became disoriented and landed his plane in Gibraltar. Two others landed in French Morocco and three in Spanish Morocco, where another Dakota dropped its paratroopers by mistake. A total of sixty-seven American troops were interned by Franco's forces until February 1943. Tafraoui and La Sénia were eventually captured but the role played by the airborne forces in Operation Torch was minimal.

British First Army & Airborne Landings 1942

Included as part of and within the airborne assault forces were the British First Army, which had been reformed during the Second World War to command the American and British land forces, which had landed in Western North Africa as part of Operation Torch, the allied invasion of French North Africa, in Morocco and Algeria on 8 November 1942. It was commanded by Lieutenant General Sir Kenneth Anderson. The First Army headquarters was formally activated on

9 November 1942 when Anderson arrived in Algiers to assume command of the redesignated Eastern Task Force.

The First Army initially consisted of American and British formations only. After the surrender of French forces following the German abrogation of their armistice agreement with Vichy France, French units were also added to the First Army's order of battle. It eventually consisted of four corps: the US II Corps, the British V Corps, British IX Corps and French XIX Corps.

The following extract is taken from the book **'Men of the Red Beret - Airborne Forces 1940-1990 by Max Arthur - Author'**, which was first published in 1990 through Hutchinson.

> *'In November 1942 the First Army, which included the 1st Parachute Brigade, landed near Algiers with the aim of advancing and capturing Tunis and Bizerte 500 miles (805 km) to the east. The 3rd Parachute Battalion, which had flown to Algiers via Gibraltar, spearheaded this advance; they seized the vital Bone airfield on 12 November by parachute assault, anticipating by minutes a German force with the same task, which it then abandoned. On 16 November the 1st Battalion dropped near Souk el Arba airfield and occupied a key road junction at Beja, only 90 miles (145 km) from Tunis, from which they actively patrolled. Both these operations were successful, and the airborne troops were quickly relieved by the advancing main force.*
>
> *The 2nd Parachute Battalion, initially held in reserve, was dropped at Depienne on 29 November to destroy enemy aircraft at Oudna. The airfield, however, was found to be abandoned while unexpectedly heavy enemy opposition halted the advance of the First Army, leaving the battalion isolated 56 miles (90 km) behind enemy lines. Lightly equipped and continuously attacked by air and ground forces, the battalion successfully conducted an arduous fighting withdrawal back to the nearest Allied positions, losing 16 officers and 250 men en route.*
>
> *The campaign now entered a new phase that developed over the winter onto a bitter slogging match. For the next five months until April 1943, the Parachute Brigade Group was required to fight in the normal infantry role. Taking part in more battles than any other formation in the First Army, they inflicted over 5,000 casualties with a loss to the brigade of 1,700 men. The brigade's actions in this operation earned them the name* ***Rote Teufel****, or the Red Devils, from the German forces.'*

Parachute Regiment

The **Parachute Regiment**, colloquially known as the **Paras**, is an airborne infantry regiment of the British Army. British Prime Minister Winston Churchill had been impressed by the success of German airborne operations during the Battle of France and directed the War Office to investigate the possibility of creating a corps of 5,000 parachute troops. No. 2 Commando was turned over to parachute duties and on 21 November, redesignated the 11th Special Air Services (SAS) Battalion, with a parachute and glider wing. The first battalion is part of the Special Forces Support Group under the operational command of the director special forces and was formed on 22 June 1940 during the Second World War and eventually raised seventeen battalions. During the Second World War, the regiment took part in six major parachute assault operations in North Africa, Italy, Greece, France, the Netherlands and Germany, often landing ahead of all other troops.

The first operation by the Parachute Regiment was Operation Biting in February 1942. The objective was to capture a Würzburg radar on the coast of France. The raid was carried out by 'C' Company, 2nd Parachute Battalion, under the command of Major John Frost.

The success of the raid prompted the War Office to expand the existing airborne force, setting up the Airborne Forces Depot and Battle School in Derbyshire in April 1942, and creating the Parachute Regiment as well as converting several infantry battalions into airborne battalions in August 1942. The 2nd Parachute Brigade was then formed from the 4th Battalion. In addition to this, the Army Air Corps was created as the command formation of the Parachute Regiment and the Glider Pilot Regiment. With two parachute brigades now in the order of battle, the 1st Airborne Division commanded by Major General Frederick Arthur Montague Browning was formed.

The Parachute Regiment had their own distinctive uniform, the maroon beret at first with the Army Air Corps cap badge and from May 1943 the Parachute Regiment cap badge which is still in use today. Parachute wings were worn on the right shoulder above the airborne forces patch of Bellerophon riding the flying horse Pegasus. British Paras did not use a reserve parachute, as the War Office considered the £60 cost a waste of money. As with the nonuse of a reserve parachute similarly the Paras were not issued any special weapons. Their small arms were the same as the rest of the army's.

Parachute training was a twelve-day course carried out at the No. 1 Parachute Training School, RAF Ringway. Recruits initially jumped from a converted barrage balloon and finished with five parachute jumps from an aircraft. Anyone failing to complete a parachute jump was returned to his old unit. On completion of the course, new paras were presented with their maroon beret and parachute wings and then posted to a parachute battalion.

Algiers

Resistance and Coup

As agreed at Chercell, in the early hours of 8 November, the 400 mainly Jewish French Resistance fighters of the Géo Gras Group staged a coup in the city of Algiers. Starting at midnight, the force under the command of Henri d'Astier de la Vigerie and José Aboulker seized key targets, including the telephone exchange, radio station, governor's house, and the headquarters of the 19th Corps.

Robert Murphy took some men and then drove to the residence of General Alphonse Juin, the senior French Army officer in North Africa. Whilst they surrounded his house (making Juin a hostage), Murphy attempted to persuade him to side with the Allies. Juin was treated to a surprise. Admiral François Darlan – the commander of all French forces – was also in Algiers on a private visit. Juin insisted on contacting Darlan and Murphy was unable to persuade either to side with the Allies. In the early morning, the local Gendarmerie arrived and released Juin and Darlan.

Invasion

On 8 November 1942, the invasion commenced with landings on three beaches – two west of Algiers and one east. The landing forces were under the overall of Major General Charles W. Ryder, CG of the US 34th Infantry Division. The 11th Brigade Group from the British 78th Infantry Division landed on the right-hand beach, the US 168th Regimental Combat Team, from the 34th Infantry Division, supported by 6 Commando and most of 1 Commando, landed on the middle beach, and the US 39th Regimental Combat Team, from the US 9th Infantry Division, supported by the remaining five troops from 1 Commando, landed on the left-hand beach. The 36th Brigade Group from the British 78th Infantry Division stood by in floating reserve. Though some landings went to the wrong beaches, this was immaterial because of the lack of French opposition. All the coastal batteries had been neutralized by the French Resistance and one French commander defected to the Allies.

The only fighting took place in the port of Algiers, where in Operation Terminal, two British destroyers attempted to land a party of US Army Rangers directly onto the dock, to prevent the French destroying the port facilities and scuttling their ships. Heavy artillery fire prevented one destroyer from landing, but the other was able to disembark 250 Rangers before it too was driven back to sea. The US troops pushed quickly inland, and General Juin surrendered the city to the Allies at 18:00 hours.

Aftermath

It quickly became clear that Giraud lacked the authority to take control of the French forces. He preferred to wait in Gibraltar for the results of the landing. However, Darlan in Algiers had such authority. Eisenhower, with the support of Roosevelt and Churchill, made an agreement with Darlan, recognizing him as French 'High Commissioner' in North Africa. In return, Darlan ordered all French forces in North Africa to cease resistance to the Allies and to co-operate instead. The deal was made on 10 November, and French resistance ceased almost at once. The French troops in North Africa who were not already captured submitted to and eventually joined the Allied forces. Men from French North Africa would see much combat under the Allies banner as part of the French Expeditionary Corps (consisting of 112,000 troops in April 1944) in the Italian campaign, where Maghrebis (mostly Moroccans) made up over 60 per cent of the unit's soldiers.

The whole outcome of Operation Torch left many French in a quandary, who to trust, who to follow and what would be best for not only the region but later, France too, Operation Overlord 1944. The fact that the Allies set out their plans to invade Western North Africa and in doing so were able to carry out the pincer movement on the Axis force's and remove them once and for all out of North Africa.

The following listed operations A, B, C, D, E, F and G were all carried out under the main operation known as Operation Torch. The operation listed as Operation Overlord, whilst listed is the operation which saw the liberation of France otherwise known as D-Day Tuesday, 6 June 1944.

A. Operation Blackstone

This operation was a part of the main operation known as Operation Torch, Allied troops landing in Western North Africa. The operation called for American amphibious troops to land and capture the French-held port of Safi in French Morocco. The landings were carried out by the 47th Infantry Regiment of the US Army and took place on the morning of 8 November 1942 as part of a larger operation to capture Casablanca.

The landings from converted destroyers were mostly successful. They were initially conducted without covering fire, hoping that the French might not resist at all. When the coastal batteries opened fire, the fleet returned fire. When CG Harmon arrived, French snipers had pinned the assault troops (most of which were in combat for the first time) on the beaches. Most of the landings occurred behind schedule; air support from the carriers destroyed a French convoy of trucks intending to reinforce the defences.

Safi surrendered on the afternoon of 8 November, but sporadic resistance continued until 10 November when the remaining defenders were pinned down and the bulk of Harmon's forces raced to join the siege of Casablanca.

B. Operation Brushwood

The operation took place on 8 November 1942, the landings were intended to capture Fédala as part of a larger operation to capture Casablanca in Morocco, 12 miles (19 km) south of Fédala.

Operation Brushwood forces landed at Fédala, Morocco, then marched to nearby Casablanca.

The landings took place on a stretch of coastline between Oued Nefifikh and Oued Mellah rivers. Singular battalion landing teams landed on four separate beaches within this 4-mile-(6 km)long zone.

A total of 19,364 officers and men from three regimental landing groups were involved in the attack.

The main goals being to capture Casablanca and silence the coastal batteries.

C. Operation Goalpost

The battle of Port Lyautey began on 8 November for the city of Port Lyautey, today known as Kenitra, in French Morocco. The battle ended with the capture and occupation by American troops, overrunning French forces after more than two days of fierce fighting.

The objectives of the operation were threefold:

1.0 Capture the beach village of Mehdita.

2.0 Capture the fortress which secured the river mouth.

3.0 Secure the airfield.

D. Operation Overlord

The name given for this operation was the codename for the Battle of Normandy, which would see the start of the major demise of Nazi Germany and their removal as an occupying force throughout the European continent.

It is not intended to elaborate or expand on Operation Overlord as this is a complete book in its own rite. The recorded date for Operation Overlord being Tuesday, 6 June 1944.

E. Operation Reservist (the operation was a failure)

This was an Allied military operation and was an attempted landing of troops directly into the harbour at Oran in Algiers.

The purpose of Operation Reservist was to capture the valuable assets and facilities at the Vichy French port of Oran before they could be destroyed. The landing of troops directly from ships was extremely risky; however, it was hoped that either the French defenders would be taken entirely by surprise, or that they would co-operate with the landing forces. Two Banff-class sloops, HMS *Walney* and HMS *Hartland* were used to land the troops.

The landing ships came under sustained fire from the defenders once they were inside the harbour boom, including four shore batteries from east to west (Mole Ravin Blanc, Mole Miller, Mole J. Giraud and Mole Centre). There were thirty-one French ships in the port which did considerable damage to the Allied vessels. Casualties during the operation exceeded 90 per cent of the Allied force. Of the 393 American infantrymen of the 3rd Battalion, 6th Armoured Infantry Regiment, 189 were killed and 157 wounded. The Royal Navy suffered 113 dead and eighty-six wounded, and a small US Navy team assigned as anti-sabotage five killed and seven wounded. HMS *Walney* made it alongside the jetty and succeeded in landing a small number of men. The survivors were captured.

The defenders surrendered two days after the invasion, but the harbour facilities had been destroyed.

Landings were carried out at the same time to invest Oran at three different beaches. Similar operations were carried out elsewhere during Operation Torch.

F. Operation Terminal: 8 November 1942

Background

Operation Terminal was an Allied operation and was part of Operation Torch. The operation required that troops would be directly landed into the Vichy

French Port of Algiers with the intention of capturing the port facilities before they could be destroyed.

The attacking forces were two Royal Navy destroyers, HMS *Malcolm* and HMS *Broke* (commanded by Henry Fancourt) carrying 600 troops of the 3rd Battalion, 135th Infantry, (commanded by Colonel Edwin Swenson), part of the US 34th Infantry Division.

The plan was to land the troops directly into the port. It was hoped that either complete surprise would be achieved or that the defenders would support the invasion to the extent at least of refusing to fire on the attackers. However, the Vichy forces opened fire on the ships, causing heavy damage to them.

Action

At 04:00 hours on the morning of 8 November 1942 HMS *Malcolm* and HMS *Broke* approached Algiers Harbor. They were regarded as hostile by the defending Vichy troops, who opened fire at 04:06 hours. HMS *Malcolm* tried to break through the boom but was hit and severely damaged by a shell fired from the shore. Ten of her crew were dead, many more were injured, and three of her four boilers were extinguished, cutting her speed to 4 knots. She was forced to retreat and played no further part in the operation. Initially, HMS *Broke* had better luck. On her third attempt, she sliced through the boom and deposited her troops under fire on the *Quai de Fécamp*, and then retreated. This was four hours after the operation had started. HMS *Broke* luck ran out as she withdrew; she was hit by shore batteries which compounded on earlier damage and after being taken in tow, she sank on 10 November.

The landed infantry was surrounded and forced to surrender seven hours later. However, they succeeded in preventing the destruction of the port before the defenders in turn surrendered to the larger invading forces.

Aftermath

A similar operation was carried out at Oran (Operation Reservist), but with even less success; however, the Operation Torch landings were overall successful, the operations Terminal and Reservist were the only setbacks in the entire operation.

G. Naval Battle for Casablanca

Date: 8–16 November 1942 **Location:** Casablanca, French Morocco **Result:** American Victory	
Belligerents	
Commanders and Leaders	
United States: Henry Kent Hewitt	**Vichy France**: Felix Michelier
	Germany: Ernst Kals

Strength	
1 aircraft carrier	1 battleship
1 escort carrier	1 light cruiser
1 battleship	2 flotilla leaders
3 heavy cruisers	7 destroyers
1 light cruiser	8 sloops
14 destroyers	11 minesweepers
15 troopships	13 submarines
347 landing craft	7 aircraft
108 aircraft	
Casualties and Losses	
174 killed	462 killed
4 troopships sunk	200 wounded
150 landing craft sunk	1 battleship damaged
5 aircraft destroyed	1 light cruiser destroyed
1 battleship damaged	4 destroyers sunk
1 heavy cruiser damaged	7 submarines sunk
2 destroyers damaged	1 submarine scuttled
1 oiler damaged	2 submarines damaged
	1 destroyer grounded
	2 flotilla leaders grounded
	1 submarine grounded
	7 aircraft destroyed

The Naval Battle of Casablanca was a series of naval engagements fought between American ships covering the invasion of North Africa and Vichy French ships defending the neutrality of French Morocco in accordance with the Second Armistice at Compiègne during the Second World War. The last stages of the battle consisted of operations by German U-Boats which had reached the area the same day the French troops surrendered.

Allied military planners anticipated an all-American force assigned to seize the Atlantic port city of Casablanca might be greeted as liberators. As an invasion task force of 102 American ships carrying 35,000 American soldiers approached the Moroccan coast undetected under cover of darkness. French defenders interpreted the first contacts as a diversionary raid for a major landing in Algeria; and Germany regarded the surrender of six Moroccan divisions to a small commando raiding force as a clear violation of French obligations to defend Moroccan neutrality under the Armistice of 22 June 1940 at Compiègne. An escalating series of surprised responses in an atmosphere of mistrust and secrecy caused the loss of four US troopships and the deaths of 462 men aboard twenty-four French ships opposing the invasion.

Background

Morocco was a protectorate of France at the time of the Second World War. The French government at Vichy had surrendered to Germany after the battle of France, signing an Armistice with Nazi Germany. General Charles de Gaulle led French forces opposed to the surrender and to the Vichy government, continuing the war on the side of the UK and the Allies. The Vichy regime – which controlled Morocco – was thus officially neutral. But in practical terms the Armistice obliged Vichy to resist any attempt to seize French territory or equipment for use against Germany. British forces had bombarded the French at Mers-el-Kébir to prevent the French fleet from falling into German hands after the French rejected demands to join the Allies or sail to a neutral port, leading to much ill-will between France and Britain. The US government had previously recognized the Vichy regime as legitimate. Military planning for Operation Torch in 1942 emphasized American troops in the initial landing forces based on intelligence estimates they would be less vigorously opposed than British soldiers.

American Forces

Troopship convoy UGF 1 left Chesapeake Bay on 23 October 1942 and was joined on 26 October by a covering force of battleships and cruisers sailing from Casco Bay and on 28 October by the aircraft carrier USS *Ranger*, and the escort carriers USS *Sangamon*, *Suwannee*, *Chenango*, and *Santee* sailed from Bermuda. These ships were screened by thirty-eight American destroyers. The resulting Task Force 34 (TF 34) included 102 ships for the invasion of Morocco under the command of Rear Admiral Henry Kent Hewitt aboard the flagship heavy cruiser USS *Augusta*. As TF 34 sailed, the British submarine HMS *Seraph* landed Major General Mark W Clark near Algiers to meet with pro-American French military officers stationed in Algeria. French officers shared information about defensive arrangements; but the Americans did not share critical invasion details of timing, strength and distribution of forces. No information was provided to key French leaders including Armed Forces Commander-in-Chief Admiral François Darlan, North African Commander-in-Chief General Alphonse Juin, or Moroccan Resident General Charles Noguès.

French Forces

In 1942, Casablanca was the principal Vichy-controlled port on the Atlantic (all of France's Atlantic coast having been occupied by Germany since 1940) and the most important Vichy-controlled naval base after Toulon. Naval gunners manned the El Hank coastal artillery battery of four 194mm (7.6in) guns and four 138mm

(5.4in) guns. One quadruple 380mm/45 Modèle 1935-gun turret of the modern battleship *Jean Bart* was operational, although the battleship remained incomplete following escape from the Saint-Nazaire shipyards during German invasion of 1940. One light cruiser, two flotilla leaders, seven destroyers (two already damaged by collision), eight slops, eleven minesweepers, and eleven submarines were in port on the morning of 8 November.

Most French personnel attending General Clark's pre-invasion meeting were army officers. Information subsequently conveyed in pre-invasion contact with army personnel stationed in Morocco was interpreted as a request for recommendations. No pre-invasion contact has been documented with Vice Admiral Michelier, who commanded naval forces responsible for the defence of Casablanca. Vice Admiral Michelier was not yet in the confidence of North African officers in contact with the Americans, since he had been a member of the Armistice Commission until assuming his Casablanca post less than a month before the invasion.

Prelude

French defenders were placed on alert status when Algerian invasion convoys were detected passing through the Strait of Gibraltar. Destinations remained unclear, and TF 34 remained undetected as it split into three groups on 7 November. Concealed by darkness, a northern group (six troopships and two cargo ships escorted by the battleship USS *Texas*, the light cruiser USS *Savannah* and six destroyers) prepared to land 9,000 troops of the 60th Infantry Regiment reinforced with sixty-five light tanks to seize Port Lyautey ai; and a southern group (four troopships and two cargo ships escorted by the battleship USS *New York*, the light cruiser USS *Philadelphia* and six destroyers) prepared to land 6,500 troops of the 47th Infantry Regiment reinforced with ninety medium and light tanks near the phosphate port of Safi to cover the southern approaches to Casablanca, whilst the centre group prepared to land the Casablanca occupation force of 19,500 troops of the 3rd Infantry Division reinforced with seventy-nine light tanks near Fédala, 15 miles (24 km) northeast of Casablanca. Naval coastal defence batteries flanked both ends of the Fédala landing beach with four 138mm (5.4in) guns on Pont Blondin to the east and three 10cm (3.9in) and two 75mm (3in) guns in Fédala on the point sheltering the western end of the beach.

Battle

8 November

Centre group troopships USS *William P. Biddle, Leonard Wood, Joseph T. Dickman, Tasker H. Bliss, Hugh L. Scott, Joseph Hewes. Edward Rutledge, Charles Carroll, Thomas Jefferson, Ancon, Elizabeth C. Stanton, Thirston, Arcturus, Procyon,* and *Oberon* anchored 8 miles <13km> (7nmi) off Fédala at midnight. Loaded landing craft rendezvoused and left the line of departure at 06:00 hours. Pont Blondin coast defence batteries were alerted by the noise of landing craft engines and illuminated the beach approaches with searchlights, but the searchlights were extinguished when the landing craft support boats opened fire with machine guns. The destroyer USS *Wilkes* and a scout boat tasked with marking Red Beach 2 moved out of position whilst manoeuvring to avoid an unidentified bat evaluated as potentially hostile; and landing craft ran onto rocks whilst running at full speed rather than reaching their intended beach. Twenty-one of the 323 landing craft from USS *Leonard Wood* were wrecked. Eight of the ship's surviving landing craft were wrecked in heavy surf waves whilst landing. Whilst the covering force engaged El Hank battery west of Casablanca, seven ships of the French 2nd Light Squadron sortied from Casablanca harbour at 09:00 hours under cover of a smoke screen to attack the troopships anchored off Fédala to the east. The French destroyer Milan sortied with destroyers Fougueux and Boulonnais. At 09:20 hours, the French squadron was strafed by fighter planes from USS *Ranger*.

French gunners sank a landing craft and scored hits on USS *Ludlow*. The French ship Milan beached after being damaged by gunfire from USS *Wilkes*, *Wichita*, and *Tuscaloosa*. USS *Massachusetts* and *Tuscaloosa* engaged the French destroyers *Fougueux* at 10:00 hours and *Boulonnaiais* at 10:12 hours. *Fougueux* sank at 10:40 hours. The French light cruiser *Primauguet* sortied with flotilla leader destroyer *Albatros* and destroyers *Brestois* and *Frondeur*. Engaged by USS *Massachusetts*, the *Primauguet* force was outgunned; *Primauguet* had been under refit and was not fully operational but returned fire, nonetheless. The French flotilla was also engaged by USS *Augusta* and *Brooklyn* from 11:00 to 11:20 hours. *Albatross* beached to avoid sinking. The remaining ships returned to Casablanca harbour where *Primauguet* beached and burnt out and the two destroyers capsized. Forty-five crew members were killed aboard *Primauguet*, and more than 200 more were wounded. The French submarine *Amazone* missed USS *Brooklyn* with a salvo of torpedoes. French submarine *Sibylle* (Q175) disappeared on a patrol station between Casablanca and Fédala, but the cause of her destruction remains uncertain. Surviving French submarines *Sidi Ferruch* and *Le Conquérant* sortied without torpedoes to avoid destruction in the harbour. *Le Tonnant* managed to load a few torpedoes before leaving. USS *Augusta* sank *Boulonnais* at noon and the only French destroyer remaining operational was *L'Alcyon*.

A less significant victim of this engagement was the boat in which General George S. Patton had intended to reach the beach from the flagship USS *Augusta*. The boat had been swung out on davits in preparation for launch when muzzle blast from the cruiser's 8-inch (20 cm) guns blew out the bottom of the boat, causing most of Patton's luggage to be lost overboard.

Three small French warships emerged from Casablanca harbour in the early afternoon to rescue sailors from the sunken destroyer *Fougueux*, but the rescue ships were turned back by shellfire from the American covering force. French planes bombed and strafed the landing beach at intervals throughout the day but caused little damage. Workmen had repaired *Jean Bart*'s turret by sundown, and El Hank battery remained operational. Nearly half of the 347 American landing craft had been destroyed, and fewer than 8,000 troops had been landed. Five French submarines still stalked the invasion fleet.

9 November

Dawn found the Fédala landing beaches lashed by 6-foot waves which greatly impeded unloading the invasion troopships. Forty per cent of the troops were ashore with barely one per cent of their supplies. These were shortages of ammunition, and inadequate medical supplies for the wounded. Communications broke down because radio equipment was still aboard the troopships. The advance towards Casablanca halted because shore parties lacked mechanized equipment to move supplies off the landing beach.

10 November

The French sloops Commandant Delage and la Gracieuse sorted at 10:00 hours to open fire on American troops advancing from Fédala to the outskirts of Casablanca. The cruiser USS *Augusta* and destroyers USS *Edison* and *Tillman* chased the minesweepers back into Casablanca harbour before being forced to retreat by gunfire from the French battleship *Jean Bart*. Nine dive bombers from USS *Ranger* hit *Jean Bart* with two 1,000lb bombs and sank her at 16:00 hours. *Jean Bart* settled into the harbour mud with decks awash. French submarines *Le Tonnant, Méduse* and *Antiope* launched unsuccessful torpedo salvos at USS *Ranger*, *Massachusetts*, and *Tuscaloosa*. Respectively. French submarine *Méduse* was crippled by counterattacks and beached off Cape Blanc.

11 November

Casablanca surrendered on 11 November whilst 11,000 tons of supplies for the invading troops remained aboard the troopships. That day German submarines were able to reach the troopships before they completed offloading cargo. In the early evening, U-173 torpedoed the destroyer USS *Hambleton*, the oiler USS *Winooski* and the troopship USS *Joseph Hewes*; around 100 men went down with USS *Joseph Hewes*. At this time USS *Bristol* spotted a surfaced submarine and engaged with her deck guns and finally with depth charges but is not believed to have sunk the French submarine. French submarine *Sidi Ferruch* was sunk by Grumman TBF Avenger torpedo bombers from USS *Suwannee*, escort carrier on 11 November.

Final Actions

The invasion troopships remained in their makeshift anchorage to keep Casablanca's harbour open to unload additional troops from the anticipated arrival of convoy of UGF 2 until U-130 – under Ernst Kals – torpedoed the troopships USS *Tasker H. Bliss, Hugh L. Scott* and *Edward Rutledge* on the evening of 12 November, killing seventy-four additional American servicemen, and prompting undamaged troopships to leave the anchorage and manoeuvre evasively at sea until they were able to moor in the lee of the Casablanca breakwater on 13 November to complete offloading supplies. Of the American ships damaged by submarine torpedoes on 11 and 12 November, all four troopships sank, but the oiler and destroyer were repaired. Surviving troopships left Casablanca when unloading was completed on 17 November. French submarines Amazone and Antiope reached Dakar, and Orphée returned to Casablanca after the city surrendered. *Le Conquérant* was sunk on 13 November by two VP-92 PBY Catalina flying boats off Villa Cisneros. *Le Tonnant* was scuttled off Cadiz on 15 November. On 16 November, U-173 was sunk off Casablanca by American destroyers.

One of the USS *Massachusetts* 41cm (16-inch) shells, weighing more than a ton, fired at the French battleship *Jean Bart*, after an unexpected rebound on the quay, caused the collapse, with the death of three of its inhabitants, of the house adjoining the Ettedgui synagogue which remained intact, in Casablanca's medina. Later, the artificer's trolley to remove defused shell having given away under the overload, it was then necessary to send for a truck.

Chapter 2

Tunisian Campaign

November 1942–May 1943 (Battle of Tunisia)

Tunisian Campaign	
Date: 17 November 1942–13 May 1942 **Location:** French Tunisia **Result:** Allied Victory **Territorial changes:** • Tunisia back under French occupation and End of the North African campaign	
Belligerents	
United Kingdom **• India** **• Newfoundland**	**Germany** **Italy**
United States **France** **Free France** **New Zealand** **Greece**	
Commanders and Leaders	
United Kingdom: Harold Alexander	**Germany**: Albert Kesselring
United Kingdom: Kenneth Anderson	**Germany**: Erwin Rommel
United Kingdom: Bernard Montgomery	**Germany**: H. J. von Arnim
United States: Dwight D Eisenhower	**Italy**: Giovanni Messe
United States: Lloyd Fredendall	
United States: George S Patton	
Free France: Charles de Gaulle	
Free France: Philippe Leclerc	
France: Alphonse Juin	
Strength	
March:	**March:**
500,000 troops	350,000 troops

1,800+ tanks	200+ tanks
1,200+ field guns	1,000+ field guns
Thousands of aircraft	Thousands of aircraft
Casualties and Losses	
76,020	290,000–362,000 (238,000–300,00 captured)
849 aircraft destroyed	2,422+ aircraft destroyed
340+ tanks lost	600+ aircraft captured
	450+ tanks lost
	1,000+ guns captured
	Thousands of trucks captured

The **Tunisian campaign** (also known as the **Battle of Tunisia**) was a series of battles that took place in Tunisia during the North African campaign of the Second World War, between Axis and Allied forces, from 17 November 1942 to 13 May 1943. The Allies consisted of British Imperial forces, including a Greek contingent, with American and French corps. The battle opened with initial success by the Germans and Italian forces, but the massive supply interdiction efforts led to the decisive defeat of the Axis. Over 250,000 German and Italian troops were taken as prisoners of war, including most of the Afrika Korps.

Background

Western Desert

The first two years of the war in North Africa were characterized by chronic supply shortages and transport problems. The North African coast has a few natural harbours and the British base at Alexandria on the Nile delta was some 1,300 miles (2092 km) by road from the main Italian port at Tripoli in Libya. Similar ports at Benghazi and Tobruk were 650 miles (1046 km) and 400 miles (644 km) west of Alexandria on the Litoranea Balbo (Via Balbia) running along a narrow corridor along the coast. Control of the central Mediterranean was contested by the British and Italian navies, which were equally matched and exerted a reciprocal constraint supply through Alexandria, Tripoli, Benghazi and Tobruk, although the British could supply Egypt via the long route through the Atlantic around the Cape of Good Hope and by the Indian Ocean into the Red Sea.

The chronic difficulty in the supply of military forces in the desert led to several indecisive victories by both sides and long fruitless advances along the coast. The Italian invasion of Egypt by the Tenth Army in 1940 advanced 60 miles (96 km) into Egypt and more than 1,000 miles (1609 km) in a straight line from Tripoli, 370 miles (596 km) from Benghazi and 200 miles (322 km) from Tobruk. The Western Desert Force (WDF) fought a delaying action as it fell back to Mersa Matruh, then began Operation Compass, a raid and counterattack into Libya.

The Italian Tenth Army destroyed and the WDF occupied El Agheila, some 600 miles (66 km) from Alexandria. With the arrival of the German Afrika Korps, the Axis counterattacked in Operation Sonnenblume and in April 1941 reached the limit of their supply capacity at the Egyptian border but failed to recapture Tobruk.

In November 1941, the British Eighth Army recovered, helped by the short supply distance from Alexandria to the front line and launched Operation Crusader, relieving the Siege of Tobruk and again reached El Agheila. The Eighth Army was soon pushed back to Gazala west of Tobruk and at the Battle of Gazala in May 1942, the Axis pushed them all the way back to El Alamein, only 100 miles (161 km) from Alexandria. In 1942, the Royal Navy and Italian Navy were still disputing the Mediterranean but the British kept hold of Malta (a strategic island during the conflict), and intelligence from Ultra allowed the RAF to sink more Italian supply ships. Large quantities of supplies became available to the British from the United States and the supply situation of the Eighth Army eventually resolved. With the Eighth Army no longer constrained, the Axis were driven westwards from Egypt following the Second Battle of El Alamein in November 1942.

Operation Torch

In July 1942, the Allies discussed relatively small-scale amphibious operations to land in northern France during 1942 (Operation Sledgehammer, which was the forerunner of Operation Roundup, the main landings in 1943), but agreed that these operations were impractical and should be deferred. Instead, it was agreed that landings would be made to secure the Vichy territories in North Africa (Morocco, Algiers, and Tunisia) and then to thrust east to take the Axis forces in the Western Desert in their rear. An Allied occupation of the whole of the North African coast would open the Mediterranean to Allied shipping, releasing the huge capacity required to maintain supplies around the circuitous route via Cape of Good Hope. On 8 November, Operation Torch landed Allied forces in Algeria (at Oran and Algiers) and Morocco (at Casablanca) with the intention that once Vichy forces had capitulated, an advance would be made to Tunis some 500 miles (805 km) to the east.

Prelude

Allied Plans

Because of the nearness of Sicily to Tunisia, the Allies expected that Axis would move to occupy the country as soon as they heard of the Torch landings. To forestall this, it would be necessary to occupy Tunisia as quickly as possible after the landings were made. However, there was a limit to how far east the Torch landings could be made because of the increasing proximity of Axis airfields in Sicily and Sardinia which at the end of October 1942 held 298 German and 574 Italian aircraft. Algiers was accordingly chosen for the most easterly landings. This would ensure the success of the initial landings in spite of uncertainty as to how the incumbent French forces would react. Once Algiers was secured, a small force, the Eastern Task Force, would be projected as quickly as possible into Tunisia in a race to occupy Tunis, some 500 miles (805 km) distance along poor roads in difficult terrain during the winter rainy season, before the Axis could get organized.

However, planners had to assume the worst case regarding the extent of Vichy opposition at Algiers and the invasion convoys were assault-loaded with preponderance of infantry to meet heavy ground opposition. This meant that at Algiers the disembarkation of mobile forces for an advance to Tunis would necessarily be delayed. Plans were thus a compromise, and the Allies could establish themselves representing a gamble which depended on the ability of the navy and air force to delay the Axis build-up. The Allies, although they had provided for the possibility of strong Vichy opposition to their landings both in terms of infantry and air force allocations, seriously underestimated the Axis appetite for and speed of intervention in Tunis.

Once operations had commenced and despite clear intelligence reports regarding the Axis reaction, the Allies were slow to respond, and it was not until nearly two weeks after the landings that air and naval plans were made to interdict Axis Sea transport to Tunis. At the end of November, naval Force K was reformed in Malta with three cruisers and four destroyers and Force Q formed in Bône with three cruisers and two destroyers. No Axis ships sailing to Tunis were sunk in November 1942, but the Allied naval forces had some in early December 1942 sinking seven Axis transports. However, this came too late to affect the fighting on land because the armoured elements of 10th Panzer Division had already arrived. To counter the surface threat, Axis convoys were switched to daylight when they could be protected by air cover, simultaneously denying the Allies the advantage of using radar in night surface combat. Night convoys resumed on completion of the extension of Axis minefields which severely restricted the activities of Force K and Force Q.

Tunisia

Tunisia is said to be shaped like a pregnant woman, with its northern and much of its eastern boundary (the head and belly) on the Mediterranean coast. Most of the inland western border with Algeria (the back) is astride the eastern line of the Atlas Mountains which run from the Atlantic coast of Morocco, 1,200 miles (1,931 km) east of Tunis. This portion of the border is easily defensible at the small number of passes through the two north-south lines of the mountains. In the south and lower range of mountains limit the approaches to a narrow gap, facing Libya to the east, between the Matmata Hills and the coast. The French had earlier constructed a 12-mile-(19 km)wide and 19-mile-(31 km)deep series of defensive works known as the Mareth Line along the plain, to defend against an Italian invasion from Libya.

Only in the north was the terrain favourable to attack; here the Atlas Mountains stopped near the eastern coast, leaving a large area on the north-west coast unprotected. Defensive lines in the north could deal with approaching forces, whilst the Mareth Line made the south secure. In between, there were only a few easily

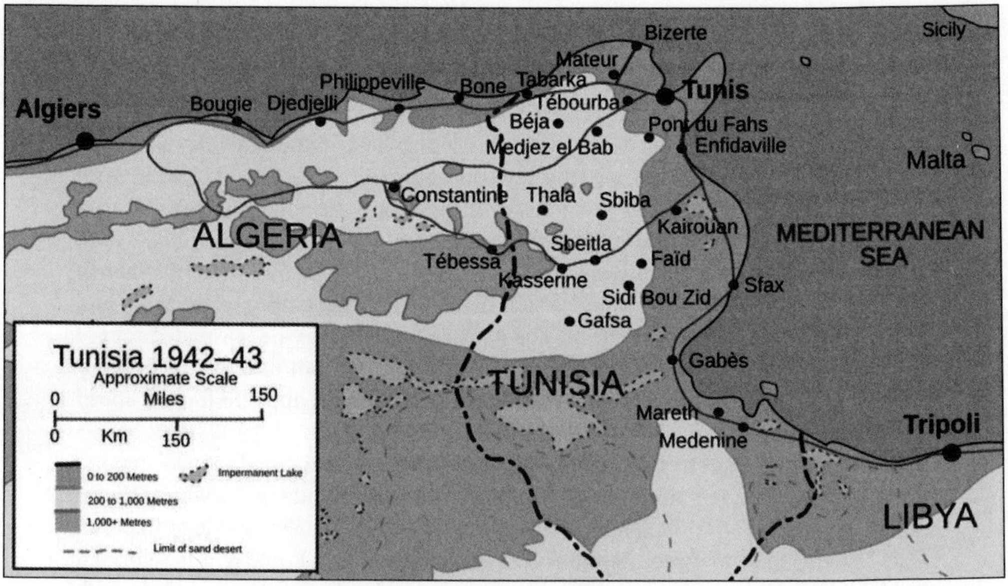

Sketch Map of Tunisia During the 1942–1943 Campaign.
(I, the copyright holder of this work, release this work into the Public Domain. This applies worldwide, in some countries this may not be legally possible; if so; I grant anyone the right to use this work for any purpose, without any conditions, unless such conditions are required by law. Source: Own work by Author–S. Kirrage File: Tunisia 1942-1943.svg Email received from Stephen Kirrage - 15:58, 2 May 2023 (UTC) giving consent.)

defended passes through the Atlas Mountains. Tunisia has two big deep-water ports in Tunis and Bizerte, only a few hundred miles from the Italian supply bases in Sicily. Ships could deliver supplies at night, safe from RAF patrols and return the next night, whilst Libya was a full-day trip, making supply operations vulnerable to daylight air attack. In Hitler's view, Tunisia could be held indefinitely, upsetting Allied plans in Europe.

Run for Tunis

By 10 November, French opposition to the Torch landings had ceased, creating a military vacuum in Tunisia. The First Army (Lieutenant General Kenneth Anderson) was immediately ordered to send the 36th Infantry Brigade Group, which had been the floating reserve for the Algiers landing, eastwards by sea to occupy the Algerian ports of Bougi, Philippeville, and Bône and the airfield at Djedjelli, preliminary to advancing into Tunisia. The CCS had decided that with the forces available, Torch would not include landings close to Tunisia. Anderson needed to get his limited force east quickly, before the Axis could reinforce Tunisia, but the Allies had only two brigade groups some additional armour and artillery for the attack.

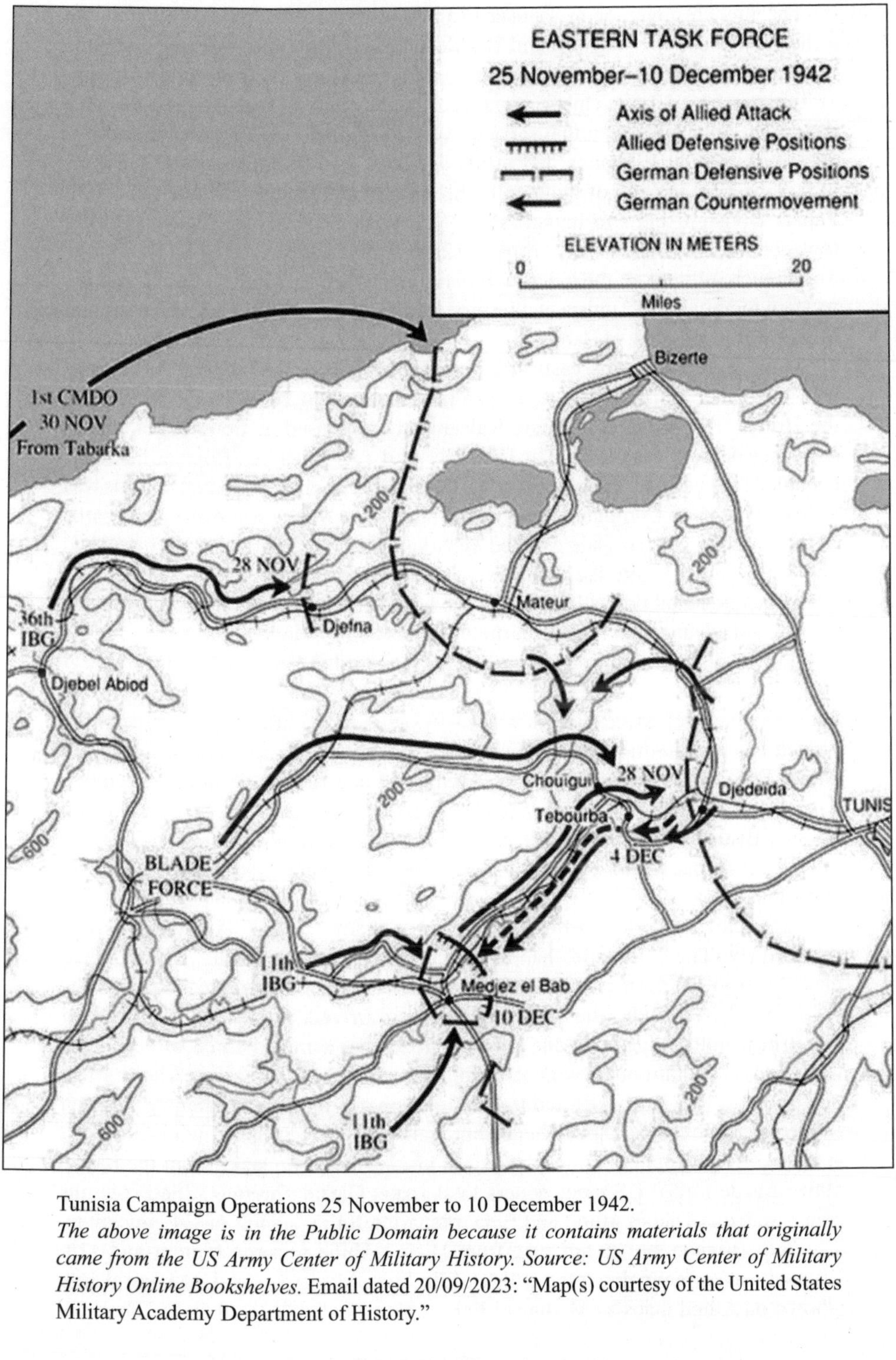

Tunisia Campaign Operations 25 November to 10 December 1942.
The above image is in the Public Domain because it contains materials that originally came from the US Army Center of Military History. Source: US Army Center of Military History Online Bookshelves. Email dated 20/09/2023: “Map(s) courtesy of the United States Military Academy Department of History.”

The French governor in Tunisia, Admiral Esteva, was afraid to support the Allies or oppose the Axis. He did not close airfields to either side; the Germans moved first and by 9 November, there were reports of forty German aircraft arriving at Tunis and by 10 November, aerial reconnaissance reported 100 aircraft. Two days later, an airlift began that carried over 15,000 men and 581 tons of supplies and ships brought 176 tanks, 131 artillery pieces, 1,152 vehicles and 13,000 tons of supplies. By the end of the month, three German divisions, including the 10th Panzer Division, and two Italian infantry divisions had arrived. Walther Nehring took command of the new XC Corps on 12 November and arrived on 17 November. The French military commander in Tunisia, General Barré, moved troops into the western mountains of Tunisia and formed a defensive line from Tebersouk through Majaz al Bab (Medjez el Bab).

There were two roads eastwards into Tunisia from Algeria. The Allied plan was to advance along the two roads and take Bizerte and Tunis. On 11 November, the British 36th Infantry Brigade had landed unopposed at Bougie, but supply shortages delayed their arrival at Djedjelli until 13 November. Bône airfield was occupied following a parachute drop by British 3rd Parachute Battalion and this was followed by No. 6 Commando seizing the port on 12 November. Advanced guards of the 36th Infantry Brigade reached Tebarka on 15 November and Djebel Abiod on 18 November where they met Axis forces. Further south, on 15 November, a US parachute battalion made an unopposed drop at Youks-les-Bains, capturing the airfield and advanced to take the airfield at Gafsa on 17 November.

On 19 November Nehring demanded passage for his forces across the bridge at Medjez and was refused by Barré. The Germans attacked twice and were repulsed, but the French defensive success was costly, and lacking armour and artillery, the French had to withdraw. Some Vichy French forces, such as Barré's, joined the Allies. But the attitude of Vichy forces remained uncertain until on 22 November, when the 'Darlan Deal' placed French North Africa on the Allied side. This allowed US and British forces that had been securing Algeria to go to the front. By this time, the Axis had deployed a corps in Tunisia and outnumbered the Allies there in almost all ways.

Two Allied brigade groups advanced towards Djebel Abiod and Béja respectively. The Luftwaffe, happy to have local air superiority whilst Allied planes had to fly from relatively distant bases in Algeria, harassed them all the way. On 17 November, the same day Nehring arrived, the leading elements of the British 36th Brigade on the northern road met a mixed force of seventeen tanks and 400 paratroopers with self-propelled guns at Djebel Abiod. The German paratroopers, with Luftwaffe and Italian fire support from the 1st Infantry Division 'Superga', knocked out eleven tanks, but their advance was halted whilst the fight at Djebel Abiod continued for nine days. On 22 November, tanks from the Italian 50th Brigade forced US paratroopers to abandon Gafsa. The two Allied columns concentrated at Djebel Abiod and Béja, preparing for an assault on 24 November. The 36th Brigade was to advance from Djebel Abiod towards Mateur and 11th Brigade was to move down the valley of the river Merjerda to take Majaz al Bab (shown on Allied maps as Medjaz el Bab or just 'Medjez') and then to Tebourba,

Djedeida and Tunis. Blade Force, an armoured regimental group made up of 37mm gun M3 Stuart light tanks and 75mm M3 GMC self-propelled anti-tank guns, was to strike across country on minor roads in the gap between the two infantry brigades towards Sidi Nsir and make flanking attacks on Terbourba and Djedeida.

The northern attack did not take place because torrential rain had slowed the build-up. In the south 11th Brigade were halted by stiff resistance at Medjez. Blade Force passed through Sidi Nsir to reach the Chouigui Pass, north of Terbourba part of B Squadron Stuart's from Blade Force infiltrated behind Axis lines to the newly activated airbase at Djedeiba in the afternoon and destroyed more than twenty Axis planes but lacking infantry support, withdrew to Chouigui.

The understrength tank Squadrons and three M3 GMC French 75s were to hold the pass. A mixed unit of Panzer III and Panzer IVs and a small Italian scouting force, around fifteen tanks all told. Frontal attacks by the GMCs and Stuarts were ineffective losing 12 tanks but allowed a rear attack by B Squadron firing into the weaker armour of the German tanks.

The German commander, believing he had encountered a much stronger force, retreated. Blade Force's attack caught Nehring by surprise and he decided to withdraw from Medjez and strengthen Djedeida, only 19 miles (31 km) from Tunis. The 36th Brigade's delayed attack began on 26 November, but they were ambushed with the leading battalion taking 149 casualties. Further attacks were driven back from the cleverly planned interlocking defences. No. 1 Commando landed 14 miles (23 km) west of Bizerte on 30 November to outflank the Jefna position but failed and re-joined 36th Brigade by 3 December. The position remained in German hands until the last days of fighting in Tunisia the following spring.

Early on 26 November, as the Germans withdrew, 11th Brigade were able to enter Medjez unopposed and by late in the day had taken positions in and around Tebourba, which had also been evacuated by the Germans, preparatory to advancing on Djedeiba. However, on 27 November the Germans attacked in strength, 11th Brigade tried to regain the initiative in the early hours of 28 November attacking towards Djedeiba airfield with the help of US armour but failed. On 29 November, Combat Command B of US 1st Armoured Division had concentrated forwards for an attack in conjunction with Blade Force planned for 2 December. They were forestalled by an Axis counterattack, led by Major General Wolfgang Fischer, whose 10th Panzer Division had just arrived in Tunisia. By the evening of 2 December, Blade Force had been withdrawn, leaving 11th Brigade and Combat Command B to deal with the Axis attack.

The attack threatened to cut off 11th Brigade and break through into the Allied rear, but desperate fighting over four days delayed the Axis advance and permitted a controlled withdrawal to the high ground on each side of the river west of Terbourba.

The Allies force initially withdrew 6 miles (10 km) to high positions on Longstop Hill (Djebel el Ahmera) and Bou Aoukaz on each side of the river. Concern over the vulnerability to flanking attacks prompted a further withdrawal west. By the end of 10 December, Allied units held a defensive line just east of Medjez el bab. Here, they started a build-up for another attack and were ready by late December 1942. The slow build-up had brought Allied force levels up to a total of 54,000 British, 73,800 American and 7,000 French troops. A hasty intelligence review showed about 125,000 combat and 70,000 service troops, mostly Italian, in front of them. The main attack began the afternoon of 22 December. Despite rain and insufficient air cover, progress was made up the lower ridges of the 900-foot Longstop Hill that controlled the river corridor from Medjez to Tebourba and thence to Tunis. After three days of to-and-fro fighting, with ammunition running low and Axis forces now holding adjacent ground, the Longstop position became untenable and the Allies were forced to withdraw to Medjez, and by 26 December 1942 the Allies had withdrawn to the line they had set out from some two weeks earlier, having suffered 20,743 casualties.

Aftermath

Whilst the battles wound down, factionalism among the French again erupted. On 24 December, François Darlan was assassinated by an anti-Vichy French monarchist, and Henri Giraud succeeded him as high commissioner. To the frustration of the Free French, the US government had displayed considerable willingness to make a deal with Darlan and the Vichyites. Consequently, Darlan's death appeared to present an opportunity to bring together the French in North Africa and Charles de Gaulle's Free French. De Gaulle and Giraud met in late January, but little progress was made in reconciling their differences or the constituencies they represented.

It was not until June 1943 that the French Committee of National Liberation (CFLN) was formed undern the joint chairmanship of Giraud and de Gaulle. De Gaulle quickly eclipsed Giraud, who openly disliked political responsibility and more or less willingly from then on deferred to the Leader of the Free French, namely, de Gaulle.

Command Changes

Nehring, considered by most to be an excellent commander, had continually infuriated his superiors with outspoken critiques. He was 'replaced' when the command was renamed the Fifth Panzer Army and Colonel General Hans-Jürgen von Arnim arrived in Tunis unannounced on 8 December, to assume command. The Army consisted of the composite von Broich battlegroup in the Bizerte area, the 10th Panzer Division in the centre before Tunis and the 1st Infantry Division 'Superga' on the southern flank, but Hitler had told Arnim that the Army would grow to three mechanized and three motorized divisions. The Allies had tried to prevent the Axis build-up with substantial air and sea forces, but Tunis and Bizerte were only 120 miles (193 km) from the ports and airfields of western Sicily, 180 miles (290 km) from Palermo and 300 miles (483 km) from Naples, making it very difficult to intercept Axis transports which had the benefit of substantial air cover. From mid-November 1942 to January 1943, 243,000 men and 870,000 tons of supplies and equipment arrived in Tunisia by sea and air.

General Eisenhower transferred further units from Morocco and Algeria eastwards into Tunisia, In the north, the British First Army, over the next three months, received three more British divisions, the 1st, 4th, and 46th Infantry divisions, joining the 6th Armoured and 7th Infantry divisions.

By late March the British IX Corps HQ (Lieutenant General John Crocker) had arrived to join the British V Corps (Lieutenant General Charles Allfrey) in commanding the expanded army. On their right flank, the basis of a two-division French XIX Corps (General Alphonse Juin) was assembling.

In the south was the US II Corps (Major General Lloyd Fredendall), consisting of the 1st and 34th Infantry divisions and the 1st Armoured Division (although the 34th Division was attached to the British IX Corps to the north). Giraud refused to have the French XIX Corps under the command of the British Army and so they, along with the US II Corps, remained under command of Allied Force Headquarters (AFHQ). New forwards airfields were built to improve air support. The Americans also began bases in Algeria and Tunisia, to form a large forwards base at Maknassy, on the eastern edge of the Atlas Mountains, well placed to cut off the Panzerarmee in the south from Tunis and the Fifth Panzer Army in the north.

Prelude

During the first half of January 1943, Anderson had with mixed results kept constant pressure through limited attacks and reconnaissance in strength. Arnim did the same and on 18 January, launched Operation Eilbote I ('Courier I'). Elements of the 10th Panzer and 334th Infantry divisions attacked from Pont du Fahs to create more space in front of the Superga Division and forestall an Allied thrust east to the coast at Enfidaville. To cut Rommel's line of communication, the westwards thrust against the right wing of the British V Corps at Bou Arada had little success but further south his attack against French positions around the 'hinge' of the Western and Eastern Dorsals succeeded, advancing 35 miles (56 km) south of Ousseltia and 25 miles (40 km) south-west to Robba. The poorly equipped defenders resisted well but were overwhelmed and the equivalent of seven infantry battalions were cut off in the mountains. Anderson sent 36th Brigade to Robba and requested Lloyd Fredendall to send Combat Command B from 1st Armoured Division to Ousseltia, to come under Juin's orders on arrival. Fierce fighting lasted until 23 January, but the front was stabilized.

The lack of Allied co-ordination led Eisenhower to change the command structure. On 21 January Anderson was made responsible for the co-ordination of the whole front and on 24 January his responsibilities were extended to include 'the employment of American troops'. That night, Juin accepted the command of Anderson, confirmed by Giraud the next day but with forces spread over a 200-mile (322 km) front and poor communication (Anderson motored over 1,000 miles (1609 km) in four days to speak to the corps commanders) the practical difficulties remained. Eisenhower appointed an air support commander, Brigadier General Laurence S. Kuter, for the whole front on 21 January.

Erwin Rommel had made plans for forces retreating through Libya to dig in in front of the defunct French fortifications of the Mareth Line. The Axis forces would control the two natural entrances into Tunisia in the north and south, with only the easily defensible mountain passes between them. In January, those parts of the German Italian Panzer Army on the Mareth Line defences were renamed First Italian Army (General Giovanni Messe), separate from the units (including the remains of the Afrika Korps) he had facing the Western Dorsal. On 23 January 1943, the Eighth Army took Tripoli, by which point the army retreating through Libya was already well on its way to the Mareth Line position. Part of the US II Corps crossed into Tunisia through passes in the Atlas Mountains from Algeria, controlling the interior of the triangle formed by the mountains, their position raised the possibility of a thrust eastwards towards Sfax on the coast, to cut off the First Italian Army at Mareth from Arnim's forces to the north around Tunis. Rommel could not allow this and formed a plan for a spoiling attack.

As part of the ongoing Tunisian campaign, the Allied command would continue planning crucial operations to relieve Tunisia of the incumbent Axis forces before further advances could be planned. The following chapters look at the battles in greater depth, some they would lose and the majority of which they would win.

Chapter 3

Battle of Kasserine Pass

February 1943

Battle of Kasserine Pass	
Date: 19–24 February 1943 **Location:** Kasserine Pass, Kasserine, Tunisia **Result:** Axis Victory	
Belligerents	
United States **United Kingdom** **Free French**	**Germany** **Italy**
Commanders and leaders	
United States: Lloyd Fredenhall	**Germany**: Erwin Rommel
United Kingdom: Kenneth Anderson	
France: Alphonse Juin	
Strength	
30,000	22,000
Casualties and Losses	
United States:	**German & Italian:**
3,300 killed and wounded	989 killed and wounded
3,000 prisoners of war (PoWs)	608 captured
183 tanks lost	20 tanks lost
616 vehicles lost	67 vehicles lost
208 guns lost	14 guns lost
(Including Sidi Bou Zid)	(Including Sidi Bou Zid)
Free French:	
500 killed and wounded	
Total: 10,000 casualties	

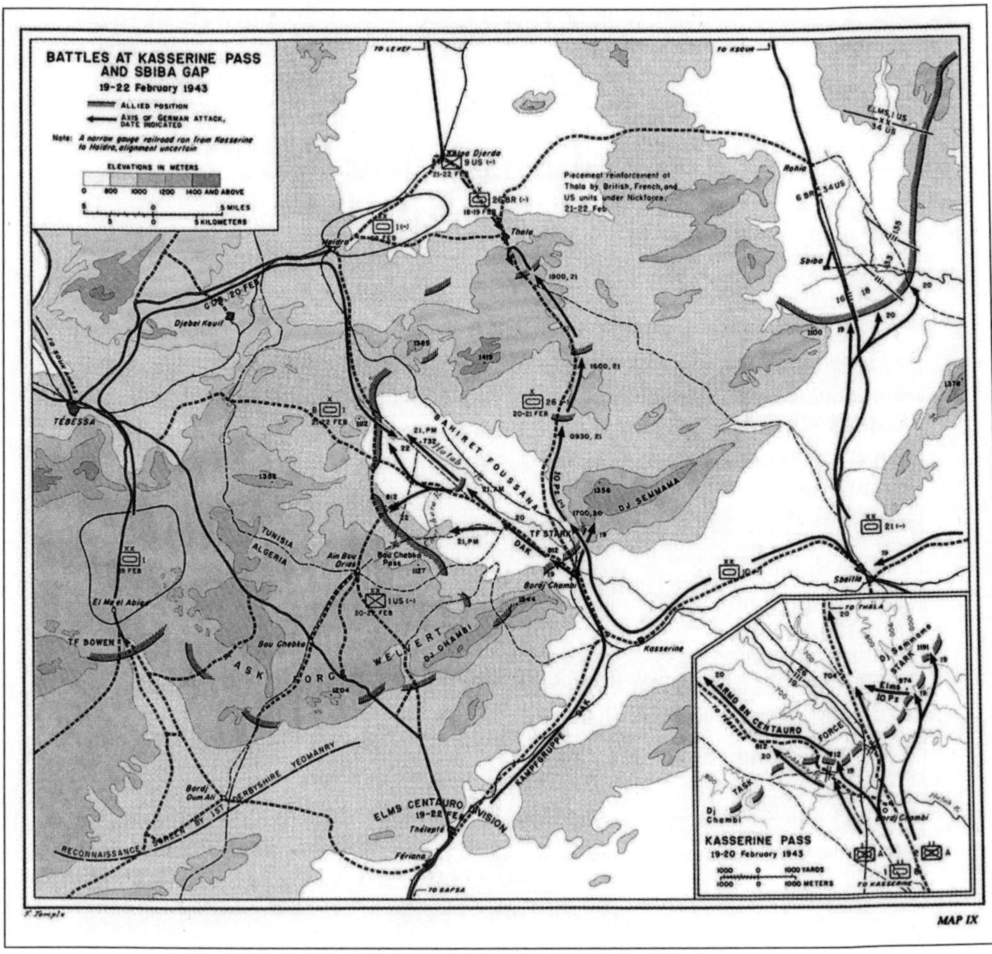

Battle of Kasserine Pass – 19–24 February 1943.
(*The above image is in the Public Domain in the United States – NO Copyright in the USA. Source: https://www.ibiblio.org/hyperwar/USA/USA-MTO-NWA/maps/USA-MTO-NWA-IX.jpg.* Email dated 20/09/2023: "Map(s) courtesy of the United States Military Academy Department of History.")

The **Battle of Kasserine Pass** took place from 18–24 February 1943 at Kasserine Pass, a 2-mile-(3 km)wide gap in the Grand Dorsal Chain of the Atlas Mountains in central Tunisia. It was a part of the Tunisian campaign of the Second World War.

The Axis forces, led by Generalfeldmarschall Erwin Rommel, were primarily from the Afrika Korps Assault Group, the Italian Centauro Armoured Division and two Panzer divisions detached from the Fifth Panzer Army, whilst the Allied forces were from the US II Corps (Major General Lloyd Fredendall), the British 6th Armoured Division (Major General Charles Keightley) and other parts of the First Army (Lieutenant General Kenneth Anderson).

The battle was the first major engagement between US and Axis forces in North Afrika. The initial handful of American battalions were inexperienced and poorly led; they suffered many casualties and were successfully pushed back over 50 miles (80 km) from their original positions west of Faïd Pass, until they met an advancing brigade of the US 1st Armoured Division. British units were also driven back, losing all their tanks in the process. After the initial defeat, Allied reinforcements with strong artillery support stopped the Axis advance, and recaptured the mountain passes in western Tunisia, defeating the Axis offensive. The Axis force was overextended and pinned down by the Allied artillery. Facing counterattacks and airstrikes, they withdrew from Kasserine Pass by 24 February.

General Anderson, the First Army commander, was judged to be at fault for, among other things, dispersing the three combat commands of the US 1st Armoured Division, despite the objections of Major General Orlando Ward, the divisional commander. As a result of lessons learned in the battle, the US Army instituted sweeping changes in unit organization and tactics and replaced some commanders and some types of equipment.

Background

US and British forces landed at several points along the coast of French Morocco and Algiers on 8 November 1942, during Operation Torch. This came only days after the breakthrough of the British Eighth Army (Lieutenant General Bernard Montgomery) following the Second Battle of El Alamein. In response, German and Italian troops were ferried in from Sicily to occupy Tunisia, one of the few easily defended areas of North Africa and only one night's sail from bases in Sicily.

This short passage made it very difficult for the Allied naval vessels to intercept Axis transports, and air interdiction proved equally difficult, because the nearest Allied airbase to Tunisia, in Malta was over 200 miles (322 km) distant.

The Run for Tunis in November and December 1942 is the term for an attempt to reach Tunis before German and Italian reinforcements could arrive. Because of the poor road and rail communications, only a small, division-sized Allied force could be supplied and due to the excellent defensive terrain, small numbers of German and Italian troops were sufficient to defeat the attempt. The Allied build-up continued, more aircraft became available and new airfields in western Algeria and Tunisia were built. The Allies reduced the flow of Axis troops and equipment into Tunis and Bizerte, but a sizeable Axis force was already ashore.

On 23 January 1943, the Allied Eighth Army took Tripoli, Erwin Rommel's main supply base. Rommel ad anticipated this, switching his line of supply to Tunis with the goal of blocking the southern approach to Tunisia from Tripoli at Gabès. The Mareth Line, which the French had built to protect against an Italian attack from Libya, was 'a line of antiquated French blockhouses, which in no way measured up to the standards required by modern warfare' (Rommel).

Allied troops had already crossed the Atlas Mountains and set up a forward base at Faïd, in the foothills on the eastern arm of the mountains, an excellent position to thrust east to the coast, split the Axis forces in southern Tunisia from the forces further north, and cut the line supply to Tunis.

Prelude

Faïd Pass

Elements of the Fifth Panzer Army, headed by General Hans-**Jürgen von Arnim** reached the Allied positions on the eastern foot of the Atlas Mountains on 30 January. The 21st Panzer Division met French troops at Faïd, and, despite excellent use of the French 2.95-inch (7.5cm) guns, which caused heavy casualties among the German infantry, the defenders were easily forced back.

US artillery and tanks of the 1st Armoured Division then entered the battle, destroying some enemy tanks and forcing the remainder into what appeared to be a headlong retreat. This was, however, a trap, and when the 1st Armoured Division gave chase, it was engaged by a screen of German anti-tank guns and sustained heavy casualties. A US forward artillery observer whose radio and landlines had been cut by shellfire recalled:

'It was murder. They rolled right into the muzzles of the concealed eighty-eights and all I could do was stand by and watch tank after tank blown to bits or burst into flames or just stop, wrecked. Those in the rear tried to turn back but the eighty-eights seemed to be everywhere.'–Westrate, 1944.

The 21st Panzer Division resumed its advance towards Faïd. American infantry casualties were exacerbated by the practice of digging shallow *shell scrapes* instead of *foxholes,* as German tank drivers could easily crush a man inside a scrape by driving into it and simultaneously making a half-turn. Several attempts were made by the 1st Armoured Division to stop the German advance, but all three combat commands found that each defensive position they tried to occupy had already been overrun, and they were attacked by German troops with heavy losses. On 2 February, the 1st Armoured Division was ordered to end its attacks and concentrate to form a reserve. The Germans capture most of Tunisia, and the entrances into the coastal lowlands were blocked. The Allies held the interior of the roughly triangular Atlas range, but with the exits blocked this was of little advantage to the Allies. For the next two weeks, Rommel and the Axis commanders further north debated what to do next.

Sidi Bou Zid

Rommel did not consider the Eight Army a serious threat because, until Tripoli was open, Montgomery could maintain only a small force in south Tunisia. Ships commenced unloading on 9 February, but the port was not fully operational until the end of the month. Rommel made a proposal in early February to Comando Supremo (Italian High Command in Rome) to attack with both battlegroups, including detachments from the Fifth Panzer Army, towards two US supply bases just to the west of the western arm of the mountains in Algeria. A quick thrust could capture the supplies and disrupt a US attempt to concentrate forces near Tébessa. Arnim objected and the attack was delayed for a week until agreement was reached to mount Operation Frühlingswind, a thrust by the Fifth Panzer Army through the US communications and supply centre of Sidi Bou Zid. Rommel's forces, 60 miles (7 km) to the south-west, would conduct Operation Morgenluft to capture Gafsa and advance on Tozeur.

On 14 February, the 10th and 21st Panzer divisions began the Battle of Sidi Bou Zid, about 10 miles (16 km) west of Faïd, in the interior plain of the Atlas Mountains. The US tanks were defeated and the infantry, poorly sited on three hills and unable to give mutual support, was isolated. A counterattack the next day was easily repulsed and on 16 February the Germans advanced towards Sbeitla. After the success at Sidi Bou Zid, Rommel ordered the Afrika Korps Assault Group to attack Gafsa on 15 February, but on the night before, Anderson ordered the defenders to evacuate Gafsa and make the main defence line the hills around Feriana, as he believed Gafsa should not be defended against a large attack. The next day, because of the threat to the southern flank, Anderson obtained Eisenhower's agreement and ordered a withdrawal from the Eastern Dorsale, to the line of the Western Dorsale from Feriana northwards. Early on 17 February, Fredendall ordered a withdrawal from Sbeitla and Feriana. The US XI Corps was able to concentrate at the Kasserine and Sbiba Passes, on the western arm of the mountains. US casualties were 2,546 men, 103 tanks, 280 vehicles, 18 guns, three anti-tank guns and an anti-aircraft battery.

Axis Plan of Attack

At this point, there was some argument in the Axis camp about what to do next; all of Tunisia was under Axis control, and there was little to do until the Eight Army arrived at Mareth. Rommel decided to attack through the Kasserine Pass into the main force of the US XI Corps at Tébessa to capture US supplies on the Algerian side of the western arm of the mountains, eliminate the Allied ability to attack the coastal corridor linking Mareth and Tunis and threaten the southern flank of the First Army. On February 18, Rommel submitted his proposals to Albert Kesselring, who forwarded them with his blessing to the Comando Supremo in Rome.

At 13:30 hours on 19 February Rommel received the Comando Supremo's agreement to a revised plan. He was to have 10th and 21st Panzer divisions transferred from Arnim's Fifth Panzer Army to his command and attack through the Kesserine and Sbiba Passes towards Thala and Le Kef to the north, clearing the Western Dorsale and threatening the First Army's flank. Rommel was appalled; the plan dispersed Axis forces and, through the passes, would expose their flanks. A concentrated attack at Tébessa, whilst entailing some risk, could yield badly needed supplies, destroy Allied potential for operations into central Tunisia and capture the airfield at Youks-les-Bains, west of Tébessa.

Battle

In the early hours of 19 February, Rommel ordered the Afrika Korps Assault Group from Feriana to attack the Kasserine Pass. The 21st Panzer Division at Sbeitla was ordered to attack northwards through the pass east of Kasserine which led to Sbiba and Ksour. The *Kampfgruppe von Broich,* the battlegroup released by Arnim from 10th Panzer Division, was ordered to concentrate at Sbeitla, where it would be ready to exploit success in either pass.

Sbiba

The Sbiba area was attacked by Battle Groups Stenkhoffnand Schuette, remnants of 21st Panzer Division. Facing the German armoured advance was the British 6th Armoured Division (less the 26th Armoured Brigade which except for the tanks of the 16/5th Lancers had been sent to Thala). Also in the line was the 18th Regimental Combat Team from the US 1st Infantry Division; and three battalions of infantry from the US 34th Infantry Division. There were also three US field artillery battalions, elements of two British anti-tank regiments and some French detachments. The Germans made little progress against the combined firepower of the defending force which had also laid minefields. The 21st Panzer Division was checked and then driven back by 20 February.

Kasserine

Defending the pass was a force consisting of the US 1st Battalion, 26th Regimental Combat Team, the US 19 Combat Engineer Regiment, the 6th Field Artillery Battalion, a tank destroyer battalion, and a battery of French artillery. On the hills to their west was French General Welvert's Task Force Welvert comprising a US Ranger and infantry battalion, three French infantry battalions, two US field artillery battalions, four French artillery batteries and engineer and anti-aircraft detachments. Further west was Task Force Bowen (consisting of the 3rd Battalion of the 26th Regimental Combat Team), blocking the track from Feriana towards Tébessa. Between Task Force Bowen and Tébessa to the north was the regrouping 1st Armoured Division although only Combat Command B was fit for combat. The positions in the pass had been placed under Colonel Alexander Stark, commander of the 26th Regimental Combat Team (RCT), on the night of 18 February and the command named Stark Force.

An attempt to surprise the Kasserine defences by the 33rd Reconnaissance Unit into the pass failed and a battalion of Panzer grenadiers was ordered into the floor of the pass and another onto Djebel Semmama, the hill on its eastern flank and slow progress was made against artillery fire. The tanks of 1/8 Panzer Regiment were committed at noon, but little progress resulted against stubborn defence. Rommel decided to commit his units from the 10th Panzer to the Kasserine Pass the next morning in a co-ordinated attack with the Afrika Korps Assault Group, which was to be joined by elements of the Italian 131st Armoured Division *Centauro*. British reinforcements from the 26th Armoured Brigade (6th Armoured Division) had been assembling at Thala and Brigadier Dunphie, making forward reconnaissance, decided to intervene. The First Army headquarters restricted him to sending Gore Force, a small combined-arms group of a company of infantry, a squadron of eleven tanks, an artillery battery, and an anti-tank troop. Brigadier Cameron Nicholson (6th Armoured Division) was given command of Nickforce, all units north-west of the pass.

During the night, the Americans positions on the two shoulders overlooking the pass were overrun and at 08:30 hours German Panzer grenadiers and Italian Bersaglieri resumed the attack. At 10:00 hours Dunphie judged that Stark Force was about to give way and ordered Gore Force to the Thala side of the pass as elements of the *Centauro* Division launched their attack towards Tébessa and continued it during the afternoon.

On 20 February during the opening attack on key American positions of the town Djebel, the 5 Bersaglieri Regiment made a frontal assault on US positions that lasted most of the morning and finally carried the position, losing the regimental commander Colonel Bonfatti in the process. The action cracked open the Allied defences, opening the road to Thala and Tébessa. By mid-day the accompanying combined Axis armoured units poured through the pass, routing US forces with the 1st US Armoured Division into one of the worst US defeats of the Tunisian campaign. The Italian regiment was complimented by General Bulowius, commander of the DAK Assault Group who cited their action as the instrumental event of the Axis victory. At 13:00 hours Rommel committed two battalions from 10th Panzer which overcame the defence. Tanks and Bersaglieri from the *Centauro* Division advanced along Highway 13 and overran the 19 Combat Engineer Regiment. The US survivors made a disorganized retreat up the western exit from the pass to Djebel el Hamra, where Combat Command B of the 1st Armoured Division was arriving. On the exit to Thala, Gore Force slowly leapfrogged back, losing all its tanks in the process, to re-join the 26th Armoured Brigade some 10 miles (16 km) further back.

Djebel el Hamra

The Afrika Korps Assault Group began moving along the Hatab River Valley towards Haidra and Tébessa in the early afternoon of 21 February and advanced until they met defenders consisting of the US 16th Infantry Regiment, 1st Infantry Division and Combat Command B of the US 1st Armoured Division at Djebel el Hamra. The German Italian force was halted and, despite heavy pressure including air attacks, failed to dislodge the American defenders. Having brought the Axis drive towards **Tébessa to a halt, General Paul Robinett and General Terry Allen now turned their** attention to planning a counterattack that was to take place the next day, 22 February. Plans made by both sides were upset by the battle, and the Axis forces (5th *Bersaglieri,* a *Semovente* group from *Centauro* and 15th Panzer) launched another assault on the US position on the morning of 22 February towards Bou Chebka Pass. Although the American defenders were pressed hard the line held and, by mid-afternoon, the US infantry and tanks launched a counterattack that broke the combined German and Italian force. More than 400 Axis prisoners were taken as the counterattack was pressed into the Afrika Korps position.

Thala

Rommel had stayed with the main group of the 10th Panzer Division on the route towards Thala, where the 26th Armoured Brigade and remnants of the US 26th Infantry Regiment had dug in on ridges. If the town fell and the southern of two roads from Thala to Tébessa was cut, the US 9th Infantry Division to the north would be cut off and Combat Command B of the 1st Armoured Division would be trapped between the 10th Panzer Division and its supporting units moving north along the second road to Tébessa. The combined force fought a costly delaying action in front of Thala, retreating ridge by ridge to the north until by dark, the force held the German attacks just south of the town. The divisional artillery (48 guns) of the 9th Infantry Division and anti-tank platoons, that had moved from Morocco on 17 February, 800 miles (1,287 km) west, dug in that night. Next day, the front was held mostly by British infantry, with exceptionally strong backing by unified US and British artillery, under Brigadier General Stafford LeRoy Irwin, the US artillery commander. The British had thirty-six guns, supported by armoured cars of the Derbyshire Yeomanry and Valentine and Crusader tanks of the 17/21 Lancers.

Anderson ordered the 9th Infantry Division and its artillery support to LeRoy to meet an expected German attack but US Major General Ernest N Harmon, who had been sent by Eisenhower to report on the battle and the Allied command, instructed the 9th Divisional Artillery to stay behind.

On the morning of 22 February an intense artillery barrage from the massed Allied guns forestalled the resumption of the 10th Panzer Division attack, destroying armour and vehicles and disrupting communications. Broich, the battle commander, decided to pause and regroup but Allied reinforcements continued to arrive. Under constant fire, 10th Panzer waited until dark to retire from the battlefield.

Withdrawal

Overextended and with supplies dwindling, pinned down by the Allied artillery in the pass in front of Thala and now facing US counterattacks along the Hatab River, Rommel realized his strength was spent. At Sbiba, along the Habab River and now at Thala, the efforts of the German and Italian forces had failed to make a decisive break in the Allied line. With little prospect of further success, Rommel judged that it would be wiser to break off to concentrate in South Tunisia and strike a blow at the Eighth Army, catching them off balance whilst still assembling its forces. He at least had the consolation that he had inflicted heavy losses on his enemy and that the Allied concentrations in the Gafsa-Sbeitla area had been destroyed.

At a meeting at Rommel's Kasserine HQ on 23 February, Kesselring and Chief of Staff Siegfried Westphal tried to change Rommel's mind, arguing that there were still possibilities for success. Rommel was adamant; Kesselring finally agreed and formal orders from the Comando Supremo in Rome were issued that evening calling off the offensive and directing all Axis units to return to their start positions. On 23 February a massive American air attack on the pass hastened the German retreat and by late 24 February the pass had been reoccupied, Feriana was in Allied hands, Sidi Bou Zid and Sbeitla followed soon after.

Aftermath

Casualties and Losses

German losses at Kasserine were 201 killed, 536 wounded and 252 missing, totalling 989 casualties. In equipment, Germans lost 20 tanks, 67 vehicles and fourteen guns. Allied forces captured 73 German and 535 Italian soldiers.

American losses totalled 300 killed, 3,000 wounded, and 3,000 missing. Losses were so high that an additional 7,000 replacements were needed to recover units to their original strength. The French losses on the 34th Division totalled fifty killed, 200 wounded and 250 missing. Regarding Allied personnel captured, Rommel and Ziegler claimed 3,721 prisoners captured but in a consolidated report of 24 February they reported 4,026 Allied prisoners of war.

Material losses of the US II Corps were staggering in total 183 tanks, 104 halftracks, 208 guns and 512 trucks and motor vehicles were lost, some of them captured by the Germans. The Allies also lost supplies and fuel, since over 215 cubic metres of gasoline and lubricants were seized along with 45 tons of ammunition.

Rommel

Rommel had hoped to take advantage of the inexperience of the new Allied commanders but was opposed by Arnim who, wanting to conserve strength in his sector, ignored Kesselring's orders and withheld the attached heavy tank unit of 10th Panzer. Rommel felt that most US units and commanders had showed their inexperience, losing sight of the broader picture. Rommel was later impressed with how quickly US commanders came to understand and implement mobile warfare and also praised US equipment. **'British experience has been put to good use in American equipment.'**

Of particular interest to the Germans was the sturdy M3 armoured halftrack, and for a time after the battle, German units deployed large numbers of captured US vehicles.

The Allies studied the results equally seriously. Positioned by senior commanders who had not personally reconnoitred the ground, US forces were often located too far from each other for mutual support. It was also noted that US soldiers tended to become careless about digging in, exposing their positions, bunching in groups when in open view of enemy artillery observers, and positioning units on topographic crests, where their silhouettes made them perfect targets. Too many soldiers, exasperated by the rocky soil of Tunisia, were still digging shallow slit trenches instead of deep foxholes.

The 1st Armoured Division was on the receiving end of German anti-tank and screening tactics and had not learned about those tactics from experienced British armoured forces. Others in the US Army were aware of the German deception tactics.

The Allies were also unable to prevent the Germans from attaining air superiority over the battlefield, limiting effective Allied air reconnaissance, and allowing relentless German bombing and strafing attacks that disrupted Allied attempts at deployment and organization. Attacks by the Luftwaffe in close support of German ground offensive often neutralized US attempts to organize effective defensive artillery fire.

Eisenhower

General Dwight D Eisenhower began restructuring the Allied command, creating the 18th Army Group, commanded by General Sir Harold R. L. G. Alexander, to tighten the operational control of the three Allied nations involved and improve their co-ordination. Major General Lloyd Fredendall was relieved by Eisenhower and sent home. Training programmes at home had contributed to US Army units in North Africa being saddled with disgraced commanders who had failed in battle and were reluctant to advocate radical changes. Eisenhower found through Major General Omar Bradley and others, that Fredendall sub-ordinates had lost confidence in him and Alexander and told US commanders, **'I'm sure you must have better men than that.'**

Fredendall took the blame but Anderson, the First Army commander, was judged to be at fault for the failure to concentrate Allied armoured units and keep forces concentrated, that later disintegrated into individual units. When Fredendall disclaimed all responsibility for the poor equipped French XIX Corps and denied French requests for support, notably when under pressure at Faïd, Anderson allowed the request to go unfulfilled. Anderson was also blamed for dispersing the three combat commands of the US 1st Armoured Division, despite the objections of Major General Orlando Ward, the divisional commander. US Brigadier General Irwin later became commander of the 5th Infantry Division in Europe and went on to higher command, as did Brigadier Nicholson, who later commanded the 2nd Infantry Division in India. Allied commanders were given greater scope for initiative and to keep forces concentrated. They were also urged to lead their units from the front and to keep command posts well forward, unlike Fredendall who had rarely visited the front line. (Ward was sent home, where he trained troops and then commanded the 20th Armoured Division in Europe.)

On 6 March, Major General George Patton was temporarily removed from planning for the Allied invasion of Sicily to command the II Corps. Bradley was appointed assistant corps commander and moved up to command of II Corps when Patton returned to planning for Sicily. Fredendall was reassigned to the United States and several other commanders were removed or promoted out of the way. Patton was not known for hesitancy and did not bother to request permission when taking action to support his command or other units requesting assistance.

During the advance from Gafsa, Alexander, the 18th Army Group commander, had given detailed orders to Patton, afterwards changing XI Corps' mission several times. Once beyond Maknassy, Alexander again gave orders Patton considered excessively detailed. From then on, Patton simply ignored those parts of mission orders he considered ill-advised on grounds of military expediency and/or a rapidly evolving tactical situation.

Efforts were made to improve the integration of immediate artillery and air support, which had been poorly co-ordinated. Whilst US artillery response times improved dramatically, co-ordinating close air support was not achieved until Operation Overlord over a year later. American anti-aircraft artillery began reforms, having learned that, whilst Stuka dive bombers were vulnerable to .50 BMG rounds fired from vehicles, field units needed dedicated autocannon to protect them from aerial attack; in one division, 95 per cent of air attacks were concentrated on its artillery.

Chapter 4

Battle of Sidi Bou Zid

February 1943

Battle of Sidi Bou Zid	
Date: 14–17 February 1943 **Location:** Sidi Bou Zid, Tunisia **Result:** German Victory	
Belligerents	
United States **Free France**	**Germany**
Commanders and Leaders	
United States: Lloyd Fredendall	**Germany**: Hans-Jürgen von Arnim
United States: Orlando Ward	**Germany**: Heinz Ziegler
United States: John K Waters (PoW)	
Free France: Alphonse Juin	
Casualties and Losses	
2,546 missing	None recorded
103 tanks	

The **Battle of Sidi Bou Zid** *(Unternehmen Frühlingswind/*Operation Spring Breeze) took place during the Tunisian campaign from 14–17 February 1943, in the Second World War. The battle was fought around Sidi Bou Zid, where a large number of US Army units were mauled by German and Italian forces. It resulted in the Axis forces recapturing the strategically important town of Sbeitla in central Tunisia.

The battle was planned by the Germans to be a two-part offensive-defensive operation against US positions in western Tunisia. Generaloberst Hans-Jürgen von Arnim commanded several experienced combat units, including the 10th Panzer Division and the 21st Panzer Division of the Fifth Panzer Army, which were to sweep north and west towards the Kasserine Pass, whilst another battle group attacked Sidi Bou Zid from the south. Facing the attack was the US II Corps under Major General Lloyd Fredendall.

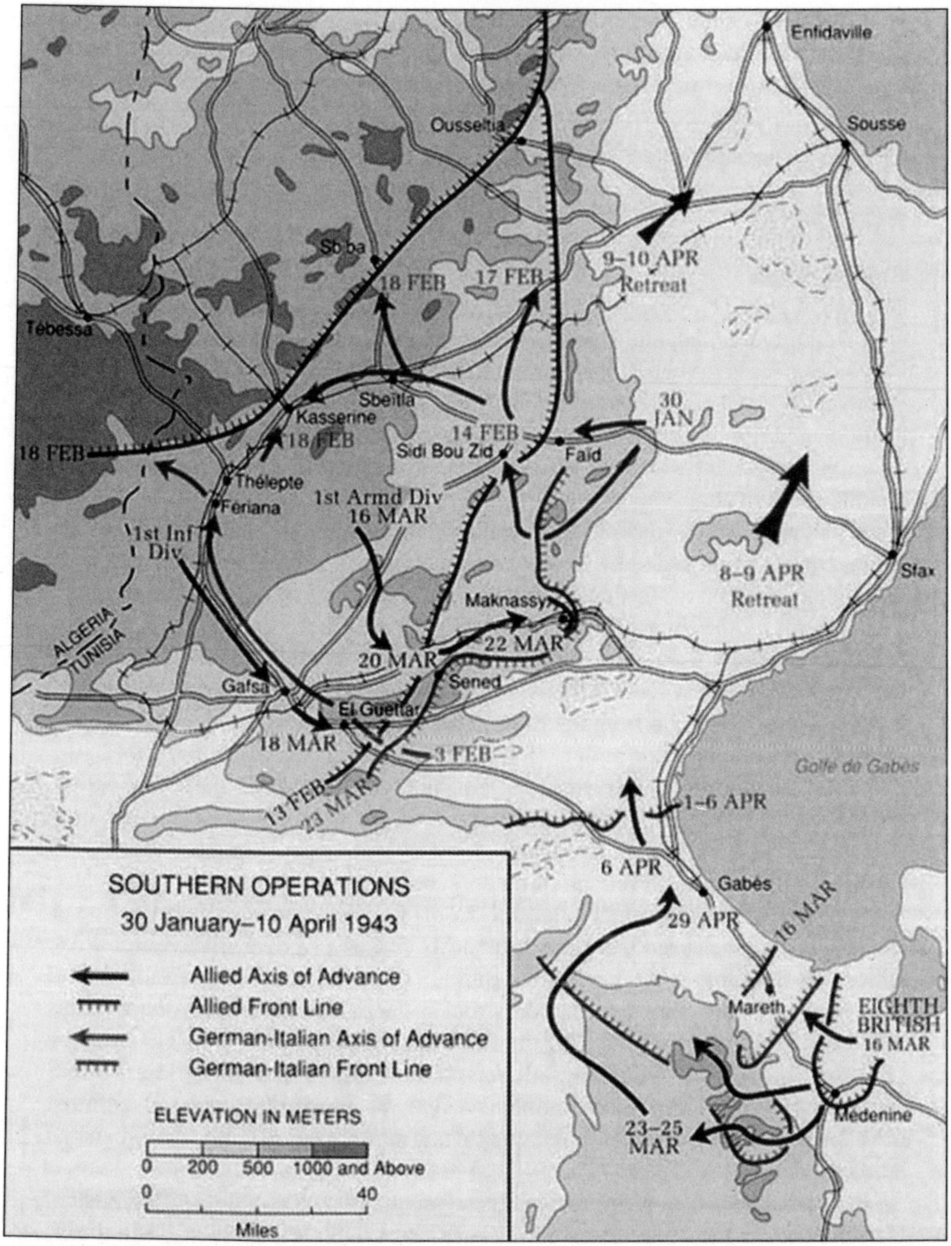

Battle of Sidi Bou Zid: 14–17 February 1943.
(The above image is in the Public Domain because it contains materials that originally came from the US Army Center of Military History. Source: US Army Center of Military History Online Bookshelves. Email dated 20/09/2023: "Map(s) courtesy of the United States Military Academy Department of History.")

In a few days, the Axis attack forced the US II Corps to take up new defensive positions outside Sbiba. Axis troops were then given time to consolidate their new front line west of Sbeitla. The success of the offensive led the German High Command to conclude that despite being well equipped, American forces were no match for experienced Axis combat troops.

Background

Run for Tunis

The Allied attempt to capture Tunis, in late 1942 after Operation Torch (refer to Chapter 1), had failed, and since the year end a lull had settled on the theatre, as both sides paused to rebuild their strength. Hans-Jürgen von Arnim had been given command of the Axis forces defending Tunisia and reinforcements led to the force being named the Fifth Panzer Army *(5. Panzer-Armee)*. Arnim chose to maintain the initiative gained when the Allies had been driven back the previous year by making spoiling attacks to keep his intentions hidden.

In January 1943, the German Italian Panzer Army (Deutsch-Italienische Panzerarmee) commanded by General Erwin Rommel had retreated to the Mareth Line, a line of defensive fortifications near the coastal town of Médenine in southern Tunisia built by the French before the war. The Axis forces joined and in the Sidi Bou Zid area there were elements from both armies, among them the 21st Panzer Division of the Afrika Korps, transferred from German Italian Panzer Army, and the 10th Panzer Division from the Fifth Panzer Army.

Most of Tunisia was under Axis occupation but in November 1942, the Eastern Dorsale of the Atlas Mountains had been captured by the Allies. The Eastern Dorsale was held by elements of the inexperienced US II Corps (Lieutenant General Lloyd Fredendall) and the poorly equipped French XIX Corps (Alphonse Juin). Fredendall made Tébessa, over 80 miles (129 km) back, his headquarters and rarely visited the front. In the absence of intelligence as to Axis intentions, Fredendall dispersed his forces to cover all eventualities, which left his units too far apart for mutual support. At Sidi Bou Zid, he had overruled his divisional commanders and ordered the defensive dispositions without studying the ground. Sid Bou Zid was defended by the 34th US Infantry Division, 168th RCT (Colonel Thomas Drake) and the tanks of the 1st US Armoured Division Combat Command A (CC A). Fredendall had caused most of this force to be placed in defensive "islands" on high ground, which risked defeat in detail.

Rommel was conscious of the danger of an attack by the Allies on the Eastern Dorsale towards the coast, about 60 miles (97 km) to the east, which could divide the Axis forces and isolate the German Italian Panzer Army from its line of supply from Tunis. On January 30, Arnim had sent the 21st Panzer Division to attack the Faïd Pass, held by the French XIX Corps. Fredendall had reacted slowly, and Arnim's troops had overcome fierce French resistance and achieved their objectives whilst inflicting heavy casualties.

Prelude

German Plan

Two offensive-defensive operations were planned, with *Unternehmen Frühlingswind* to be conducted by the 10th and 21st Panzer divisions against US positions at Sidi Bou Zid, west of Faïd, after which the 21st Panzer Division would join a battlegroup of the First Italian Army to attack Gafsa in *Unternehmen Morgenluft* and the 10th Panzer Division moved north for an attack west of Kairouan. *Unternehmen Frühlingswind* was to begin from 12–14 February.

Battle

At 04:00 hours on 14 February four battle groups totalling 140 German tanks drawn from 10th and 21st Panzer divisions (Lieutenant General Heinz Ziegler), advanced through Faïd and Maizila passes, sites that General Dwight D. Eisenhower had inspected three hours earlier, to attack Sidi Bou Zid. The attack started with tanks of the 10th Panzer Division under cover of a sandstorm advancing westwards from Faïd in two battle groups (the Reimann and Gerhardt groups). Elements of CC A tried to delay the German advance by firing a 105 mm M101 howitzer mounted on an M4 Sherman tank. The Germans responded by shelling the American battle positions with 88mm guns. By 10:00 hours the Germans had circled Djebel Lessouda (defended by Lessouda Force, an armoured battalion group commanded by Lieutenant Colonel John K. Waters, George S. Patton's son-in-law) and joined up north of Sidi Bou Zid.

Kampfgruppe Schütte and *Kampfgruppe Stenckhoff* of the 21st Panzer Division had secured the Maizila Pass to the south and *Kampfgruppe Schütte* headed north to engage two battalions of the 168th RCT on Djebel Ksaira whilst *Kampfgruppe Stenckhoff* headed north-west to Bir el Hafey in order to swing round and make the approach to Sidi Bou Zid from the west during the afternoon. Under heavy shelling from *Kampfgruppe Schütte,* Colonel Thomas Drake requested permission to retreat, which was denied by Fredendall, who ordered him to hold his position and wait for reinforcements, which never arrived. By 17:00 hours *Kampfgruppe Stenckhoff* and the 10th Panzer Division had attacked CC A which had been driven nearly 15 miles (24 km) west to Djebel el Hamra, with the loss of forty-four tanks and many guns. The infantry was marooned on the high ground at Djebel Lessouda, Djebel Ksaira and Djebel Garet Hadid.

During the night, 1st US Armoured Division Commander Orlando Ward moved up Combat Command C (CC C) to Djebel Hamra, to counterattack Sid Bou Zid on 15 February, but the attack was over flat exposed terrain and was bombed and strafed early in the move, then found itself between the two Panzer divisions, with more than eighty Panzer IV, Panzer III and Tiger I tanks. CC C retreated, losing forty-six medium tanks, 130 vehicles and nine self-propelled guns, narrowly regaining the position at Djebel Hamra. By the evening, Arnim had ordered three of the battle groups to head towards Sbeitla and were engaged by remnants of CC A and CC C which were forced back. On 16 February, helped by intensive air support, they drove back the fresh Combat Command B (CC B) and entered Sbeitla.

Aftermath

The experienced Germans performed well and caused many US losses before General Anderson, who had been appointed to co-ordinate Allied operations in Tunisia, ordered an Allied withdrawal on 17 February. The left (northern) flank of the First Army retreated from a line from Fondouk to Faïd and Gafsa to better defensive positions in front of Sbiba and Tébessa. Eisenhower blamed himself for trying to do too much and the sudden French collapse in the central mountains.

Confusing and overlapping command arrangements made things worse. When the US II Corps was forced out of Sbeitla on 17 February and Axis forces converged on Kasserine, the Axis lack of unity of command and unclear objectives had a similar effect on Axis operations.

The poor performance of the Allies during the actions of late January 1943 and the first half of February 1943, as well as at the later Battle of Kasserine Pass, led the Axis commanders to conclude that, whilst US units were well equipped, they were inferior in leadership and tactics. This became received wisdom among the Axis forces and resulted in a later underestimation of Allied capabilities as they gained experience and replaced poor commanders.

Chapter 5

Battle of Médenine

March 1943

Battle of Médenine	
Date: 6 March 1943 **Location:** Médenine, Tunisia **Result:** Allied Victory	
Belligerents	
United Kingdom **New Zealand** **Free French**	**Germany** **Italy**
Commanders and Leaders	
United Kingdom: Bernard Montgomery	**Germany**: Albert Kesselring
	Italy: Giovanni Messe
Strength	
2 Infantry Divisions	2 Infantry Divisions
1 Armoured Division	3 Panzer Divisions (understrength)
1 Armoured Brigade	
Casualties and Losses	
130 killed/missing	635 killed/missing
6 tanks	41 to 52 tanks
49 vehicles	
32 guns and anti-tank guns	

The Battle of Médenine (*Unternehmen Capri*/Operation Capri) was an Axis spoiling attack at Médenine in Tunisia on 6 March 1943. The operation was intended to delay an attack by the British Eighth Army on the Mareth Line. The British had been forewarned by Ultra Decrypts of German wireless communications and rushed reinforcements from Tripoli and Benghazi before the Axis attack, which was a costly failure. General Erwin Rommel, the commander of Army Group Africa

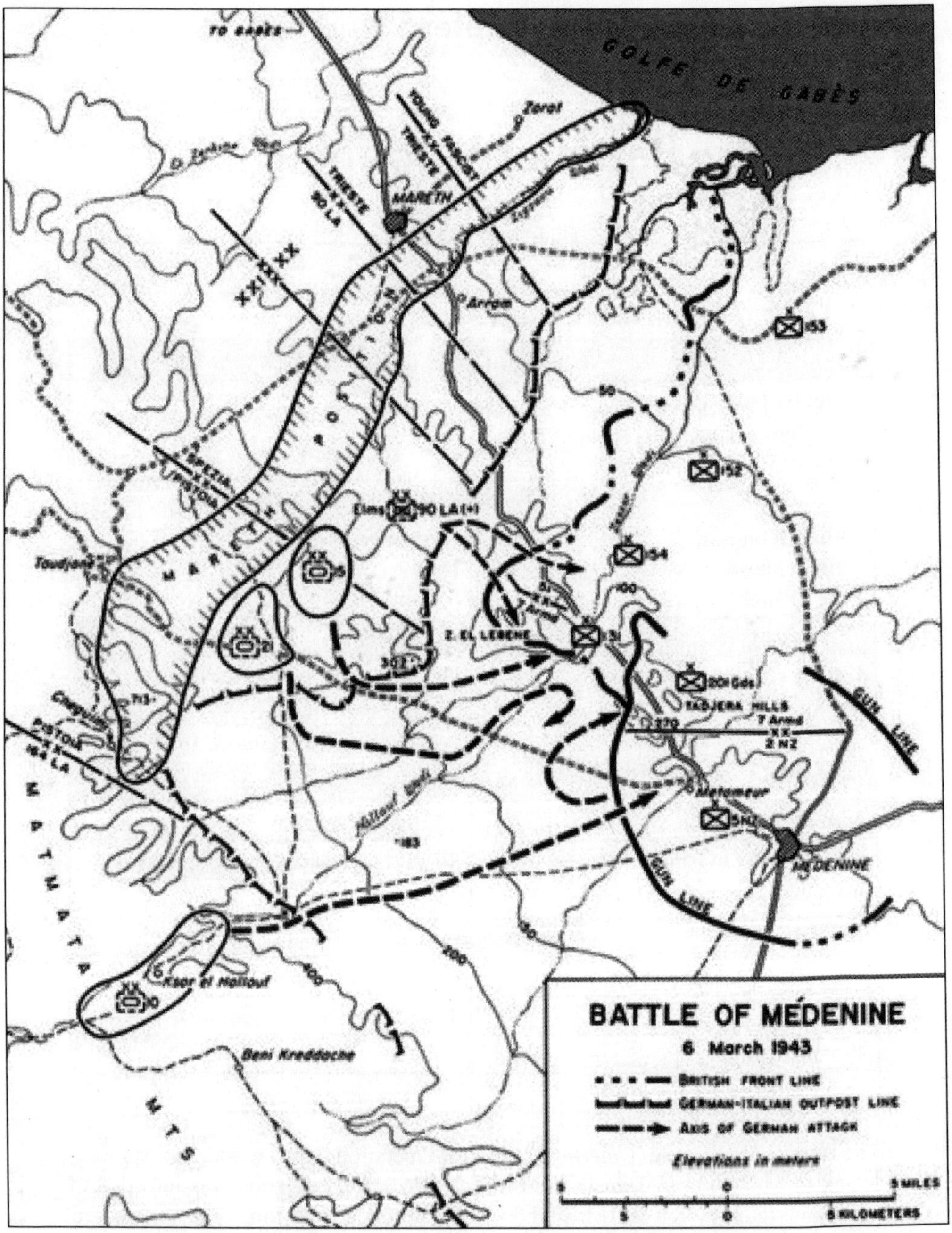

Battle of Médenine–6 March 1943.

(Author: Office of the Chief of Military History, Department of the Army. Source: http://www.ibiblio.org/hyperwar/USA/USA-MTO-NWA/USA-MTO-NWA-26.html Email dated 20/09/2023: "Map(s) courtesy of the United States Military Academy Department of History.")

(Heeresgruppe Afrika), could not afford to lose forces needed for the defence of the Mareth Line and the effort was abandoned at dusk that day.

During the night, the Eighth Army remained alert for the possibility of another Axis attempt and sent forward patrols to carry out reconnaissance and to demolish/knock-out Axis tanks. During the day the Luftwaffe and *Regia Aeronautica* had made a maximum effort with little effect against the Allied anti-aircraft defence and the Desert Air Force (DAF). On 7 March the Axis forces began a withdrawal northwards towards the Mareth Line, the Eighth Army pursuit being slowed by rain. The Battle of Médenine was the last battle commanded by Rommel in the North African campaign, who returned to Europe for good soon afterwards.

Background

Axis Retreat from El Alamein

The retreat of Deutsch-Italienische Panzerarmee took place from 5 November 1942–15 February 1943 and on 8 November, Operation Torch began in Morocco, Algeria and Tunisia. The Panzerarmee evaded British outflanking moves but traffic jams, fuel shortage, poor weather and air attacks reduced the retreat to 6–7 miles (10 – 11 km) per day. Commando Supremo (Supreme Command) in Rome was the highest command echelon of the Italian Armed Forces between June 1941 and May 1945. Its predecessor, the Stato Maggiore Generale (General Staff), was a purely advisory body with no direct control of the several branches of the armed forces and with very little staff, created amidst the exigencies of the Second World War. Commando Supremo was a large organization with several departments and operational command of the armed forces on the active fronts. At the end of the Second World War, it was reduced to a purely advisory role again. The Oberkommando der Wehrmacht (OKW, Armed Forces High Command) in Berlin was created in 1938. The OKW succeeded the Reich Ministry of War, becoming the supreme military command and control staff of Nazi Germany during the Second World War, directly subordinate to Adolf Hitler. Comando Supremo in Rome and OKW in Berlin took an optimistic view of the situation and Comando Supremo chose the Mersa-el-Brega–El Agheila position as the terminus of the retreat, despite the position having a front 110 miles (177 km) long, strong points up to 5 miles (8 km) apart, too far for mutual support and being protected by only 30,000 mines. When the Panzerarmee arrived, the Afrika Korps had only 5,000 men, 35 tanks, 16 armoured cars, 12 anti-tank guns, 12 field howitzers and deliveries of only 50 long tons of the 400 long tons of supplies needed daily.

Rommel had wanted to retreat to Wadi Akarit in the Gabès area, 120 miles (193 km) further west, where the nonmotorized troops could defend the narrow gap between the Mediterranean and the Chott Djerid. The tanks and motorized infantry could join the Fifth Panzer Army (Colonel General Hans-Jürgen von Arnim) further north, drive back the First Army from Tunisia into Algeria, then swiftly return to force back the Eighth Army, preparatory to embarkation to Europe. At a meeting with Hitler on 28 November 1942, Rommel discussed the proposal but only received a promise of more supplies. On the night of 11/12 December, the British attacked and on the following evening the Panzerarmee resumed its retreat and despite the chronic fuel shortage, evaded another outflanking move. The Panzerarmee took up a defensive position at Buerat on 29 December, but this was poorly fortified, wide open to an outflanking manoeuvre and vulnerable to being cut off by an attack on Gabès by the First Army from southern Tunisia. The supply situation was a little better, with 152 long tons of the 400 long tons daily requirement being delivered and 95 per cent of the fuel being used to distribute supplies or for withdrawals.

The Long-Range Desert Group (LRDG) attacked Axis supply lines and hundreds of lorries were stranded along roads for lack of fuel, whilst the Eighth Army massed petrol and ammunition for its next attack. On 13 January 1943, the infantry of the 21st Panzer Division were sent north to the Fifth Panzer Army, to guard against the loss of Gabès and on 15 January, the Eighth Army attacked with 450 tanks against thirty-six German and fifty-seven Italian tanks; in the evening Rommel ordered another withdrawal.

Lack of fuel and apprehension about the threat to Gabès, led to the retreat passing beyond the Tarhuna to Hom's line and Tripoli was occupied by the British on 23 January, the Axis retreat from El Alamein having covered 1,400 miles (2,253 km). On 13 February, the last Axis soldiers left Libya and on 15 February, the rear-guard reached the Mareth Line, 80 miles (129 km) inside Tunisia. Comando Supremo intended the line to be held indefinitely but Rommel considered it too vulnerable to another flanking move, unlike the Wadi Akarit position, another 40 miles (64 km) back.

Operation Torch

This operation by the Allied forces is well recorded and documented in Chapter 1 of this book, and it is not intended to expand further here on the operation that took place on 7 November 1942 other than to say: Refer to Chapter 1.

Mareth Line

Southern Tunisia is a region of broken terrain, with rocky ridge lines and desert, which obstruct manoeuvre; opposite a bight where the north-south coast opens to the east, a semi-arid, scrub covered coastal plain is met inland by the Matmata Hills which run south to north; North of Gabès, the road to Sfax passes between the sea and the Chotts, the only route north for the Eighth Army. Access the plain in a line roughly south-west to north-east, lay the Mareth Line, a fortification built by the French in the 1930s. In the north, the hills and line of forts terminated at the Tebaga Gap, a low pass between Matmata Hills and the Djebel Tebaga, another line of high ground to the west of the gap running east-west. North and west of this feature is the Chott el Djerid; west of the Matmata Hills lies dry Jebel Dahar country, and then the impassable sand of the Grand Erg Oriental. Gabès is on the coast where the plain meets the route from the Tebaga Gap.

Th Mareth Line followed the line of **Wadi Zigzaou**, a natural tank obstacle, with steep banks rising to 70 feet; (21 m) the north-west side had been fortified by the French and was further reinforced by Axis engineers. The wadi crosses the coastal plain from Zarat to Toujane and into the Matmata Hills beyond. In 1938, the French judged Jebel Dahar to be impassable to motorized transport and had not extended the Mareth Line any further inland, but 1943 motor vehicles had much better performance.

The Italian First Army (General Giovanni Messe) occupied the Mareth Line with the 90th Light Division, 164th Light Afrika Division, and the 10th Panzer Division, 15th Panzer Division and the 21st Panzer Division of the Afrika Korps with about 200 tanks and the 80th Infantry Division 'La Spezis'.

Prelude

Axis Preparations

On 28 February, Rommel, Messe and the senior armoured unit commanders met to discuss an attack on Médenine, the junction of several roads and tracks an attack from three directions was suggested, from Toujane to Metameur on the left, an attack in the centre and an attack on the right from the Hallouf Pass to Médenine. Rommel suggested an attack nearer the coast to create the possibility of attacking from an unexpected direction, but the sub-ordinates disagreed because of information from rcconnaissance by the Afrika Korps that the coastal approaches were difficult, mixed and covered by many guns. There was no room for manoeuvre and the tanks would be easy targets for British artillery and aircraft. Rommel gave way and the plan was drawn up by Messe and Lieutenant General Heinz Ziegler, the temporary commander of the Afrika Korps.

The attack was set for 6 March, to give time for the units involved in *Unternehmen Morgenluft* (the battle of Sidi Bou Zid) to replace casualties and reorganize. Messe planned to encircle the British troops between the Mareth Line and Médenine with the DAK Group (Generalleutnant Hans Cramer) formed from the three Afrika Korps Panzer divisions, Reconnaissance units 3 and 33, a battalion of the 164th Light *Afrika* Division, a parachute battalion, seven field artillery batteries and two anti-aircraft battalions and Column Bari (Generalleutnant Theodor von Sponeck) a battlegroup with two battalions of Panzergrenadier Regiment 200, two batteries of Panzergrenadier Regiment 361, the *La Spezia* and the *Trieste* battle groups with two battalions each, a battery of German field guns and several *Nebelwerfer,* seven Italian field batteries and part of three anti-aircraft batteries; both columns had attached anti-tank and engineer units.

Axis Plan

The DAK was to capture a line from Hir en Nraa to Ksar Rebounten and then circle north or north-east, the 10th Panzer Division advancing from Hallouf valet to capture Metameur. The 21st Panzer Division was to emerge from the south end of Djebel Tebaga and attack Hir Ksar Koutine. The 15th Panzer Division was to move from Djebel er Remtsia towards Hir en Nraa followed by its infantry and the Reconnaissance units were to cut the Foum Tathouine-Médenine road to prevent the movement of British reinforcements. Column Bari was to make a frontal attack at Zemiet el Lebene with Battle Group *Spezia* on the right flank, Panzer Grenadier Regiment 200 in the centre and Battle Group *Trieste* on the left. On 5 March, the Luftwaffe and *Regia Aeronautica* were to bomb Allied airfields and cover the assembly of the ground force and on 6 March, were to attack British artillery positions east of Zemlet el Lebene, close the forward Allied airfields, provide fighter escorts for the ground attack and reconnoitre from Tatahouine to Ben Gardane.

British Preparations

Long before the Eighth Army reached the port of Tripoli, thought had been given to an attack on the Mareth Line and the LRDG had been sent to survey the land south of the Matmata Hills. Despite maps and reports indicating that the ground was impossible for tanks and lorries. The LRDG found a route inland southwards and around the hills to the Tebaga Gap, between the Chott el Fejaj salt marsh and the hills.

The 7th Armoured Division (Major General George Erskine) had probed forwards from Tripoli, whilst the 51st (Highland) Division (Major General Douglas Wimberley) and the 2nd New Zealand Division (Major General Bernard Freyberg) rested at the port. Winter rains turned the ground into a swamp, until a short lull beginning on 15 February, when the 7th Armoured and the 51st (Highland) divisions moved forwards and captured airfields at Médenine on 17 February. The next day the **Free French Flying Column** and the 1st Infantry Battalion Marine and Pacific arrived with General Philippe Leclerc, after a march across the Sand Sea from Lake Chad to join the Eighth Army XXX Corps (Lieutenant General Oliver Leese) brought the 2nd New Zealand Division forward from Tripoli, which had the 8th Armoured Brigade and the 201st Guards Brigade under command.

The Allied code breakers of the Government Code and Cipher School at Bletchley Park, in England, read Axis Enigma codes and on 26 February, warned Montgomery that Rommel had ordered the termination of the Battle of Kasserine Pass (19 24 February 1943). On 28 February, they decrypted orders from Rommel for a reconnaissance to be conducted by the First Italian Army, preparatory to an attack on the Eighth Army by 4 March and a fuel return on 1 March showed that the Axis forces had sufficient for a three-day operation. On 6 February, the Eighth Army had only about one division at Médenine, most of its tanks were with X Corps (Lieutenant General Brian Horrocks) at Benghazi, 1,000 miles (1609 km) away, and an attack on the Médenine Line could not be ready before 20 March. Montgomery thought that XXX Corps at Médenine would not be able to withstand an attack before 7 March, but over three days and nights, reinforcements were rushed forwards and by 4 March, 400 tanks, 350 field guns and 470 anti-tank guns had been moved up.

The DAF had also increased the number of aircraft in the area to double that of the Axis air forces. At 05:36 hours on 6 March, Allied code breakers sent notice to Montgomery of the thrust line of the attack and that it was to begin at 06:00 hours.

Battle

6 March

It was foggy when the Axis bombardment of the British forward positions began at 06:00 hours, and for ninety minutes tanks, guns and other vehicles emerged from the heights between Toujane and Kreddache. Tanks of the 15th Panzer Division moved along the Toujane-Médenine road and then turned north against the positions of the 7th Armoured Division and were engaged by the anti-tank guns of the 131st Infantry Brigade and the 2nd Battalion Scots Guards. On the 2nd New Zealand Division front, 164th Light Afrika Division was engaged by Bren carriers of the 21st New Zealand Battalion, which met seven vehicles carrying infantry and anti-tank guns at close range in the fog. The New Zealanders inflicted many casualties, for the loss of two casualties and a carrier. Small parties of Axis infantry probed the front and as the fog dispersed, artillery was seen moving up. The British artillery did not reply, being under orders to wait until the attackers were in range of the maximum number of guns; the anti-tank guns were only to commence firing at short range. The 5 Field Regiment Royal Artillery (RA) did not begin to fire until Axis tanks were engaged by the forward 6-pounders and then bombarded infantry and lorries following the tanks, isolating them.

At about 08:30 hours, tanks were reported to be converging on Tadjera Kbir (Point 270) and the 28th NZ Battalion reported ten tanks and thirty trucks moving up the wadi to its right. The tanks reached a dummy minefield and then diverted towards rising ground, as had been intended, two 6-pounder anti-tank guns from the 73rd Anti-Tank Regiment RA opened fire and knocked out four Panzer III Specials at 400 yards and the mortars of the 28th New Zealand Battalion knocked out a fifth tank, When the crews alighted, mortars, machine guns and artillery joined in. The attackers were taken by surprise and disorganized but then spotted the anti-tank guns and returned fire.

A 6-pounder was damaged, and two men wounded but the rest kept firing until the other weapons commenced fire, and the surviving tanks retired. Fifteen prisoners from the 10th Panzer Division, including the tank company commander, were taken.

Just after 09:00 hours, the 21st Battalion mortar fire dispersed a group of infantries dismounting from vehicle and by about 10:00 hours the remaining infantry withdrew and dug in 3–4 miles (5 – 6 km) to the rear. The British artillery fired everywhere, especially on areas registered beforehand, and as soon as Axis troops or vehicles moved into them. The leading tanks of the 21st Panzer Division crossed a skyline and were engaged, observers of the 201st Guards Brigade reporting that they 'wandered rather vaguely'. The 2nd New Zealand Division was not attacked again during the morning, but much disorganized movement of tanks and transport was seen. It was realized that the main Axis effort was against Tadjera Kbir and further north. On the left flank, reconnaissance units 3 and 33 and the headquarters *Kampfstaffel* with nine tanks worked round to the Foum Tatahouine-Médenine road against the Free French Flying Column, which repulsed attacks along the road from a point 12 miles (19 km) south of Médenine, losing twenty-seven casualties during the day.

In the afternoon, Axis infantry joined in the attacks and from about 15:30 hours were dispersed by the 2nd New Zealand Division artillery. At 17:45 hours, about 1,000 Axis infantry with tank support advanced west of Point 270 and were devastated by the by the 2nd New Zealand Division artillery, the 5th Army Group RA field and medium regiments and the heavy anti-aircraft guns on a landing ground nearby. A troop of captured 88 mm guns with RA crew operated as anti-aircraft guns.

On the 51st (Highland) Division and 7th Armoured Division fronts, the Axis attacks were more determined but had little success and Tadjera Kbir was never threatened. At 18:00 hours, twenty-seven Axis tanks and infantry were engaged by the New Zealand field artillery, after which there were no more attacks on the New Zealand front. At about 20:30 hours, Rommel accepted a suggestion from Messe to end the attack, since it could not be continued without risking losses which would compromise the defence of the Mareth Line.

Sorties by Luftwaffe and *Regia Aeronautica* fighter-bombers and fighters were made during the day but had little impact as the DAF controlled the air above the battlefield. Two New Zealanders were killed and two wounded in a raid over the 4th Field Ambulance and Bf 109 was shot down by the 26th Battalion with a captured Breda machine gun. As dusk fell, the attackers withdrew, a detachment of the King's Royal Rifle Corps and other units at Haddada having remained undisturbed, despite being isolated when the FFF Column on the right was forced back, during an Axis outflanking move. During the night of 6/7 March, XXX Corps patrols went out to find out if the attack would resume on 7 March, despite the Axis tank casualties, which as dark fell on 6 March, were already known to be 40–50, making another attack unlikely. On the New Zealand Division front, vigilance was maintained in case of an outflanking move south of the defensive line. After dark the five tanks knocked out on the 28th Battalion front were demolished, along with the others disabled along the XXX Corps front. Some tanks of the Staffordshire Yeomanry were moved forwards slightly in the New Zealand area, but the night was quiet except for British artillery harassing fire until 03:30 hours.

Aftermath

Analysis

In 1966, Ian Playfair, the British official historian, wrote that 'during the attack, the XXX Corps artillery fired about 30,000 shells and that the Luftwaffe had made a maximum effort attacking DAF airfields, and attempting close support of the First Italian Army, which railed against British anti-aircraft fire and the DAF, only tactical reconnaissance sorties, having many successes.'

In 1978, Matthew Cooper wrote **'that had the Axis attacked the previous week, it might have found the Eighth Army unprepared, having attacked at short notice to divert attention from the British First Army during Untemehmen Ochsenkopf.'** The rapid preparations made to receive the Axis attack enabled the Eighth Army easily to defeat the offensive and Rommel wrote **'that the failure to delay the British attack on the Mareth Line, caused "a great gloom" and that for the Axis to remain in Africa was suicide.'**

Casualties

- In 1943, Montgomery made a diary note **'that the Eighth Army had lost 130 casualties'.**
- In 1957, G. F. Howe, the US official historian, **'recorded German losses of 61 killed, 388 wounded, and 32 missing. Italian losses of 33 killed, 122 wounded, and 9 missing. A minimum of 41 Axis tanks were lost.'** The Germans claimed six British tanks, sixteen scout cars, thirty-three motor vehicles, thirty-two anti-tank and anti-aircraft guns and fifty-one prisoners.
- In 1966, Ian Playfair, the British official historian, called the Eighth Army losses *trifling* and recorded 635 Axis casualties, mostly German, and 44–56 Axis tanks.

Subsequent Operations

At dawn on 7 March, some groups of Axis transport were seen moving to the north and quickly drew out of range as they were engaged by artillery. There were rear-guard actions from 7–8 March, as the Germans withdrew to the Mareth Line and Gabès, but British attempts at pursuit were frustrated by the weather and the speed of the Axis withdrawal. On 10 March, some heights were still occupied and there was sporadic long-range artillery fire. Rommel left Africa the same day for the last time, leaving Arnim in command. The defeat had been so comprehensive that it caused the Germans to question their security, and Montgomery was rebuked for not taking greater steps to hide the source of his information.

On 6 March, Montgomery wrote to General Sir Alan Brooke, the chief of the Imperial general staff (the professional head of the British Army).

'He is trying to attack me in daylight with tanks, followed by lorried infantry. I have 500 6pdr atk guns dug in…I have 400 tanks…good infantry…and a great weight of artillery. It is an absolute gift, and the man must be mad.'

Note: '6pdr atk' is the 6 pounder anti-tank gun. The ordnance quick-firing 6-pounder 7cwt or just 6-pounder, was a British 57mm gun, serving during the Second World War as a primary anti-tank gun of both the British and US Army (as the 57mm gun M1). It was also used as the main armament for a number of armoured fighting vehicles. Although designed before the start of the Second World War, it did not reach service until the North African campaign in April 1942. There, it replaced the 2-pounder as an anti-tank gun, allowing the 25-pounder gun-howitzer to revert to its intended artillery role.

Allied plans for the attack on the Mareth Line continued virtually undisturbed. On 17 March, the US II Corps began Operation Wop (sic), an attack towards Gafsa, the Eighth Army began the preliminary Operation Walk and Operation Canter and then began Operation Pugilist, the Battle of the Mareth Line on 19 March.

Chapter 6

Battle of the Mareth Line

March 1943

Battle of the Mareth Line	
Date: 16–31 March 1943 **Location:** Southern Tunisia **Result:** British Victory	
Belligerents	
United Kingdom • **British India** **New Zealand** **Free France** **Greece**	**Germany** **Italy**
Commanders and Leaders	
United Kingdom: Bernard Montgomery	**Italy**: Giovanni Messe
Free France: Philippe Leclerc	
Units Involved	
United Kingdom: Eighth Army	**Italy:** First Army
Strength	
90,000 of 123,600 men	73,500 of 115,000 men
	455 guns
	139–220 tanks
	480 anti-tank guns
	75 88-mm guns
Casualties and Losses	
4,000 killed/wounded	7,000 (PoWs)
	Equipment: none recorded

Note: Before we go into the detail of the battle for the Mareth Line, it is worth recording what the Mareth Line was and when it was built.

The Mareth Line was a system of fortifications built by France in southern Tunisia in the late 1930s. The line was intended to protect Tunisia against an Italian invasion from its colony in Libya. The line occupied a point where the routes into Tunisia from the south converged, leading towards Mareth, with the Mediterranean Sea to the east and mountains and a sand sea to the west.

The line ran along the north side of Wadi Zigzaou for about 31 miles (50 km) south-westwards from the Gulf of Gabès to Cheguimi and the Djebel (mountain) Matmata on the Dahar plateau between the Grand Erg Oriental (Great Eastern Sand Sea) and the Matmata hills. The Tebaga Gap, between the Mareth Line and the Great Eastern Sand Sea, a potential route by which an invader could outflank the Mareth Line, was not surveyed until 1938.

After the French Armistice of 22 June 1940, the Mareth Line was demilitarized under the supervision of an Italo-German commission. Tunisia was occupied by Axis forces in 1942 after Operation Torch (refer to Chapter 1) and the line was refurbished and extended by Axis engineers into a defensive position by building more defences between the line and Wadi Zeuss 3.5 miles (6 km) to the south, but French-built anti-tank gun positions were too small for Axis anti-tank guns, which had to be sited elsewhere.

Battle of the Mareth Line or the Battle of Mareth

The battle was an attack in the Second World War by the British Eighth Army (General Bernard Montgomery) in Tunisia, against the Mareth Line held by the Italo-German First Army (General Giovanni Messe). It was the first big operation by the Eighth Army since the **Second Battle of El Alamein** in November 1942. On 19 March, **Operation Pugilist**, the first British attack, established a bridgehead, but a breakout attempt was defeated by Axis counterattacks. Pugilist established an alternative route of attack and **Operation Supercharge II**, an outflanking manoeuvre via the Tebaga Gap, was planned. Montgomery reinforced the flanking attack, which from 26–31 March, forced the Italo-German First Army to retreat to Wadi Akarit, another 40 miles (65 km) back in Tunisia.

Background

Axis Retreat from El Alamein

The retreat of Panzer Army Africa (known as the Deutsch-Italienische Panzerarmee/ Armata Corazzata Italo-Tedesca from October 1942) took place from 5 November 1942 to 15 February 1943. On 8 November, Operation Torch (refer to Chapter 1) began in Morocco, Algeria, and Tunisia, as the Panzerarmee Afrika in Egypt managed to evade British outflanking moves but traffic jams, fuel shortages, poor weather and air attacks reduced the speed of their retreat to 6–7 miles (10–11 km) per day. Comando Supremo in Rome and OKW (refer to refer to Chapter 5) in Berlin took an optimistic view of the situation and Comando Supremo chose the Mersa-el-Brega–El Agheila position as the terminus of the retreat, even though the position had a front of 110 miles (177 km), its strongpoints were up to 5 miles (8 km) apart, too far for mutual support, and only 30,000 mines. When the Panzerarmee arrived, the Afrika Korps had only 5,000 men, 35 tanks, 16 armoured cars, 12 anti-tank guns, 12 field howitzers and only 50 long tons of the required 400 long tons of supplies it needed daily.

Rommel wanted to retreat to Wadi Akarit in the Gabès area, 120 miles (193 km) further west, where the nonmotorized troops could defend a narrow gap between the Mediterranean and the Chott el Djerid.

The tanks and motorized infantry would join the Fifth Panzer Army (Colonel General Hans-Jürgen von Arnim) further north, drive back the British First Army from Tunisia into Algeria, then swiftly return to force back the Eighth Army. At a meeting with Hitler on 28 November, Rommel discussed the proposal but received only a promise of more supplies. On 11/12 December, he British attacked and on the following evening, the Panzerarmee resumed its retreat, and despite its chronic fuel shortages, evaded another outflanking move. The Panzerarmee took up a defensive position at Buerat on 29 December, but it was poorly fortified, wide open to an outflanking manoeuvre and vulnerable to an attack on Gabès by the First Army in southern Tunisia. The supply situation was a little better, with 152 long tons of the required 400 long tons it needed daily, but 95 per cent of the fuel had been used distributing supplies or in retreat.

The LRDG attacked Axis supply lines to great effect, leaving hundreds of Axis lorries stranded along the roads for lack of fuel, whilst the Eighth Army amassed fuel and ammunition for its next attack. On 13 January 1943, the infantry of the 21st Panzer Division were sent north to the Fifth Panzer Army to protect Gabès. On January 15, the Eighth Army attacked with 450 tanks against thirty-six German and fifty-seven Italian tanks. That evening Rommel ordered another retreat. Lack of fuel and apprehension about the threat to Gabès led the retreating infantry to pass beyond the Tarhuna-Hom's line. The British occupied Tripoli and on 23 January (the Axis retreat from El Alamein had covered 1,400 miles [2,253 km]). On 13 February the last Axis soldiers left Libya and on 15 February the rear-guard reached the Mareth Line, 80 miles (129 km) inside Tunisia; Comando Supremo intended them to hold the line indefinitely, but Rommel considered it too vulnerable to another flanking move, unlike the Wadi Akarit position further back.

Terrain

The broken terrain of southern Tunisia, with difficult rocky ridge lines and desert, limited manoeuvrability; opposite the bight where the north-south cost opens to the east, a semi-arid, scrub covered coastal plain is met inland by the Matmata Hills which lie south to north. Across the plain in a line roughly south-west to north-east was the Mareth Line, fortifications built by the French in the 1930s. In the north, the hills and the line of forts ended at the Tebaga Gap, a mountain pass between the Matmata Hills and the Djebel Tebaga, another line of high ground to the west of the gap, running east-west. North and west of this feature is the Chott el Djerid and west of the Matmata Hills, dry Jebel Dahar country and then the impassable sand of the Grand Erg Oriental. Gabès lies on the coast, where the plain meets the route from Tebaga Gap. North of Gabès, the rod to Sfax passes between the sea and the chotts, was the only route north for the Eighth Army and it was blocked by the Mareth Line.

The Mareth Line followed the line of Wadi Zigzaou, a natural tank obstacle with steep banks rising to 70 feet (21 m) high, the north-west side had been fortified by the French and subsequently reinforced. The wadi crosses the coastal plain from Zarat to Toujane and into the Matmata Hills beyond. In 1938, the French judged Jebel Dahar impassable for motorized transport, and so had not been extended the Mareth Line any further inland. However, by the time of 1943 motorized vehicles had much better performances than their predecessors had. The British had an advantage because General Georges Catroux, the designer and garrison commander of the Mareth Line in the 1930s, was available in Algiers, to provide information and advice for the attack. In the original plan, Montgomery wrote **'...the object of Operation Pugilist is to destroy the enemy now opposing Eighth Army in the Mareth Line and to advance and capture Sfax'.**

Prelude

Battle of Médenine

In this chapter, it is intended to concentrate on the Battle of the Mareth Line. Whilst the Battle of Médenine was an integral part of the Allies' overall plan, the Battle of Médenine is covered in depth in Chapter 5.

Battle

Operation Pugilist

On 19 March 1943, XXX Corps (Lieutenant General Oliver Leese) commenced Operation Pugilist. The 50th (Northumbrian) Infantry Division (Major General John Nichols) managed to penetrate the line held by the 136th Armoured Division 'Giovanni Fascisti' near Zarat. Rain and the nature of the terrain prevented the deployment of tanks, aircraft, or anti-tank guns, which left the infantry isolated. A counterattack by 15th Panzer Division and the 'Giovanni Fascisti' on 22 March, recaptured much of the bridgehead, which included thirty-five British tanks and 200 prisoners. British forces held their positions until darkness. On 24 March, all the British attacking forces were recalled. XXX Corps prepared a new attack towards Tallouf, in which the 4th Indian Infantry Division (Major General Francis Tuker) would make a night attack on 23/24 March, around the inland end of the line, coinciding with a wide left hook manoeuvre by Montgomery.

Left Hook

In early January 1943, a LRDG patrol had found a pass in the Jebel Dahar, which was given the name Wilder's Gap. A later patrol penetrated to the Tebaga Gap and proved that the route was practicable. The patrol demonstrated the weakness of

Axis defences by going further north to Gafsa and on 2 February, and made contact with the First Army, advancing from the west. Montgomery reinforced the 2nd New Zealand Division (Lieutenant General Bernard Freyberg) and renamed it the New Zealand Corps, for an attack through the Matmata Hills via Wilder's Gap, into Jebel Dahar, with the assembly of the force concealed from Axis reconnaissance. Staff from X Corps (Lieutenant General Brian Horrocks) were seconded to provide adequate HQ personnel for the new, New Zealand Corps, too big for one divisional staff, which caused some friction between the two generals.

The New Zealand Corps advance was planned in three stages, from a 20-mile (32 km) night march to Wadi bel Krecheb 19 March, a second night march of 40-miles (64 km) to just short of the Tebaga Gap and then the capture of the entrance to the gap at first light on 21 March, or as soon as possible afterwards. The corps would then advance to El Hamma, which overlooks the coast road north of Gabès. The flank of the advance was to be protected by Free French forces (General Philippe Leclerc) and the 1st King's Dragoon Guards. An attack by X Corps from El Hamma to Gabès would cut off the First Army defenders of the Mareth positions

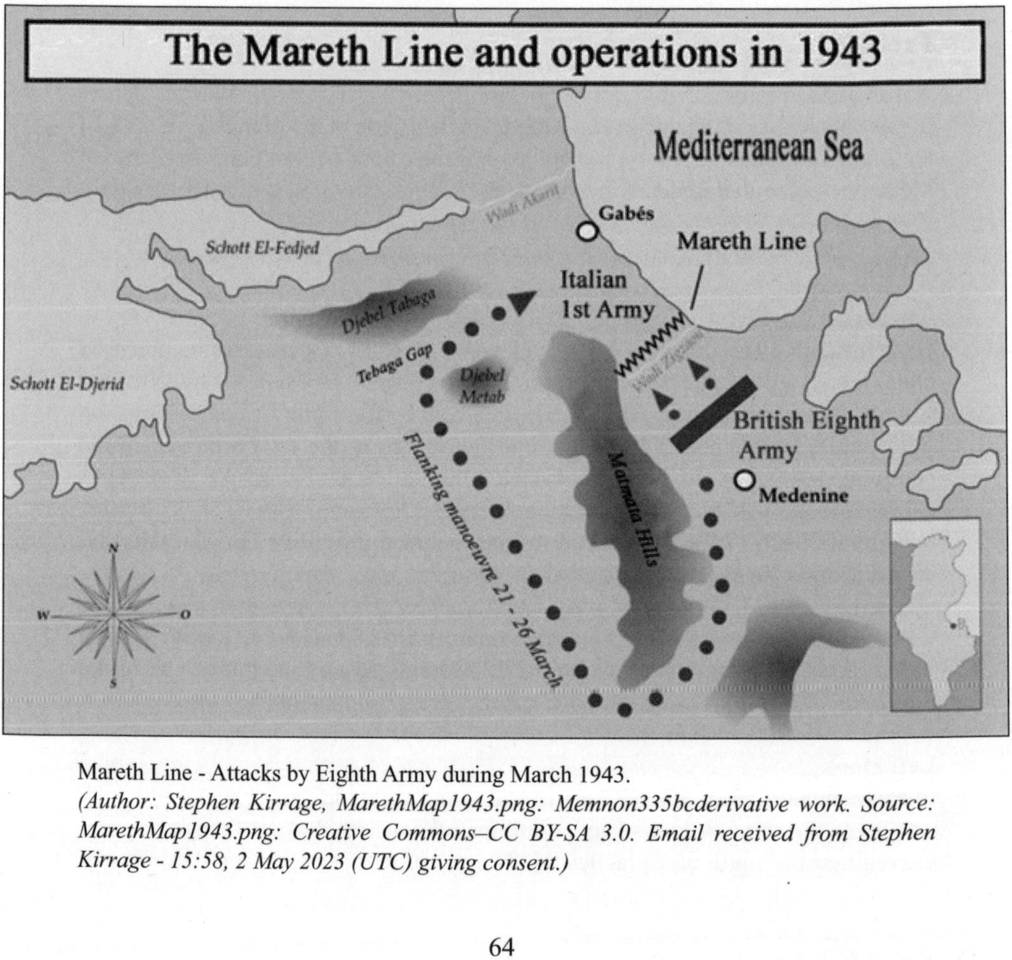

Mareth Line - Attacks by Eighth Army during March 1943.
(Author: Stephen Kirrage, MarethMap1943.png: Memnon335bcderivative work. Source: MarethMap1943.png: Creative Commons–CC BY-SA 3.0. Email received from Stephen Kirrage - 15:58, 2 May 2023 (UTC) giving consent.)

and give the New Zealand Corps the opportunity to advance 80-miles (129 km) up the coast to Sfax and the landing grounds on the west side of the town.

The planning emphasized surprise and the ability to blitz Axis positions. The corps had relatively few infantries and relied on its artillery to break Axis troop morale, with air support provided by fighters and bombers. A simultaneous frontal attack by XXX Corps on the Mareth Line would divide enemy attention and hamper an Axis counterattack; the US II Corps of the First Army would advance through El Guettar to threaten Axis communications and pin down reinforcements from Sfax.

Tebaga Gap

The New Zealand Corps engaged the Axis troops in the Tebaga Gap on 21 March, but progress over the next four days against the 164th Light Afrika Division and 21st Panzer Division was very slow, although they did secure the entrance to the gap. On the Mareth Line, XXX Corps made some progress but did not break through. On 23 March, Montgomery ordered the 1st Armoured Division of Major General Raymond Briggs of X Corps to reinforce the New Zealand Corps from reserve, where it was waiting to exploit the anticipated breakthroughs by either XXX Corps or the New Zealand Corps and Horrocks, with the X Corp Headquarters to take control of operations in the Tebaga Gap.

Operation Supercharge II

The operation was planned to start on the afternoon of 26 March, with a preliminary operation on the night of 25/26 March, to capture Height 184. The New Zealand Corps was to attack into the Tebaga Gap on a two-brigade front and capture the Axis defences from Djebel Tebaga to Djebel Melab, which would be exploited by the 1st Armoured Division. After assembling during the night and lying in concealed positions all day, the 5 New Zealand Brigade was to attack on the right and the 6 New Zealand Brigade on the left, preceded by the 8 Armoured Brigade and a creeping barrage by the New Zealand and X Corps artillery. The attacking troops were to move to high ground 2,000 yards forwards and then to a second objective at a Wadi 2,500 yards further on. The 1st Armoured Division, led by the 2 Armoured Brigade, was to move through at 18:15 hours to an area 3,000 yards beyond the New Zealand Corps' final objective, and as soon as the moon rose (at about 23:15 hours), advance to El Hamma.

RAF heavy bombers would begin harassment of the Axis defenders led by General Messe the night before, with attacks on transport and communications until 15:30 hours. Day bombers would then begin low-altitude pattern bombing, to add to Axis disorganization, followed by relays of fighter-bombers every 15 minutes for 2½+ hours. Spitfires would escort the bombers and fighter-bombers, and the remainder of the Northwest African Tactical Air Force (NATAF) would bomb Axis airfields. An RAF forward observation officer was to brief pilots by nominating landmarks, making targets with red and blue smoke; friendly troops to use orange smoke and the artillery would fire smoke shells to signal to the aircrews.

On 24 March, Arnim doubted that an Eighth Army attack was likely and was more concerned about Maknassy further north. Despite the slow advance in the south, Arnim wanted First Army to withdraw to Wadi Akarit on 25 March, but Liebenstein and Messe preferred to counterattack with the 15th Panzer Division. The threat to Maknassy and the possibility of the US II Corps reaching Gabès and cutting off the First Army meant that they had to retire from Mareth and then from Tebaga.

Height 184 fell at 02:50 hours to the 21st New Zealand Battalion and the Allied artillery commenced firing at 16:00 hours. The attack began with the 8 Armoured Brigade, followed by infantry battalion carriers and then infantry on foot. It appeared that the 164th Light and 21st Panzer divisions had not expected a daylight assault and had been surprised; the setting sun, wind and dust had made observations difficult. The British tanks had been ordered to press on and the infantry also managed a quick pace, arriving on the first objective and then kept going, despite increasing resistance and delays. An armoured regiment pressed on to Wadi Aisoub beyond the second objective, followed by the 23rd New Zealand Battalion. On the left, a minefield covered by anti-tank guns was bypassed on both sides to close-up to the second objective, clearing a gap for the 1st Armoured Division, despite many Axis posts holding out in the vicinity.

By dark, a gap in the defences had been made; pausing until moonrise at 23:00 hours, the 1st Armoured Division advanced through the gap and rapidly moved on El Hamma, 20 miles (32 km) to the north-east, halfway to Gabès on the coast. On the morning of 27 March, the 15th Panzer Division was brought out of reserve to counterattack the New Zealand Corps on their flank. By 09:00 hours the attack had been repulsed and the New Zealand Corps advanced into the hills on their right. By the evening of 27 March, German resistance had been broken and the line of communication forward to the 1st Armoured Division secured, the division having been halted by the defences of El Hamma, whilst the tanks had waited for the moonlight, Freyberg persuaded Horrocks that the New Zealand Corps, en route to El Hamma to link with the 1st Armoured Division, should branch off to the right to avoid the Axis defences at El Hamma and head across the broken ground direct to Gabès.

By 28 March, General Messe gave the order that all Axis forces on the Mareth Line be withdrawn to face the X and New Zealand corps on their right flank, but by holding up the 1st Armoured Division at El Hamma, managed to avoid encirclement. On 29 March, the New Zealand Corps took Gabès, which forced a further Axis withdrawal to a new line 15 miles (24 km) to the rear of Gabès at Wadi Akarit, whilst the 164th Light, 15th Panzer and 21st Panzer divisions fought rear-guard actions. El Hamma was evacuated of 29 March, leaving the way open for the 1st Armoured Division to advance northwards with the New Zealand Corps on their right.

Aftermath

Casualties

On 31 March, Operation Supercharge II was terminated, having cost the Eighth Army 4,000 casualties, many from the 50th Division, and a large number of tanks; the New Zealand Corps lost 51 tanks and 945 men.

The corps was disbanded, and its elements were distributed between X and XXX corps. On 30 March, Montgomery sent the following message to Freyberg,

'My very best congratulations to NZ Corps and 10 Corps on splendid results achieved by the left hook. These results have led to the complete disintegration of the enemy resistance and the whole Marth position. Give my congratulations to all your officers and men and tell them how pleased I am with all they have done.'

Montgomery

The Axis forces, despite withdrawing in relatively good order, lost over 7,000 men now (PoW), of whom 2,500 were German. The 15th Panzer Division had suffered many losses, the 164th Light Afrika Division lost most of its weapons and vehicles. The 80th Infantry Division 'La Spezia' suffered losses of nearly 50 per cent and the 16th Infantry Division 'Pistoia' was almost annihilated; several Italian divisions were amalgamated. The First Army withdrew in good order to Wadi Akarit.

Other Operations Carried Out by Montgomery When Taking the Mareth Line–19 March to 31 March 1943

[Contributor–C. Peter-Chen, ww2dbase]

Operation Pugilist

With Ermin Rommel recalled to Europe, Italian General Giovanni Messe assumed command of Axis forces in North Africa, which by this time had been pushed into Tunisia from both east and west; German Major General Fritz Bayerlein served under Messe as the German Liaison.

On 19 March, British General Bernard Montgomery launched Operation Pugilist, attacking the Axis Mareth Line defences, and penetrating near Zarat. On 21 March, Lieutenant General Bernard Freyberg's New Zealand Corps troops bypassed the line by passing through Wilder's Gap undetected, attacking Axis positions in the Tebaga Gap; surprise was initially achieved, but German 164th Division and German 21st Panzer Division pinned down the New Zealand attack. On 22 March, German 15th Panzer Division counterattacked near Zarat, recapturing the territory previously lost in the opening of Operation Pugilist; the Allied troops fell back in the face of German tank fire as the terrain prevented Allied tanks from playing a significant role. During the day of 23 March, Montgomery sent the British 1st Armoured Division from the reserve to reinforce the New Zealand troops at the Tebaga Gap. During the night of 23 March, Indian 4th Infantry Division attacked the western end of the Mareth Line.

Operation Supercharge II

On 26 March, Montgomery launched a renewed offensive, codenamed Operation Supercharge II. At 15:30 hours, aircraft dropped bombs on German positions at the Tebaga Gap in front of the New Zealand troops' positions. At 16:00 hours, as the aircraft departed, Allied artillery commenced a brief barrage, and then the

New Zealand troops charged in on a two-brigade front. The German troops were taken again by surprise, and the Allies were able to open a gap in the defences. At 23:00 hours, as the moon rose to provide some light, tanks of the British 1st Armoured Division charged through the gap towards El Hamma 20 miles (32 km) to the northeast. To defend against this attack, tanks of the German 15th Panzer Division was ordered out of the reserve, counterattacking by dawn of 27 March, halting the tank attack just before El Hamma by 09:00 hours; meanwhile, the New Zealand troops were able to capture high grounds near the Tebaga Gap, securing the area rear of the British tanks. By 28 March, Axis defences had shifted out of Mareth Line to form a new defensive line before the forces engaged in Operation Supercharge II.

On 29 March, New Zealand troops captured Gabès, forcing the Axis to form a new line 15 miles (24 km) to the north of Wadi Akarit, while German 164th Light Division, German 15th Panzer Division and German 21st Panzer Division fought a delaying action campaign against the advancing Allies; on the same day, Axis forces at El Hamma were withdrawn. Operation Supercharge II was concluded with success on 31 March.

Chapter 7

Battle of El Guettar

March–April 1943

Battle of El Guettar	
Date: 23 March–3 April 1943 **Location:** El Guettar, Tunisia **Result:** Indecisive	
Belligerents	
United States	**Germany** **Italy**
Commanders and Leaders	
United States: George S Patton	**Germany**: Hans-Jürgen von Arnim
	Italy: Giovanni Messe
Casualties and Losses	
22 tanks lost	37 tanks lost
4 halftracks lost	4,000–6,000 killed or wounded in three weeks
4,000-5,000 killed or wounded	

The **Battle of El Guettar** was a battle that took place during the Tunisian campaign of the Second World War, fought between elements of the Army Group Afrika under General Hans-Jürgen von Arnim, along with Italian First Army under General Giovanni Messe, and US II Corps under Lieutenant General George S. Patton, in south Tunisia. It was the first battle in which the US forces were able to defeat the experienced German tank units, but the follow-up to the battle was inconclusive.

Background

The US II Corps had been badly mauled in its first encounter with Axis forces in Tunisia during a series of battles that culminated in the disastrous battle of the Kasserine Pass (refer to Chapter 3) in late February 1943. Erwin Rommel – *poised on the threshold of a complete tactical victory* – turned from the battle to return to his eastwards-facing defences at the Mareth Line when he heard of the approach of Bernard Montgomery's British Eighth Army. Thus, the battle concluded with the US forces still in the field, but having lost ground and men, and with little confidence in some key commanders.

In the last week of January 1943, despite a massive artillery bombardment, the Italian 14th Bersaglieri Battalion of the 131st Armoured Division Centauro dug in near Djebel Rihana. Harold V. Boyle, an Irish war correspondent, wrote **'that a second attack was required using grenades and bayonets in order to evict the Italians'.**

'Artillery and aircraft may harass but cannot dislodge him. Only bullets and bayonets of rival riflemen can do that. This was well illustrated in the Ousseltia Valley campaign in January when tanks and artillery laid down one of the finest barrages of the campaign but couldn't rout Italians dug in like moles in the hills bordering the rod to Kairouan. The artillery was beautiful to see but they couldn't do the job alone. Finally American infantry swarmed up the hills at night and flushed the Italians out in droves with hand grenades and the pointed persuasion on their bayonets.'

The American command reached to its reverses against German and Italian forces with a prompt and sweeping series of changes in command, discipline and tactics. Also, large units were kept massed rather than being broken up into smaller, unsupported elements as had been done under US II Corps Commander Lloyd Fredendall. Close air support was also improved.

On 6 March, 1943, George S. Patton took command of the US II Corps from Lloyd Fredendall, who had been in command before and during the Kasserine engagement. His first move was to organize his US II Corps for an offensive back towards the Eastern Dorsal chain of the Atlas Mountains. If successful, this would threaten the right rear of the Axis forces defending the Mareth Line facing Montgomery's Eighth Army and ultimately make their position untenable. Patton's style of leadership was very different from his predecessor; he is reported to have issued an order in connection with an attack on a hill position ending, **'I expect to see such casualties among officers, particularly staff officers, as will convince me that a serious effort has been made to capture this objective'.**

On 17 March, the US 1st Infantry Division moved forwards into the almost abandoned plains, taking the town of Gafsa and preparing it as a forward supply base for further operations. On 18 March, the 1st Ranger Battalion – led by Colonel William O. Darby – pushed ahead, and occupied the oasis of El Guettar, again meeting with little opposition. The Italian defenders instead retreated and took up positions in the hills overlooking the town, thereby blocking the mountain pass (of the same name) leading south out of the interior plains to the coastal plain. Another operation by the Rangers raided an Italian position and took 200 prisoners on the night of 20 March, scaling a sheer cliff and passing ammunition and equipment up hand-over-hand.

Battle

The Axis army commanders had become aware of US movements and decided that the 10th Panzer Division should stop them. Rommel had departed Tunisia

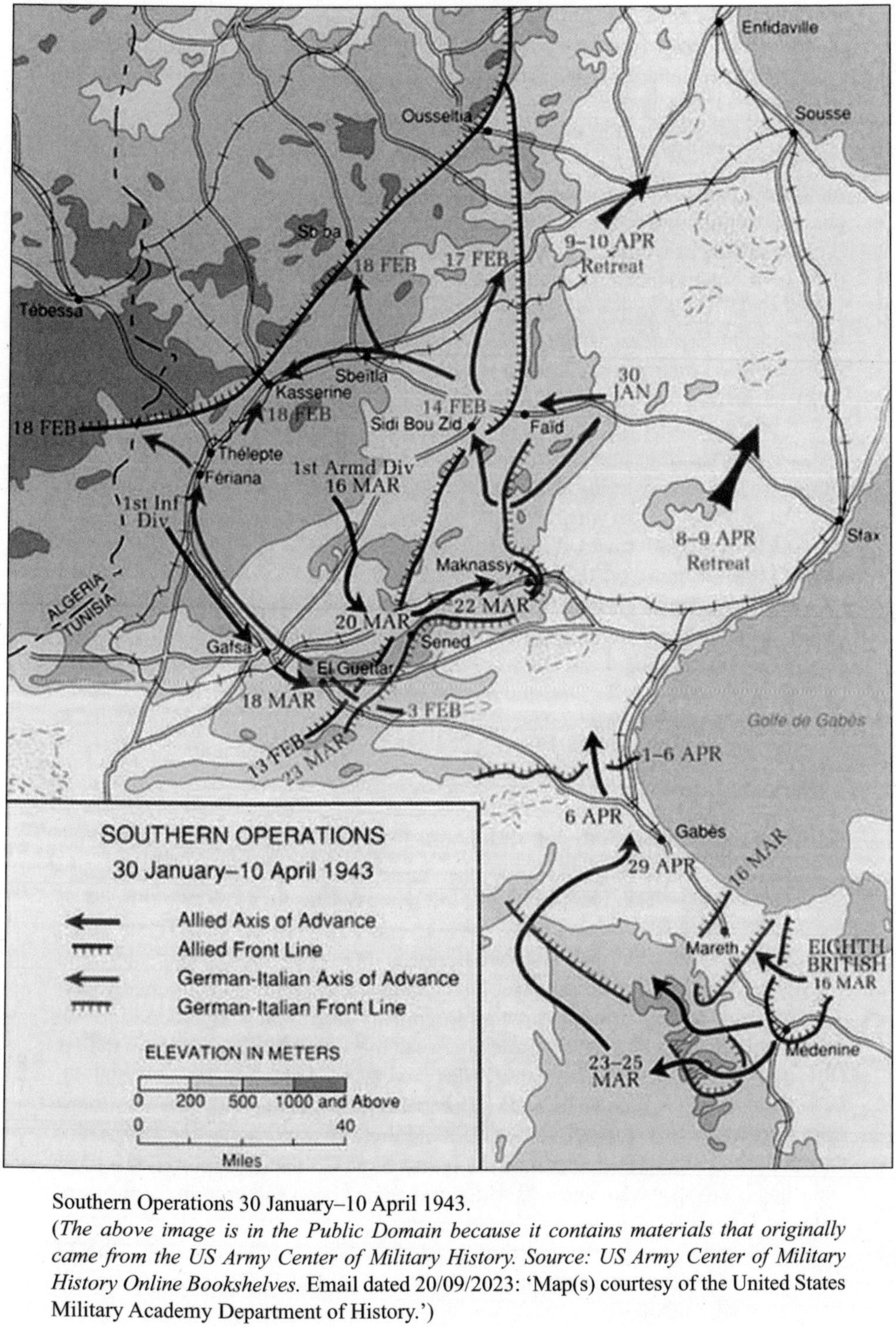

Southern Operations 30 January–10 April 1943.
(*The above image is in the Public Domain because it contains materials that originally came from the US Army Center of Military History. Source: US Army Center of Military History Online Bookshelves.* Email dated 20/09/2023: 'Map(s) courtesy of the United States Military Academy Department of History.')

for Germany on 9 March, before the battle, leaving Arnim in control of the newly named Afrika Korps. Arnim also held Rommel's opinion on the low quality of the American forces and felt that a spoiling attack would be enough to clear them from the Eastern Dorals again.

At 06:00 hours on 23 March, 50 tanks of Broich's 10th Panzer Division emerged from the pass into the El Guettar valley at ***34° 20' 12" N 8° 56' 53" E***. German motorized units in halftracks and motorcycle sidecars broke off from formation and charged the infantry on the top of the hill.

The halftracks would move up the hill as far as they could, and then the infantry they carried would dismount whilst covered by fire from 88mm guns. The Germans were manoeuvring to hit American artillery anchored on the hill. They quickly overran front-line infantry and artillery positions. Major General Terry de la Mesa Allen Sr – commanding the US 1st Infantry Division – was threatened when two tanks came near his headquarters, but he shrugged off suggestions of moving, **'I will like hell pull out, and I'll shoot the first bastard who does'.**

The German attack lost momentum when it ran into a minefield. When the Germans slowed to reorganize, US artillery and anti-tank guns engaged, including 31 M10 tank destroyers which had recently arrived. Over the next hour, thirty of the 10th Panzer's tanks were destroyed, and by 09:00 hours they retreated from the valley.

A second attempt was made at 16:45 hours, after waiting for infantry to form up. Once again, the US artillery was able to disrupt the attack, eventually breaking the charge and inflicting heavy losses. Realizing that further attacks were hopeless, the rest of the 10th Panzer Division dug in on hills to the east or retreated back to the German headquarters at Gabès.

Allied Attacks

On 10 March, the British Eighth Army launched their attack on the Mareth Line, at first with little success.

Over the next week, the US forces slowly moved forwards to take the rest of the interior plains and set up lines across the entire Eastern Dorsals. The German and Italian defences and reserves were heavy, and the progress was both slow and costly. On 23 March, the 10th Panzer Division attacked Lieutenant Colonel Robert H. York's 1st Battalion, 18th Infantry Regiment, 1st Infantry Division, and the German tanks broke through the valley between the 3rd and 1st battalions of the 1st Division, reaching a position about 6 miles (10 km) to the rear of the 1st Battalion. In the action, the German tanks and self-propelled guns, along with German troops riding in carriers and trucks, overran the 32nd Field Artillery Battalion and part of the 5th Field Artillery Battalion, and the Italian High Command reported that forty tanks had been destroyed, and 170 Allied troops had been captured in 'central and southern Tunisia'.

By 30 March, the US forces were in position for an offensive south from El Guettar. In order to start a breakout, the two original Italian strongpoints on Hill

369 ***34° 14' 29" N 9° 7' 16" E*** and Hill 722 ***34° 12' 7" N 8° 59' 36" E*** had to be taken, one after the other.

The US plan involved the US 1st and 9th Infantry divisions, and Combat Command 1/3 of the US 1st Armoured Division, collectively known as 'Benson Force'. This force attacked Hill 369 on the afternoon of 30 March, but ran into mines and anti-tank fire, losing five tanks and a rifle company from the 2nd Battalion of Colonel Edwin H. Randle's 47th Infantry Regiment that was forced to surrender. The tanks were withdrawn, and the 1st and 9th attacked again the next day at 06:00 hours, gaining some ground and taking several hundred prisoners.

However, an Italian counterattack drove them back from their newly gained positions, and by 12:45 hours they were back where they started with the loss of nine tanks and two tank destroyers. A further attempt the next day, 1 April, also failed, after barely getting started. Private Emil J. Dedonato remembers that Patton drove up to the 47th Regiment's command post, unhappy that the initial attacks had failed:

'Patton was in a huffy mood and stormed over to see Colonel Randle in his Jeep. It was obvious he wasn't pleased with the initial results of the night attacks. I'll never forget Colonel Randle's instructions as they moved into El Guettar, **"Where we're going you won't need a psychic!"'**

At this point Patton received orders to start the attempt on Hill 772, even though Hill 369 was still under Italian control. The 9th was moved to Hill 772, leaving the 1st on Hill369. By 3 April, the 1st had finally cleared Hill 369, but the battle on Hill 772 continued. The Italian commander – General Messe – then called in support from the German 21st Panzer Division, further slowing progress. The tempo of the operations slowed, and the lines remained largely static.

Aftermath

On 6 April, the British Eighth Army once again overran the Axis lines at the Battle of Wadi Akarit, and a full retreat started. On the morning of 7 April, Benson Force moved through the positions held by the 1st and 9th divisions and raced down the abandoned El Guettar to Gabès Road, where it met the lead elements of the Eighth Army at 17:00 hours. With the last Axis line of defence in the south of Tunisia broken, the remaining forces made a run to join the other Axis forces in the north. Tunis fell to the Allies in early May 1943.

Chapter 8

Operation Flax

April 1943

Operation Flax	
Date: 5–27 April 1943 **Location:** Tunis and Cap Bon, Tunisia **Result:** Allied Victory	
Belligerents	
United Kingdom **United States**	**Germany** **Italy**
Commanders and Leaders	
United Kingdom: Arthur Tedder	**Germany**: Martin Harlinghausen
United Kingdom: Arthur Conningham	**Italy**: Rino Corso Fougier
United States: Carl Spaatz	
United States: James H. Doolittle	
Units Involved	
Mediterranean Air Command	II Flieger Korps
Casualties and Losses	
35 aircraft in aerial combat	4 Savoia-Marchetti S82
	123–157 Junkers Ju 52
	21 Messerschmitt Me 323
	432 Axis aircraft to all causes

Operation Flax

Operation Flax was a western Allied air operation during the Tunisian campaign, as part of the larger North African campaign of the Second World War. It was designed to cut air supply between Italy and the Axis armies in Tunis, Tunisia, in April 1943. The parallel Allied naval effort was Operation Retribution.

In November 1942, American and British forces landed in North Africa under Operation Torch (refer to Chapter 1). Allied thrusts overran Vichy French Morocco and Algeria and advanced into Tunisia. The danger for the Axis powers was now apparent. American forces advancing eastwards and the British Eighth Army advancing westwards after the victory at the Second Battle of El Alamein threatened to trap and destroy the remaining Axis forces in North Africa, reinforcements for the German Afrika Korps, Italian Army and Luftwaffe were dispatched by sea and air. These reinforcements staved off an immediate defeat in Tunisia, the last African region still in Axis hands. The poor state of the roads and rail lines in Algeria meant Allied forces faced supply difficulties which helped the Axis prolong their defence. The inexperience of the US forces was exposed at the Battle of the Kasserine Pass. The growing number and experience of Allied forces squeezed the Axis towards the northern tip of Tunisia. The RAF and Royal Navy operating from Malta took a heavy toll on Axis shipping. Axis supplies were still reaching the Afrika Korps by air and by early April 1943, many Axis personnel were being evacuated by air. Although the Allies held air superiority by this time, Luftwaffe transports were operating with impunity during darkness hours.

To prevent these operations, the RAF and the United States Army Air Forces (USAAF) were ordered to attack Axis aircraft by day and night. Owing to bad weather and the need to gather intelligence, Operation Flax, did not begin until 5 April. Although the Axis put up a determined resistance with large air battles taking place, the Allied air forces cut the aerial link from Axis-held Sicily and Italy. During the operation, an air battle known as the 18 April, *Palmsonntag Massaker* (Palm Sunday Massacre) took place, in which German Junkers JU 52 transport aircraft suffered many losses over Cape Bon whilst evacuating *Heer* (German Army) forces escaping from the Allied ground offensive, Operation Vulcan (refer to Chapter 11). The air operation continued until 27 April and did great harm to the Axis supply effort. Along with the attempted airlift during the Battle of Stalingrad, Operation Flax was so costly to the German transport fleet that it was unable to recover.

Background

Strategic Situation

The Axis campaign in North Africa was characterized by supply shortages. The failure was one of the primary reasons that Field Marshal Erwin Rommel could not defeat the Eighth Army throughout 1941–1942. Rommel, at points, had recognized Malta as a serious obstacle to Axis supply between Axis-held Europe and their forces in North Africa. Malta lay across their lines of communication, and, despite the two-and-a-half-year Siege of Malta, it remained a base for Allied naval and air forces to attack Axis supply lines for much of this period. Rommel failed to apply enough pressure on OKW (refer to Chapter 5) to invade the island in Operation Herkules. Although Malta was mostly neutralized as an offensive base in mid-1942, later that year the Allied offensive from Malta became increasingly effective. The Axis defeat at the Second Battle of El Alamein and the Allied landings, Operation Torch, in Western North Africa, threatened to crush the Axis from east and west. The Germans sent reinforcements to Africa through Vichy-held Tunisia, but by the start of 1943, they were suffering increasing shipping losses to Malta-based forces. Some respite was won for the Axis when the Allies lost the 'Run for Tunis' in part owing to rapid German reactions and the difficulty in supplying their armies through the poor Algerian infrastructure. By early 1943, the Axis had numerical superiority in aircraft; 690 to the Allied's 480.

The campaign from Malta caused chronic supply shortages in Africa. By April 1943, the Allied armies had pushed the Axis force to the northern tip of Tunisia, near its capital, Tunis. Despite the desperate situation, OKW continued to send reinforcements and supplies to the besieged Axis forces by air.

To prevent prolonged resistance, the Allies, now aware of the German supply timetables through the use of British *Ultra,* began an aerial offensive to cut the link. The operation was due to begin in the last week of March 1943 but bad weather over Tunisia meant that it was delayed until 5 April.

Axis Supply

The Axis situation in the air, on land and at sea was gradually deteriorating, Axis supply ships had suffered many losses between Cape Bon and Sicily, 67 per cent of which were down to Allied aircraft. Theo Osterkamp was appointed Fighter Leader Sicily to fly over the area. On 7 April 1943, the organization was given 148 fighters for these operations. The Luftwaffe reorganized its forces in Tunisia, Hans Seidemann was appointed Flying Corps Tunisia with three commands: Flying Leader Tunis, Middle and Gabès, after its headquarters' location. Seidemann had the equivalent of twelve groups and maintained around 300 fighters until mid-April. The German fighter defences also benefited from a rudimentary radar supported early-warning network.

Major General Ulrich Bucholz, the wing commander of KGzbV 3, was appointed air transport leader II, Mediterranean Sea, on 15 January 1943. His forces were organized under the Naples-based KGzbV N (N for Neapel, or Naples) and the Trapani-based KGzbV S. KGzbV S had to make two missions a day; KGzbV S made only one. The formations would be eighty to 120 aircraft strong. Operations were to be flown at only 150 feet (46 m), arriving around noon to operate during the Allied 'lunch' period. The units operated mostly the Junkers Ju 52, which brought in 89 long tons daily, and the giant Messerschmitt Me 323s brought in some 30 long tons with their smaller numbers. The logistical effort was made using Indian prisoners of war, who helped unload supplies. The operational method usually involved escort fighters picking up the formation en route. Only one fighter for every five transports was made available owing to various shortages. The Naples units were met near Trapani and on the return leg fighters, including Bf 110 *Zerstorer,* escorted them home. The end of the airlifts at Stalingrad and in the Kuban allowed the number of Axis transport aircraft to reach 185 by 10 March. By the beginning of April, it rose to 426. The force flew much-needed ammunition and fuel to the Axis in Africa.

Allied Plan

James H Doolittle commanding Northwest African Strategic Air Force (NASAF) was ordered to formulate an air interdiction campaign. He named it Operation Flax.

Flax called for Allied fighters to intercept the aerial convoys over Sicily-Tunisia strait. Allied units were also briefed to carry out attacks against Axis airfields in Tunisia and the overcrowded staging fields in Sicily. They were also ordered to carry out anti-shipping sweeps. Flax was an operation which was unlikely to work more than a few times, as shown by the relative impunity with which the surviving Axis air transports operated at night after the operation had begun. The flight time across the Strait of Sicily was so short aerial interception could be made only with precise intelligence. The Germans understood this but did not know that their communications had been compromised and were being read by Allied intelligence. Ignorant of their intelligence leaks, they operated by day. Since their enemy had the option of flying by night, and the weather conditions were not ideal, the allies delayed Flax until the most German transport aircraft were in operation so that the blow would be as great as possible. Allied intelligence listened to the Y-stations until they were sure they could strike.

The plan included co-ordinated attacks on Axis airfields carried out by Boeing B-17 Flying Fortress groups to tie down Axis fighters. Medium bomber units operating the North American B-26 Mitchell would fly sweeps over the Gulf of Tunis; they were to be joined by Lockheed P-38 Lightning heavy fighters, which were also detailed to sweep the area.

The presence of the B-25s would allow the P-38s to operate in the area without raising the Axis suspicions. It would seem as if they were there to escort the B-25s, rather than to attack Axis air transports. Supermarine Spitfire units would sweep the straits further north, catching any enemy aircraft that evaded the P-38s. More B-25 and B-17 units were detailed to bomb Sicilian airfields to catch transports on the ground. The USAAF 9th Air Force was detailed to send its Consolidated B-24 Liberator bomb groups against airfields in and around Naples in this capacity as well. On 2 April, Doolittle's superiors – supreme commander of all Allied Air Forces in the Mediterranean, Arthur Tedder, and commander of Allied Air Forces in Western North Africa, Carl Spaatz – decided to wait for the next suitable window to launch the offensive.

Order of Battle

Allied

The Allied order of battle involved all the main commands in the area. The Supreme Allied Air Force Command was the Mediterranean Air Command (MAD) under Air Chief Marshal Arthur Tedder. Below the supreme command were the sector organizations, the Northwest African Air Forces (NAAF) commanded by Carl Spaatz. Directly sub-ordinated to Spaatz was the NASAF under James H. Doolittle. The second command was the operational/tactical force, the NATAF under Air Marshal Arthur Coonningham, nicked named 'Maori'.

Axis

Martin Harlinghausen commanded Air Corps II, which controlled Luftwaffe operations in Africa, as part of Air Fleet 2; sub-ordinate to Fliegerkorps II were seven Kampfgeschwader (bomber wings). Several Jagdgeschwader (fighter wings) were also on-call for support.

American Operations

Closing the Straits

At 06:30 hours on 5 April, twenty-six P-38s of the US 1st Fighter Group conducted a sweep over the Sicilian Strait; eighteen B-25s of the 321st Bomb Group, escorted by thirty-two P-38s off the 82nd Fighter Group, set out on a maritime interdiction operation. Six of the P-38s returned to base for unrecorded reasons. The B-25s claimed two ferries damaged and a destroyer sunk. One B-25 was shot down.

The 1st Group arrived over Cape Bon at 08:00 hours; they reported contact with several formations of Axis aircraft, estimating fifty to seventy Ju 52s, twenty Bf 109s, four Fw 190s, six Ju 87s and a Fw 189. The German formation had only thirty-one Ju 52s, ten Bf 109s, six to seven Bf 110s, four Ju 87s and one Fw 190. The US fighters attacked, and a large air battle developed, the 82nd Fighter Group also engaged, the 1st Fighter Group claimed eleven Ju 52s, two Ju 87s, two Bf 109s and the Fw 189 for three P-38s lost. The 82nd claimed seven Ju 52s, three Ju 87s, three Bf 109s, one Bf 110 and one Me 210 for four P-38s. German losses were about half this total: thirteen to fourteen Ju 52s and about three fighters. In 2003, Weal wrote of the loss of thirteen Ju 52s and two Bf 109s, from 5./JG 27.

Bomber Offensive

Later that day, eighteen B-17s from the 97th Bomb Group bombed Axis airfields at El Aounina, with two Me 323s, two Ju52s and five Italian transports being destroyed. A second mission was flown to Sid Ahmed, both raids with Spitfire escorts. Only a few German fighters intercepted, without success. The bombers claimed one German fighter destroyed. An hour later, thirty-five B-25s from the 310th Bomb Group and eighteen P-38s from the 82nd Fighter Group raided Axis airfields in Sicily near Borizzo. Some eighty to ninety Axis aircraft were counted, poorly camouflaged and vulnerable. The attack achieved good results with fragmentation bombs. The attackers were intercepted by fifteen Bf 109s, losing two B-25s. The bombers claimed three Bf 109s whilst the P-38s claimed two of the German fighters. The 301st Bomber Group attacked Milo airfield, claiming fifty-two destroyed on the ground. Actual Axis losses were thirteen German, and eight Italian aircraft destroyed with eleven German and thirty Italian aircraft damaged. Some 72 B-17s of the 99th Bomber Group bombed the airfield at Bocca di Falco. They claimed to have seen 100-150 aircraft, but the raid only destroyed four Axis aircraft and damaged several. Spitfires claimed two Bf 109s for two losses. Two sweeps by P-38s found nothing further. The NASAF claimed 201 Axis aircraft destroyed including forty in the air battles. German sources list the loss of fourteen Ju 52s in aerial combat and eleven Ju52s and Me 323s on the ground with sixty-seven damaged. Aside from combat aircraft, the British Official History concludes that twenty-seven German and three Italian transports were lost on 5 April.

Fighter Offensive

Flax merged into the preparatory phase of the Sicilian campaign as air attacks were eroding the Axis air defences on the island. Whilst Flax continued, albeit on a smaller scale, the emphasis was on fighter operations. On 10 April, Flax was renewed and about seventy-five P-38s of the 1st Fighter Group intercepted twenty Italian Savoia-Marchetti SM.82 and around six Macchi C.200s. The battle resulted in ten transports and two Italian fighters being shot down. Later that morning, twenty-seven P-38s of the 82nd Fighter Group were escorting 18 B-25s of the 310th Bomb Group over Cape Bon when thirty Ju 52s were spotted with two Bf 110s, two Ju 87s and just three Ju 88s with them. At first, eleven P-38s stayed with the B-25s but then the bombers joined in, flying past the transports, and firing on them with their gunners. Around fifteen Bf 109s were scrambled from Tunisia to help the transports and they destroyed one P-38 and damaged three more. The Germans had already suffered many losses; one P-38 pilot was killed when he flew into a Bf 110 and some B-25s were shot up. The Americans claimed twenty-five victories. The Germans recorded the loss of ten Ju 52s, one Ju 88, one Bf 109 and one Bfd 110. Some Ju 52s managed to ditch, and their crews survived. A Spitfire patrol later shot down four more Ju 52s. It is likely the Bf 110s 'spotted' in the formation were in fact German Me 210s planes from Zerstörergeschwader 1. RAF and USAAF units also shot down a SG 2 Fw 190 on a ferry flight and another from SKG 210. An SG 2 Hs 129 was also shot down and a JU 88 from III./KGH77 was also shot down.

On 11 April, the 82nd ran into twenty Ju52s, four Ju 88s, four Bf 110s and seven Bf 109s. The Americans claimed all of the Ju 52s and seven escorts. Actual losses are unclear; in the afternoon, twenty of the 82nd ran into thirty unescorted Ju 52s. The transports fought back, losing only five and shooting down one P-38, its pilot killed. The day's total amounted to seventeen Ju52s, one SM.82 and two Bf 110s destroyed. The RAF had also been involved in the day's operations; 152 Squadron sent thirty-four Spitfires to intercept twelve Ju52s escorted by a handful of Bf 109s. Three Ju52s were shot down for the loss of two Spitfires, both claimed by Wolfgang Tonne of I./JG 53; the German units reported no losses. It had been a bad day for the Luftwaffe, losses amounted to eighteen Ju 52s; four from III./KG.z.b.V 1. Raids by RAF Vickers Wellington bombers continued during the night. Ju 88-night fighters from NJG 2 shot down two; the results of the rads are not known.

On 13 April, B-17s from 97th and 301st Bomb Groups bombed Sicilian airfields at Castelvetrano and Trapani. The Italians lost eleven SM.82s destroyed and sixteen damaged on the ground.

At Trapani the Germans lost eight aircraft and forty damaged for the loss of two B-17s to the island's fighter defences consisting of Bf 109s from JG 27. Battles over the airfields in the afternoon were inconclusive, costing the Axis one Ju 88 from II./KG 26 and the Allies lost an RAF Spitfire from 232 Squadron. That night, air raids killed four German fighter pilots from I./JG 53 and two Ju 88s from II./NJG 2 and III./KG 76 were lost.

DAF Operations

Early Sweeps

On 12 April, the RAF DAF took command over most of the Flax operations. The RAF used sea-looking radar, which was less effective than it could have been as the German formations flew low. The considerable ranges stretched the Curtiss P-40 Warhawks and Spitfires to the limit. The British spread their forces more thinly to maintain continuous coverage and on 16 April, thirteen Spitfires ran into a large formation of Axis aircraft. The Spitfires shot down seven SM 82s and a Bf 109 for the loss of two, German fighters claiming three Spitfires. One of the two confirmed victims was Wing Commander Ian 'Widge' Gleed of 244 Wing. Gleed was possibly the victim of a Lieutenant Ernst-Wilheim Reinert of 4 Staffel of JG 77; Gleed had had fourteen victories.

The setback meant small operations were abandoned and missions continued with three P-40 squadrons covered by the Spitfire squadron. On 16 April, in a small counterattack, eight SchlG 10 Fw 190s, escorted by sixteen Bf 109s of JG 27, led an attack on Allied airfields near Souk el Khemis. They destroyed six Douglas A-20 Havoc bombers. The next day, II./ZG 26 several Bf 110s were shot down by 260 Squadron Curtiss P-40 Warhawks. The American 97th Bomb Group dispatched seven B-17s covered by forty P-38s to bomb Palermo airfields. A large air battle developed when thirty Bf 110s and Bf 109s from ZG 26 and JG 27 intercepted. The Bf 110s attacked the bombers whilst the JG 27 Bf 109s tackled the escorts. The Germans claimed five bombers and one fighter for the loss of one Bf109. Actual Allied losses are unknown.

Palm Sunday Massacre

The patrols failed to intercept any formations of transports on the afternoon 18 April. In the evening, the 9th Air Force 57th Fighter Group sent out all its squadrons, including the 314th Fighter Squadron of the 324th Fighter Group, under its command. The 57th had already flown unproductive sorties in the afternoon. Still, forty-seven USAAF P-40s arrived in the sweep area with twelve Spitfires from 92 Squadron RAF. The Spitfires flew high cover at 15,000 feet (4,572 m) whilst the P-40s stayed at around 4,000 feet (1,219 m). Soon enough, a large formation of thirty Ju 52s was reported by Allied pilots at an altitude of only 1,000 feet (305 m), flying northeast on a return flight. There were sixty-five Ju52s, sixteen Axis fighters and five Bf 110s. As the Allied fighters began their attacks, the passengers fired machine guns out of the Junkers' windows in desperation to fend off the attack. In the air battle that followed, six Curtiss P-40 Warhawks and a Spitfire were shot down. The Americans claimed 146 victories, which was later reduced to fifty-eight or fifty nine Ju 52s, fourteen Macchi C.202s and Bf 109s and two to four Bf 110s. Actual German losses were twenty-four Ju 52s, nine Bf 109s and one Bf110. Some Italian fighters may also have been shot down. Along with the twenty-four Ju 52s destroyed, another thirty-five were damaged and managed to crash-land all along the Sicilian coastline. The battle became known as the 'Palm Sunday Massacre'.

Continuation of Offensive

The following day, 7 Wing SAAF shot down another sixteen Italian SM.82s. The ease with which they caught fire led the Allied pilots to believe they were carrying fuel. Among these units involved were 54 Squadron and 2 Squadron SAAF.

Another source gives Axis losses as ten destroyed and four crash-landed. On 22 April, the 7 Wing sent out thirty-six P-40s which intercepted a well-escorted Italian formation. The South Africans claimed twelve Ju 52s, two SM 79s, a Ju 87 towing a glider, a Reggiane Re 2001, two Bf 109s and a Ju 88 for the loss of five Spitfires and three P-40s. Known Axis loses were twelve SM 79s and a Macchi C.202; RAF Spitfires flying from Malta shot down another two transports. Later, a flight made in the daylight cost the Axis sixteen to seventeen Me 323 Transports all destroyed, plus a Macchi C.202, three German fighters and a RE-2001, when they were intercepted by thirty-six Australian, British, and South African P-40s covered by South African, British and Polish Spitfire units.

Four P-40s were lost and one Spitfire had to force land. The main combatants in the battles were 1 Squadron SAAF, 112 Squadron RAF, 450 Squadron RAAF, I./JG 27 and II./JG 27. Hermann Göring ordered that no more transport flights be made. Albert Kesselring complained that this would deny the Axis forces supplies, and Göring once again permitted flights. This time they were to travel via Sardinia, but no more than sixty to seventy flights would be allowed per night; some 250 had been mounted daily before Flax. The transports also had to run the gauntlet of radar-equipped Bristol Beaufighters, but these were rarely successful at intercepting them. One Allied effort was made by seventy B-24 Liberators, which bombed airfields around Bari in Italy, some fifty-four German aircraft were destroyed and thirteen damaged on the ground. The USAAF units claimed fifty.

Aftermath

The aerial operation had a considerable effect in strangling Axis supply. The stores reaching Axis units dwindled and the Axis armies and air units remaining in Tunisia gradually ran out of fuel, ammunition, and other supplies. Having lost most of its airbases, the Luftwaffe evacuated most of its units. By early May 1943, only the Italian fighter units and one German Gruppe (I./JG 77) remained, as the Axis held on to a narrow strip of African coastline near Tunis. Allied air superiority was so overwhelming, that Luftwaffe personnel climbed into fighter fuselages, or squeezed into cockpits of Bf 109s alongside the pilot rather than risk flying in transport aircraft. Most ground crew and pilots attempted to escape this way. Flying large numbers of personnel in one go and by transport was too dangerous; sixteen personnel were killed in a crash on 29 or 30 April. The last transport missions were flown on 4 May, in which 117 tons of fuel and ammunition were brought in. Some supply drops were attempted (by II./Kampfgeschwader 1), but most of the remaining signals, *Flak,* transport and administration staff left were captured when the campaign ended on 13 May 1943.

Chapter 9

Battle of Longstop Hill

April 1943

Battle of Longstop Hill	
Date: 22–23 April 1943 **Location:** Djebel el Ahmera, Djebel el Rhar, Tunisia **Result:** British Victory	
Belligerents	
United Kingdom	**Germany**
Commanders and Leaders	
United Kingdom: Vyvyan Evelegh	**Germany**: Ernst-Günther Baade
Strength	
78th Division	999th Light Arika Division
Casualties and Losses	
Roughly 400 killed and/or wounded	Roughly 500 killed and/or wounded
	Roughly 600 captured (nonwounded)
	Equipment none recorded

2nd Battle of Longstop Hill or the Capture of Longstop Hill

This battle took place in Tunisia during the Tunisian campaign of the Second World War from 21 to 23 April, 1943. The battle was fought for control over the heights of Djebel el Ahmera and Djebel el Rhar, together known as Longstop Hill and vicinity, between the British forces of the First Army and German units of the Fifth Panzer Army. The infantry of the 78th Battle-axe Division and Churchill tanks of the North Irish Horse captured Longstop Hill after bitter fighting, in which the tanks created a measure of tactical surprise by driving up the hill, a manoeuvre that only Churchill tanks could achieve. The attackers broke through the German defences, which were the last great natural barrier on the road to Tunis.

Background

The Run for Tunis, an Allied effort to capture Tunis in late 1942 following Operation Torch (refer to Chapter 1) had failed, and since the end of the year, a stalemate had settled on the theatre as both sides paused to rebuild their strength.

The Fifth Panzer Army (Hans-Jürgen von Arnim) defending Tunisia was being strengthened as was the Allied First Army (Kenneth Anderson).

In January 1943, the German–Italian Panzer Army (Erwin Rommel) on confronting the Eighth Army (Bernard Montgomery) had withdrawn westwards and joined the Fifth Panzer Army. Army Group Afrika was formed, with two Axis armies under command of Rommel. In March, the Army Group Afrika was defeated by the Eighth Army at the Battle of Médenine and the Battle of the Mareth Line, which fell after Rommel's return to Germany. In the central west, north of Medjez el Bab and some 30 miles (48 km) from Tunis, the First Army continued to fight for the dominating, German-held peaks in the Medjerda Valley. This included a massif with the hills known as Djebel el Ahmera and Djebel el Rhar.

First Battle

On the night of 22/23 December 1942, the 2nd Battalion, Coldstream Guards, mounted an attack in heavy rain, capturing what they thought to be the whole massif, before being relieved by the US 18th RCT. The Germans counterattacked, driving the Americans off Djebel el Ahmera, but the next night the Guards recaptured the hill only to find, when daylight came, that another summit, Djebel el Rhar, remained to be assaulted. During the night, the Guards attacked once again and captured the second hill, but they were later driven off by a German counterattack on Christmas Day. Progress towards Tunis was blocked, so the senior Allied commanders, General Dwight D. Eisenhower, the supreme Allied commander in North Africa, and General Sir Harold Alexander agreed that further advances were to be delayed. Thereafter the massif was known by the Allies as 'Longstop Hill' and by the Germans as *'Der Welhnachtsberg'*. The name Longstop is taken from the lay-back position behind the wicket keeper near the boundary of the cricket field. By mid-April 1943, because of increasing German pressure the British had withdrawn and had lost possession of 'Longstop' and all of the higher ground to the north-west, culminating in the Djebel et Tanngoucha.

Plan

On 20 April, the British troops of the 1st Battalion East Surrey Regiment supported by the 48th Royal Tank Regiment took nearby hill known as Djebel Djaffa from the Germans, managing in the process to capture several panzers. On 22 April, the 38th (Irish) Infantry Brigade of the 78th Division captured the fortified town of Heidous and the craggy slopes of Tanngoucha. The capture of these positions made sure that the high ground behind Medjez was taken and the next objective would be Longstop.

The 78th Division commander, Vyvyan Evelegh, ordered the 36th Infantry Brigade (Brigadier Bernard Howlett) to seize Longstop Hill by an attack from the south-west. The brigade comprised the 6 Battalion Queen's Own Royal West Kent Regiment, the 5th Buffs (Royal East Kent Regiment), the 8th Argyll and Sutherland Highlanders, and the 1 East Surrey Regiment, all detailed for the attack on Longstop, supported by the North Irish Horse equipped with Churchill tanks and by most of the 78th Division artillery.

The Royal West Kents and the Buffs were to lead the attack whilst the Argylls, who were to be held back in reserve at the start, were to pass through the Kents and seize Djebel el Rhar, the right-hand higher end of Longstop. If successful, the Surreys with the North Irish Horse were to be prepared to exhibit north-eastwards along the road to Terbourba. Defending the position was the 999th Light Afrika Division (Generalmajor Ernst-Günther Baade) which was composed of the 962 Afrika-Schützen-Regiment and the III/745 Grenadier Regiment. They had adequately prepared the area for defence and were supported by anti-tank guns, mortars and dug in machine gun nests.

Battle

On 22 April, the Surreys, Buffs, West Kents and Argylls dug in, using shallow gullies and depressions wherever they could find them in the open ground, in

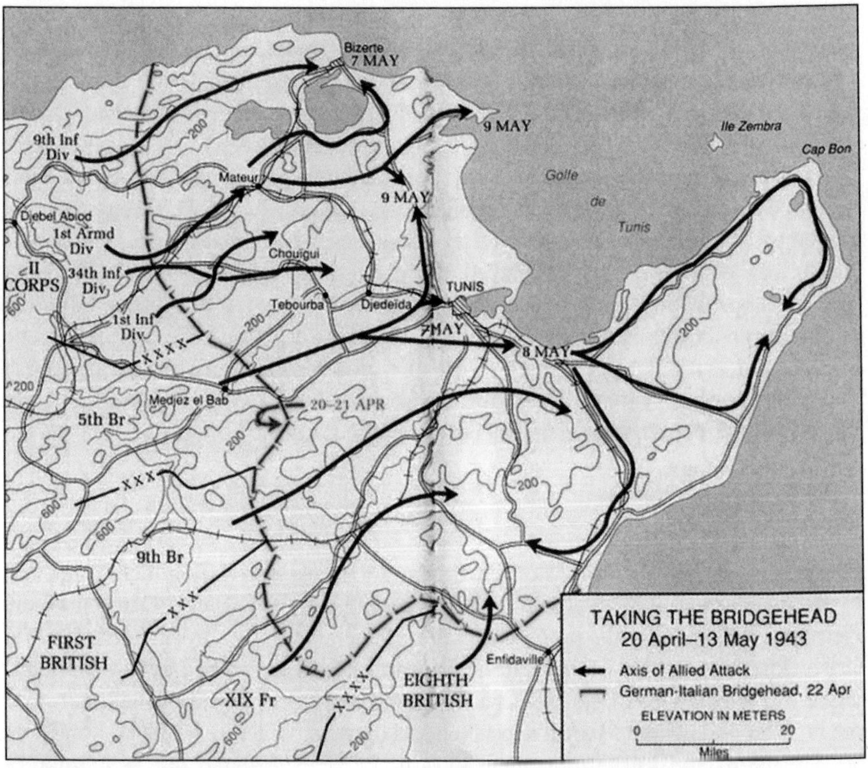

Tunisia Campaign Operations 20 April to 13 May 1943.
(This file is a work of a US Army soldier or employee, taken or made as part of that person's official duties. As a work of the US Federal Government, it is in the Public Domain in the United States. Source: http://www.army.mil/cmh-pg/brochures/tunisia/p22-23(map).jpg. Email dated 20/09/2023: 'Map(s) courtesy of the United States Military Academy Department of History.')

preparation for the attack. At 20:00 hours the artillery fire of 400 guns, which would last all night, signalled that the battle for Longstop Hill had begun. At 11:30 hours the next morning the Surreys and the Argylls advanced but German machine guns and mortars began to inflict casualties on the start line. The German 962 Regiment repulsed the attacks of the West Kents and the Buffs trying to capture Djebel el Rhar. This delay had made it impossible for the Argylls to capture the main hills during the hours of darkness. Soon after dawn, Howlett, seeing that his original plan had been too ambitious, went forwards and made another plan for the Argylls and the Surreys, supported by the North Irish Horse, to seize the Djebel el Ahmera (the western half of Longstop).

Djebel el Ahmera

The Argylls were supported along the southern slopes of Longstop by two squadrons of North Irish Horse. Behind heavy concentrations of artillery, the Highlanders went up the Djebel el Ahmera ridge through heavy machine gun fire, advancing in box formation through a cornfield. As they reached the base of the hill the commanding officer, Colin McNabb, was killed by shellfire and the attack soon lost cohesion but Major John 'Jock' Anderson soon took command and urged the Argylls to press on. Despite heavy casualties, the Argylls climbed up the hill and were soon among the defenders and started to eliminate the ring of machine gun nests. For inspiring his men and eliminating strong points during the fighting around Djebel el Ahmera, Anderson was later awarded the **Victoria Cross**. The citation for Anderson's award stated: **'Major Anderson re-organized the battalion, led the assault on the second objective, and, despite a leg wound, captured Longstop Hill with a total force of only four officers and less than forty other ranks. He personally led attacks on at least three enemy machine gun positions and in every case was the first man in the enemy gun-pits.'**

By nightfall, the Argylls, reinforced by the Surreys, had managed to complete the capture of Djebel el Ahmera along with 200 prisoners and held the hill. The West Kents had moved closer up in reserve but an attempt during the night to capture the next higher peak of Djebel el Rhar failed, owing to heavy mortar fire on their forming-up place.

Sidi Ahmed

On 24 April, an attempt was made by the Surreys, the 5th (Huntingdonshire) Battalion, Northamptonshire Regiment, and a squadron of tanks, to clear Sidi Ahmed ridge just north of Longstop Hill, which contained a white mosque occupied and used as a defensive position by the Germans. In this attack the tanks helped infantry on to the ridge, which was captured in spite of intense mortar and machine gun fire. The positions were reinforced by anti-tank guns and mortars in anticipation of a counterattack which never came.

Djebel el Rhar

During 25 April, a further advance was made by the British, but troops on Djebel el Ahmera strengthened their positions and the tanks remained upon the southern slopes. The capture of Djebel el Rhar was to take place the next day. A diversionary attack started on 26 April, at 08:30 hours but the Germans brought down heavy mortar fire on the southern flanks of the hill. The attack mopped up a number of snipers who lay hidden on the southern slopes in ravines and also resulted in the capture of a number of prisoners. On the left at the same time, the Buffs left their start line and worked forwards with a squadron of tanks, on the lower northern slopes of the hill and another squadron supporting them on their main line of advance.

The Churchill tanks descended the gully between Djebel el Ahmera and Djebel el Rhar and with the Buffs appeared on the north-west slopes; the tanks had remarkably traversed the steep southern slopes. With tanks and infantry working together, they were heavily engaged with mortars and small arms fire. The tanks then reached the defensive rim, eliminating the surprised German strong points one-by-one with Besa machine guns and 6-pounder fire. A tank led by Sergeant O'Hare was the first to reach the summit, breaching the headquarters and capturing fifty prisoners; three more tanks followed having finished their extraordinary drive, getting up inclines that were so steep that in places they had gradients of 1:3. The rest of the regiment arrived and headed up the slopes and with the Buffs eliminated more strong points and cut off escape routes, completing the capture of Longstop, and by 11:00 hours on 26 April, the battle was over.

Aftermath

The Buffs had lost nine killed and eighty-three wounded, but between them and the North Irish Horse, they had captured over 300 prisoners making the total 650, including all of the III./754 Grenadier Regiment's senior officers. One of the German officers noted that when he saw the tanks coming over the summit, 'I knew all was over'. Other prisoners simply could not believe that tanks had played a role in the capture of the position until they were shown; another called the Churchill tanks 'metal mules'. With the summit in the hands of 78th Division, the British began to consolidate Longstop Hill against counterattack and the fire from nearby hills. By 27 April, the whole of Longstop Hill and Djebel el Rhar had been secured, enabling Wilberforce and the Surreys to be relieved. Longstop was the last great natural barrier barring movement towards Tunis.

On 7 May, British armour rolled into Tunis, taking the Axis forces there by surprise, some were caught emerging from shops and bars. By 15 May, all Axis forces had been cut off and soon surrendered with more than 250,000 taken prisoner. Joseph Goebbels admitted it was on the same scale as the Third Reich's disaster at the Battle of Stalingrad and the name 'Tunisgrad' was coined for the defeat.

Grenadier Guards, 1st Guards Brigade - Grich El Oued: 23 April 1943

The following extract is taken from the Panzer Grenadier Headquarters (https://pg-hq.com)

> 'In the early morning of April 23, 1943, British Forces of the Grenadier Guards, 1st Guards Brigade advanced along a road leading to the town of Grich el Oued. Two Churchill VII platoons were east of the road, while 3-inch mortar units were advanced on Bren carriers along with 4 infantry units emerging from the woods. One additional British infantry unit was situated on the rocky ground west of the 20-metre hill. The Axis comprised of a combination of former Vichy French, now referred to as "Phalange Afrique" platoons and elements of the 334th German Infantry Division. The Phalange Afrique infantry were dug in both on the southwest of 20-metre hill and east of the road 800 metres south of the town. All remaining Axis units were in Grich el Oued under the direction of Lt. Gruyere. British units moved slowly north at 03:00 hours, and the Axis infantry near the road retreated toward the town. By 04:00 hours, all Axis units present were in the town except for the infantry on the west, central of the 20-metre hill. By 04:15 hours, the British had the town surrounded on three sides and were assaulting the 60mm and NW41 units *[*15cm Nebelwerfer 41 – German multiple rocket launcher]* in the northeast sector of the town. The German captain and Lt. Gruyere were booth killed in action (KIA) by 04:45 hours, and the entire town was under British assault. The British had control of the northwest sector of the town by 05:30 but could not dislodge the Axis units from the south and northwest sectors until 07:00 hours resulting in the Axis forces claiming a minor victory.'

Scenario

This is a short scenario with a lot of tactics in it due to the limited sight range for much of the scenario. The basic objective for the British was the control of the town Grich el Oued, and the sooner the better. In this instance, the Axis forces showed remarkable resistance in avoiding elimination in the town itself despite some serious assault odds to the contrary. It took five attempts to dislodge a single NW41 unit*, and nine attempts to clear HMG (Heavy Machine Gun) from the northwest part of the town. One British unit had moved to the north of the town to tie up a returning Axis infantry unit so that the HMG could not be reinforced. The British finally cleared the town on 'Turn 17' when a DM HMG (Designated Marksman/sniper operating a 15cm Nebelwerfer 41) unit finally had to flee, holding the Axis to a minor victory. The key for the Axis was to slow down the British advance by spotting for the NW41 and 60mm units, whilst regrouping to put the greatest strength in the town itself. Then it was a question of endurance. In this scenario, the British only lost two steps to the Axis loss of eight, and they had multiple action segments to open eleven of the seventeen actions taken.

The following extract is taken from the war magazine 'The Army At War: Tunisia–published in 1944'. The magazine was prepared for the War Office by The Ministry of Information under Crown Copyright Reserved.

Extract taken from pages 43 to 45: - 22 to 24 April 1943

> 'Some infiltration took place, but after confused fighting our positions were all firmly held by the British 1st Division. By dawn the enemy had started to withdraw, having lost 33 tanks destroyed (including some Mark VI's) and leaving 500 prisoners in our hands. Not only was the enemy repulsed, but he failed completely in his object of spoiling our dispositions for attack. For on the very next day, 22 April, the First Army launched a strong offensive eastwards from the line of the Bou Arada-Goubellat Road. On the right, north-east of Bou Arada, the 46th Division advanced to the high ground south of Sebkra el Kourzia, from which, however, they had to make a slight withdrawal under pressure from an enemy counterattack. Farther north our troops, although held up at first, made good progress and reached and reached Argoub Sellar.
>
> On 23 April our troops in the Bou Arada area resumed their advance and occupied the features of Mehalla and Argouf. On the left, tanks of the 6th Armoured Division advanced and continued to press eastwards, engaging enemy armour, and reaching a line north-east of Sebkra el Kourzia. The number of enemy tanks destroyed during the day was 16.
>
> Father to the left, an attack was launched east of Medjez el Bab by troops of the British 1st Division who captured their first objectives and retained them with the exception of one point, after strong enemy counterattacks.
>
> North of Medjez el Bab British troops of the 78th Division succeeded in capturing Jebel Ahmera ('Longstop Hill'), except for the north-eastern slopes. In all sectors, the enemy put up a fierce resistance and advance of our troops was difficult and costly.
>
> Meanwhile, in the Sidi Nsir and Sedjenane sectors, the US II Corps, coming into action for the first time on this part of the front, scored an immediate success, gaining all their first objectives and capturing many prisoners. To the north of them. On the coast, French Goums [lethal Moroccan fighters], who had throughout given proof of their excellent fighting qualities, advanced some ten miles (16 km) east from Cap Serrat.'

Chapter 10

Battle of Hill 609

27 April–1 May 1943

Tunisian Campaign	
Date: 27 April–1 May 1943 **Location:** Djebel Tahent, Tunisia **Result:** American Victory	
Belligerents	
United States	**Germany**
Commanders and Leaders	
United States: Omar N. Bradley	**Germany**: Hans-Jürgen von Arnim
United States: Charles W. Ryder	
United States: Terry Allen	
United States: Manton S. Eddy	
Strength	
II Corps	Afrika Korps
Casualties and Losses	
2,453 killed or wounded	Unknown

Battle of Hill 609

The battle took place at Djebel Tahent in north-western Tunisia during the Tunisian campaign of the Second World War. The battle was for control over the key strategic height of Hill 609 and its surrounding area between the American forces of the US II Corps and German units of the Afrika Korps. The battle proved a formative experience for the American forces–in their first clear-cut victory of the campaign and has been called **'the American Army's coming of age'.**

Battle

In late April 1943, Hill 609 was the key to the German defensive line facing the US II Corps, commanded by Major General Omar Bradley. The German general, Hans-Jürgen von Arnim, used the hill for artillery fire and observation. From the

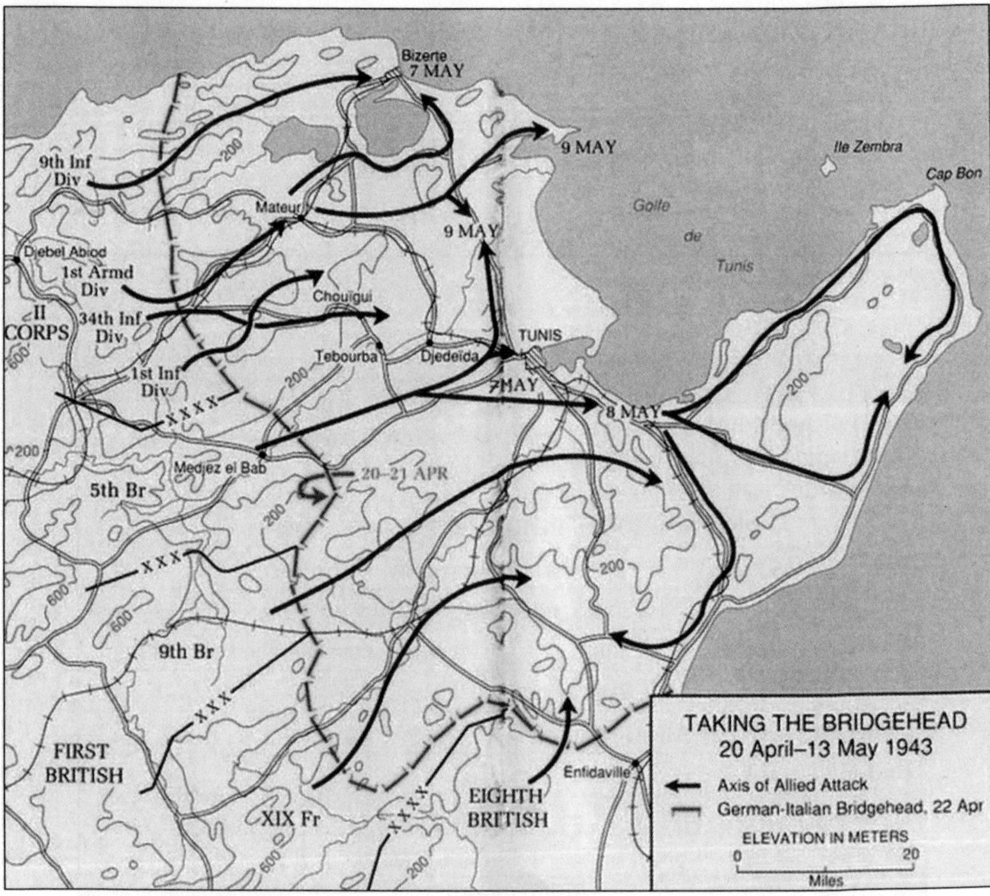

Tunisia Campaign Operations 20 April to 13 May 1943.
(*This file is a work of a US Army soldier or employee, taken or made as part of that person's official duties. As a work of the US Federal Government, it is in the Public Domain in the United States. Source: http://www.army.mil/cmh-pg/brochures/tunisia/p22-23(map).jpg.* Email dated 20/09/2023: 'Map(s) courtesy of the United States Military Academy Department of History.')

hill, the Germans could also prevent movement by both the 1st Infantry Division, commanded by Major General Terry Allen, to the south and the 9th Infantry Division, commanded by Major General Manton S. Eddy, to the north. Hill 609 was deemed one of the most difficult objectives in Tunisia, not only protected by steep slopes and artillery but also by fire from nearby high grounds, which gave the Germans a crossfire on the slopes leading up to it. After rejecting the proposition of bypassing the mountain, Bradley ordered the 34th Infantry Division, commanded by Major General Charles W, Ryder, to take the hill. After heavy fighting and high casualties, the 4th Infantry Division managed to take the hill by 30 April, and the following day repelled several German counterattacks.

Chapter 11

Operation Vulcan, April 1943, and Operation Strike, May 1943

Operations Vulcan and Strike	
Date: Vulcan 22 April–6 May 1943 Strike 6–12 May 1943 **Location:** Tunis, Cape Bon and Bizerte, Tunisia **Result:** Allied Victory	
Belligerents	
United Kingdom **United States**	**Germany** **Italy**
Commanders and Leaders	
United Kingdom: Harold Alexander	**Germany**: Hans- Jürgen von Arnim
United Kingdom: Kenneth Anderson	**Germany**: Gustav von Vaerst
United Kingdom: Brian Horrocks	**Italy**: Giovanni Messe
United States: Omar N. Bradley	
Casualties and Losses	
None recorded	240,000 captured
	Equipment none recorded

Operation Vulcan (22 April–6 May 1943) and Operation Strike (6–12 May 1943)

These two operations were the final ground attacks by the Allied forces against the Italian and German forces in Tunis, Cape Bon, and Bizerte, the last Axis toeholds in North Africa, during the Tunisian campaign of the Second World War.

Background

Generalfeldmarschall Erwin Rommel believed that the Axis position in Tunisia was untenable, and he had recommended the evacuation of all German troops to

Italy, where he believed they could be more useful. His advice was rejected by Adolf Hitler. In April 1943, a major Allied air force effort (Operation Flax) (refer to Chapter 8), had cut off Axis supplies to North Africa. US II Corps, commanded by Major General Omar N. Bradley, surrounded the last defenders at Enfidavlle, ending the Axis effort in North Africa. Operation Retribution (refer to Chapter 12), and the control of the air and the sea prevented any large-scale evacuation of Axis troops to Italy. The initial offensive was codenamed Vulcan.

Operation Vulcan

The fighting was costly against German units in well-prepared and dug-in defences. In the advance on Tunis, the British 4th Infantry Division (British IX Corps, Lieutenant General Brian Horrocks) was opposed by German paratroopers (Fallschirmjager) of the elite Hermann Göring Parachute Division. At Cactus Far, the British infantry was faced by extensive defensive fire from well-concealed German paratroopers. Churchill tanks of the 12 Royal Tank Regiment (21 Tank Brigade), advanced without infantry support and the tanks were assaulted by the defenders using Molotov cocktails and sticky 'teller' anti-tank mines. Twelve tanks were destroyed, and, in some cases, their crews were rescued from the burning wrecks by Germans.

Operation Strike

On 30 April, it was realized that a revision was necessary to achieve success. The revised final phase of the assault on Tunis was codenamed Strike and launched six days later. On that day, the British First Army (Lieutenant General Kenneth Anderson), took Tunis and American troops reached Bizerte. The German commander General Hans-Jürgen von Arnim, finally surrendered on 12 May 1943.

Aftermath

On 13 May, all remaining Axis forces in Tunisia, under the command of Marshal Giovanni Messe, surrendered unconditionally. Messe had, with Mussolini's approval, tried to negotiate an 'honourable surrender' the previous day; but this had been rejected. Earlier in the morning he was promoted to the rank of field marshal, but the Allies would not accept anything but an unconditional surrender and threatened to resume their attacks, which had been halted the day before. At 12:20 hours Messe gave the orders. He and the remaining German commander, Kurt von Liebenstein, surrendered late in the day. By the close of the operation, in excess of 250,000 German and Italian troops had been captured.

Chapter 12

Operation Retribution

May 1943

Operation Retribution	
Date: 8–13 May 1943 **Location:** Sicilian Channel and Cape Bon, Tunisia **Result:** Allied Victory	
Belligerents	
United Kingdom **United States**	**Germany** **Italy**
Commanders and Leaders	
United Kingdom: Andrew Cunningham	Unknown

Operation Retribution

The operation was the Second World War air and naval blockade designed to prevent the seaborne evacuation of Axis forces from Tunisia to Sicily. Axis forces were isolated in northern Tunisia and faced a final Allied assault. The equivalent blockade of air evacuation was Operation Flax (refer to Chapter 8).

British Admiral Andrew Cunningham – Allied naval commander – began the operation on 7 May 1943, with the colourful signal to **'Sink, burn and destroy. Let nothing pass'.** He had also named the operation Retribution in recognition of the losses that his destroyer forces had endured during the German occupations of Greece and Crete. The Germans were unable to mount a significant rescue effort.

The Axis' predicament had been recognized earlier and a large-scale effort to evacuate Axis personnel was expected. So, all available naval light forces were ordered to concentrate at Malta or Bône, with specified patrol areas. In order to achieve this, convoy movements were restricted to release their escorts. The Italian Fleet was expected to intervene, so the battleships HMS *Nelson* and *Rodney* and the aircraft carrier HMS *Formidable* were moved to Algiers in readiness for a major action.

In the event, the Italian Fleet did not leave port (due to the imposing threat of the British navy in much of the Mediterranean Sea) and there was no organized attempt to evacuate Axis forces by sea.

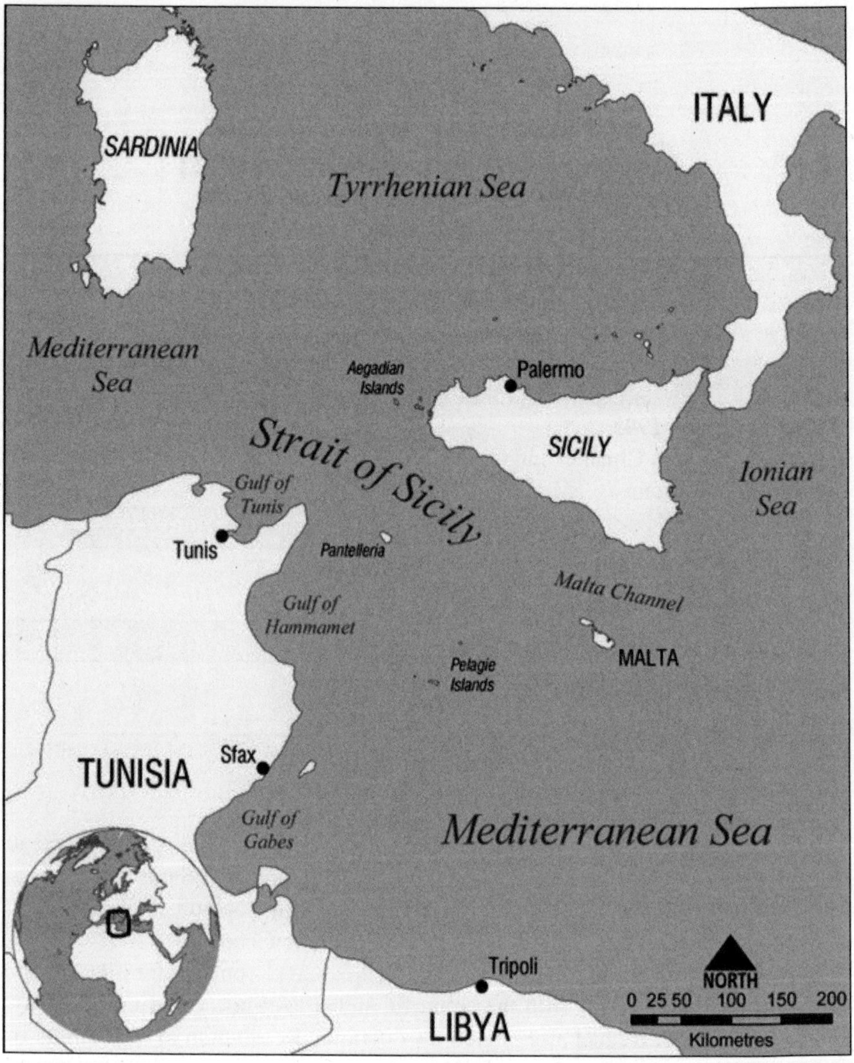

Map Showing the Location of the Strait of Sicily. [Between Sicily, Italy in Europe, and Tunisia in Africa.]
(Author: Norman Einstein–own work. Source: File; Strait of Sicily map.png Creative Commons BY-SA 3.0. Email dated 20/09/2023: 'Map(s) courtesy of the United States Military Academy Department of History.')

Two supply ships en route to Tunisia were intercepted and sunk. Inshore flotillas of British MTBs and American PT boats intercepted small craft and raided the waters around Ras Idda and Kelibia. The only significant threat to the sea forces were friendly fire attacks by Allied aircraft, after which red recognition patches were painted on the ships. The Allies captured 897 men; 653 Germans and Italians are thought to have escaped to Italy and an unknown number drowned.

Axis forces in North Africa, squeezed into a small area with minimal supplies and facing well-supplied opponents, surrendered on 13 May. The North African ports were rapidly cleared and readied to support the forthcoming invasions of southern Europe. The 12th, 13th, and 14th Minesweeping Flotillas from Malta, two groups of Minesweeping trawlers and smaller vessels cleared a channel through the minefields of the Sicilian Channel to Tripoli, removing nearly 200 moored mines. On 15 May, Cunningham signalled that **'the passage through the Mediterranean was clear'** and that convoys from Gibraltar to Alexandria could be started at once. Thus, the direct route between Gibraltar and Alexandria – closed since May 1941 – was reopened with prodigious savings in shipping and their escorts.

With the surrender of the Axis forces on 13 May 1943, the battle was far from over, as groups of isolated pockets of Axis forces were still fighting and it would take the remaining days of May 1943 to fleece them out and be taken prisoners (PoWs). In all more than 250,000 Axis troops were taken prisoner, thus denying the Germans of valuable troops that would be needed in future battles in Sicily and Italy.

Axis Force Final Surrender: 13 May 1943

The Captured Axis Force

The Tunisian campaign in North Africa was set around the countries of Morocco, Algiers, Libya and Tunisia. This campaign by the Allied forces ended after six months of combat with the unconditional surrender of Axis powers at 8.15 pm on 13 May 1943. Allied forces captured German Commander-in-Chief Jürgen von Arnim, eleven other generals, and at the first count, over 150,000 enemy troops, a mix of German and Italian.

The Axis Force had started to surrender on 5 May 1943, and from that day the number of prisoners captured had been climbing and was expected to climb even further during the coming days. Out of the initial 150,000 captives, it was estimated that about 110,000 were Germans and the remainder Italians. On top of this the American forces had reportedly taken 25,000 prisoners, including six of the twelve generals captured, in their northern sector of the Tunisia front.

The French to have also reported the capture of two generals named Yelich and Pfeiffer and between the two, the French had captured over 25,000 Axis troops, including the Italian Superba Division. Although the Italian First Army still fought on, their General Giovanni Messe was due for capture soon.

Commander-in-Chief General Dwight D. Eisenhower motivated the troops, declaring, 'As long as a single German is on African soil, there is still a battle to be fought and won, I want to destroy the rest of the Axis resistance.'

The defeat, which took place in Northern Tunisia, was swift and relentless. Remaining Axis forces split up in desperate attempts to flee. Von Arnim and his men took to the Cap Bon Peninsula, hoping to escape to Sicily, but were cut off by a deadly British air-sea blockade, where they surrendered almost without opposition. American forces several miles below the peninsula set up blockades where groups attempting to leave the peninsula were blocked.

The prisoners were rounded up into an enormous 'Bull Pen' in a Tunisian wheat field to be counted and fed before they were moved. Isolated groups of resistance are still active in a 9-mile (14 km) circle in the Zaghouan Mountains, but the campaign was considered to be nearly over, and it was believed that the remaining resistance would soon be overrun. The French infantry had already deeply penetrated Djebel Zaghouan, the highest mountain in Tunisia, and advanced four miles (6 km) towards the circle.

The quality of military equipment captured from the Axis forces was huge: hundreds of vehicles, such as armoured cars, trucks, and tanks, along with hundreds of thousands of guns.

A captured Nazi order dated 18 April 1943 revealed that dissatisfaction had been spreading among German troops in Tunisia, so much so that Nazi headquarters issued a threat of reprisal. Any relative of soldiers who surrendered 'without due cause', and the men themselves after the war, were to be punished. From the document, it can be asserted that non-commissioned officers leading platoons had encouraged their men to surrender, although their situations were not hopeless.

Despite this threat, numbers of Axis surrenders continued to rise on a daily basis. Allied forces, in demanding unconditional surrender and the immediate delivery of all materials, had their desires met. Outside of the 9-mile (14 km) circle in the Zaghouan Mountains, it was unclear as to how many Nazi forces were left, but British forces had been performing wide sweeps on both sides of the range, rounding up over 20,000 prisoners.

The Tunisia campaign took up after Operation Torch ended on 11 November 1942. Operation Torch, the invasion of Vichy French-held North Africa, was a success that ended with the cessation of armed resistance in Morocco and Algeria. Following this, the main Tunisia campaign started, with the advance into Tunisia, which would allow Allied forces to cross into Europe and invade Sicily.

Since the North Africa campaign began two years before, eleven German divisions and twenty-six Italian divisions had been destroyed. Over 400,000 total Axis prisoners had been captured. There were no official figures of Allied losses during the campaign; suffice to say that the losses were relatively light.

Axis Casualties and Captured Troops as of May 1943

The Axis armies suffered casualties of 170,000 to 180,000 men; the losses are uncertain, but it is estimated that the German army suffered 8,500 men killed during the campaign and that the Italians lost 3,700 men killed; another 40,000 to 50,000 Axis soldiers were wounded. In the British official history, Playfair wrote that the Allies took 238,243 unwounded prisoners: 101,784 German, 89,442 Italian and 47,017 others. In 2004, Rick Atkinson wrote that a quarter of a million prisoners is a reasonable estimate. Playfair wrote that G. F. Howe, the American official historian, recorded the capture of 275,000 Axis soldiers; an 18th Army Group calculation of 244,500 prisoners (including 15,000 Germans). Rommel estimated 130,000 Germans were taken prisoner, whilst Arnim estimated 100,00 German and 200,000 Italian prisoners of war.

Conclusion

In considering the above physical numbers of Axis troops captured and taken prisoner after the Tunisian campaign, and with the Allies planning to invade Normandy on the 6 June 1944, had these Axis forces managed to escape and get evacuated to Sicily, Italy and then onto mainland Europe, that D-Day (as it was termed) would most definitely have been a harder nut to crack. It was hard enough as it was, but most definitely a protracted and longer invasion would have taken place with more lives lost.

Sources

Kluckhohn, Frank. "AFRICAN WAR OVER: 100,000 of Captive Total Believed German." *New York Times.* May 13, 1943. Pg 1.

"Story of German Surrender; Berliners Stunned by News: The War Today Can't Believe It." *The Washington Post.* May 11, 1943. Pg 1.

Kennedy, Edward. "11 Other Generals Captured; Vast Quantities of Material Seized in Final Allied Drive; Axis Prisoners Total 400,000: All French Africa Now in Allied Hands." *The Washington Post.* May 13, 1943. Pg1.

"ENEMY CASUALTIES IN TUNISIA 324,000: 267,000 Captured, 30,0000 Killed and 27,000 Wounded Since Start of Campaign." *The New York Times.* May 20, 1943. Pg 5.

Boyle, Harold "Prisoners Stream In: Story of Germans' Africa Surrender." *The Washington Post.* May 11, 1943. Pg 1.

"NAZIS TO PUNISH KIN OF TROOPS WHO QUIT: Order Captured in Tunisia Also Threatens Reprisals on Soldiers Themselves." *The New York Times.* May 5, 1943. Pg 3.

King, William. "British Armor Forces Race Up Both Sides of Peninsula: 200,000 More Nazi Troops Surrender." *The Washington Post.* May 12, 1943. Pg 1.

Chapter 13

The Eighth Army

1941 to 1943

Any book written about the North African campaign of the Second World War from 1940 to 1943 would not be complete without a chapter on the formation of and the actions and battles undertaken and so vigorously fought by the Eighth Army from the time of its inception on the 10 September 1941 through the North African campaign up to and including the Tunisian campaign of November 1942 to May 1943, of which the Eighth Army became instrumental in the capture of in excess of 250,000 Axis forces, which included 150,000 German troops, and thus preventing them getting to Sicily and possibly on to Europe.

The following paragraphs – 'The First Offensive: Thrust and Parry, Foreword' and 'The Eighth Army Is Born' are extracts taken from the booklet 'The Eighth Army - September 1941 to January 1943, which was first printed in 1944 reference S.O. CODE 70-437* priced at the cost of 1 shilling, and at the time could be purchased from *'His Majesty's Stationary Office.'*

The First Offensive: Thrust and Parry

Foreword

'The first occasion on which the name "The Eighth Army" appeared in print was when General Sir Alan Cunningham was appointed as its' commander on 18th November 1941, though it was officially known as the English from 26th-27th September. After the landing of the Americans and the First Army in French North Africa on 8th November, 1942, there was always a sense of strategic co-ordination of the operations of the two Armies, since the plain strategic purpose was to pinch the Axis out of the continent between them; but there was no direct tactical co-ordination until the amalgamation of the First, Eighth, American and French Armies into the Eighteenth Army Group on 20th February, 1943, when all had reached Tunisia.'

The Eighth Army Is Born

'The British Eighth Army represents the most modern and most powerful force to be found (at that time) on the different chessboards of the world war. The infantry is perfectly trained, shows great fighting spirit and has armament and equipment better than those of any other infantry in the world. The British artillery is well provided with excellent guns and is splendidly organised, and the British armoured units are among the best in the world. Its leaders and staffs are carefully chosen and have proved their worth on the battlefield. Finally, the Eighth Army has some 10,000 motor vehicles and has both a naval and an air fleet at its disposal. The co-operation between the R.A.F. and the land forces can serve as an example for everyone.'

This extract from an official Italian report on the Mareth and Akarit gives an opinion of the Eighth Army which modesty would prevent a British writer from inscribing. Though the estimate of the Army's motor vehicles was, in fact, a gross understatement, the general verdict should be taken with a pinch of salt. Given comparable opportunities and leadership, other British armies have proved to be on the same high level; and the Italian commentator may well have been influenced by the fact that nothing puts a beaten army in a better light than praise of its victorious opponents. But in substance it was true when written in April 1943 and has remained true since; and there is some gratification in noting that the Eighth Army, in the opinion of its adversaries, was a better military instrument than the African Korps.

It was not always so. The Eighth Army was born at a critical moment in Britain's fortunes. It was the child of the Army of the Nile, which, under General Wavell, had utterly destroyed the Italian Army in Libya, only to be brought to the brink of destruction itself by a German counter-offensive launched when it had been greatly weakened to keep the promise given to Greece.

The credit for holding the enemy on the Egyptian frontier and for holding on to the outpost of Tobruk belongs not only to the men on the spot, but to those at home who had the courage and vision steadily to reinforce the Middle East whilst Britain was still threatened with imminent invasion.

But nothing which could be sent over lines of communications 12,000 miles (19,312 km) long could make the Eighth Army into a formidable striking force for many months; and there were distractions which prevented entire concentration in Libya.

- In the first place, Syria had to be rescued against Axis infiltration, and Iraq rescued from a pro-Axis rebellion.
- Secondly, after the German assault on Russia in June 1941, the road from the Persian Gulf to the Caucasus had to be secured and improved.
- Thirdly, the ever-growing menace of Japan dictated some measure of precautionary reinforcement of the Far East.

All these things had to be done at a time when, with notable exception of the people of the British Empire themselves, most of the world was expecting an early Axis victory; and human nature being what it was at the time was not enthusiastic as its inclinations might otherwise have prompted it to be.

- There was one other factor which would have had to have been taken into serious account when assessing the tasks and achievements of the Eighth Army, namely the very special character of the country in which it had to fight in. What may be called the cinema impression of a desert is nothing like the Western Desert. 1) There is much less sand than one expects. 2) The sandstorms so often mentioned are more frequently choking clouds of dust rather than sand. 3) Vast stretches are hard, firm going (except after rain), and resemble flat rock more than anything else. 4) There are practically no features in the landscape, other than occasional shallow depressions which allow tanks to get into hull-down positions.

- Where the Western Desert is true to convention is in its lack of water and a pipeline had to be built all the way from Alexandria and nearly to Tobruk, and this supply eked out with the brackish water retrieved from the local wells and aquifers.
- Among the more disagreeable features are the flies. They were a filthy, pertinacious, excruciating pestilence.
- As for the climate, it was, once acclimatized, not so trying after a time, with most people finding it quite healthy, except when the hot winds, or *Khamsin* would blow. (These winds would prove to be completely horrible; physically, seemed devoid of oxygen, and morale-wise, they made the most placid temperament morose.)

In Conclusion

The peculiarities of the desert can be best summed up by **General von Ravenstein**, the captured commander of the 21st German Armoured Division. **'The desert', he said, 'is the tactician's paradise, but the quarter-master's hell!'**

Eighth Army Background and Formation

The Eighth Army was a field army of the British Army during the Second World War and was formed as the **Western Army** on 10 September 1941, in Egypt, before being renamed the **Army of the Nile** and then the Eighth Army on 26 September 1941. The Western Army Headquarters was needed and established in Cairo to direct these formations. **Winston Churchill, the British prime minister**, sometimes referred to the army as the Western Desert Force. One of the prime reasons for its creation was for better control of the growing Allied forces based in Egypt and to direct their efforts to lift the siege of Tobruk via Operation Crusader.

Churchill had suggested General Henry Maitland Wilson for command of the army, but the final decision was left in the hands of General Sir Claude Auchinleck, who oversaw all British-led forces in the region. Auchinleck selected Lieutenant General Alan Cunningham, who had led the British effort from Kenya during the East African campaign. Then, on 29 August 1941, due to the success he had achieved, he was ordered to Egypt to take command of the forming Eighth Army, which he did on 24 September 1941.

The Eighth Army was responsible for operations in the Western Desert and was supported by the existing command, British Troops in Egypt, that controlled the lines of communication, the Egyptian anti-aircraft defences, and internal security behind the front.

It later directed Allied forces through the remaining engagements of the Western Desert campaign, oversaw part of the Allied effort during the Tunisian campaign and finally led troops throughout the Italian campaign. During 1943, it made up part of the 18th Army Group before being assigned to the 15th Army Group (later, the Allied Armies in Italy).

It is worth noting that throughout its campaigns, it was a multi-national force, and its units came from Australia, British India, Canada, Czechoslovakia, the Free French Forces, Greece, New Zealand, Poland, Rhodesia, South Africa, Mauritius, as well as the United Kingdom. Significant formations that the army controlled included the British V, X, XIII, and XXX Corps, as well as the Canadian I Corps and the Polish II Corps.

Throughout the North African campaign, the Allied forces would, when facing up to the Axis forces in what could be described as ferocious combat, gain hard fought ground, only then to have to retreat when faced with counterattacks from Axis forces commanded by Erwin Rommel, an inspirational leader of his time.

After the surrender of Tobruk in June 1941 and the Allies' retreat, back across North Africa towards Egypt, it was imperative that the Allies regroup and establish a force that could front up and take on the formidable Axis Force. As previously detailed, the Eighth Army had been formed in September 1941; now, under command of General Claude Auchinleck, it employed delaying tactics whilst withdrawing a further 100 miles (161 km) to a more defensible position near El Alamein. The Allied command chose to dig in and prepare for what was to be a defining moment in the history of battles fought in the North African campaign and that of the Eighth Army. In choosing El Alamein, the Allies had established a strong position to defend in having the Mediterranean Sea to the North and the Qattara Depression to the South.

In July/August 1942 and after a visit to Cairo by Prime Minister Winston Churchill and General Sir Alan Brooke (CIGS), General Claude Auchinleck (CIC MEC) was removed and replaced by his successor General William Gott, only for him to be killed on his way to take up his command of the Eighth Army. The powers that be at the time appointed Lieutenant General Bernard Montgomery, who went on to lead the Eighth Army offensive.

- The First Battle of El Alamein (1–27 July 1942) stopped the advance of Rommel and his Afrika Korps from entering Egypt.
- The Second Battle of El Alamein (23 October–4 November 1942) saw the British Army go on the attack and inflict a heavy defeat on the Axis forces, from which they would not recover.

Prime Minister Winston Churchill said of the victory, 'Now this is not the end, it is not even the beginning of the end. But it is, perhaps, the end of the beginning.'

After the war he wrote: **'Before Alamein we never had a victory. After Alamein, we never had a defeat.'**

With the battle fought at El Alamein and the defeat of the Axis force, the Eighth Army pressed forwards to drive the Axis force across North Africa and trap them in Tunisia. Whilst pressing on with their advantage it became apparent that the Axis force were but a spent force, which is further highlighted by the fact that on reaching Tobruk in November 1942, the Eighth Army walked in unopposed.

As the Eighth Army pushed on across North Africa and, on reaching Benghazi, General Montgomery is said to have said, **'This time . . . Having reached Benghazi and beyond, we shall not come back.'**

The best tribute to the Eighth Army's exploits, material and moral, is the fact that when **Marshal Messe**, the Italian C.-in-C., had to surrender in Tunisia, he insisted on surrendering to the Eighth Army and nobody else.

'You are entitled to dwell upon these things', said Mr Churchill in an address to the troops in Tripoli on 3 February 1943:

- 'With the satisfaction which men, in all modesty, feel when a great work has been finally done.'
- 'You have rendered a high service to your country and the common cause.'
- 'In the words of the old hymn. You have "nightly pitched your moving tents a day's march nearer home."'
- 'The achievements of the Eighth Army will gleam and glow in the annals of history.'
- 'The days of your victories are by no means at an end.'

So be it, and so it has been.

It is not intended in this book to write about **Operation Husky–Sicily campaign** nor **Operation Avalanche–Italy** (the landings at Salerno), as these operations are a follow on from the Tunisian campaign, all of which have been well covered/documented/ written about by many eminent authors and historians, including myself in my book *The Second World War North Africa & Italy 1940 to 1945 'One Man's Story'*.

However, Chapter 16 of this book makes a brief reference to both operations as a way of linking the operations carried out during the war in the Mediterranean.

In completion of this chapter, it would be remiss of the author not to make mention of the king of the United Kingdom and the Dominions of the British Commonwealth. George VI became king on the 11 December 1936, after the abdication of his brother King Edward VIII in December 1936 – a conscientious and dedicated man who worked hard to adapt to the role into which he was suddenly thrown. After the culmination of the Tunisian campaign from November 1942 to May 1943, the king wrote: 'Under your leadership, forces diverse in nationality and race have been knit into one united and successful whole. Their task has not been easy, and the resistance of the enemy has been determined and desperate. But now, with the capture of Tunis and Bizerta, your campaign is almost concluded; the last enemy forces in Africa are being captured or destroyed, and the debt of Dunkirk repaid.'

The above extract is taken from the King's message of the 9 May 1943 to General Eisenhower, supreme commander, Allied forces, North Africa. Taken from the Magazine–'The Army At War TUNISIA' Prepared for the War Office by the Ministry of Information, 1944.

Chapter 14

Allied Air Forces and RAF 73 & 79 Squadrons' AIRs

1942 and 1943

Allied Air Forces

During the Tunisian campaign, the Allied command were planning and co-ordinated a number of operations that were required on a stage-by-stage basis to ensure that the overall plan to remove the Axis forces from North Africa came to fruition. This included fighting on the ground, fighting in the air and fighting on the sea, all of which now included the United States.

In December 1941, the Japanese attacked American strongholds in Hawaii, the major one being Pearl Harbor. The day after the attack, the United States declared war on Japan and on the 8 December 1941 the British followed, also declaring war on Japan, once they realized that British colonies had been attacked. With this happening, the Allied command was further strengthened with the United States joining forces with the Allies.

During the early part of the Second World War, the United States had been supplying equipment to the British front to help with their ongoing war in Europe; fighting forces were never included until the Japanese attacked the United States in early December 1941.

With the United States now fully ensconced in the war, they brought much-needed additional forces albeit not having been tried and tested in the field of battle. This can be witnessed in the preceding chapters in which the various operations are set out.

The battles planned would include ground forces (infantry, tanks guns, etc.) along with aircraft (fighters and bombers) and naval forces.

Whilst the chapters consider the valued service of the USAAF, they do not include the British RAF.

The following AIRs cover and relate to those listed for 73 Squadron during 1943 and are only a small selection of RAF squadrons used throughout the war in North African and latterly the Tunisian campaign.

The Allied forces were further boosted when the Second Battle of El Alamein, 23 October–11 November 1942 saw the defeat and retreat of the Axis forces, which was further enhanced when the Allies walked unopposed into Tobruk on the 4 November 1942.

RAF 73 Squadron's AIRs

The following information has been collated from the Squadrons operations Record Books [AIRs], which are kept at the National Archives–Kew. Due to the level of content, it has not been possible to record every finite detailed daily input in each AIRs daily/monthly report and the following is a snapshot in the days/months of the Squadrons exploits during the Second World War, both in North Africa and Italy.

LEGEND: a/c–aircraft, e/a–enemy aircraft, LG–Landing Ground, MT–motor transport, CO–Commanding Officer, Sq/Ldr–Squadron Leader, Fl/Lt–Flight Lieutenant, F/O–Flight Officer, W/O–Warrant Officer, P/O–Pilot Officer, Fl/Sgt–Flight Sergeant, Sgt–Sergeant

Note: The following AIRs of 73 Squadron detail the operations carried out during the Tunisian campaign, from November 1942 through to May 1943.

73 Squadron's AIRs

AIR 27/631/21 & AIR 27/631/22 Pilot Ops Report November 1942	
31 October & 1 November LG 89	Several patrols were made over the line without result. For the second night our pilots were subjected to bofor gun fire from our own lines. Long-range patrols were sent out over the Heneish are tom intercept possible e/a JU 87's but no activity was seen except our own bombers attacking Heneish station. Some MTs was strafed on the road East of Daba.
1 & 2 November LG 89	No e/a activity was observed during our patrols over the line. Sgt Edwards reported that our army had broken through the enemy lines in the Northern Sector and was pushing West and South.
2 & 3 November LG 89	Line and layer patrols were maintained throughout the night. A twin-engine a/c was seen but not contacted by Fl/Sgt Phillips. During long-range intruders to Heneish flares and bombs were being dropped on Daba without opposition.
3 & 4 November LG 89	A good night's work of strafing MTs in the Fuka area was marred by the failure of F/Lt Miller to return. F/O Waechter was also reported missing but returned to the Squadron the following day. The controls had seized, and his a/c burnt out after crashing. Sq/Ldr J.B. Selby, DFC. F/O McGill. P/O L. P. Jones and P/O Gill were all successful in strafing MTs, tents, and huts. ***The days on which Tobruk was recaptured from the German & Italian AXIS Forces by the Allied Forces. 'The Allied Forces walked in unopposed.'***

4 & 5 November LG 89	2 a/c were 'scrambled' at dawn over Alamein line but saw no e/a. In the morning "A" party move off to unknown destination. All pilots and a/c remain behind with "B" party to continue operations.
5 & 6 November LG 89	Gala Night – All a/c were fitted with long-range tanks ready for a dusk and dawn strafing attack on the retreating enemy. 12 a/c operating in pairs arrived in the Garawla – Fuka area just before dusk and strafed hundreds of MTs on the roads, many were carrying troops. Heavy and light Ack-Ack also intense Breda fire was encountered – various gun positions were strafed and at least 1-Breda silenced. All a/c returned to base but 2 were minus long-range tanks, another had been hit in the wing and another in the main tank. The dawn effort was not nearly as successful. Our army had pushed so rapidly that it was impossible to distinguish enemy troops near Garawla. Layer patrol was operated by 2 a/c along the coast to Heneish, but no hostiles were seen. The pilots reported everything quiet as far as Fuka. Orders came in the morning for "B" party to be one, one hour's notice Tents were struck, and everybody was straining at the leash. The move was delayed, and night operations went forward as usual.
6 & 7 November LG 89	The first long-range patrol however encountered heavy rain cloud before reaching Daba and had to return. Meanwhile another patrol had taken off and was recalled. At midnight a weather recce was made which confirmed the above report but at dawn the weather had cleared, and 6 a/c went on a layer patrol Heneish to Matruh. No hostiles were seen.
7 & 8 November LG 21	Orders were received for the a/c to proceed to LG 21 where "A" were established. "B" party after seeing the a/c off proceeded in convoy to LG 13 near Sidi Meneish. Movement in convoy was slow and tedious, particularly along the coast road where jams occurred every few minutes. Night operations were limited to 3-line patrols and 2 scrambles. No e/a were seen. The tightening of belts was already in force; water also being rationed. Beer became a memory and cigarettes a highly rated acquisition. But spirits are high because we are no longer stagnating. There is plenty of work for everyone and no time to brood. Evidence of the enemy's rapid retreat is seen everywhere. Burnt out tanks and lorries littered the roadside and scores of planes, many of which were serviceable, had been abandoned on the LG's.

8 & 9 November LG 21	Another night of anti-strafing Patrols passed uneventfully and by morning "B" party had reached LG 13 and were ready to receive a/c. "A" party were quickly on the move for LG 155 away South of Barrani. The wreckage of Fl/Lt. Miller's a/c and his grave close by were seen near Fuka.
9 & 10 November LG 13	Opportunities arose during the day for a swim at Heneish. A great refresher. 2 mines exploded on the LG but did not cause any damage to the Squadron. During the night 4 a/c carried out a dusk patrol between base and Sidi Barrani in anticipation of e/a strafing then road but there was no hostile activity. At dawn a smaller patrol of 4 a/c but again there was no enemy activity.
10 & 11 November LG 13	3 a/c carried out a dusk layer patrol between base and Sidi Barrani but there was no enemy activity. In the morning "B" party were on the move to LG 155.
11 & 12 November LG 155	3 a/c carried out a dusk patrol over Halfaya but found no enemy activity. Between 05:15 and 07:25 hours 12 a/c flown by the CO, P/O Chandler, F/O Thompson, P/O Smyth, Fl/Lt. Ellis DFM, F/O Pain, P/O Wiseman, Fl/Sgt Phillips, and Sgts. Davies, Wright and Beard and Fl/Lt Ambrose DFC strafed the road between Tobruk and Gazala. Much MTs was found travelling West at least 3 fires were started. Tobruk was being evacuated by the enemy who was setting alight very many of his abandoned dumps and vehicles.
12 & 13 November LG 155	"B" party arrived in the morning and were straightaway re-directed to Gambut West. 11 a/c took off shortly before dawn to strafe the rad between Gazala and Tmimi but did not find many targets. There was, however, some MT activity on Tmimi LG and this was attended to. On returning to base, they found a thick mist over the LG 7 a/c landed at other aerodromes where conditions were better.
13 & 14 November Gambut West	On the13th the remainder of the Squadron started for Gambut West and arrived in the evening of the 14th. The Squadron did not operate.
14 & 15 November Gambut West	At 04:30 hours 4 a/c flown by the CO, W/O Plenderleith, F/O Waechter and Sgt Davies took off for Benghazi area and strafed MTs on the roads in that area.
15 & 16 November Gambut West	At dusk F/O/Thompson took off to patrol the Sollum area but had to abandon patrol as cloud was 10/10 at 1,500 feet and much haze, He took off again at dawn accompanied by P/O Gill, Sgt Gadd, and F/Sgt Marsh to patrol between Sollum and Gazala but there was no e/a activity.

16 & 17 November Gambut West	The Squadron maintained continuous patrols over Sollum and Tobruk between dusk and dawn, 10 a/c participating. No enemy activity was seen. In the morning, the Squadron moved to El Adem aerodrome for the purpose of talking over the night defence of Tobruk.
17 & 18 November El Adem	Did not operate. No ground controls.
18 & 19 November El Adem	At 17:35 hours 4 a/c took off and carried out a layer patrol over Tobruk at 2,000 – 8,000 feet. There was no enemy activity. At 19:20 hours Fl/Sgt Phillips and Sgt Hiltz took off to strafe El Magrun aerodrome but could not locate it. At dawn 4 a/c patrolled Tobruk but again no enemy activity.
19 & 20 November El Adem	At 17:20 hours 4 a/c carried out a layer patrol over Tobruk at 2, 4, 6 and 8,000 feet. No enemy activity Sgt Beard crashed on landing. At 23:00 hours 6 a/c 'scrambled' after e/a reported in the Gazala - Tobruk area. Flares were seen over Gazala, but no other evidence of the enemy's presence was encountered.
20 & 21 November El Adem	Between 00:55 and 05:00 hours 4 a/c carried out a layer patrol off Tobruk without incident. The Squadron carried out dusk and dawn patrols of Tobruk. Each patrol comprising 4 a/c. There was no enemy activity. During the night 1 a/c was 'scrambled' North of Tobruk but did not make contact with the intruder.
21 & 22 November El Adem	4 a/c took off and patrolled Tobruk without incident. During the night, 3 a/c 'scrambled' after an intruder who was strafing the road North of Gazala. 1 pilot, P/O Jones got a visual of a JU 88 and closed the range to 20 yards where he opened fire. Unfortunately, only one of his cannons worked and immediately afterwards he lost sight of the e/a. P/O Wiseman patrolled the Tobruk – Gazala road between 00:35 and 01:15 hours, but there was no enemy activity, P/O Jones saw an e/a strafing underneath him. He followed the strafing as far as Derna, but could not see the e/a, so re-joined the patrol which was completed without incident.
22 & 23'November El Adem	2 a/c took off at 16:40 hours and patrolled above a convoy North of Tobruk. They received several vectors but were unable to make contact with the hostile e/a. 2 other a/c carried out a patrol of Tobruk between dusk and dark without incident. During the night 1 a/c was 'scrambled' over Tobruk but did not see any enemy activity. In addition, 7 a/c maintained a continuous patrol over Tobruk – Gazala road during the night without seeing any hostile activity. Except for P/O Charlesworth, who got a visual of a low flying JU 88 strafing the road. He gave chase, but the e/a disappeared rapidly to the North Werst and was lost sight of.

23 & 24 November El Adem	At 05: 05 hours 3 a/c carried out a patrol over Tobruk at 2, 4 and 6,000 feet without incident. 1 a/c was 'scrambled' and vectored 80 miles Northwest of Tobruk but did not see the hostile e/a. At 17:15 hours 4 more a/c took off simultaneously and carried out a layer patrol without incident, Fl/Lt Ambrose DFC crashed on landing, a/c Cat. II. A similar patrol of 4 a/c maintained a continuous patrol of the Tobruk – Gazala road without seeing any e/a.
24 & 25 November El Adem	4 a/c carried out a dusk layer patrol of Tobruk and 3 a/c a dawn layer patrol. In both cases the duty ended without incident. Continuous patrols by 6 a/c over the Tobruk – Gazala road between dusk and dawn were similarly uneventful. In addition, there were 3 'scrambles' of 1 a/c during the night but nothing was seen of the e/a.
25 & 26 November El Adem	3 a/c carried out the dusk patrol and 4 a/c the dawn patrol of Tobruk. The patrols ended without incident, except that Sgt Wright crashed on returning at sunrise, a/c Cat. II. In addition 2 a/c patrolled the Tobruk – Gazala road without seeing any e/a.
26 & 27 November Detachment: Bu Amud	A detachment of 7 a/c and pilots flew to Bu Amud providing dusk to dawn patrols of 3 a/c each of Tobruk and also a patrol of Tobruk – Gazala road. The night was uneventful. The detachment consisted of Fl/Lt Ellis DFM as CO, F/O Waechter, P/O Wiseman, P/O Jones, P/O Warburton, Fl/Sgt Marsh, and Sgt Hiltz. The remainder of the Squadron at El Adem did not operate.
27 & 28 November Detachment: Bu Amud	The detachment carried out dusk and dawn patrols of Tobruk, 3 a/c in each case, and also 3 patrols of 1 a/c over the Tobruk – Gazala road and a standing patrol over El Adem between the 21:30 and 01:00 hours while a force of 40 Wellingtons was taking off to bomb Marble Arch aerodrome. All the patrols were without incident.
28 & 29 November El Magrun	2 a/c from Bu Amud went to on dusk patrol and 1 a/c on dawn patrol of Tobruk. No e/a was seen. At El Magrun where the strength of the Squadron was now established, 3 a/c were 'scrambled' at dawn when bombs were dropped nearby. Sgt. Davies saw road strafing as far as Aghelia but could not make contact with the e/a. F/O Davis and Sq/Ldr. J.B. Selby DFC both saw bombs exploding but did not obtain a visual. F/O Smith closed with an ME 110 which was road strafing from 2,000 feet and attacked from astern at a range of 300 yards. He saw strikes on the fuselage and then gave a final burst as the e/a turned out to sea.

29 & 30 November El Magrun	The detachment put up dusk and dawn patrols of 2 a/c over Tobruk and in addition 2 a/c were 'scrambled' and given vectors. No e/a were seen. The defiles West of Agheila were the objective of 4 strafing patrols, one of which returned early with engine trouble. The only car seen was hit by Fl/Sgt. Phillips. Otherwise, there were no other objectives seen. 2 a/c which were on readiness at Benina were 'scrambled' at dawn. Flares and strafing were reported by Fl/Lt. Ambrose DFC, but he did not get visual. F/O Davis saw bombs exploding, then contacted a JU 88, 3 miles out to sea off Tocra. He closed to 150 yards at 7,000 feet, fired and saw a strike on the port wing. He received return fire and lost sight, but the e/a was seen to burst into flame and crash Northeast of Benghazi. 3 road patrols were made at dawn between Benghazi and Agedabia. Flares strafing and bombing were seen but no e/a could be contacted.
30 November & 1 December El Magrun & El Adem	At Bu Amud 2 a/c did dusk patrol over Tobruk without result. P/O Jones was 'scrambled' before dawn and F/O Waechter did the dawn patrol. Neither of these pilots saw any e/a. 2 a/c which were at readiness at Benina did a dawn patrol of Benghazi and the area North of Tocra but saw no e/a. 4 a/c from base strafed the roads from Agheila to Marble Arch. A few lorries were seen and 2 were hit. Tentage was also strafed. P/O Smyth had a visual of a JU 88 but lost sight when it entered cloud. Breda fire was encountered at various points along the road. A road protection patrol was made at dawn by 4 a/c between Benghazi and Agedabia without signs of enemy activity.

Note: For daily pilot records of flight operations carried out by 'A' Flight of 73 Squadron refer to AIR 27/631/22. These records detail the a/c number, the pilot's name and the sortie carried out.

AIR 27/631/23 & AIR 27/631/24 Pilot Ops Report December 1942	
1 & 2 December El Magrun & Bu Amud	At Bu Amud Fl/Lt. Ellis DFM and P/O Jones made a dusk patrol of Tobruk without incident. P/O Warburton and Fl/Sgt Marsh were 'scrambled' at 04:25 hours but saw no e/a, they continued to patrol Tobruk until 07:00 hours. F/Sgt Marsh saw a stick of incendiaries dropped across the road 8 miles Northwest of Gazala but did not get a visual of the e/a. 3 strafing patrols on the roads West of Agheila. No transport was seen but tentage and huts were strafed, and 2 fires were started. Very accurate Breda fire from the defiles. 6 a/c patrolled the roads from Tocra to Agedabia but saw no enemy activity.

2 & 3 December El Magrun & Bu Amud	2 a/c made a dusk patrol of Tobruk and in addition 4 a/c were 'scrambled' at 18:25 hours to intercept 6 e/a. These e/a were seen to come in South of Tobruk, but contact was not made. Later P/O Wiseman and Sgt Hiltz saw an e/a in the light of flares, but no contact was made, On the dawn patrol of 2 a/c P/O Jones was vectored on to returning Liberators. Operations from Magrun were restricted on account of bad weather. 1 road patrol as far as Benghazi was flown between 17:10 and 19:10 hours but no e/a were seen. At 02:00 hours 2 a/c took off to strafe Ras el Aali; 1 a/c returned early owing to the weather but the other continued and reached the target which he duly strafed apparently successfully. The target, a jetty was well defended, and he received much accurate Breda fire, a projected dawn patrol was cancelled because of heavy rain.
3 & 4 December El Magrun & Bu Amud	At Magrun a dusk patrol was carried out between Benghazi and Agedabia, but no enemy activity was seen. At the same time 4 a/c provided protection for a convoy which was then 560 miles out to sea from Benghazi. At 04:50 hours 4 a/c took off and were ordered to proceed to Tocra to intercept e/a. Flares were seen over Benghazi and also 3 to 4 bombs were dropped but the e/a themselves were not seen. At 06+:00 hours another a/c took off on seeing flares and Ack-Ack over Benghazi, but this had ceased by the time he reached there, and no e/a were seen. The detachment at Bu Amud, 2 a/c carried out a dusk patrol over Tobruk and a dawn patrol of 3 a/c without incident. Later on, in the morning when the detachment was off duty and resting a JU 88 was seen and 3 pilots were in the air within 3 to 4 minutes. The JU 88 however pulled away fast and was not seen again.
4 & 5 December El Magrun & Bu Amud	2 a/c patrolled the road between Benghazi and Agedabia at dusk and at dawn and a further 2 a/c patrolled from Magrun to Benghazi. Both patrols were without incident.at 23:55 1 a/c was 'scrambled' after an e/a dropping flares over base and to the North, but no visual was obtained. At dawn 1 a/c patrolled Benghazi but saw nothing. A further a/c patrolled the coast 30 miles North of Benghazi and investigated a dozen small explosions but did not get a visual on an e/a. Dusk and dawn Patrols over Tobruk were made by 2 a/c in each case. At 20:00 hours 1 a/c was 'scrambled' but without results.
5 & 6 December El Magrun & Bu Amud	3 dawn strafing patrols were made on the road West of Agheila and past Marble Arch. A convoy of 20 MT's were strafed, and strikes were scored; also, a single vehicle was hit. 2 or more a/c operating from Benina made a dawn patrol of

	the road from Tocra to Benghazi without seeing any signs of enemy activity. At Bu Amud 2 a/c made a dusk Patrol over Tobruk without incident.
6 & 7 December El Magrun & Bu Amud	Operating base 4 a/c strafed the road from Agheila to Marble Arch at dawn. There was much MTs on the road and some Breda fire was experienced. Also, at dawn 4 a/c patrolled Benghazi and to the North of it. There were some hostile e/a about and visuals of 2 JU 88's were obtained but our pilots were unable to close the range before they disappeared. The detachment at Bu Amud carried out dusk and dawn patrols of 2 a/c each over Tobruk without incident.
7 & 8 December El Magrun & Bu Amud	At Magrun 2 a/c carried out a patrol over Benghazi at dusk and 10 a/c carried out a patrol at dawn in layer formation between 2 and 4,.000 feet; no e/a were observed on either occasion. At dawn also 1 a/c made a tactical recce of the road West of Agheila as far as Ras el Aali and saw only 2 small convoys of MT's one of 6 vehicles and the other 4 vehicles going Wets, nothing going East. The detachment at Bu Amud carried out a dusk patrol of 2 a/c over Tobruk and a dawn patrol of 3 a/c over the same, without seeing any e/a, or enemy activity. During the day, 2 a/c which were at readiness with 80 Squadron were 'scrambled' at 14:00 hours but no contact was made with e/a.
8 & 9 December El Magrun & Bu Amud	Operating from Magrun 4 a/c took off at 17:00 hours to provide protection for a convoy which was then 25 miles North of Benghazi. On the way to pick up the convoy, one of the pilot's F/O Smith saw 2 – JU 88's but was unable to intercept either of them. A little however, another JU 88 passed close overhead and P/O Smyth was able to get within 250 yards of him from which range he gave him 2 x 1 second bursts and saw strikes on the porty engine and fuselage. A large piece flew off from close to the wing root and a cloud of smoke appeared. The pilot turned to make another attack but lost sight of the e/a so he went down to 1,500 Feet and saw a large patch oil spreading on the water and dark objects floating in it. The pilot was credited with a JU 88 destroyed. At dusk also 1 a/c patrolled over an MT convoy between Agedabia and Mersa el Brega and a similar patrol was flown at midnight without incident on both occasions. At dawn 1 a/c carried out a recce of the road West of Agheila and saw only about 5 MTs going West and a similar number going east near Ras el Aali. Also, at dawn, a layer patrol of 9 a/c between 2 and 11,000 feet was carried out over Benghazi, flares and

	bombs were seen near Tocra but no e/a. The detachment at Bu Amud at dusk put up a patrol of 2 a/c over Tobruk but no e/a seen. During the day of the 9th 2 a/c at readiness with 80 Squadron were 'scrambled' but no engagement took place. The detachment did not operate again from Bu Amud and re-joined the Squadron at El Magrun on the 11 December.
8 & 9 December El Magrun	At 17:00 hours 4 a/c did a layer patrol over Benghazi but did not see e/a. Sgt Rawson did a dawn recce West of Agheila as far as Marble Arch and back along the road to Mersa el Brega, but there was not much to be seen except for a handful of MTs moving West.
9 & 10 December El Magrun	7 a/c did a dawn layer patrol over Benghazi, but the results being the same as the previous evening, no e/a seen.
10 & 11 December El Magrun	4 a/c took off on a patrol of Benghazi, no enemy activity seen though the weather was excellent for the enemy to take advantage of. At 05:35 hours the CO took off and patrolled the road at 500 feet between Ras el Aali and Mersa-el-Brega, saw no MT's. He then went to see if there were any ships alongside Ras el Aali pier but saw none, on the way home he got some Breda fire from one-gun East of the defiles. At dawn 8 more a/c took off to keep a watchful eye on Benghazi, and a sharp look out for any e/a that tried to approach, but nothing was seen.
11 & 12 December El Magrun	4 a/c patrolled South of Agedabia and 4 a/c over Benghazi, on both trips no enemy activity was seen. Weather very poor with 10/10 cloud at 2,500 feet.
12 & 13 December El Magrun	The weather being very bad during the morning and afternoon and owing to the very heavy rainstorm which made the aerodrome unserviceable, all operations were cancelled.
13 & 14 December El Magrun	At 4 a/c took off on a layer patrol over Benghazi, and 4 more a/c at dawn, on both occasions no enemy activity was seen. At 19:50 to 20:30 hours 5 a/c were 'scrambled' over Benghazi the CO, Sgt Thomas, P/O Smyth, P/O Wiseman, and F/Sgt Logan. Flares were seen being dropped North on Benghazi but could not make out any interceptions. Fl/Sgt Logan got a visual of a JU 88 going into cloud, he gave it a few seconds burst and also sprayed the cloud, later on an e/a was reported to have crashed at the same time and place and he was credited with the destruction of a JU 88. 5 a/c took off at intervals on strafing patrols to the defiles but found no suitable targets, the road was deserted. One pilot did see some dark objects which he thought were tents so gave them a burst but saw no results.

14 & 15 December El Magrun	At dusk a layer patrol of 4 a/c was carried out over Benghazi at 3, 6, 8 and 10,000 feet. No enemy activity was seen. Between 19:35 and 23:55 hours 7 a/c strafed the road between Marble Arch and Bir el Ahmar, many targets were found amongst MT's and huts and several fires were started in various places. Night accurate Breda gun fire was experienced. 1 a/c provided protection to a MT convoy on the road near Mersa Brega between 22:20 and 11:20 hours. No e/a were encountered. 4 a/c carried out a dawn patrol over Benghazi without incident. At dawn 1 a/c did a recce of the road between Mersa Brega and Nofilia, much enemy MTs was seen moving Westwards ingroups of 15, all along the road the pilot received accurate Breda fire. Marble Arch was found the be evacuated by the enemy.
15 & 16 December El Magrun	4 a/c made a dusk patrol of Benghazi area but no enemy activity. Immediately after their return 6 a/c were 'scrambled' to intercept a formation approaching the coast from the North. This formation however proved to be friendly, and our a/c returned to base without incident. From 18:35 to 00:30 hours 7 a/c made individual strafing patrols West of Nofilia LG Many hits were scored on MT's and at least 4 fires were started. Very Accurate Ack/Ack was encountered from the coast North of Nofilia along with some machine gun fire. The dawn patrol of 4 a/c over Benghazi had nothing to report. A tactical recce of Nofilia LG and the road East to Marble Arch was made just after dawn by F/O McGill. No e/a were on the LG and only 3 transport and 7 Stukas could be seen. Enemy troops were withdrawing Westwards with a large force West of Marble Arch. Some of our transports were seen about 6 miles inland approx. halfway between Marble Arch and Nofilia. This recce was made at 0 feet in the facc of intense Breda fire.
16 & 17 December El Magrun	During and between 17:50, 19:00, 19:05 and 20:30 hours several patrols were carried out. The dusk patrol of 2 a/c over Benghazi saws no enemy activity. 4 a/c were 'scrambled' to intercept raiders over Benghazi but though they saw flares and bombs explosions they were unable to get any visuals except F/O Davis, who confirmed a JU 88 destroyed by Fl/Sgt Beard who just returned from dusk patrol and was preparing to land saw bofor gun fire over Benghazi and returned to investigate. He Had a visual on a JU 88 at a range of 20 yards gave a short burst and followed him down in a dive through the barrage to 1,000 feet when after another short burst he saw strikes on fuselage and port engine and the

	e/a crashed into the sea in flames. During and between 17:30 and 02:15 hours 8 a/c patrolled in the vicinity of Nofilia LG, but no e/a took off or landed there. A dim flare path was seen and a White Beacon to the North of the LG was in use.
17 & 18 December El Magrun	During and between 05:00 and 08:05 hours 1 a/c strafed about 200 MTs to the West of Nofilia and saw many strikes. A recce to Sirte was of little use owing to heavy rain and poor visibility. Some MTs was seen on the road to the Southeast of Sirte. Weather continued to be bad during the day and night. 2 a/c on dusk patrol over Benghazi saw nothing. The first 2 strafing patrols over the road West of Nofilia encountered heavy rainstorms though some MTs was seen and strafed. Further operations were cancelled after a weather recce had been to Marble Arch. At dawn Sgt Davies flew to Marble Arch LG to test the serviceability of the aerodrome.
18 & 19 December El Magrun	During and between 17:30 and 20:35 hours 4 a/c made dusk layer patrols over Benghazi but saw no enemy activity. On their return to base the controller told them there was 1 e/a over Benghazi, which they went to investigate but saw nothing. During and between 21:30 and 23:35 hours 4 a/c were 'Scrambled' over Benghazi and patrolled at height of 4,000 to 7,000 feet, they received various vectors but saw no e/a Fl/Lt. Ellis DFM saw a light out to sea about 20 miles North-North-West of Benghazi, went to investigate and found light appeared to be on the water, he circled it several times losing height each time. He then made a run across it from 20 feet with his landing light on and received MG fire, called up Controller and asked them to plot him which they did. He also requested permission to fire and was told he could with caution. He thought it to be a sub. But did not fire in case it was a crew in a boat.
19 & 20 December El Magrun	During and between 05:40 and 07:30 hours 4 a/c made a dawn layer patrol over Benghazi but saw no enemy activity. Dusk to dawn patrols were made by 4 a/c in each case, nothing was seen. Between 20:30 and 21:40 hours 4 a/c were 'scrambled' over base and told by the Controller bandits going South over base, pilot saw flares dropped about 6 miles Southeast of Beacon also incendiaries but was unable to get a visual. On his return to base saw an explosion, investigated, and thinks it was ammunition.
20 & 21 December El Magrun	At Magrun 3 a/c carried out a patrol over Benghazi at dusk, and 4 a/c carried out a similar patrol at dawn, no enemy activity was observed on either occasion. Sq/Ldr J.B. Selby DFC made a patrol over Benghazi; whilst on patrol was told by Controller bandits were about 100 miles off approaching Benghazi. They turned into Benghazi, and he saw two very

	bright lights, went, and investigated and found e 2 a/c with navigation lights on. These were so bright that he was unable to get a silhouette of them. He informed Controller who told him to open fire as they were 'definitely', bandits. He then got close to one and gave him a short burst but saw no results. He then flew under him to see if he could identify the a/c and found it to be a Liberator and told the Controller. The second a/c was also identified as a Liberator.
21 & 22 December El Magrun	The usual dusk to dawn patrols were carried out over Benghazi, in each case 4 a/c did the patrol without incident. At 22:25 to 23:20 hours 1 a/c Fl/Lt. Thompson was 'scrambled' over Benghazi. When he was 2 miles South of Benghazi and 5 miles out up to 5,000 feet got a visual of a JU 88 beneath him, got within 300 yards range and fired at him, he received no return fire, so gave another burst, and then another one, the JU 88 was losing height all the time. He gave him a 4th burst from 1,000 feet; the aircraft dived down straight into the sea. He circled it for a few minutes and gave a D/F plot to 2.2 Group. The JU 88 confirmed destroyed by No. 89 Squadron (Beaufighter).
22 & 23 December Merduma	The Squadron moved from El Magrun and arrived at Merduma this morning. Owing to the bad condition of the LG the usual operations were not carried out, but 4 a/c, was at readiness all night.
23 & 24 December Merduma	4 a/c were at readiness from the Moonrise. At 23:25 hours 2 a/c were 'scrambled' North of Bask. But saw no e/a. They returned to base and landed at 00:35 hours.
24 & 25 December Merduma	Again 4 a/c were at readiness from Moonrise all through the night, but the Hun failed to turn up.
25 & 26 December Merduma	To-day. Christmas Day, a good time was had by all, thanks to Sq/Ldr J.B. Selby DFC when things looked black in the morning as the Christmas had not arrived, after a lot of hard work on the part of the CO we had our dinner, and a good time followed.
26 & 29 December Merduma	4 a/c were at readiness all night, but nothing came over. Owing to the very bad conditions of the LG the usual operations were unable to take place, but 4 a/c were on readiness each night in case the Hun dared to come over.
29 & 30 December Merduma	4 a/c at readiness from Moonrise, at 05:10 hours 1 a/c was 'scrambled' 10 miles North of base and then given a vector and told bandits in the immediate vicinity at 8,000 feet. He did not see him. Returned to base and landed at 06:15 hours. At between 05:25 and 06:30 hours 1 a/c was 'scrambled' 5 miles South of base and given various vectors, but saw no e/a.

30 & 31 December Merduma	4 a/c were at readiness from Moonrise, but no operations took place. 1 a/c was due to take off on a dawn recce, but owing to heavy rain during the night, which made the LG unserviceable, it was cancelled.

Note: For daily pilot records of flight operations carried out by 'A' Flight of 73 Squadron refer to AIR 27/631/24. These records detail the a/c number, the pilot's name and the sortie carried out.

AIR 27/632/1 & AIR 27/632/2 Pilot Ops Report January 1943	
31st December 1942 to 1 January 1943 Merduma	From moonrise one aircraft was at readiness but was not called upon. 1st Jan/2nd Jan. The main part of the squadron moved off for a new landing ground at Alem el Chel on the afternoon of the 1 January 1943. There were no operations that night.
2 & 3 January Alem el Chel	Established at Alem el Chel by mid-day of the 2 January 1943, and the remainder of the squadron arrived the same evening. A strafing programme had been arranged for dawn but had to be cancelled because of weather conditions.
3 & 4 January	Sandstorms all day long, made flying impossible. No night operations.
4 & 5 January	Weather continued poor during the day and only one aircraft operated during the night. 05:20 – 07:20. Sq/Ldr J.B. Selby DFC, made a reconnaissance of the enemy front line and the area bounded by road and coast as far North as GIODA. Visibility was very bad and only 20-30 headlights were seen in convoy moving North near TAOURGA with a few vehicles on the tracks East and West of the road.
5 & 6 January	05:30 to 08:00. Three aircraft started out on a strafing rid, consisting of P/O M.S. Jones, Fl/Lt R.V. Ellis DFM and Fl/Sgt E.T. Bennett. The two former returned owing to low cloud and rain as far as Buerat, but Fl/Sgt E.T. Bennett continued and found the weather clear. He strafed and scored strikes on 3 MT vehicles in Garibaldi and also shot up Gioda where several lights were showing. Another reconnaissance was made by F/O J.H. Fairbairn. Some lights were seen on the roads and at Crispi and Gioda. Taourga LG still appeared to be in use as the flare path was switched on twice on approach. Forty miles of the coastal track gave no signs of MTs'.

6 & 7 January Alem el Chel	3 a/c made dawn staffing attacks on the roads and settlements east of Tripoli. These were flown by Fl/Lt C.P. Ambrose, DFC, P/O H.C. Charlesworth, and P/O R. Chandler. Visibility was not good because of the mist and two a/c returned after strafing a car and stationary lights at Hom's and Gioda. The third a/c piloted by P/O Chandler made a reconnaissance up to Castel Verde after dawn had broken and saw hundreds of MT's moving West between Zliten and Castle Verde. He used up all his ammunition and started at least two fires in the MTs'. he ran into a concentration of light Ack-Ack at Garibaldi so went out to sea round Misurata then recrossed the coast and flew south down the road to the front line. From Taourga southwards British troops and transport were seen on the road.
7 & 8 January	5 a/c piloted by F/O J.H. Fairbairn, F/O D.E. Warburton, Fl/Sgt D.R. Beard, Fl/Sgt J.D.A. Wright and Fl/Sgt E.A. McCready made strafing raids as on the previous night. Lights at Zliten and Garibaldi were hit causing two minor explosions and a large white explosion at the latter town. Fires near Hom's were strafed and also a camp 10 miles south of Garabaldi. At the same time a reconnaissance was made of the road from the line up to Zliten. Only occasional MTs were seen together with a few fires.
9 & 10 January	The same MT concentration was the objective of 6 a/c piloted by Fl/Lt J.F. Pain, F/O J. McGill, P/O D.R. Wiseman, P/O M.S. Jones, Sgt D. Gadd, and Fl/Sgt E.T. Bennett which took off just before dusk. They were, however, unable to locate the MTs and did individual strafing to the North. Results were poor due to poor visibility. A dawn reconnaissance was made over Wadi Zem Zem where no MTs were seen by the pilot, P/O D.E. Warburton. About 60 MTs with British roundels were seen in the districts round about.
10 & 11 January Hamraiet (Main)	The Squadron moved off during the day and arrived at Hamraiet the same afternoon. Landing ground already full and consequently no operations.
11 January Wadi Tamet Satellite	In the afternoon the Squadron moved to Tamet satellite landing ground, arriving shortly before the attack by e/ac, which besides destroying one of our Hurricanes on the ground, and damaged another, also destroyed a Lysander on the ground and several damaged Baltimore's. The attacking force was 18 - Macchi 200s, with a top cover of Me 109s, they were engaged by a formation of Spitfires who destroyed four without loss to themselves.

11 & 12 January	There were no operations as the runways were unserviceable on account of enemy action and could not be made serviceable in the time available.
12 & 13 January	8 a/c were engaged in strafing between 19:10 hours and 22:45 hours. These were piloted by Sq/Ldr J.B. Selby DFC, Fl/Lt R.V. Ellis, F/O G.P. Leggett, F/O J.H. Fairbairn, P/O M.W. Smyth, Fl/Sgt D.M. Logan, Fl/Sgt R.C. Dolan, and Sgt J. Rawson. Traffic on the roads near Hom's was attacked and some hits were observed. Lights and buildings were also strafed, and a couple of fires started. All a/c returned safely from the operations but 2 other a/c which it was intending to employ came to grief. One of these flown by F/O E.D. Savage punctured a tyre on take-off and tipped upon to its nose. The other one, flown by Sgt W.J. MyGind, had taken off shortly before returned with R/T trouble and taxied into it before its pilot had time to mark the obstruction. Both a/c were wrecked, F/O Savage sustained a compound fracture of the arm and the other pilot Sgt MyGind a sprained wrist. He was lucky considering he had to be dug out from under his a/c which had turned over on its back. In the morning one a/c carried out a reconnaissance of the road between Misurata and Cheddabia and found only 20 MTs moving North. There were 50 more MTs dispersed on track near Taourga.
13 & 14 January Tamet Satellite	6 a/c were engaged in strafing behind enemy lines. These were flown by Sq/Ldr J.B. Selbey DFC, Fl/Lt J.F. Pain, F/O D.K. Warburton, F/O/ S.P. Davis, Fl/Sgt E.T. Bennett, Fl/Sgt E. McCready, and Sgt D. Gadd. All were engaged in strafing behind enemy lines. They attacked a few isolated MTs near Zliten and Bir Dufan and also some lights and buildings near Misurata and Taourga. MT targets were scarce however, and those that were about quickly extinguished their headlights on our approach. One a/c scrambled (20:08 – 2:45 hours) after an e/a over base but although he got two visuals of it and it fired at him, he was unable to get into a position to attack and finally lost touch with it.
06:30/07:50	A reconnaissance in the morning made by Sgt G. Gadd showed only 12 MTs moving North near Taourga.
14 & 15 January 19:00/01:40	6 a/c, piloted by Fl/Sgt D.R. Beard, P/O M.S. Jones, P/O D.R. Wiseman, P/O H.C. Charlesworth, Fl/Sgt J.D.A. Wright, and Sgt J. Rawson, patrolled the Gioda and Misurata and Zliten area without finding suitable targets to Strafe. A ship was seen 25 miles North of Garibaldi and there were frequent explosions on board suggestive of an ammunition ship blowing up.

19:15/02:15	6a/c, piloted by F/O J. McGill, P/O R. Chandler, F/O W.T.H. Gill, W/O R. Plenderleith, Fl/Sgt R.H. Phillips, and Fl/Sgt R.C. Dolan, patrolled Gheddahia-Sedada and Bir Dufan area. There was a white revolving beacon at Bir Dufan and a flare path was alight. It had a dark object at the end which F/O McGill strafed. 20 stationary MTs near Tauorga were also strafed. A similar number 10 miles South of Bir Dufan and 6 more at the North end of Wadi Sopeggin. 2 pilots were attacked by hostile e/a over the coast near Buerat but neither sustained damage.
19:05/02:05	3 a/c, piloted by F/O S.P. Davis, Sq/Ldr J.B. Selby DFC, and Sgt D.H. Thomas maintained a local defence patrol between Buerat and Sirte but saw no e/a. 1 a/c flown by Sq/Ldr J.B. Selby DFC, was scrambled at 19:45 hours and landed at 20:40 hours. A hostile e/a approaching base had been reported but did not materialise.
05:50	In the morning F/O S.P. Davis took off on a reconnaissance of the Misurata and Taourga areas. He found about 20 e/a on Taourga landing ground and 3 MTs on the track leading West. He strafed the latter and saw some strikes. There was some ground activity and artillery fire near Gheddahia and much dispersed in the Wadi Zem Zem area.
15 & 16 January 03:10 Tamet	10 a/c flown by Sgt D. Gadd, F/O G.P. Leggett, Sq/Ldr J.B. Selby DFC, P/O D.K. Warburton, F/O J.H. Fairbairn, Fl/Lt J.F. Pain, Fl/Lt R.V. Ellis DFM, Fl/Sgt D.M. Logan, and P/O M.W. Smyth, carried out offensive patrols in the Gheddahia, Sedada, Taourga and Misurata areas. They strafed MTs near Gheddahia, Wadi Sabba, Taourga, Homs, Bir Dufan and Buerat, scoring many hits and some fires resulted. There was much MTs going West through Garibaldi and North through Zliten. Considerable artillery fire was seen near Taourga and between Sedada and Churgia. In the neighbourhood of Churgia an anti-tank trench was blown up. Much MTs' were seen in the marshes making for the road.
22:05/02:40	2 a/c flown by P/O M.S. Jones and Sgt F. Davies patrolled the road between Neurat and Sirte but saw no enemy activity.
05:50	In the morning 1 a/c, flown by Fl/Sgt R.H. Phillips took off on a reconnaissance of the Taourga area. The flare path was found to be alight, and an e/a took off. There were only a few MTs' on the road moving North and South of Misurata the pilot strafed two cars successfully.

16 & 17 January 19:15/04:20 Tamet	8 a/c flown by Sq/Ldr J.F. Selby DFC, F/O J. McGill, P/O D.R. Wiseman, P/O R. Chandler, P/O H.C. Charlesworth. W/O R. Plenderleith, Fl/Sgt J.D.A. Wright, and Fl/Sgt R.H. Edwards maintained defensive patrols between Sirte and Buerat but there was no enemy activity. 2 a/c flown by Sq/ Ldr J.B. Selby DFC, and F/O S.P. Davis took off to petrol near Taourga landing ground in order to prevent the enemy from ploughing it up on his evacuation as his custom is. The CO found that the landing ground had already been ploughed up, so he strafed some machine gun nests which were still occupied sites to the North and South of it and returned safely at 9:3 hours. The other plot however F/O S.P. Davis did not return and at present the only clue as to his possible fate is provided by a strategical reconnaissance which found a previously un-observed and indistinguishable object on the ground a few miles east of Gioda (Misurata sheet 1:500000 Ref. (R.) s.3080). It was surrounded by a group of MTs'.
18:05/04:45	7 a/c flown by Fl/Lt J.F. Pain, F/O W.T.W. Gill, F/O R.V.D. Smith, Fl/Sgt McCready, Fl/Sgt R.C. Dolan, and Sgt D.H. Thomas patrolled over Bir Dufan landing ground. There was a white flash beacon there and 20 dispersed e/a. The latter were strafed and strikes seen among them. The landing ground was defended by a searchlight and Heavy and Light Ack-Ack gun fire, which however did no damage. 6 MTs about 8 miles North of the landing ground were strafed also about 8 MTs near Misurata and 50 dispersed South of Taourga landing ground. In the morning 1 a/c flown by FL/Lt C.F. Ambrose DFC, took off at 06:00 hours on a reconnaissance of the road as far North as Gioda where he observed a slight degree of activity, but none to the Southeast of it.
17 & 18 January Tamet	20 a/c, counting the double sorties of some pilots, piloted by Sq/Ldr J.B. Selby DFC (2), P/O M.W. Smyth (2), P/O M.S. Jones, F/O J.H. Fairbairn (2), F/O Leggett, Fl/Lt R.V. Ellis, Fl/Sgt E.T. Bennett, Fl/Sgt D.R. Beard (2), Fl/ Sgt D.M. Logan, Fl/Sgt R.H. Phillips (2), Sgt D. Gadd (2), Sgt F. Davies (2), and Sgt D.N. Green, operating between 18:35 hours and 04:45 hours strafed three to four hundred MTs in the Tarhuna area. Many strikes were observed and about 40 fires and one explosion caused. In addition, a warehouse was strafed, and an explosion followed causing part of the roof to fly off.

	Much Breda and Machine Gun fire was experienced. In addition, 4 a/c, comprising of two sorties each by F/O D.K. Warburton and Fl/Sgt R.D. Marsh maintained local defence patrols between 19:00 hours and 03:35 hours. Saw no enemy activity. In the morning 1 a/c piloted by Fl/Sgt E.T. Bennett, carried out a reconnaissance of the coast road, as far North as Misurata but found the road empty of traffic except for a few British vehicles South of Taourga.
18 & 19 January Tamet	13 a/c, the pilots of which in some cases did two sorties, Sq/Ldr J.B. Selby DFC, Fl/Lt C.F. Ambrose DFC, Fl/Lt J.F. Pain (2), Fl/Lt R.V.D. Smith (2), F/O W.T.H. Gill (2), P/O R. Chandler (2), P/O D.R. Wiseman (2), P/O H.C. Charlesworth (2), W/O R. Plenderleith (2), Fl/Sgt R.H. Edwards (2), Fl/Sgt Wright (2), Sgt J. Rawson (2), and Sgt D.N. Green (2), operating between 18:45 hours and 04:20 hours strafed approximately 100 MTs in the area West of Tarhuna and the defiles towards Castel Benito. One large explosion and five small fires were started. A train of 25 trucks was strafed North of Azzia and brought to a halt. 2 a/c were maintained at readiness for local defence but as there was no enemy activity they did not operate.
19 & 20 January Tamet	15 a/c flown by Sq/Ldr J.B. Selby DFC (2), Fl/Lt C.F. Ambrose DFC, F/O J. McGill, F/O D.K. Warburton, F/O Henderson, F/O J.H. Fairbairn, P/O M.S. Jones, Fl/Sgt Bennett, Fl/Sgt D.R. Beard, Fl/Sgt R.H. Phillips, Fl/Sgt D.M. Logan, Fl/Sgt R.C. Dolan, Sgt D. Gadd, and Sgt D.H. Thomas, operating between 19:10 hours and 05:15 hours, strafed 5-600 MTs in the Tripoli area, chiefly between Zania and 20 miles East where they were parked under trees in groups of 5 or 6 vehicles. Many strikes were observed and at least one fire caused. There was much Ack-Ack Defence including 30 Breda's East of Zania. In addition, buildings in Azzia, Zania and Binanchi were attacked, and a camp of 25 tents and petrol dump. One Breda gun was silenced near Castel Verde and an ammunition trailer, and an ammunition dump or lorry were blown up. The railway goods yard at Sabratha was also strafed. One pilot Sgt E.T. Bennett had a glimpse of a Ju 87, which jettisoned two bombs over Castel Benito (then in enemy hands) and disappeared into cloud after seeing our a/c. Later another pilot Sgt D.H. Thomas saw another Stuka in the same area and scored hits on its tailplane before it also disappeared into cloud.

20 & 21 January Tamet	11 a/c piloted by Sq/Ldr J.B. Selby DFC, Fl/Lt R.V. Ellis DFM, Fl/Lt J.F. Pain, Fl/Lt R.V.D. Smith, F/O G.P. Leggett, P/O D.R. Wiseman, P/O M.W. Smyth, W/O R. Plenderleith, Fl/Sgt J.D.A. Wright, Sgt J. Rawson, and Sgt D.N. Green, operating from an advanced landing ground (Bir Dufan) between 19:25 hours and 23:15 hours strafed roads and MTs in the coastal area West of Tripoli. About 70 MTs were seen and strikes secured on some of them followed by a large fire in one case. Two camps of 85 and 7 tents were also strafed and some lights extinguished. Two railway trucks near Memlita were also attacked. Considerable Breda gun fire was experienced. At dawn 1 a/c flown by Fl/Sgt R.H. Edwards made a reconnaissance of the road West of Tripoli.
21 & 22 January Bur Dufan	During the day "B" Party left Tamet satellite and arrived at Bir Dufan by mid-day of the 22nd. 16 a/c flown by F/O G.P. Leggett, F/O J. McGill, F/O W.T.H. Gill, Fl/Sgt E.A. McCready, P/O H.C. Charlesworth, Fl/Sgt D.R. Beard, Fl/Sgt R.H. Phillips, F/O Henderson, Fl/Sgt R.D. Marsh, F/O D.K Warburton, Fl/Lt R.V. Ellis DFM, P/O M.W. Smyth, Fl/Sgt J.D.A. Wright, W/O R. Plenderleith, Sq/Ldr J.B. Selby DFC, and Fl/Lt J.F. Pain, operating between 20:00 and 03:35 hours strafed MTs in the Tripoli – Ben Gardane area. Targets were found on the coastal road and also parked in the vicinity. Some strikes were observed and at least one explosion. The landing ground at Ben Gardane was strafed and an e/a seen to take off, but no interception was made. Breda gun and Ack-Ack gun fire was experienced on the roads upon which much traffic was moving Westwards from Ben Gardane.
22 & 23 January Bir Dufan	12 a/c piloted by F/O J.H. Fairbairn, P/O M.S. Jones, P/O D.R. Wiseman, Fl/Sgt R.H. Edwards, Fl/Sgt D.M. Logan, Fl/Sgt D.M. Logan, Fl/Sgt R.C. Dolan, Fl/Sgt E.T. Bennett, Sgt J. Rawson, Sgt F. Davies, Sgt D.N. Green, Sgt D.H. Thomas, and Sgt D. Gadd operating between 19:10 hours and 00:50 hours strafed about 140 MTs between Zania and Médinine. The vehicles were dispersed singly and in small groups. Many strikes were observed. Sgt R.H. Edwards found in Sormom a building showing a light, strafed, and set it on fire. Near Sobratha P/O Jones silenced a Breda gun which was firing on other a/c. In addition, various tents and lights were attacked. Much Breda gun fire especially along the coast road was experienced, also Heavy Ack-Ack gun fire North of Ben Gardane and at Sormom. Many tents and MTs were

	found dispersed in small groups about 10 miles Southeast of Ben Gardane. There were 8 or 9 burning MTs 5 miles South of the coast road near Sabratha and several large fires burning in Tripoli. Artillery fire 10miles Southwest of Azizia was observe. Sgt D.H. Thomas did not return from these operations but later in the day it was learned that he had crash-landed some miles East of Castel Verde and was uninjured.
23 & 24 January Bir Dufan	Between 19:20 hours and 03:55 hours 12 a/c operating West of Zuara fund a negligible amount of traffic along the coast road between there and Ben Gardane. In all a total of about 80 MTs was observed and strafed and a 30lb bomb dropped amongst a group of 15 vehicles. The MTs which were chiefly in the area 10 miles Southeast of Ben Gardane were dispersed singly and in small groups. Some strikes were seen and at least two fires followed. A small group of tents in the same area was also attacked and one caught fire. A few buildings in the Zeltan area were strafed. Only slight Breda and machine gun fire was experienced. The names of the pilots who took part on these operations are Fl/Lt R.V. Ellis DFM (who flew twice), F/O D.K. Warburton, Fl/Lt R.V.D. Smith, F/O J. McGill, F/O Henderson, F/O W.T.H. Gill, P/O R. Chandler, Fl/Sgt R.D. Marsh, Fl/Sgt E.A. McCready, Fl/Sgt R.H Phillips, and Fl/Sgt D.R. Beard.
24 & 25 January	***From this night until February 1943, the Squadron was released, and no operations were carried out.***
25 & 26 January	***From this night until February 1943, the Squadron was released, and no operations were carried out.***
26 & 27 January	***From this night until February 1943, the Squadron was released, and no operations were carried out.***
27 & 28 January	***From this night until February 1943, the Squadron was released, and no operations were carried out.***
28 & 29 January	***From this night until February 1943, the Squadron was released, and no operations were carried out.***
29 & 30 January	***From this night until February 1943, the Squadron was released, and no operations were carried out.***
30 & 31 January	***From this night until February 1943, the Squadron was released, and no operations were carried out.***

Note: For daily pilot records of flight operations carried out by 'A' Flight of 73 Squadron refer to AIR 27/632/2. These records detail the a/c number, the pilot's name and the sortie carried out.

AIR 27/632/3 & AIR 27/632/4 Pilot Ops Report February 1943	
1 February Bir Dufan Gasr Garabulli	**There were no operations during the opening days of the month.**
2 February	**There were no operations during the opening days of the month.**
3 February	On this day, the Squadron's "A" Party moved on to Gasr Garabulli.
4 February	On this day the Squadron's "B" Party and the aircraft moved to Gasr Garabulli.
5 February	**No records of the day's operations were posted.**
6 February	On this day F/O D.K. Warburton and P/O D.R. Wiseman were posted from the Western Desert to Middle East Headquarters as ***'operationally tired'*** having completed their tour of duty.
7 February	**No records of the day's operations were posted.**
8 February	**No records of the day's operations were posted.**
9 February	**No records of the day's operations were posted.**
10 February	**No records of the day's operations were posted.**
11 February	**No records of the day's operations were posted.**
12 February	There were no further operations or developments of interest until the 12th when it was learned that the CO, Sq/Ldr J.B. Selby DFC had been awarded the D.S.O., F/O J. McGill, F/O W.T.H. Gill, P/O M.S. Jones, and P/O D.R. Wiseman, had received the DFC, and Fl/Sgt D.R. Beard the DFM.
13 February	**No records of the day's operations were posted.**
14 February	**No records of the day's operations were posted.**
15 & 16 February El Assa Castel Benito	On this date "A" Party arrived at El Assa landing ground. The following pilots flew up to El Assa during the day, F/O W.T.H. Gill, Fl/Lt D.F. Ambrose, P/O M.W. Smyth, P/O R.H. Phillips, P/O D. Gadd, Fl/Sgt D.M. Logan, Fl/Sgt J.F.A. Wright, Fl/Sgt D.R. Beard, Fl/Sgt F. Davies, Fl/Sgt D.J. Green, W/O R.C. Dolan, Fl/Sgt R. Marsh, Sgt J. Rawson, Sgt D.N. Green, and Sgt D.H. Thomas. \a detachment consisting of Fl/Lt R.V.D. Smith, F/O R.J.D. Henderson, P/O R. Chandler, Fl/Sgt R.H. Edwards, and Fl/Sgt E.T. Bennett went to Castel Benito and will later be joined by Fl/Lt C.F. Ambrose DFC who will command the detachment, and a similar detachment from No. 213 Squadron, which it is intended to employ in the night defence of Tripoli.

16 & 17 February 18:30/20:00	Fl/Lt R.V.D. Smith, and F/O J.D.A. Henderson took off and patrolled Tripoli area in company with a Beaufighter of 89 Squadron, but no e/a was seen.
17 February Castel Benito	The new CO, Sq/Ldr R.V. Ellis DFM, re-joined the detachment at Castel Benito after a period of leave and a junior commander's course (administration) in Cairo.
17 & 18 February	At dusk F/O Chandler and Fl/Sgt E.L. Bennett carried out a patrol over Tripoli in formation with Beaufighters of 89 Squadron and a similar patrol was flown by the same pilots at dawn without seeing any e/a on either occasion.
18 & 19 February	There was no dusk patrol because of bad weather but at 05:35 hours 2 a/c were scrambled (F/O R.J.D. Henderson and Fl/Sgt R.H. Edwards) and 05:50 P/O M.W. Smyth also took off on a scramble. No e/a were seen by these pilots.
19 & 20 February 06:35	There was again no dusk patrol because of bad weather but in the morning Fl/Lt Ambrose DFC, and Fl/Lt R.V.D. Smith carried out a convoy patrol, they received various vectors but saw no enemy aircraft and landed at 08:10 hours.
2o & 21 February	At 05:30 hours, P/O M.W. Smyth and Fl/Sgt E.L. Bennett scrambled to intercept e/a over Tripoli and at 06:00 hours were followed by F/O R.J.D. Henderson and Fl/Sgt R.H. Edwards. They did not make contact with hostile e/a but saw 2 e/a go down in flames, whether as a result of Ack-Ack gun fire or action by Beaufighters of 89 Squadron is not known. As in all, 4 e/a were shot down that night, 2 e/a by Beaufighters and 2 e/a by Ack-Ack gun fire.
22 & 23 February	The detachment carried out no flying as the duties were taken over by No. 213 Squadron.
23 & 24 February	At 18:10 hours, Fl/Lt C.F. Ambrose and Fl/Lt R.V.D. Smith carried out a patrol of Tripoli without seeing any enemy activity and landed safely at 19:20 hours. At 05:15 hours P/O R, Chandler and P/O R.H. Phillips took off on a similar patrol which was also without incident and landed at 6:30 hours.
24 & 25 February El Assa	The detachment re-joined the Squadron at El Assa with the exception of Fl/Lt C.F. Ambrose DFC, F/O R.J.D. Henderson, and Sgt W.J. Mygind, all of whom went on leave.
24 & 25 February	At 04:40 hours, P/O D, Gadd and Fl/Sgt F. Davis took off to reconnoitre the first 50 miles of the Gabès – Gafsa road and the Gabès – Mareth Road. Low cloud (at 800 feet) and thick mist at ground level prevented them finding the Gabès – Gafsa road, but in good visibility the Gabès – Mareth Road

24 & 25 February [continued]	was investigated and found to be devoid of MTs. On the Gabès – Hamma Road 6 miles West of Gabès 12 isolated stationary MTs were seen and near Cekhira (about 30 miles North of Gabès) a convoy of 10 MTs was moving North. Heavy Ack-Ack and Breda gun fire was experienced near Gabès.
25 & 26 February	Fl/Lt J.H. Pain was posted away from the Squadron and left on the 25th. There were no operations required on the Squadron.
26 & 27 February	Ay 04:00 hours a signal was received calling for reconnaissance's of the Gabès – Sfax road and the Gabès – Gafsa road. Immediate steps were taken to carry out the instruction and at 04:50 hours, P/O R, Chandler and Sgt J. Rawson were airborne. The former reconnoitred the Gabès – Sfax road and found only 13 isolated MTs in all going North and South. He received both Heavy and light Ack-Ack gun fire at both Gabès and Sfax. On the coast visibility was good. About 10 miles inland there was a thick low ground mist. Because of this Sgt Rawson was unable to investigate the Gabès – Gafsa road only as far West at Djebel Haidondi (TY 9848) and on this stretch found only 3 isolated MTs.
27 & 28 February	At 04:55 hours F/O H.C. Charlesworth and Fl/Sgt D.J. Green took off on a reconnaissance of the Gabès – Sfax, Gabès – Gafsa and Gabès – Mareth roads but on account of poor visibility, were able only to find the Gabès – Sfax road and even then, could not see whether there was any MTs moving on it. There was 9/10ths at 500 feet and also ground mist. At Gabès, much light Ack-Ack gun fire was encountered.
28 February & 1 March	At 04:40 hours, F/O J.H. Fairbairn and Fl/Sgt E.L. Bennett took off on a reconnaissance of the Gabès – Sfax road and found no MTs moving on it but received much Breda fire from various places along the road. There was 8/10ths cloud at 800 feet and visibility was fair. The pilots landed safely at 07:00 hours. Fl/Sgt R.H. Edwards was posted from Squadron and went to Ballah on a conversion course to Spitfires.

Note: For daily pilot records of flight operations carried out by 'A' Flight of 73 Squadron refer to AIR 27/632/4. These records detail the a/c number, the pilot's name and the sortie carried out.

AIR 27/632/5 & AIR 27/632/6 (1) Pilot Ops Report March 1943	
1 & 2 March 04:45 El Assa	2 a/c took off on an armed reconnaissance of the Gabè – Sfax, Gabès – Gafsa and Gabès – El Hamma roads. F/O G.P. Leggett had to return to base early with engine trouble. With fair visibility through ground haze Fl/Lt R.V.D. Smith found only 6 isolated MTs on the first mentioned road and saw nothing on the other two roads.
2 & 3 March	Fl/Sgt J.D.A. Wright who took off with Fl/Lt W.T.M. Gill DFC, on an armed reconnaissance of the first 25 miles of the Gabès - Sfax and Gabès - Gafsa roads and the road between Gabè and Mareth, failed to return, Fl/Lt W.T.H. Gill DFC, found only a few vehicles on the Gabès – Sfax road and a small group of dispersed MTs at Z.0045. Nothing was seen on the Gabès – Mareth Road. Accurate Breda gun fire was encountered at various points in the roads.
3 March 16:45 El Assa, Castel Benito 18:00–1940	A detachment of 6 a/c to do dusk to dawn patrols over Tripoli took off for Castel Benito. Fl/Lt W.T.H. Gill DFC was accompanied by P/O D. Gadd, F/O J.H. Fairbairn, and Fl/Sgts D.R. Beard, D.J. Green. and J. Rawson. Shortly after arrival at Castel Benito, F/O J.R. Fairbairn, P/O D/ Gadd, Fl/Sgt Rawson and Fl/Sgt D.R. Beard DFM, made a layer patrol at angels 4, 6, 8 and 10 to the east of Tripoli. No enemy activity was observed.
4 March 04:30–06:35 05:30–06:35 18:00	From El Assa, Fl/Sgts F. Davies and R.D. Marsh, went out on an armed reconnaissance of the roads leading out of Gabès but with good visibility found only a few less vehicles moving on the roads. Fl/Lt W.T.H. Gill DFC, F/O J.H. Fairbairn as one section and Fl/Sgts D.J. Green and D.R. Beard DFM as another, patrolled to the East and West of Tripoli but had nothing to report on their return to base. As on the previous day, 4 a/c piloted by Fl/Lt W.T.H. Gill DFC, P/O D. Gadd, and Fl/Sgts D.J. Green and J. Rawson, made a layer patrol over the area just East of Tripoli.
5 March 05:15 El Assa and Castel Benito	This morning the same pilots in sections of two patrolled to the East and West of Tripoli. Both patrols were without incident.

5 March 04:30 [continued]	From El Assa Fl/Sgt D.M. Logan and W/O R.C. Dolan started out on an armed reconnaissance of the area 10 miles North of Mareth to Bir Tonjane. Neither of these pilots returned.
18:00	The dusk layer patrol East of Tripoli was made by F/O J.H. Fairbairn and Fl/Sgts D.R. Beard DFM, J. Rawson, and D.J. Green. No e/a were seen.
20:15	At El Assa 6 pilots had been detailed to make a standing patrol to the East of Sfax for the purpose of intercepting transport Ju, 52s operating between Sicily and Tunisia. Bad weather however upset the plan when P/O R. Chandler and W/O R. Plenderleith had to return to base and reported 8/10 low cloud in patrolling area.
6 March 05:10	A dawn patrol to the east and West of Tripoli was made by Fl/Lt W.T.H. Gill DFC, P/O D, Gadd, F/O J.H. Fairbairn and Fl/Sgt D.R. Beard DFM, in two sections. No e/a were seen.
18:00	A layer patrol to the East of Tripoli was carried out by the same four pilots as at dawn. No incidents were reported.
7 March 18:00	Fl/Lt W.T.H. Gill DFC, and Fl/Sgts D.R. Beard DFM, D. J. Green, and J. Rawson made a layer patrol to the East of Tripoli without sighting any e/a.
8 March 05:15	At dawn 4 a/c piloted by F/O J.N. Fairbairn, P/O D.G. Gadd, Fl/Sgt D.J. Green, and Fl/ Sgt J. Rawson patrolled to the East and West of Tripoli without incident.
18:00–19:25	A further layer patrol East of Tripoli was made by Fl/Lt W.T.H. Gill DFC, F/O J.H. Fairbairn, P/O D. Gadd, and Fl/Sgt D.J. Beard DFM. No e/a were seen.
9 March 05:00	Convoy protection patrol by two sections was carried out by Fl/Lt W.T.H. Gill DFC, P/O D. Gadd, Fl/Sgts D.J. Green and J. Rawson.
07:10	No e/a activity was observed.
10 March 17:55 El Assa and Castel Benito	The layer patrol East of Tripoli was made by F/O J.H. Fairbairn and Fl/Sgts D.R. Beard DFM, J. Rawson, and D.J. Green. No e/a were seen.
11 March 05:15-06:45	Fl/Lt W T H. Gill DFC, F/O J.II. Fairbairn, P/O D. Gadd and Fl/Sgt D.J. Green patrolled East and West of Tripoli without incident.
17:55-19:40	No e/a were observed during the layer patrol East of Tripoli made by Fl/Lt W.T.H. Gill DFC, P/O D. Gadd, Fl/Sgt D.R. Beard DFM, and Fl/Sgt J. Rawson.

12 March 05:30-07:00 18:00-19:40	F/O J.H. Fairbairn, Fl/Sgt D.R. Beard DFM, Fl/Sgt J. Rawson, and Fl/Sgt D.J. Green took part in a dawn patrol East and West of Tripoli. No enemy activity was reported. 4 a/c piloted by Fl/Lt W.T.H. Gill DFC, P/O D. Gadd, Fl/Sgt J. Rawson, and Fl/Sgt D.J. Green, made a layer patrol to the East of Tripoli at Dusk, and patrols to the
13 March 05:00–06:40 18:00 - 19:30	East and West of Tripoli at dawn without seeing any e/a. A convoy protection patrol was carried out by F/L J.H. Fairbairn, Fl/Sgt E.L. Bennett, Fl/Sgt J. Rawson, and Fl/Sgt D.J. Green without incident.
13 & 14 March	From the 6th to the night 13th/14th instant, no operations were carried out from El Assa.
14 March El Assa 19:55-21:55	Today the a/c at Castel Benito returned to the Squadron. Fl/Sgt R.D. Marsh made an armed reconnaissance of the Mareth–Gabès Road saw only 4 single MTs moving North. Visibility was good.
15 March 19:55-21:55	Sq/Ldr R.V. Ellis DFM went off on a reconnaissance of the Mareth–Gabès Road but saw nothing. At the same time, 2 a/c piloted by Fl/Sgt G.J.E. Hiltz and Sgt D.H. Thomas, which were airborne on night tests were told to investigate flares dropping to the Northwest of base. Upon investigation, flares were found to be near Mareth Line and though one pilot reported seeing four bomb bursts, no e/a were seen.
16 & 17 March 18:55-01:15 El Assa	During these times, 9 a/c made intruder patrols in the Gabès area. P/O Phillips and P/O R. Plenderleith took off together but though vectored on two occasions by Commander, saw no e/a. P/O D. Gadd and Fl/Sgt J. Rawson were the next two off and did similar patrols at 6,000 and 10,000 feet. One vector was received but with no results. Fl/Sgt C.F. Ambrose DFV, and F/O G.P. Leggett relieved as the next patrol and received vectors without seeing any e/a. The three remaining patrols were made by Fl/Lt W.T.H. Gill DFC, Sgt D.H. Thomas, and F/O J.H. Fairbairn. Fl/Lt W.T.H. Gill DFC had a visual of a Ju.88 at 3,000 feet over Djerba Island but lost sight before contact could be made. As he was approaching Gabès the flarepath at Gabès West came on and upon investigation he received accurate fire from both heavy and light Ack-Ack gun fire. During all these patrols much artillery fire was seen near the Mareth Line.

16 & 17 March [continued] 19:15-21:35	Whilst the intruders were in progress, Sq/Ldr R.V. Ellis DFM, and Fl/Sgt D.R. Beard DFM, made a patrol over the Mareth area under control of Commander. One unidentified twin-engine a/c was seen but could not be contacted. Several bombs were seen to burst West of Médenine and flares were also being dropped.
17 & 18 March 19:05-22:05	To-night's operations were curtailed by bad weather. 4 a/c piloted by Fl/Lt C.F. Ambrose DFC, F/O G.P. Leggett, F/O H.C. Charlesworth, and Fl/Sgt F. Davies went out as intruder patrols over Sfax but were recalled by the controller. No e/a were seen.
19:30	Sq/Ldr R.V. Ellis DFM made a weather reconnaissance of the Mareth area, he reported bad conditions for bombers.
20:15-05:00	4 a/c were at readiness at Nefatia during the night and one of the pilot's F/O R.J.D. Henderson did a dawn weather reconnaissance.
06:20	Weather was not good but likely to improve.
18 & 19 March 18:05-19:10	4 a/c at readiness at Nefatia and two a/c at base were not scrambled. Three weather reconnaissance's were made. The first by F/O R.J.D. Henderson; rain locally and thick cloud up to 7,000 feet West of Médenine.
06:00-07:20	W/O Hewitt made a dawn reconnaissance in the Mareth area and reported similar conditions with strong Northly winds.
20:00-21:00	P/O R. Chandler also went over the Mareth area and made similar observations.
19 & 20 March 18:35-20:10 El Assa	Sq/Ldr R.V. Ellis DFM reported local storms in the Mareth area moving Eastwards.
20:50-22:50	A further reconnaissance was made by P/O R. Plenderleith, very high cloud being observed, otherwise clear over Mareth. In the Gabès and Toujane area cloud at 8-10,000 feet with a thin layer at 5,000 feet.
05:00-06:15	P/O R. Plenderleith carried out a further weather reconnaissance of the Mareth Line reported no cloud and very slight mist.
20 & 21 March 19:55-22:30 Nefatia South	Just before dusk 13 /c took off for Nefatia South for night operations from the landing ground. Fl/Lt W.T.H. Gill DFC, and F/O R.J.D. Henderson went off on intruder patrol over Sfax. Both saw several RED and GREEN Verey lights West of Sfax, and F/O R.J.D. Henderson damaged a Ju.88, which

20 & 21 March 19:55-22:30 Nefatia South	was approaching from the Southwest when he made a quarter attack on the port side from ranges of 300 and 100 yards, scoring strikes on port main plane. At his second attempt from 100 yards his cannons jammed but he saw a marked glow from the enemy's port engine.
19:45-20:15	F/O H.C. Charlesworth made a weather reconnaissance of the Mareth area reporting no cloud and fair visibility over land and 8/10 cloud at 7,000 feet out to sea.
20:30-22:05	Fl/Sgt D.R. Beard DFC, was scrambled to investigate flares to the North but saw no e/a.
21:30-22:45	F/O J.H. Fairbairn made a reconnaissance of the Gabès – Marta track and saw only a few MTs parked in the South, on returning to base he investigated flares to the North of base and had a visual of an e/a going rapidly out to sea. He could not make contact.
21:50-22:50	P/O R.H. Phillips was scrambled to investigate more flares but returned to base without success.
22:05-23:45	Sgt D.H. Thomas was also scrambled North of Base without success
21 March Nefatia South	In the morning the ground personnel moved to Nefatia and the rest of the Squadron, two of whom had been at readiness, and also included two new pilots, Fl/SGT J.F. Farrell, and Sgt A. Cenitch joined the other a/c, which had stayed at Nefatia. A detachment of 821 Squadron, F.A.A., comprising 3-Albacores have been temporarily adapted for victualling and night flying aids.
21 & 22 March 19:55-21:45	Fl/Lt W.T.H. Gill DFC made a weather reconnaissance of the Mareth area for the information of bombers.
19:15-o1:25	During this period Fl/Sgt J. Rawson, Fl/Sgt E.L. Bennett, F/O G.P. Leggett, Fl/Lt C.F. Ambrose DFC, Fl/Sgt D.J. Green, and Fl/Sgt F. Davies, were out on patrol in the Mareth area. No enemy air activity was reported until the last patrol, when Fl/Sgt F. Davies investigated flares to the North of Base without result. Continuing his patrol, he sighted a Ju.88, which however was going too fast to be caught. Fl/Sgt D.J. Green in addition to patrolling, was ordered to make a reconnaissance of the Mareth-Gabès and Marta-Gabès Road. Slight traffic was seen and small group of parked MTs about 150 vehicles in all respectively on each road.

21 & 22 March [continued] 19:50-04:30	Intruder patrols over Sfax were made by W/O N.F. Hewett, Sq/Ldr R.V. Ellis DFM, Fl/Sgt G.J.E. Hiltz, Fl/Sgt R.D. Marsh, and P/O R.H. Phillips without results. Fl/Sgt J.F. Farrell also took off but returned early with engine trouble.
01:40-03:15	F/O H.C. Charlesworth was scrambled over Bou Grara and later investigated strafing and bombing near Médenine but saw no e/a. Heavy rain over base during the last two hours of operations made landing hazardous, but all a/c returned safely.
22 & 23 March 19:15-04:45	12 a/c piloted by F/O G.P. Leggett, P/O D. Gadd, Sgt D.H. Thomas, Sq/Ldr R.V. Ellis DFM, Fl/Sgt D.R. Beard DFM, F/O H.C. Charlesworth, Fl/Sgt F. Davies, F/O R.J.D. Henderson, Fl/Lt W.T.H. Gill DFC, P/O R. Plenderleith, Sgt A. Cenitch and Fl/Lt C.F. Ambrose DFC, patrolled El Hamma and the coastal area between Gabès and Mareth. Visuals of 4 e/a were obtained including 2 – Ju.88's, one of which was hit in a one second burst by F/O R.J.D. Henderson. The pilots were instructed to strafe suitable targets and about 35 MTs in small groups were accordingly attacked, but without observed results.
20:00-21:00	Fl/Sgt R.D. Marsh was scrambled after e/a bombing and strafing West of Mareth but made no contact.
23 & 24 March 18:55-05:45 Nefatia South	A continuous patrol was kept up by 13 a/c over the Mareth area. Pilots were Fl/Sgt J. Rawson, Fl/Sgt G.J.E. Hiltz, Fl/Sgt D.J. Green, Fl/Sgt R.D. Marsh, Fl/Sgt F Davies, W/O N.F. Hewitt, Sq/Ldr R.V. Ellis DFM, P/O R. Plenderleith, F/O H.C. Charlesworth, Fl/Sgt E.L. Bennett, P/O R. Chandler, Fl/Sgt J.F. Farrell, and P/O R.H. Phillips. Flares and bombs were dropped over Médenine but only visual was obtained, without result. No road movements were seen. A few parked MTs were strafed, and several attempts were made to extinguish a navigation beacon West of Toujane without success. Fl/Sgt J.F. Farrell had a force landing but came down safely near Bou Grara and was reported safe at 244 Wing.
20:30-21:25	Sgt D.H. Thomas was scrambled to investigate flares near Médenine and received vectors from 211 Group without avail.
05:55	Fl/Lt W.T.H. Gill DFC, and F/O R.J.D. Henderson took off together in search of Fl/Sgt J.F. Farrell whose R/T had apparently broken down between Mareth and Gabès. No success but all ended happily.

24 & 25 March 20:55-05:15	Night patrols over the front-line area were made by F/O R.J.D. Henderson, F/O J.H. Fairbairn, F/O R. Plenderleith, Fl/Sgt G.J.E. Hiltz, Fl/Lt W.T.H. Gill DFC, F/O G.P. Leggett, Sgt A. Cenitch and Fl/Sgt E.L. Bennett. Flares were seen at Médenine, Foum Tathouine and to the South of El Hamma. One Ju.88 was seen but lost sight of. The Toujane beacon was once more unsuccessfully strafed.
21:00	Intruder patrols over Sfax made by P/O R. Chandler, Sq/Ldr R.V. Ellis DFM, Fl/Ly G.F. Ambrose DFC, P/O D, Gadd, Fl/Sgt R.D. Marsh, Fl/Sgt D.J. Green, and P/O R.H. Phillips met with some success. P/O R. Chandler, after being fired at by a Ju.88 got in a couple of bursts at short range and blew off half of the starboard wing. One Ju.88 destroyed.
04:15-04:55	P/O R. Plenderleith took after an e/a in the vicinity of base but was unable to make contact.
25 & 26 March 22:15-04:45	Nothing was seen during this period when 6 a/c did intruder patrols over Sfax. Pilots were Sgt A. Cenitch, P/O R.H. Phillips, F/C H.C. Charlesworth, W/O N.F. Hewitt, Fl/Sgt J.F. Farrell, and Sgt D.H. Thomas. The last named returned early because of bad weather.
22:50-05:25	Line interception patrols were carried out by Fl/Lt G.P. Ambrose DFC, Fl/Sgt D.R. Beard DFM, P/O D. Gadd, F/O J.H. Fairbairn, P/O R. Chandler. No enemy air activity was seen.
00:15-02:10	P/O D. Gadd strafed the Toujane beacon without result. Sq/Ldr R.V. Ellis DFM took off with 2 x 250 lb bombs in an attempt to blast the beacon out of its hole, but after they exploded, the light was still winking at him.
26 & 27 March 23:30-01:35	P/O D. Gadd took off on an interception patrol of the front line but saw no sign of enemy activity. High wind and sandstorms over base made landing very difficult. Emergency patrol flares were lit, and a good approach was made ending however in a CAT II. The pilot was unhurt.
O4:25-06:30	Continued bad weather stopped further operations, till P/O B. Bretherton took off as a weather reconnaissance of the front line.
27 & 28 March	Lack of target information and bad weather stopped operations for this night.

28 & 29 March 01:20-05:20	Once again, the enemy's defensive positions have been outflanked and smashed by the 8th Army, and tonight's programme consists of 10 Strafing sorties along the Gabes-Sfax road. F/O G.P. Leggett, F/Sgt E.L. Bennett, Sgt D.H. Thomas, F/O H.C. Charlesworth, W/O N.F. Hewitt, F/C R.J.D. Henderson, Fl/Sgt F. Davies, Fl/Sgt R.D. Marsh, F/C J.H. Fairbairn, and Sgt A. Cenitch took off at five-minute intervals. Visibility was not good owing to haze but in all about 35 MTs and various dark objects on and beside the road were strafed. Cekhira was well guarded by Breda's and heavy Ack-Ack gun fire combining with searchlights. Some fire was also encountered at Gabès.
29 & 30 March	The moon was blacked out by heavy rain clouds. Sq/Ldr R.V. Ellis DFM went up but found generally bad weather conditions spreading from the West.
04:40	Operations were cancelled until 04:40 hours when Fl/Sgt D.J. Green made a weather reconnaissance along the coast to Gabès. Rain with low cloud base was encountered over the sea, with slightly better conditions inland.
30 & 31 March 03:30-06:00	Very little traffic was found to strafe on the Sfax-Cekhira road by P/O R. Chandler, Fl/Lt W.T.H. Gill DFC, and Fl/Sgt J. Rawson, 18 MTs in all were attacked and strikes were seen on one vehicle towing a gun. Some tentage was also strafed near Graiba.
04:30-05:40	Fl/Sgt C.F. Ambrose DFC made a weather reconnaissance of the Sfax area reporting 5-7/10ths cloud at 4-6,000 feet. Visibility was fair with ground base.
06:40-08:00	Search for a Wellington ditched in the Zarzis area was made by Fl/Lt W.T.H. Gill DFC, P/O B. Bretherton, and F/O H.C. Charlesworth. The a/c was seen badly broken up on the beach about 11/2 miles North of Zarzis.
31 March & 1 April 21:00-22:45	P/O J. McGill DFC, who has just returned to the Squadron after a period of night instructing at Misurata made a short strafing flight to the coast road near Meharas without visible success.
04:05-05:10	A newcomer to the Squadron, Sgt D. Ross set out on a weather reconnaissance of the Sfax area reported visibility excellent and no cloud.

Note: For daily pilot records of flight operations carried out by 'A' Flight of 73 Squadron refer to AIR 27/632/6. These records detail the a/c number, the pilot's name and the sortie carried out.

AIR 27/632/7 & AIR 27/632/8 Pilot Ops Report April 1943	
1 & 2 April Nefatia South	There were no operations today.
2 & 3 April	No operations to report. 1 e/a intruder in vicinity of base at dawn.
3 & 4 April 04:55-06:15	Fl/Sgt D. Beard DFM went up on local patrol to forestall a repetition of previous morning, but there was no e/a activity.
4 & 5 April 17:15-18:30	6 a/c piloted by Fl/Lt W.T.H. Gill DFC, F/O J.H. Fairbairn, F/O G.P. Leggett, P/O R. Chandler, P/O R.H. Phillips and P/O E.T. Bennett landed at El-Hamma in preparation for front-line protection patrols but were forced to leave when the enemy shelled the landing ground.
18:45-20:10	A further patrol of the Gabès area was scheduled, but Sq/Ldr R.V. Ellis DFM, F/O J.R.D Henderson, W/O N.F. Hewitt, Fl/Lt C.F. Ambrose DFC, and F/O H.C. Charlesworth, were all told to return to base before they had reached the box.
04:35-06:10	In the early morning a defensive patrol of the front line was carried out by Fl/Lt W.T.H. Gill DFC, P/O E.T. Bennett, F/O J.H. Fairbairn, F/O J.R.D. Henderson, F/O J. McGill DFC, P/O B. Bretherton, F/C G.P. Leggett, P/O R.H. Phillips, P/O R. Chandler, Fl/Lt C.F. Ambrose DFC, and Sq/Ldr R.V. Ellis DFM, without incident.
5 & 6 April 19:05-05:55 Nefatia South	25 a/c operating singly made patrols over the front-line area. Bombs were seen to burst near Oudref and visuals were obtained of 4 Ju.88's, a Heinkel III, two unidentified twin-engine and one single-engine aircraft. Fl/Lt W.T.H. Gill DFC had a burst at a twin-engine aircraft, which was dropping flares, and he registered strikes on the tailplane and fuselage before losing sight in a turn. Various minor targets were strafed on the Cekhira-Sfax road and one uncountable light in the air was chased by F/O J. McGill DFC, from 3,000 to 12,000 feet. Pilots on patrol were P/O R.D. Marsh, Fl/Sgt J. Rawson, Sgt W.J. MyGind, Fl/Lt P.H.V, Wells, Sgt D.H. Thomas, Sgt A. Cenitch, P/O R.H. Phillips, F/O J. McGill DFC, Fl/Sgt D.J. Green, Sgt T.H. Ross, F/O J.H. Fairbairn, F/O H.C. Charlesworth, Fl/Sgt D.R. Beard DFM, P/O E.T. Bennett, Fl/Sgt G.J. Hiltz, F/O J.R.D. Henderson, P/O B. Bretherton, and Fl/Lt W.T.H. Gill DFC, Fl/Sgt F. Davies, P/O D. Gadd. Two sorties were made by F/O H.C. Charlesworth, Sgt D.J. Thomas, and Sgt W.J. MyGind.

6 & 7 April 18:35-06:05	Continuous patrol of the front-line – Gabès area was carried out by 17 a/c operating singly. Four JU.88's and four unidentified twin engine aircraft were seen. One Ju.88 was attacked and destroyed by F/O J.R.D. Henderson a few miles Northeast of Gabès. On patrol were, P/O R. Chandler, P/O R.D. Marsh, Fl/Sgt D.J. Green, Sgt T.H. Ross, P/O E.T. Bennett, W/O N.F. Hewitt, P/O R.H. Phillips, F/O J.H. Fairbairn, Sq/Ldr R.V. Ellis DFM, Fl/Lt W.T.H. Gill DFC, Sgt A. Cenitch, F/O J.R.D. Henderson, F;/Sgt J. Rawson, P/O B. Bretherton, Fl/Lt C,F, Ambrose DFC, F/O J. McGill DFC, and Fl/Sgt F. Davies.
7 & 8 April 18:40-21:15 03:05-05:50	A dusk patrol of the Gabès area was made by F/O J.H.D. Henderson, P/O E.T. Bennett, F/O G.P. Leggett, Fi/Sgt G.J.E. Hiltz, Sgt D.H. Thomas and Sgt A. Cenitch. These a/c operating singly saw, in all, 16 Ju.88's and attacked 5 of them, hits being scored on 3. One light MT vehicle on the Sfax- Mahares road was also hit. Three of the pilots also were attacked by Ju.88's, but no damage was sustained. Fl/Lt C.F. Ambrose, P/O R. Chandler, Fl/Lt W.T.H. Gill DFC, F/O J.H. Fairbairn, P/O D. Gadd, P/O B. Bretherton, Sgt T.H. Ross, and Fl/Sgt D.H. Beard DFM patrolled in the Gabès area. Flares and bomb bursts were seen and visuals of 4 JU.88's were obtained. One Ju.88 was attacked and damaged.
8 April Gabes Main	Immediately after the night operations were finished and all q/c refuelled they were flown up to Gabès Main Aerodrome, the "A" party followed by road, The camp was pitched in and around the houses and between two cemeteries and the town though badly damaged was quite worth visiting with additional attraction of swimming.
8 & 9 April 19:10-20:45 Gabes Main 20:00-21:30 21:30-03:35	F/O G.P. Leggett, F/O J.R.D. Henderson, P/O R.H. Phillips, and P/O D. Gadd made a patrol of the Gabès area but there was no enemy activity. Late news of MTs on the Mahares-Sfax road, sent out Sgt T.H. Ross, F/O J. McGill DFC, W/O N.F. Hewitt, Sgt A. Cenitch, and Fl/Sgt G.J.E. Hiltz, on individual strafing sorties. The first to arrive, Sgt T.H. Ross strafed and set on fire one MT, but there were no targets to be found when the others arrived. A Breda gun and a few old lights were strafed without visible results. A patrol of the Gabès area made by Fl/Sgt J. Rawson, F/O R.C. Charlesworth, P/O J. McGill DFC, Fl/Lt W.T.H. Gill DFC, F/O P.H.V. Wells and Fl/Sgt C.J.E. Hiltz without incident.

9 & 10 April 19:05-19:55	Gabès area was patrolled by Sq/Ldr R.V. Ellis DFM, \f/C J. McGill DFC and F/O P.H.V. Wells without incident.
04;25-05;50	In the morning, Fl/Sgt D.J. Green, P/O E.T. Bennett, P/O R. Chandler and F/O G.P. Leggett patrolled Gabès but there was no enemy activity.
10 & 11 April 19:05-20:45	2 a/c piloted by F/O H.C. Charlesworth and Fl/Sgt D.R. Beard patrolled Gabes without incident.
19:00-20:40	F/O J.H. Fairbairn, P/O D. Gadd and F/O B. Bretherton, patrolled Sfax but there was no enemy activity. A light was reported South of Kerkenna Isles.
04:15-06:00	P/O R.H. Phillips and Sgt W.J. MyGind patrolled Gabès without incident.
04:10-06:15	Fl/Lt W.T.H. Gill DFC, Fl/Lt C.F. Ambrose and F/O J.R.D. Henderson patrolled Sfax. Flares were seen to the West but were too far for investigation. F/O J.R.D. Henderson did not return; wreckage of his a/c has since been found in the sea near Mahares.
11 & 12 April 18:40-21:05	W/O N.F. Hewitt and Fl/Sgt F. Davies made patrols of the Sfax and front-line area without seeing any enemy air activity.
21:20	Air to air firing was seen in the vicinity of base and Sgt T.H. Ross scrambled to investigate but no further signs of e/a were seen.
03:45-06:05	A patrol of the Sfax and Sousse area was made by P/O R. Chandler and Sgt A. Cenitch without results. "A" party with "A" Flight moved off Sfax El Maou and operated from there at night.
12 & 13 April Sfax El Maou	Sgt D.H. Thomas and P/O R.H. Phillips at dusk and Fl/Lt C.F. Ambrose DFC, F/O H.C. Charlesworth, and P/O R.D. Marsh at dawn, patrolled the Sousse area but saw no enemy air activity. "B" party and "B" Flight came up from Gabes during the day.
13 & 14 April	2 a/c made a patrol of Sousse at dusk and dawn; The pilots were P/O R.D. Marsh and Fl/Sgt C.J.E. Hiltz. Fl/Lt W.T.E. Gill DFC and F/O J.E Fairbairn nothing to report.
14 & 15 April 18:50-20:05	P/O M.W. Smyth and W/O N.F. Hewitt patrolled Sfax but had nothing to report.
18:50-00:40	P/O R. Chandler, Sgt T.H. Ross, F/O P.H.V. Wells, P/O D. Gadd, Fl/Sgt F. Davies, P/O B. Bretherton, Sgt A. Cenitch, Sq/Ldr R.V. Ellis DFM, P/O R.H. Phillips, Sgt D.H. Thomas made Intruder Patrol along the coast between Hammamet and Rass

14 & 15 April 18:50-00:40 [continued]	Mostefa. The patrols were mainly directed to finding shipping and 20 – 50 footers were seen in Hammamet harbour, a few, 4 miles North and one 15 miles East of Hammamet. All were strafed and some strikes seen. Wharf buildings at Hammamet and 20 MTs slightly inland were also strafed. Breda gun searchlights and night fighters provided opposition.
03:50-05:50	Fl/Sgt J.Rawson and Sgt W.J. Mygind patrolled the frontline for 30 miles West of Enfidaville but saw no enemy activity.
04:00-05:45	Fl/Lt C.F. Ambrose DFC, and F/O H.C. Charlesworth patrolled the coast between Hammamet and Rass Mostefa but saw no shipping.
04:35-06:05	Fl/Lt WE.T.H. Gill DFC, and P/O R.D. Marsh made a defensive patrol of Sfax without incident.
15 & 16 April 18:45-20:05	Fl/Sgt D.J. Green and Sgt D.H. Thomas made a convoy protection patrol Southeast of Mahdia. No enemy activity.
19:25-21:55	Fl/Sgt D.R. Beard DFM, and P/O M.W. Smyth on patrol in the Hammamet – Rass Mamoura area was attacked by Ju.88 which, however, was evaded. Then they encountered a formation of 7 Ju,52s, two of which they destroyed with one probable and one damaged. P/O R.D. Marsh and P/O E.T. Bennett also patrolled in the same area without result.
21:10	F/O J.H. Fairbairn and P/O R. Chandler were scrambled over base to investigate flares. One unidentified T/E a/c was seen and fired at without visible result.
20:30-22:55	Patrols in the Hammamet – Manoura area were continued by F/O G.J. McGill DFC, Fl/Lt W.T.H. Gill DFC, Fl/Sgt G.J.E. Hiltz, and P/O D. Gadd. No enemy shipping was seen but one large a/c, possibly a JU.52 was seen flying at deck level by Fl/LT W.T.H. Gill DFC and strikes were scored.
22:15-00:40	4 a/c patrolled the same area but saw no shipping. 1 a/c piloted by Fl/Lt P.H.V. Wells was attacked by a T/E a/c near Hammamet but evaded him and got in a burst without result.4 searchlights were also strafed, and much heavy and light Ack-Ack gun fire was encountered. Fl/Sgt F. Davies, P/O B. Bretherton, and Sgt A. Cenitch, were also on patrol.
00;30-01:50	Fl/Sgt D.R. Beard DFM went off on a patrol of Hammamet but returned because of bad weather.
04:15-06:05	Fl/Sgt J. Rawson patrolled over convoy in Maldia Bay and saw no enemy activity. P/O R. Chandler took off on the same duty but crashed almost immediately and was killed.

16 & 17 April 18:45-20:55	On defensive patrol of Sousse, Fl/Lt P.H.V. Wells saw no enemy activity.
19:00-04:50	During this period, 15 a/c patrolled North of Hammamet but saw no signs of enemy air activity or shipping. Four of our MTBs were seen approaching Hammamet from the Northeast. Pilots taking part were F/O H.C. Charlesworth, P/O M.W. Smyth, Sq/Ldr R.V. Ellis DFM, W/O N.F. Hewitt, Fl/Sgt F. Davies, P/O R.E. Phillips, Fl/Lt W.T.H. Gill DFC, P/O E.T. Bennett, Fl/Sgt C.J.E. Hiltz, P/O B. Bretherton, Fl/ Sgt J. Rawson, |F/\o J. McGill DFC, Fl/Sgt D.J. Breen, and P/O D. Gadd.
03:55-05:35	Sgt T.H. Ross, patrolled Sousse without incident.
17 & 18 April 18:35-20:10 Sfax El Maou	P/O M.W. Smyth, patrolled Sousse without incident.
19:15-05:35	Patrol of the coast between Hammamet and Cap Bon was made by Fl/Sgt D.R. Beard DFM, Fl/Lt P.H.V. Wells, F/O G.T. McGill DFC, Fl/Sgt D.J. Green, P/O R.H. Phillips, Sgt T.H. Ross, Fl/Sgt G.T.E. Hiltz, F/O J.H. Fairbairn, P/O R.D. Marsh, Sgt W.J. MyGind, Sgt A. Cenitch, Fl/Li C.F. Ambrose DFC, and Sgt H. Wilkinson. A flat square shaped object about 100 feet long two miles off the shore was strafed and hit. Machine gun fire was returned.
04:15-05:45	Fl/Sgt F. Davies patrolled Sousse and Fl/Sgt J. Rawson patrolled Sfax without incident.
18 & 19 April 18:45-20:50	Patrols over Sousse and Sfax by P/O E.T. Leggett and Sgt T.E. Ross respectively reported no enemy activity.
19:15	Fl/Sgt F. Davies and P/O D. Gadd were already on patrol in the Hammamet–Cap Bon area when news came through that several JU.52s had been forced down on the beaches in the vicinity of Cap Bon. Despite bad weather which forced Sgt A. Cenitch and P/O R.D. Marsh to turn back, Sgt T.E. Ross and Sgt H. Wilkinson both found some targets. Three Ju.52s were set on fire and two others were strafed, strikes being seen on one. F/O J.H. Fairbairn was also forced to return, visibility being practically NIL.
04:30-06:15	W/O N.F. Hewitt patrolled Sousse without incident.
19 & 20 April 20:00-05:25 Alem	In the morning the squadron moved up to Alem near Kairouan.

19 & 20 April 20:00-05:25 Alem [continued]	6 a/c visited the Cap Bon area on strafing and anti-shipping patrols. Two Ju.52s on the beach were strafed, on blew up and many strikes were seen on the other one. A barge was set on fire at the Isle Zemira, and a searchlight was strafed at Hammamet. Pilots taking part were Fl/Sgt J. Rawson Sgt D.H. Thomas, Fl/Sgt D.J. Green, Fl/Lt P.H.V. Wells, F/O H.C. Charlesworth, and Fl/Lt C.F. Ambrose DFC.
22:40-00:30	Fl/Sgt G.J.E. Hiltz was scrambled and ordered to patrol East of Sousse and the front line. No e/a were seen.
01:45-02:40	P/O M.W. Smyth scrambled and saw bombs drop 30 miles Southeast of base but had no visual.
20 & 21 April 22:30-00:10 Monastir	Sgt W.J. MyGind was also scrambled over the El Djem area without result. Bombs were dropped before he arrived on patrol.
00:15	Readiness only was carried out by the squadron as weather conditions were unsuitable for operational intruders. Fl/Sgt R.D. Marsh was scrambled after bandits approaching Gouerine but saw no signs of e/a.
21 April	The whole Squadron moved to MONASTIR.
21 & 22 April 19:25-20:00 Monastir	Fl/Sgt D.J. Green and Fl/Sgt F. Davies started on an intruder patrol of the Cap Bon area but returned early as weather unfit. Rain and low cloud cancelled all other intruders.
23:45-00:10	W/O N.F. Hewitt made a further attempt, but conditions were the same.
23:15	F/O J. McGill DFC was scrambled to intercept hostiles approaching from the Northeast.
04:20	Received several vectors and hostiles jettisoned bombs two miles Southeast of Monastir. F/C J.H. Fairbairn was scrambled with Fl/Sgt J. Rawson. They patrolled Sousse, Monastir and Gouerine without result. The enemy appeared to be bombing from cloud base of 10 – 11,000 feet. P/O R.H. Phillips, P/O B. Bretherton and P/O J. McGill DFC were all scrambled in turn to patrol the same area. One visual of a Ju.88 was obtained but contact could not be made.
03:40 04:30	Sgt W.J. MyGind made a weather reconnaissance of the coast up to Korba for information of day fighter-bombers.
22 & 23 April 21:30-22:15	Sgt T.H. Ross on intruder to Cap Bon returned early as conditions bad.

22 & 23 April Monastir 21:50-01:15	5 a/c were scrambled during this period without success. One visual was obtained but contact and identification could not be made. The pilots were Fl/Lt P.H.V. Wells, P/O D, Gadd, Fl/Lt W.T.H. Gill DFC, Fl/Sgt G.J.E. Hiltz, and P/O M.W. Smyth.
03:50-05:10	Sgt H. Wilkinson made a weather reconnaissance of the coast as far as Cap Bon.
23 & 24 April 22:45-04:00 Monastir	Patrols in the Cap Bon area were carried by P/O E.T. Leggett, P/O B. Bretherton, Sgt W.J. MyGind, F/O H.C. Charlesworth, Sgt T.H. Ross and W/O N.F. Hewitt without incident. Quayside buildings in Kelibia were strafed and a revolving beacon seen at Hammamet.
23:45-03{10	Sq/Ldr R.V. Ellis DFM, P/O R.D. Marsh, Fl/Sgt D.R. Beard DFM, Sgt D.H. Thomas, and Sgt A. Cenitch were off to patrol North of Tunis. Weather unsuitable. Ack-Ack gun fire was encountered by Sgt A. Cenitch who returned with a holed elevator.
24 & 25 April 00:05-00:20 Monastir	F/O G.J. McGill DFC and Fl/Sgt D.J. Green returned from patrol of Tunis as weather was unsuitable. A weather test was made by Fl/Sgt J. Rawson at 03:00 hours but cloud still 10/10ths at 1,000 feet.
25 & 26 April Monastir	There were no operations.
26 & 27 April 01:55-04:45 Monastir	8 a/c taking off two at a time patrolled Cap Bon area. P/O R. Plenderleith and Sgt H. Wilkinson, Sgt W.J. MyGind and Sgt J.L. Horn, Sgt D.H. Thomas and Fl/Sgt F. Davies, Fl/Sgt D.R. Beard DFM and Sgt E.M. Karatau took part. No aircraft or shipping was seen. One beacon 14 miles inland from Hammamet was strafed.
27 & 28 April 02:15-02:45	Shortly after take-off on a patrol to Cap Bon Sgt A. Cenitch reported weather unfit for flying. Visibility almost nil due to low clouds, mist, and haze. Further operations were cancelled.
28 & 29 April	Bad weather cancelled operations for tonight.
29 & 30 April	Programme of operations again cancelled because of weather.
30 April & 1 May	No operations again tonight.

Note: For daily pilot records of flight operations carried out by 'A' Flight of 73 Squadron refer to AIR 27/632/8. These records detail the a/c number, the pilot's name and the sortie carried out.

AIR 27/632/9 (1) & AIR 27/632/10 (1) Pilot Ops Report May 1943	
1 & 2 May 03:45-04:15 Monastir	Sgt A. Cenitch took off to patrol the Cap Bon area but turned back as the weather was unfavourable. Low cloud and fog made visibility practically nil.
2 & 3 May 00:35-00:45 Monastir	Fl/Sgt D.J. Green went up on a weather reconnaissance and reported visibility poor due to thick mist.
3 & 4 May Monastir	There were no operations.
4 & 5 May 20:10-21:20 Monastir	Sgt A. Cenitch and Sgt E.M. Karatau patrolled coast to Cap Bon on anti-shipping and Ju.52 look out but saw nothing.
5 & 6 May 20:00-21:35 Monastir	P/O R.H. Phillips and Sgt T.H. Ross on anti-shipping patrol up to Cap Bon had nothing to report whilst on patrol. Sgt T.H. Ross strafed a searchlight at Kabeul and a car and light at Hammamet.
6 May Monastir	It has been reported that Fl/Sgt J.D.A. Wright and Fl/Sgt D.M. Logan, reported missing on dawn reconnaissance of the 3rd and 5th March respectively, are now prisoners of war.
6 & 7 May 01:15-03:25 Monastir	6 a/c were ordered to patrol Hammamet to Cap Bon. Visibility was very poor, however because of low cloud and haze nothing was seen by the pilots. W/O N.P. Hewitt had engine trouble; P/O R. Plenderleith and Fl/Sgt J. Rawson returned early, and Sgt J.L. Horn, Fl/Sgt D.J. Green and Sgt H. Wilkinson completed their patrols.
7 & 8 May 19:50-20:10 Monastir 03:05-05:00	F/O J. McGill DFC, and Sgt T.H. Ross started off to patrol Cap Bon but returned almost immediately as there was heavy rain and low cloud spreading North. Four patrols were made of the Cap Bon area where the weather was clearer though bumpy. Flare paths were seen at Ras El Melah and El Haguaria and strafed without visible result. Later an unidentified a/c was attacked when flying East from Cap Bon and strikes were scored, return fire was made by the rear gunner which Sgt W.J. Mygind evaded. The other pilots on patrol were Fl/Lt P.H.V. Wells, Fl/Lt C.F. Ambrose DFC, and Fl/Sgt F. Davies.
8 & 9 May 19:45 Monastir	22 a/c piloted by W/O W.F. Hewitt, F/O G.J. McGill DFC, F/O J.H. Fairbairn, Sgt D.H. Thomas, Sq/Ldr R.V. Ellis DFM, Fl/Sgt F. Davies, Fl/Lt W.T.H. Gill DFC, P/O R.H. Phillips, Sgt T.C. Stonehouse, P/O B.T. Bennett, Sgt E.M. Karatau,

	Sgt A. Cenitch, P/O R. Plenderleith, Sgt H. Wilkinson, Sgt T.H. Ross, P/O M.W. Smyth, Sgt J.L. Horn, Fl/Sgt J. Rawson, Fl/Sgt D.J. Green, F/O H.C. Charlesworth, Sgt D.E. Thomas (2nd time) and Fl/Lt F.H.V. Wells made patrols of the Cap Bon area. Flare paths were on at Menzel Temime and El Haouaria and, in all, 10 e/a were seen. Sgt A. Cenitch chased a three-engine a/c out to sea from Ras El Melah and after four short bursts it crashed into the sea. F/O J.H. Fairbairn attacked 2 e/a which were attempting to land at El Haouaria and scored strikes on one. P/OR.H. Phillips also scored strikes on an e/a landing at the same place, whilst Fl/Sgt D.J. Green hit a large three-engine e/a landing at Menzel Temime. Other targets were strafed including ten small boats off Sidi El Daoud and 4 MTs on the Soliman - Cap Bon Road.
9 & 10 May 19:30-05:00 Monastir	Patrols of the Cap Bon area were made by Fl/Sgt G.J.E. Hiltz, Fl/Sgt D.R. Beard DFM, P/O B. Bretherton, Fl/Lt P.H.V. Wells, P/O M.W. Smyth, P/O R.H. Phillips, Sgt A. Cenitch, Sgt D.H. Thomas, Fl/Sgt D.J. Green, W/O N.F. Hewitt, Sgt T.H. Ross, Sgt W.J. MyGind, Sgt E.M. Karatau, Sgt T.C. Stonehouse, Sgt J.L. Horn, Fl/Sgt F. Davies, Fl/Lt C.F. Ambrose DFC, F/O J.H. Fairbairn. 3 e/a Ju.52s and one unidentified aircraft were seen. Fl/Sgt D.R. Beard destroyed one e/a at Menzel Temime and one approaching Kelibia where flare paths were alight, both burned on the ground. Fl/Sgt D.J. Green gave a burst at long range to s Ju.52 landing at Menzel Temime but saw no results. Various ground targets were strafed, 3 MTs being hit and another caught fire; one H.A.A. gun was silenced and 6 boats near Kelibia were damaged.
10 & 11 May 19:45-04:30 Monastir	In all 20 patrols were made of the Cap Bon area by the following pilots: - F/O R.D. Marsh, Fl/Lt C.F. Ambrose DFC, Sgt E.M. Karatau, F/O N.T. Bennett, Sgt N. Wilkinson, Fl/Lt W.T.H. Gill DFC, F/O R. Plenderleith, Sgt J.L. Horn, Sgt W.J. Millard, Sgt T.C. Stonehouse, P/O M.W. Smyth, Fl/Sgt G.J.H. Hiltz, F/O J.M. Fairbairn, F/O R. Bretherton, Fl/Sgt D.R. Beard DFM, W/O H.F. Hewitt, P/O R.H. Phillips, F/O J. McGill DFC, Fl/Lt P.H.V. Wells and Fl/Sgt D.J. Green. One Ju.52 was attacked and destroyed as it came into land at El Haouarla by P/O B. Bretherton at Menzel Temime, W/O H.F. Hewitt attacked a Ju.52 making its final approach; he claims a probable. Later, the same pilot scored a strike on a Ju.52 landing at Kelibia. Fl/Lt W.T.H. ill DFC, added to the nights bag when he saw several strikes on a Ju.52 at deck level. Many ground targets were strafed, 6 MTs being hit and

10 & 11 May 19:45-04:30 Monastir [continued]	4 of them caught fire. Another fire was started at Kelibia L.G. and the jetty at the village was strafed. Whilst going out on patrol, several of the pilots unloaded leaflets in the battle area and along the peninsula.
11 & 12 May 19:50-04:45	All enemy attempts to escape by air from the Cap Bon peninsula seem to have been abandoned. Neither e/a nor flare paths were seen when 17 Hurricanes patrolled in the area from dusk to dawn. Many fires were seen, however, between Korba and Menzel Temime. The pilots were Sgt A. Cenitch, P/O R.H. Phillips, P/O R. Plenderleith, Sgt T.H. Ross, W/O N.F. Hewitt, Fl/Lt W.T.H. Gill DFC, Fl/Sgt C.J.E. Hiltz, Sgt J.L. Horn, F/O J. McGill DFC, Fl/Lt P.H.V. Wells, P/O M.W. Smyth, P/O E.T. Bennett, P/O B. Bretherton, Sgt T.C. Stonehouse, Sgt E.M. Karatau and F/O J.H. Fairbairn.
12 May	**All organised resistance in Tunisia came to a finish today and for a short spell, operations continued until the 16th of this month.**
13 May	**On this day, 13 May 1943, the day on which the Axis Forces in North Africa surrendered.** **However, the fighting in Tunisia would continue for some time after, due to isolated groups of Axis Forces being unaware that a surrender had taken place.**
14 May	**No operations carried out.**
15 May	**No operations carried out.**
16 May	**No operations were carried out during the daytime.**
16 & 17 May 19:45 Monastir	9 a/c were ordered to patrol Pantelleria Island but bad weather conditions between base and target resulted in 5 a/c either being recalled or turning back. Two searchlights were in action along the coast and one pilot strafed a lighthouse. Otherwise, nothing was seen except low cloud and haze. Those taking part were F/O J. McGill DFC, P/O R.H. Phillips, Sq/Ldr R.V. Ellis DFM, Sgt A. Cenitch, P/O R. Plenderleith, Fl/Sgt F. Davies, Sgt J.L. Horn, Fl/Lt P.H.V. Wells and Fl/Lt C.F. Ambrose DFC.
17 May	F/O H.W. Coussens has just returned to the Squadron for his second tour of duty.
18 May	**No recorded daily operations detailed. Refer to 17 to 30 May records below.**
19 May	**No recorded daily operations detailed. Refer to 17 to 30 May records below.**
20 May	**No recorded daily operations detailed. Refer to 17 to 30 May records below.**

21 May	Sq/Ldr R.V. Ellis DFM announced today that the Squadron will shortly be re-equipped with SPITFIRES.
22 May	The Fleet Air Arm detachment of 821 Squadron who had moved up with us from Nefattia were today ordered back to MALTA; regrets were mutual.
17 to 30 May	During this period there were no operational flights. On the 29th the Squadron moved to La Seballa No. 2 Landing Ground, 30 kilometres West of TUNIS. 12 new pilots have joined the Squadron, six of whom are new night operational having undergone a night flying instructional courses at Zuara. Those operational are P/O G.A. Martin, Fl/Sgt J.C. McCall, Fl/Sgt E.F. Bramley, Sgt F.J. Bailey, Sgt C.J.A. Edwards and Sgt P.H. Cashen.
31 May–1 June La Seballa No. 2 LG.	Night operations recommenced with intruder patrols over Pantelleria lasting all night. The main object was to keep the defences on the "qui vive" so that no respite be given either night or day. No targets were strafed but six pilots emptied their cannons mainly in the harbour area. P/O B. Bretherton was first over the island followed by Sgt W.J. MyGind, Sgt J.L. Horn, Sgt H. Wilkinson, P/O G.A. Martin and Sgt A. Cenitch. 2 a/c piloted by P/O M.W. Smyth and P/O E.T. Bennett returned to base without reaching the island as they had trouble with their instruments. Considerable Ack-Ack gun fire opposition was met with at first, particularly as our bombers were also on the job.

Note:
For daily pilot records of flight operations carried out by 'A' Flight of 73 Squadron refer to AIR 27/632/10 (1). These records detail the a/c number, the pilot's name and the sortie carried out.

With the Axis forces surrendering on the 13 May 1943, it is necessary to complete the history of RAF 73 Squadron by detailing their further operations from the 14 May 1943 in North Africa, then onto the Sicilian campaign 9 July to 17 August 1943 (Operation Husky). Refer to Chapter 16 of this book.

However, RAF 73 Squadron AIRs from September through to December 1943 are not included as the AIRs for this period of time. Refer to the Invasion of Italy from September to October 1943 (Operation Avalanche) and beyond. Details of the Allied assault and landings are further covered. Refer to Chapter 16 of this book.

It is worth noting that RAF 73 Squadron was just one of many Allied squadrons that carried out the operations throughout the Mediterranean area to remove the German and Italian Axis forces to ensure that their forces were depleted ahead of the main battles in Europe being planned: Operation Overlord (Battle for Normandy, France), 6 June 1944 'D-Day' to 30 August 1944.

AIR 27/632/11 (1) & AIR 27/632/12 Pilot Ops Report June 1943	
1 & 2 June La Sebala [No. 2 LG]	Early on the morning of the 1st, a ground party set off for an advanced landing ground in the vicinity of Cap Bon and were ready by dusk to receive 11 a/c flown up from base.
20:30-22:10	Four of the a/c were held at readiness during the night whilst four were piloted by Sq/Ldr R.V. Ellis DFM, Fl/Lt F.H.V. Wells, P/O R. Plenderleith, and P/O R.D. Marsh patrolled over a convoy of 4 Warships 25 miles South of Pantelleria. There was no incident on patrol but in landing Fl/Lt F.H.V. Wells had a burst tyre rendering the a/c Cat. II and himself slightly damaged by a cut over the eye.
04:10-06:00	Sgt F.J. Bailey and Sgt T.C. Stonehouse made individual intruder raids over Pantelleria continuing the nerve breaking policy. They both strafed at random in the harbour area. The a/c returned to base by 07:00 hours.
2 & 3 June	Out of 12 a/c that flew up to Cap Bon for night operations only, 2 a/c went up on weather tests. P/O E.T. Bennett took off at 21:00 hours and reported visibility was nil with heavy ground haze. Conditions were even worse at midnight when P/O R.H. Phillips made another short test. At dawn the a/c returned to La Sebala.
3 & 4 June	The weather was still a bit doubtful and only 7 a/c went up to Cap Bon in the evening. At 21:30 Sgt H. Wilkinson, on weather test, reported heavy low cloud below1,000 feet with haze and storms out to sea. By 04:00 hours the weather had cleared, and P/O G.A. Martin with Fl/Sgt D.J. Green went on intruder patrol over Pantelleria strafing in the harbour area and receiving some light Ack/Ack.
4 & 5 June	Many of the long desert services ground personnel have recently left the Squadron, some of them bund for South Africa, others for the Delta and Palestine. One who was with the Squadron before it went to France, namely F/O CG Reed had just received a commission and left today for H.Q.M.E.

5 & 6 June 04:20-06:05	At dawn Sgt A. Cenitch and Sgt F.J. Bailey were on patrol over Pantelleria. The harbour area was strafed without visible result and some light Ack/Ack was received.
6 & 7 June 04:20-06:05	Bad weather again restricted night operations until dawn when with poor visibility, patrols were made over Pantelleria by Fl/Sgt E.F. Bramley and Sgt C.J.A. Edwards. Buildings and fires near the harbour were strafed, also buildings in the Southeast of the island.
7 & 8 June 22:10-05:30	5 a/c went on patrol over Pantelleria despite generally bad weather when visibility was bad due to haze. Fl/Sgt D.J. Green, Sgt H. Wilkinson, Sgt T.C. Stonehouse, P/O D. Gadd, all arrived over target and strafed various points. Fl/Sgt G.J.E. Hiltz had to return to base early.
8 & 9 June 21:15-23:40 04:05-06:10	Fl/Lt G.P. Leggett Fl/Sgt E.F. Bramley, P/O E.T. Bennett and Fl/Sgt F.J. Davies strafed Pantelleria and reported the flare being on, but no e/a taking off. Sgt E.M. Karatau patrolled Pantelleria and on return to Cap Bon, which is in use as an advanced Landing Ground, saw another aircraft which he presumed hostile above him, so he took evading action in cloud and finally landed at Cap Bon LG.
9 & 10 June 20:50-22:15 21:30-22:10 23:45-01:00	Operating from our advanced landing ground near Cap Bon, P/O B. Bretherton, and W/O N.P. Hewitt patrolled 5 warships which were proceeding in the direction of Pantelleria Island. Fl/Sgt J.C. McCall, a new pilot who recently joined the Squadron, went up on an intruder patrol over Pantelleria Island but unfortunately had to return early owing to engine trouble. F/O H.C. Charlesworth did a similar patrol of Pantellieria strafing two fires that were already there without any opposition from ground defence. The pilots finally returned reporting weather not so good.
10 & 11 June 04:45-06:45	Fl/Lt C.F. Ambrose, F/O H.W. Coussens, P/O B. Bretherton, Fl/Sgt F. Davies, Sgt C.J.A. Edwards, Fl/Sgt D.R. Beard, Sgt W.J. MyGind and Fl/Sgt J.C. McCall patrolled a convoy off Korba on the Eastern side of the Cap Bon peninsula. No incident.

10 & 11 June [continued] 04:00-05:40	Sgt F.J. Bailey and Sgt F.H. Cashen, operated from our A.L.G. patrolled Pantelleria Island strafing the town and harbour where again there was no opposition, but a few rounds of Breda gun fire were noticed from or near the island's only landing ground. A large grass fire was also observed on the island.
00:01-01:00	Sgt T.R. Ross also patrolled and strafed various targets on the island including the quayside, town, North of the landing ground and harbour. The latter was well illuminated by flares that had been dropped earlier by other aircraft. No Ack-Ack was encountered.
22:05-22:55	Fl/Lt W.T.H. Gill carried out an intruder and weather test over the island reporting visibility, bad and haze over the sea and in the meantime the pilot strafed a target near the landing ground.
11 & 12 June 20:05-21:35	12 a/c piloted by Sq/Ldr R.V. Ellis DFM, Fl/Lt G.P. Leggett, P/O D. Gadd, F/O H.C. Charlesworth, P/O R. Plenderleith, Fl/Lt P.H.V. Wells, Fl/Sgt J. Rawson, Sgt J.L. Horn, Sgt E.M. Karatau, Sgt T.H. Ross, Sgt H. Wilkinson, and Sgt D.H. Thomas patrolled a convoy about 30 miles South-South-East of Pantelleria without incident.
05:05-06:05	The same 12 pilots as above again carried out a dawn convoy patrol 7 miles Northwest of Pantelleria but owing to the poor state of the weather – with cloud 8/10 at 1,000 feet, mist at 500 feet and visibility very poor – the majority of the pilots were unable to join up together which resulted in them doing individual patrols. No incidents.
12 & 13 June	The good news has already spread throughout the Squadron that the first two SPITFIRES have arrived this afternoon through the good effort of CO Sq/Ldr R.V. Ellis DFM.
19:00-20:30	13 a/c which included one pilot to act as duty pilot took off in the early evening to proceed to the advance landing ground to prepare for the night operations.
20:30-21:30	F/O DFC McGill, F/O R.D. Marsh, P/O B. Bretherton, P/O G.A. Martin, Sgt T.C. Stonehouse and Sgt F.J. Bailey patrolled the coast of Pantelleria but saw nothing in the way of enemy surface or aircraft. The weather on this occasion was 6-7/10 cloud at 2,000 feet with heavy ground haze.

20:40-22:00	Fl/Lt W.T.H. Gill DFC, Fl/Sgt D.R. Beard, Fl/Sgt D.J. Green, Sgt A, Cenitch, and Sgt P.H. Cashen took off to patrol a convoy off Mostefa and Kelibia areas but did not contact the convoy.
05:15-06:15	11 a/c F/O J. McGill DFC, P/O R.D. Marsh, P/O B. Bretherton, P/O G.A. Martin, Sgt T.C. Stonehouse, Sgt F.J. Bailey, Fl/Lt W.T.H. Gill DFC, Fl/Sgt D.R. Beard, Fl/Sgt D,J, Green, Sgt A. Cenitch, and Sgt P.H. Cashen carried out a dawn patrol between main land and coast and Pantelleria Island again without incident but Sgt F.J. Bailey had the bad luck of crashing on landing. Aircraft Cat. II. W/O N.F. Hewitt was unable to carry out patrols owing to breaking a tail strut on landing at Cap Bon in the early morning.
13 & 14 June	13 a/c again took off at 19:00 hours including P/O F.C. Bremner as duty pilot for the advanced Landing Ground.
20:15-21:40	Fl/Lt C.F. Ambrose, P/O M.W. Smyth, P/O R.H. Phillips, P/O E.T. Bennett, and Sgt C.J.A. Edwards patrolled between Rass Zebib and Rass Sidi Ali which is a strip of coast West of Bizerte.
14 & 15 June	In recognition of their services to the Squadron, the undermentioned paragraph appeared in today's Routine Orders. ***'His Majesty the King has been graciously pleased to give orders for the publication of the names of the undermentioned personnel of this unit who have been mentioned in dispatches by the Air Officer Commanding-In-Chief, Royal Air Force, Middle East.'*** ***336711 Fl/Sgt Haynes, F.W. 1182585 CPL. Humphries, K.W.*** ***1170775 CPL. Castle, A.F. 1258028 CPL. Palmer, F.L.*** ***639555 CPL. Gerry, T.J. 1359078 LAC. Gannon, W.E.*** This afternoon 3 Hurricanes piloted by Fl/Lt C.F. Ambrose, Fl/Sgt D.J. Green, and F/O J. McGill DFC, flew to Setif to collect three Spitfires, bringing our total of Spitfires to five.

14 & 15 June [continued] 20:15-21:45	Operating from advance Landing Ground Sq/Ldr R.V. Ellis DFM, F/O H.C. Charlesworth, P/O B. Bretherton, W/O N.F. Hewitt, Fl/Sgt J.C. McCall, and Sgt H. Wilkinson took off to patrol Bizerte to Cap Bon, which was carried out without incident, the leader reporting weather rather hazy.
04:45-06:30	A dawn patrol over Pantelleria was carried out by Sq/Ldr R.V, Ellis DFM, Fl/Lt G.P. Leggett, P/O D. Gadd, Sgt A. Cenitch, Sgt D.H. Thomas, and Sgt T.H. Ross with nothing to report other than the weather, which was none too good.
15 & 16 June 20:20-22:10	Operating from advance Landing Ground, Fl/Lt C.F. Ambrose, P/O B. Bretherton, P/O G.A. Martin, P/O R.D. Marsh, Fl/Sgt C.J.E. Hiltz, and Sgt T.C. Stonehouse patrolled Pantelleria again. This time the a/c patrolled South of the harbour where there were two minesweepers operating.
04:05-06:05	Fl/Lt W.T.H. Gill DFC, Sgt J. Rawson, Sgt P.H. Cashen, Sgt W.J. MyGind, and Fl/Sgt E.M. Karatau patrolled a convoy Southwest of Pantelleria. No incident.
16 & 17 June 04:50-06:35	On the morning of the 17th Fl/Lt P.R.V, Wells, P/O E.T. Leggett, Fl/Sgt E.F. Bramley, and Fl/Sgt J.G. McCall were on convoy patrol 14 miles Southeast of Cap Mamoar. No incident.
04:45-06:30	4 a/c piloted by P/O R.H. Phillips, P/O R. Plenderleith, Fl/Sgt F. Davies, and Sgt T.H. Ross patrolled a convoy 11 miles Southwest of Cap Mostefa without incident.
17 & 18 June	This afternoon the Squadron at 100% strength paraded under the Commanding Officer for an inspection by His Majesty the King. His Majesty who had arrived at Sebala 1 in a four engine "YORK" air transport machine, took the salute passing between the paraded units in an American little car commonly known as a "JEEP".
20:20-22:10	Fl/Lt G.P. Leggett, P/O M.W. Smyth, P/O D. Gadd, W/O N.F. Hewitt, Fl/Sgt E.M. Karatua, and Sgt H. Wilkinson patrolled a convoy North of Bizerte, the convoy was steering in a Westerly direction.

04:20-06:10	At dawn we were on convoy patrol again Fl/Lt P.R.V. Wells, P/O R.D. Marsh, Fl/Sgt W.J. Mygind, Sgt D.H. Thomas, Sgt N. Cenitch, and Sgt F.J. Bailey patrolled a convoy proceeding towards Pantelleria harbour. No incident on patrol but the day's good work was marred by the fatal accident of one of our youngest pilots who had only joined this Squadron about a month ago. The pilot was Sgt P.H. Cashen. The accident happened when he was returning early to base on an operation flight, through some technical trouble. The a/c was burnt out when he crash-landed.
18 & 19 June 20:15-21:55	6 Hurricanes piloted by Fl/Lt W.T.H. Gill DFC, P/O D. Gadd, P/O G.A. Martin, Fl/Sgt G.J. Green, Sgt T.H. Ross, and Sgt C.J.A. Edwards took off from base and patrolled Cap Mostefa to Cap Memoura, patrolled the area at 3–5,000 feet, the weather again being fairly good. At dawn, we again paid a visit to Pantelleria, which by this time had changed from Italian to Allied hands. F/O H.C. Charlesworth, P/O M.W. Smyth, Fl/Sgt G.J.E. Hiltz, P/O E.T. Bennett, Fl/Sgt E.F. Bramley, and Fl/|Sgt J.C. McCall arrived over the island about 05:05. During the patrol they were vectored towards 3 hostile e/a but were unable to make contact with the e/a as they had to break off and return to base owing to getting short on petrol.
19 & 20 June 20:20-21:50 04:30-06:30	This afternoon Sgt P.H. Cashen was buried in TUNIS. The Squadron now have 19 Spitfires Mark VC type to increase the Squadrons strength and many training hours have been flown in them since their arrival here. This evening F/O J. McGill DFC, Sgt A. Cenitch, Fl/Sgt E.F. Bramley, Sgt H. Wilkinson, and Sgt P.J. Bailey patrolled about 30 miles north of Bizerte. No incident. This morning, again operating from base 8 of our pilots, Fl/Lt C.F. Ambrose DFC, P/O R.H. Phillips, F/O H.W. Coussens, Fl/Sgt F. Davies, Fl/Sgt J. Rawson, Fl/Sgt J.G. McCall, Sgt W.J. MyGind, and Sgt T.C. Stonehouse were on convoy patrol East of Cap Berrat. "Once more nothing to report" are the words of the pilots.

20 & 21 June 20:15-21:40	7 a/c piloted by Fl/Lt W.T.H. Gill DFC, P/O E.T. Bennett, P/O R.D. Marsh, Fl/Lt G.P. Leggett, Sgt J.L. Horn, Sgt T.H. Ross, and Fl/Sgt D.R. Beard (the latter carrying out his last patrol with the Squadron) this evening patrolled two convoys between Rass Mostefa and Rass Mamoura with nothing to report apart from the weather which was rather good. Sgt G.J.A. Edwards, eighth a/c did not take off owing to bursting his tail wheel when landing at advanced landing ground earlier in the evening.
04:50-06:15	This morning Sq/Ldr R.V. Ellis DFM, Fl/Lt P.H.V. Wells, W/O N.F. Hewitt, F/O J. McGill DFC, and Fl/Sgt G.J.E. Hiltz patrolled a convoy located East of and proceeding towards Bizerte.
21 & 22 June 20:15-21:55	P/O D. Gadd, P/O M.W. Smyth, P/O G.A. Martin, Fl/Sgt D.J. Green, Sgt A. Cenitch, and Sgt D.H. Thomas operating at 5,000 feet, patrolled the Bizerte area. The only incident of interest was the reporting of two lights on the water about 5 miles North of Cap Rass Sidi Ali-El Mekki and another light about 15 miles Northwest of the same place.
22 & 23 June 20:30-21:45 La Sebala	6 a/c keeping up their dusk and dawn patrols of Bizerte. On this patrol the pilots flying at 8,500 feet were F/O H.G. Charlesworth, P/O E.T. Bennett, Fl/Sgt J. Rawson, Fl/Sgt W.J. MyGind, Fl/Sgt F. Davies, and Sgt C.J.A. Edwards. No incident apart from the weather being reported as fair.
05:15-06:45	F/O H.W. Coussens, P/O R. Plenderleith, P/O B. Bretherton, Fl/Sgt E.F. Bramley, Fl/Sgt J.C, McCall, and Sgt T.H. Ross patrolled East of Bizerte reporting rain showers and visibility fair.
23 & 24 June 20:05-21:30	Today the Squadron lost two of their long service pilots on posting to H.Q.M.E., namely F/O J.H. Fairbairn who was a most popular officer and pilot on the Squadron and whose name has appeared in this Diary many times, the other pilot being Fl/Sgt D.R Beard,
04:45-06:10	Fl/Lt G.P. Leggett, P/O R.E. Phillips, Fl/Lt P.H.V. Wells, Sgt F.J. Bailey, and Sgt J.L. Horn patrolled Bizerte without incident.

23 & 24 June	***SPITFIRES: For the first time in the history of the Squadron.*** Spitfires were on patrol, patrolling East of Bizerte, the first five Spitfire pilots were, Fl/Lt W.T.H. Gill DFC, P/o D. Gadd, Fl/Lt C.F. Ambrose DFC, P/O M.W. Smyth, and Fl/Sgt D.J. Green. There was no incident apart from the behaviour of the new machines which were reported as **"beautiful"**.
24 & 25 June 20:10-21:40 04:30-06:10 04:30-06:20	5 - Hurricanes piloted by F/O J. McGill DFC, W/O N.F. Hewitt, Sgt T.C. Stonehouse, Fl/Sgt E.F. Bramley, and Fl/SGT J.C. McCall patrolled a convoy way out to sea from East to West of Cap Bon without incident with the weather closing in on leaving the convoy. 5 – Spitfires piloted by Fl/Lt W.T.H. Gill DFC, F/O H.C. Charlesworth, P/O R.H. Phillips, P/O E.T. Bennett, F/O R. Bretherton, and Fl/Sgt E.M. Karatau patrolled a convoy between Rass Fortass and Rass Ahmar. No incident other than the Flight Leader Fl/ Lt W.T.H. Gill DFC experienced R/T trouble. 4 – Hurricanes as well carried out a dawn patrol. W/O W.F. Hewitt, Fl/Sgt G.J.E. Hiltz, Sgt D.H. Thomas, and Fl/Sgt J. Rawson patrolled a convoy about 10 miles off Rass Mostefa at 5,000 feet. The convoy was travelling in a North Easterly direction.
25 & 26 June 20:15-21:40 04:45-06:25	6 – Hurricanes piloted by P/O R.D. Marsh, P/O G.A. Martin, P/O E.T Bennett, Sgt T.H. Ross, Sgt A. Cenitch, and Fl/Sgt E.M. Karatau patrolled North of Bizerte. No incident. 6 – Hurricanes again were up on a dawn patrol. Fl/Lt W.T.H. Gill DFC, P/O D. Gadd, Fl/Lt C.F. Ambrose DFC, P/O R. Plenderleith, Sgt J.L. Horn, and Sgt F.J. Bailey patrolled the usual line East of Bizerte without incident. Our a/c returned owing to engine trouble.
26 & 27 June ***[LAC Lamb's Diary records of this day, states 'Going into Tunis', and it is highly likely that he attended the show in Tunis].***	Last night (26 June) an **E.N.S.A. concert party**, which has been touring the Middle East during the last three and half years under the direction of Mr Reg Lever and are now presenting **"Hello Happiness" in TUNIS**, were entertained to dinner in the Pilot's Mess. Special efforts were made to provide this veteran troupe with the sort of fare to which neither they nor we were accustomed to in the Western Desert and a most enjoyable evening followed.

26 & 27 June [continued] 20:15-22:10	6 - Spitfires piloted by Fl/Lt W.T.H. Gill DFC, F/O J. McGill, P/O R.H. Phillips, P/O D. Gadd, F/O H.C. Charlesworth, and Fl/Sgt D.J. Green, patrolled a convoy 10-15 miles East of Menzel Temime. The convoy was steering South. While the pilots were over the convoy, they were informed of hostile e/a in their vicinity, but the e/a did not approach the convoy. One ship in the convoy which were 50 strong appeared to catch fire. This was the only incident.
20:30-22:10	5 - Hurricanes piloted by Fl/Lt G.P. Leggett, P/O B. Bretherton, P/O E.T. Bennett, Fl/Sgt J.C. McCall, and Fl/Sgt J. Rawson were patrolling a convoy of about 7-ships just North of Cap Bon where again the enemy were in the vicinity. Our pilots were vectored to intercept. In all about 20 Ju.88's and HE 111's was encountered. The Flight Leader Fl/Lt G.P. Leggett saw two Ju.88's attacking a convoy which was near Menzel Temime. F/O B. Bretherton engaged and shot down one of the Ju.88's. The e/a just blew up in the air. Fl/Sgt J.C. McCall damaged one HE 111 during the engagement.
04:30-06:20	6 - Hurricanes including 5 - pilots which had the engagements with the Huns last night Fl/Lt G.P. Leggett, F/O B. Bretherton, P/O E.T. Bennett, Fl/Sgt J.C. McCall, Fl/Sgt J. Rawson, and Fl/Sgt C.J.A. Edwards were up on a dawn patrol Northeast of Bizerte. No incident.
04:40-06:15	S second dawn patrol was carried out this morning by 6 - Spitfires. Fl/Lt G.F. Ambrose DFC, Fl/Lt EW.T.H. Gill DFC, P/O W.M. Smyth, W/O N.F. Hewitt, and Sgt T.C. Stonehouse patrolled a convoy located about 10 miles Northwest of Bizerte.
27 & 28 June 20:10-21:45 La Sebala	6 - Spitfires piloted by F/O J. McGill DFC, P/O W.M. Smyth, P/O R. Plenderleith, W/O N.F. Hewitt, Fl/Sgt E.M. Karatau, and Sgt E.C. Stonehouse did a dusk patrol of Bizerte. During the patrol P/O W. M. Smyth and W/O N.F. Hewitt were vectored for about 50 miles to the North of Bizerte, to intercept 2 - e/a but returned reporting nothing seen.
20:15-21:45	6 - Hurricanes piloted by Fl/Lt P.H.V. Wells, P/O R.D. Marsh, Fl/Sgt W.J. MyGind, Fl/Sgt E.F. Bramley, and Sgt T.H. Ross were also on dusk patrol, patrolling two convoys which were Southeast of Cap Bon. No incident.

27 & 28 June 04:15-06:00	6 - Hurricanes piloted by Fl/Lt P.H.V. Wells, P/O R.D. Marsh, P/O G.A Martin, Fl/Sgt W.J. MyGind, Fl/Sgt E.F. Bramley, and Sgt T.H. Ross, the same 6 - pilots, patrolled Bizerte This morning reporting no incident.
28 & 29 June 20:10-21:55	6 - Hurricanes piloted by P/O R.H. Phillips, P/O E.T. Bennett, Fl/Sgt F. Davies, Fl/Sgt D.J. Green, Sgt D.R. Thomas, and Sgt J.L. Horn were on a patrol near Bizerte with nothing to report, weather being poor.
04:50	6 - Spitfires, continuing their patrols at dawn patrolled the Bizerte area. The pilots Fl/Lt C.F. Ambrose DFC, Fl/Lt C.F. Leggett, F/O H.W. Coussens, P/O D. Gadd, W/O N.F. Hewitt, and Sgt F.J. Bailey patrolled a line running Southeast - Northwest about 10 miles off Bizerte without incident.
29 & 30 June 20:10-21:45 La Sebala No. 2 LG.	6 - Hurricanes piloted by Fl/Lt P.H.V. Wells, Fl/Sgt E.F. Bramley, Sgt D.H. Thomas, Sgt A. Cenitch, Sgt H. Wilkinson, Sgt C.J.A. Edwards patrolled Northeast of Bizerte reporting the weather as cloud 7/10 at 10,000 feet with visibility poor.
04:40-06:25	Again, this morning, Fl/Lt W.T.H. Gill DFC, P/O R.H. Phillips, P/O R. Plenderleith, Sgt J.L. Horn, Sgt F.J. Bailey, and Sgt T.C. Stonehouse flying Spitfires, patrolled Northeast of Bizerte without incident.
20:30-21:30	We had 6 - Hurricanes at readiness but were not called upon for operations.
	June 1943 ends with RAF 73 squadron still at La Sebala No. 2 LG, with a few changes of personnel to and from the Unit, including pilots. Also 19 - Spitfires on the strength where many operational and training hours have been carried out in them.

Note: For daily pilot records of flight operations carried out by 'A' Flight of 73 Squadron refer to AIR 27/632/12. These records detail the a/c number, the pilot's name and the sortie carried out.

Other related AIRs

AIR 27/638-1 (1) General news & Reports & AIR 638-2 (1) Sortie Reports.

AIR 27/633 Operations Record Book

30/6/1943 - Seballa II Tunisia N.A.

On this day and during the Tunisian campaign the monthly hygiene review/report was undertaken - Impressions of First Army Hygiene.

The inspection was deemed necessary as the report states, and I quote:

> 'Owing to the large number of cases of Gastro-enteritis occurring in neighbouring Units, special interest was aroused in their Sanitary arrangements. One Unit, recently formed, was found to have very primitive Sanitary standards, due to; (a) complete lack of any sanitary knowledge, (b) complete lack of any disinfectants and sanitary equipment.'

AIR - Daily records and Pilot Ops Reports: From July 1943 & August 1943 are listed below. As for the AIRs from September 1943 to December 1943, these are not included as these predominantly deal with Operation Avalanche, 'The Battle for Italy'.

The AIR daily report sheets and the Pilot Operational Reports listed below complete the operational duty of 73 Squadron, just one (of many) squadrons who carried out sorties during the Tunisian campaign, the Battle for Sicily and then finally the Battle for Italy.

From the squadron's written reports, RAF 73 Squadron was involved in all of the battles listed above and it is only fitting to have these detailed and further recorded to show the extent of which both officers, pilots and ground crew served unconditionally, working long hours day and night in the fight against the Axis forces.

AIR 27/632/13 (1) & AIR 27/632/14 Pilot Ops Report July 1943	
1 & 2 July La Sebala (No.2)	Today the 1st of July, has seen the return to the Squadron of one of our old timers. The officer is Fl/Lt E.L. Joyce DFM. Fl/Lt E.L. Joyce has done one tour of duty with this Squadron. His reputation as a pilot and flight commander stands exceptionally high.
04:35-06:30	6 - Spitfires on dawn patrol - Fl/Lt W.T.H. Gill DFC, F/O J. McGill DFC, F/O G.H.C. Charlesworth, P.O.D. Gadd, F/O R. Bretherton, and Fl/Sgt D.J. Green started the month providing an escort to a convoy about 15 miles out to sea from Enfidaville, without incident. Fl/Sgt D.J. Green stayed a little too long on his patrol resulting in his having to land at a neighbouring 'drome' to refuel.

04:45-06:40	6 - Hurricancs pilot by P/O M.W. Smyth, P/O G.A. Martin, P/O E.T. Bennett, Fl/Sgt E.M. Karatau, Fl/Sgt W.J. MyGind and Sgt T.H. Ross were also on early morning patrol. The Hurricanes whilst patrolling Bizerte, observed a convoy coming from the West.
20:15-21:50	8 - Spitfires piloted by Fl/Lt G.P. Leggett, F/O R. Bretherton, P/O E.T. Bennett, P/O R. Plenderleith, Fl/Sgt E.M. Karatau, Sgt F.J. Bailey, Sgt T.C. Stonehouse, and Sgt J.L. Horn, were up on a dusk convoy patrol which was located off Bizerte. The weather was none to good - cloud 6/10 at 7,000 feet.
20:00-21:30	4 - Hurricanes piloted by Fl/Lt P.H.V. Wells, P/O R.D. Marsh, Fl/Sgt E.F. Bramley, and Fl/Sgt F. Davies were also up on dusk convoy patrol. Their convoy was located about 25 miles off Mostefa.
04:20-06:25	4 - Hurricanes piloted by Fl/Lt P.H.V. Wells, P/O R.D. Marsh, Fl/Sgt E.F. Bramley, and Fl/Sgt F. Davies - patrolled Bizerte as it is about this particular hour of the morning that the Huns (Germans) try to make their so-called sneak raids.
2 & 3 July 20:10-21:55	6 Hurricanes piloted by P/O R.H. Phillips, P/O R. Plenderleith, Fl/Sgt J.C. McCall, Fl/Sgt W.J. MyGind, Sgt D.H. Thomas, and Sgt T.H. Ross, were on a dusk patrol over Bizerte, with nothing to report.
04:30-06:35	6 - Spitfires piloted by Fl/Lt C.F. Ambrose DFC, Fl/Lt W.T.H. Gill DFC, P/O M.W. Smyth, Fl/Sgt J. Rawson, Sgt H. Wilkinson, and Sgt A. Cenitch, carried out the dawn patrol of Bizerte. A few ships in small groups were noticed around the harbour area.
3 & 4 July 20:15-21:35 La Sebala (No. 2)	Fl/Lt E.L. Joyce DFM, on his first operational flight on his return to the squadron, led the 6 - Hurricanes which did this evening's patrol of Bizerte. The other pilots were: - F/O J. McGill DFC, P/O E.T. Bennett, W/O K.F. Hewitt, Fl/Sgt C.J.A. Edwards, and F/Sgt E.F. Bramley - no incidents.
04:25-06:30	6 - Spitfires piloted by Fl/Lt G.P. Leggett, F/O H.W. Coussens, Fl/Sgt E.M. Karatau, Sgt T.H. Ross, Sgt T.C. Stonehouse, and Sgt J.L Ross - patrolled a convoy about 10 miles Northwest of Cap Serrat.
4 & 5 July 20:20-21:35	4 - Hurricanes piloted by P/O G.A. Martin, Fl/Sgt G.J. MyGind, Sgt A. Cenitch, and Sgt H. Wilkinson patrolled a convoy from South of Zemera Island heading towards Cap Bon.

4 & 5 July [continued] 20:20-21:35	5 - Spitfires piloted by Fl/Lt W.T.H. Gill DFC, F/O H.C. Charlesworth, F/O B. Bretherton, P/O R.H. Phillips, and Fl/Sgt D.J. Green patrolled the same convoy as the 4 - Hurricanes above.
05:00-06:35	2 - Hurricanes piloted by P/O M.W. Smyth, and Fl/Sgt G.J.E. Hiltz with 2 - Spitfires as top cover piloted by Fl/Sgt J. Rawson and SGT J.L. Horn were on dawn patrol over Bizerte, Sgt J.L. Horn returning early with R/T trouble.
5 & 6 July La Sebala (No.2)	The temperature now is almost unbearable and lasts few days, the readings were up to an average of 112°F in the shade - yesterday it was 120 degrees. Unfortunately for us La Sebala lies low with rather high hills on all sides. Today's routine orders contain another message of congratulations from the A.O.C. of the Northwest African Coastal Air Force for the convoy escort squadrons in the Tunis section. These are the A.O.C.'s own words: ***'Please convey my heartiest congratulations to all concerned for the magnificent performance in protecting the 26 ships East bound convoy through your dangerous sector. Not one ship was hit by enemy action. This reflects great credit on all concerned. The only damaged sustained while in your sector was on a landing craft when a cook upset some gravy on his fire. The convoy went through. Well, done.'*** The convoy in question passed through our sector about a week ago and was covered at various times by our squadron with both Hurricanes and Spitfires.
20:00-22:00	4 - Hurricanes piloted by P/O R.D. Marsh, Fl/Sgt E.F. Bramley, Fl/Sgt J.C. McCall, and Sgt D.H. Thomas as low cover, with 6 - Spitfires piloted by F/O J. McGill DFC, P/O E.T. Bennett, W/O N.F. Hewitt, Fl/Sgt E.M. Karatau, Sgt F.J. Bailey, and Sgt T.H. Ross as top cover at 12,000 feet, patrolled East of Bizerte without incident.
04:40-06:30	2 - Hurricanes piloted by Sgt F.J. Bailey and Sgt T.H. Ross along with 8 - Spitfires piloted by Fl/Lt G.P. Leggett, Fl/Lt W.T.H. Gill DFC, Fl/Lt P.H.V. Wells, P/O D. Gadd, P/O R.H. Phillips, Fl/Sgt D.J. Green, Sgt T.C. Stonehouse and Sgt J.L. Horn, patrolled Bizerte at various heights without incident.
6 & 7 July	Today we had another pilot posted to the squadron. The officer, Fl/Lt J.P. Mills arrived from No. 71 O.T.U.

20:20-20:30 04:40-06:30	12 - Spitfires piloted by Fl/Lt W.T.H. Gill DFC, F/O J. McGill DFC, F/O H.C. Charlesworth, F/O B. Bretherton, P/O M.W. Smyth, P/O D. Gadd, P/O E.T. Bennett, Fl/Sgt F. Davies, Fl/Sgt E.M. Karatau, Fl/Sgt D.J. Green, Sgt J.L. Horn and Sgt H. Wilkinson took off to patrol Bizerte but owing to the weather closing in, were ordered to patrol base by "Whipanade" (Ground Control) a few minutes after take-off. Fl/Sgt F. Davies returned early due to engine trouble. 7 - Spitfires piloted by Fl/Lt C.F. Ambrose DFC, Fl/Lt E.L. Joyce DFM, Fl/Lt P.H.V. Wells, P/O R. Plenderleith, W/O N.F. Hewitt, Fl/Sgt F. Davies, and Sgt A. Cenitch were this morning on rather a long job. They patrolled a convoy of about 25 large ships, some of them liners up to 20,000 tons. The ships were sighted taking an Easterly course between Rass Zebib and Cap Bon. It is interesting to note that since the fall of Tunis, quite a large number of our convoys have sailed through (in both directions) between Cap Bon and Sicily, yet only once have our pilots come into contact with e/a.
7 & 8 July 20:10-22:05 La Sebala (No.2) 20:15-22:10 04:30-06:25	4 - Spitfires piloted by Fl/Lt G.P. Leggett, P/O R.H. Phillips, Sgt T.H. Ross, and Sgt F.J. Bailey patrolled about 20 miles North of Zemera Island without incident. 6 - more Spitfires operated this evening piloted by P/O D. Gadd, P/O R. Plenderleith, W/O R.F. Hewitt, Fl/Sgt E.M. Karatau, Fl/Sgt D.J. Green and Sgt J.L. Horn. They patrolled Rass Sidi Ali-El Mekki without incident. 6 - Spitfires piloted by Fl/Lt W.T.H. Gill DFC, F/O H.W. Coussens, P/O E.L. Bennett, Sgt J.L. Horn, Sgt A. Cenitch, and Sgt T.H. Ross, patrolled a convoy off Cap Zebib; and 5 - Spitfires piloted by Fl/Lt C.F. Ambrose DFC, F/O H.C. Charlesworth, P/O M.W. Smyth, Sgt H. Wilkinson, and Sgt D.H. Thomas patrolled another convoy off Cap Bizerte. Today, 6 of our pilots led by Fl/Lt P.H.V. Wells flying Hurricanes proceeded to MALTA. The detachment which was of pilots and a/c only, is expected to be away only for a few days in which they will carry out a very important job. The other 5 pilots are Fl/Lt J. P. Mills, P/O R.D. Marsh, P/O G.A. Martin, Fl/Sgt E.F Bramley, and Fl/Sgt C.J.A. Edwards.
8 & 9 July 19:35-21:35	6 - Spitfires piloted by Fl/Lt W.T.H. Gill DFC, P/O R. Plenderleith, P/O E.L. Bennett, Fl/Sgt D.L. Green, Fl/Sgt E.M. Karatau, and Sgt J.L. Horn, patrolled a convoy about 10 miles North of Korlea. The pilots had to return early from

8 & 9 July 19:35-21:35 [continued]	patrol as the weather, which was continually getting worse, was down to 5 miles visibility, with cloud 6/10 at 1,000 feet, also rain squalls.
19:55-22:25	Also, this evening five other Spitfires piloted by Fl/Lt E.L. Joyce DFM, F/O B. Bretherton, Fl/Sgt F. Davies, Sgt H. Wilkinson, and Sgt T.C. Stonehouse were on convoy patrol. They located their convoy about 12 miles East West of Pantellaria. They too returned early owing to foul weather.
04:40-04:45	6 - Spitfires piloted by Fl/Lt W.T.H. Gill DFC, F/O H.W. Coussens, P/O D. Gadd, Fl/Sgt J. Rawson, Fl/Sgt E.M. Karatau, and Sgt A. Cenitch, patrolled a Southeast bound convoy off Rass Zebib. No incident lost sight, bad weather was again experienced this morning. 5 - Spitfires piloted by Fl/Lt C.F. Ambrose, F/o H.C. Charlesworth, F/O J. McGill DFC, Sgt F. Bailey, and Sgt D.H. Thomas patrolled a convoy travelling East just off Cap Negro. The convoy was covered with mist when the pilots left.
La Seballa (No. 2)	3 - Hurricanes piloted by Fl/Sgt G.J.E. Hiltz, Fl/Sgt J.C. McCall, and Fl/Sgt W.J. MyGind set off this morning for MALTA, to make our detachment out there to 9 a/c.
20:15-22:25	10 - Spitfires this evening was on convoy patrol, led by Fl/Sgt G.F Leggett. The other pilots were Fl/Lt WE.T.H. Gill DFC, P/O E.L. Bennett, P/O M.W. Smyth, P/O R.H. Phillips, W/O E.F. Hewitt, Fl/Sgt E.M. Karatau, Sgt F. Bailey, Sgt T.H. Ross, and Sgt T.C. Stonehouse. The convoy was located and patrolled a few miles North of Bizerte where it was anchored. At 21:00 hours 4 of the 10 Spitfires were ordered to patrol another convoy which was near Cap Serrat.
04:30-06:15	6 - Spitfires piloted by Fl/Lt E.L. Joyce DFM, F/O H.W. Coussens, F/O B. Bretherton, Fl/Sgt J. Rawson, Sgt A. Cenitch, and Sgt D.H. Thomas, patrolled the same convoy as was patrolled last night where it is was still anchored North of Bizerte. No incident. Below are the individual reports of 4 Hurricane pilots operating (on detachment) from Luqa in Malta on intruder anti-searchlight patrol of Landing Ground area in Sicily.
20:30-00:30	Fl/Lt J.P. Mills patrolled Cap Mira di Parco and saw searchlights switching off and on intermittently, but he was unable to find any suitable targets to strafe.

9 & 10 July 20:35-00:50	Fl/Lt P.H.V. Wells patrolled Gira to Ponte Olive did not see anti-searchlights but however he strafed an Ack-Ack gun position outside Ponte Olive.
20:40-00:35	P/O G.A. Martin also patrolled Ponte Olive, but his report was nil.
21:10-23:10	P/O R.D. Marsh patrolled Cap Mira di Parco, but this pilot also had nothing to report as far as searchlights were concerned. Two other pilots were on intruder patrols with their Hurricanes but unfortunately have not yet returned to their base. They had just joined the squadron about six weeks ago but were fully operational.
21:30-22:20	Fl/Sgt C.J.A. Edwards was the first of the missing pilots to go on patrol. After patrolling Gerbini he returned to Malta, circled the island and disappeared. The other pilot Fl/Sgt E.F. Bramley patrolled Biscari-Comiso and when about 15 miles North of Malta on the return trip he was heard transmitting the distress call which was the last heard from him.

Assault on **Sicily** began on the **9 July 1943 - Operation Husky**

10 & 11 July 21:15-22:05 La Sebala (No. 2)	5 - Spitfires piloted by F/O J. McGill DFC, F/O H.C. Charlesworth, Fl/Sgt D.J. Green, Fl/Sgt F. Davies, and Sgt H. Wilkinson patrolled a convoy about 20 miles North of Bizerte from 12 - 15,000 feet. 6 other Spitfires piloted by P/O R. Plenderleith, P/O D. Gadd, W/O N.F. Hewitt, P/O R.H. Phillips, Sgt E.M. Karatau, and Sgt J.L. Horn patrolled the same convoy as above as low cover patrolling at 5,000 feet.
04:35-06:50	At dawn 4 more Spitfires piloted by Fl/Lt W.T.H. Gill DFC, P/O E.T. Bennett, P/O P.D. Jones, and P/O D. Draper patrolled two convoys in the Bizerte and Cap Bon area. Both convoys were covered at 12-15,000 feet. Hostile e/a were reported between Cap Bon and Bizerte, but the only a/c encountered by our pilots was one Wellington.
04:45-06:20	2 other Spitfires piloted by Fl/Lt C.F. Ambrose DFC, and P/O M.W. Smyth this morning, also patrolled a convoy between Cap Bon and Bizerte. Their covering was at 2,000 feet - no incidents.

11 & 12 July	Today Fl/Lt E.L. Joyce DFM was promoted to Sq/Ldr and assumed command of the squadron from Sq/Ldr R.V. Ellis DFM whom we regret to say, will shortly be leaving the Unit. Sq/Ldr E.L. Joyce DFM has been much welcomed on the Squadron as a CO and we are proud to say that through his previous efforts as a pilot and flight leader, will have the confidence of all pilots.
20:15-21:50	6 - Spitfires piloted by Fl/Lt W.T.H. Gill DFC, P/O R. Plenderleith, P/O E.T. Bennett, Fl/Sgt J. Rawson, Fl/Sgt D.J. Green, and Sgt A. Cenitch patrolled a convoy near Zemera Island.
20:25-22:10	6 - Spitfires piloted by Sq/Ldr E.L. Joyce DFM, Fl/Lt G.P. Leggett, F/O B. Bretherton, Sgt T.C. Stonehouse, Sgt F.J. Bailey, and Sgt H. Wilkinson patrolled a convoy of ten warships about 35 miles North of Bizerte and at dawn 10 more Spitfires were airborne, continuing their early patrols.
04:35-06:40	First four piloted by F/O H.W. Coussens, P/O D. Gadd, P/O P.D. Jones, P/O S.D. Thistleton patrolled a convoy near Cap Serrat, reporting no incident.
05:00-06:45	The other 6 Spitfires piloted by Fl/Lt C.F. Ambrose DFC, Fl/Sgt F. Davis, P/O R.H. Phillips, P/O H.C Charlesworth, P/O M.W. Smyth, and Sgt T.H. Ross patrolled a convoy near Rass Sidi Ali El Mekki.
Luqa, Malta	Continuing their anti-searchlight intruder patrols from Malta our detachment of Hurricanes was again active last night. Although the weather was none too good, 4 a/c managed to take to the air.
21:00-21:40	The first pilot off P/O G.A Martin found the weather too poor and had to return to base after 40 minutes flying.
21:10-23:40	Fl/Sgt W.J. MyGind patrolled Agrigento-Conicatti area but did not see any searchlights or receive any Ack-Ack gun fire.
21:15-22:05	Fl/Sgt G.J.E. Hiltz was the third pilot to report nothing seen, the weather again being the reason with visibility poor and cloud down to 10/10 at 1,000 feet.
22:40-01:00	Fl/Lt J.P. Mills patrolled Catania-Gerbine area and strafed two light Ack-Ack guns. No searchlights were observed, or road movements seen.

12 & 13 July La Sebala	This morning Sq/Ldr R.V. Ellis DFM, our late CO, we are sorry to say, left the squadron on his way to Rear Air Headquarters, Western Desert. Enough cannot be said about our late CO for his leadership and interest in the squadron. Sq/Ldr R.V. Ellis DFM had risen from the ranks, becoming an N.C.O. pilot in this same squadron in France and has been an operational pilot with us ever since, apart from a few months while on rest after completing his first tour of duty. His record as a pilot need not be mentioned here but can be found in earlier entries in this diary. But one incident does stand out was the destroying of 3 e/a one morning before breakfast while patrolling Tobruk. Before leaving us Sq/Ldr Ellis had the satisfaction of seeing the squadron re-equipped with Spitfires. The squadron's best wishes go with Sq/Ldr R.V. Ellis DFM.
20:00-22:05	6 - Spitfires piloted by P/O H.W. Coussens, P/O D. Gadd, W/O N.F. Hewitt, Fl/Sgt J. Rawson, Fl/Sgt E.M. Karatau, and Sgt J.L. Horn patrolled a convoy off Cap Serrat. 4 a/c patrolled at 15,000 feet and the remaining 2 a/c covered the ships at 5,000 feet. The leader was informed of e/a in their area but all they saw was only a single Hudson.
20:20-22:10	5 more Spitfires piloted by F/O J. McGill DFC, F/O R. Bretherton, F/O H.C. Charlesworth, Fl/Sgt F. Davis, and Sgt T.H. Ross - at the same time patrolled North of Bizerte at 15/20,000 feet.
04:45-06:45	In the morning Bizerte was again patrolled by 6 more Spitfires piloted by Fl/Lt G.P. Leggett, Fl/Lt W.T.H. Gill DFC, Sgt T.C. Stonehouse, Sgt F.J. Bailey, and Sgt A. Cenitch at 2/12,000 feet.
	The night of the 12/13 July was the last of our Hurricane detachment operated from Malta, this being the third but most successful night.
12 & 13 July Luqa, Malta 20:55-23:20	Fl/Lt P.E.V. Wells failed to find any searchlights and only a few MTs were seen but he strafed a part of the coast road Southwest Sicily also two MT vehicles.
20:55-23:15	Fl/Sgt G.J.E. Hiltz patrolled the coast road from Agrigento to Palermo but did not observe anything of a military nature so flew on to Menfi where he strafed a light.
21:10-23:15	P/O R.D. Marsh patrolled some roads in central Sicily where he strafed a couple of parked MTs, but again little activity was noticed.

12 & 13 July [continued] 21:20-00:10	Fl/Sgt C.J.A. McCall strafed two searchlights near Menfi which resulted in one going out but at the same time received some light and heavy Ack-Ack gun fire which did not do any damage. Continuing his patrol, he strafed some more MT vehicles near Rimera.
22:00-01:20	F/O G.A. Martin strafed four searchlights near Sciacca. One of these exploded and the other three extinguished. He also strafed MT vehicles in the same area and at Parto Palo some accurate Breda gun fire was encountered.
22:95-00:20	Fl/Sgt W.J. MyGind patrolled the roads and railways Northwest of Agrigento and strafed one MT vehicle which caught fire.
13 & 14 July 20:15-21:50 La Sebala (No 2)	6 - Spitfires piloted by Fl/Lt W.T.H. Gill DFC, P/O M.W. Smyth, P/O R. Plenderleith, P/O R.H. Phillips, Fl/Sgt D.J. Green, and Fl/Sgt J. Rawson - patrolled a convoy near Rass Sidi Ali-El Mekki without incident.
04:25-06:30	6 - Spitfires piloted by Fl/Lt C.F. Ambrose DFC, Fl/Lt G.P. Leggett, F/O D. Draper, P/O P.D. Jones, Sgt T.C. Stonehouse, and Sgt H. Wilkinson - were this morning airborne to cover a West bound convoy off Cap Serrat but by the time they had arrived, the convoy had gone far West. The weather in the Cap Serrat area was 8/10 at 4,000 feet.
14 & 15 July 20:10-22:20	This evening's convoy patrol was led by the CO The other 5 Spitfires were piloted by F/O H.W. Coussens, F/O B. Bretherton, P/O P.D. Jones, and Sgt A. Cenitch. The convoy was located about 12 miles (19 km) off Cap Bon.
04:20-06:30	6 - Spitfires piloted by Fl/Ly W.T.H. Gill DFC, P/O D. Gadd, P/O S.D. Thistleton, Fl/Sgt D.J. Green, Fl/Sgt F. Davies, and Sgt D.H. Thomas this time covered an anchored convoy North of Bizerte. 4 of the a/c patrolled at 10,000 and 15,000 feet and the other 2 a/c at 5,000 feet. No incident.
	Today also saw 6 of our remaining Hurricanes (on detachment) in Malta return to La Seballa 2. The pilots enjoyed their short stay in Malta and would have liked to stay much longer. Some of them met W/CDR J.B. Selby DSO & DFC, who commanded our squadron before Sq/Ldr R.V. Ellis DFM. Sq/Ldr E.L. Joyce DFM also flew over to Malta while the detachment was there.

15 & 16 July	**During the last 24 hours, the squadron flew 24 convoy sorties.**
20:05-22:00	6 - Spitfires piloted by F/O H.C. Charlesworth, F/O M.W. Smyth, F/O D. Draper, P/O S.D. Thistleton, Sgt H. Wilkinson, and Sgt F.J. Bailey - patrolled an East bound convoy which was 10 miles North of Cap Negro.
20:15-22:20	6 more Spitfires piloted by F/O J. McGill, P/O P.D. Jones, P/O E.T. Bennett, W/O N.F. Hewitt, Sgt T.H. Ross, and Sgt T.C. Stonehouse - patrolled a convoy between Pantelleria Island and Kélibia. No incident.
03:50-06:50	12 Spitfires this morning, all on the one convoy piloted by Sq/Ldr E.L. Joyce DFM, Fl/Lt G.P. Leggett, F/O H.W. Coussens, P/O R.H. Phillips, P/O R.D. Marsh, P/O R. Plenderleith, Fl/Sgt E.M. Karatau, Fl/Sgt F. Davies, Fl/Sgt J. Rawson, Sgt D.H. Thomas, Sgt A. Cenitch, and Sgt J.L. Horn - patrolled the convoy which was 15 miles Southeast of Kélibia. It was covered at various heights. P/O R.D. Marsh who remained in Malta when the other six pilots arrived back yesterday, arrived back here today.
16 & 17 July 19:40-21:55	6 - Spitfires piloted by Fl/Lt G.P. Leggett, P/O R.D. Marsh, F/O M.W. Smyth, P/O D. Gadd, Fl/Sgt D.J. Green, and Sgt F.J. Bailey - patrolled a convoy which was just East of Bizerte.
04:25-06:40	6 - Spitfires piloted by F/O R. Bretherton, F/O D. Draper, P/O E.T. Bennett, W/O N.F. Hewitt, Sgt D.H. Thomas, and Sgt A. Cenitch - patrolled a convoy proceeding South of Mostefa. F/O D. Draper returned early owing to engine trouble.
17 & 18 July 20:10-21:55	This morning again, 6 more Spitfires piloted by F/O H.C. Charlesworth, P/O D. Draper, P/O R.H. Phillips, P/O R. Plenderleith, Sgt H. Wilkinson, and Sgt T.C. Stonehouse - patrolled a convoy near Bizerte without incident.
04:30-06:40	At dawn 6 other Spitfires piloted by F/O J. McGill, P/O R.D. Marsh, P/O P.D. Jones, P/O S.D. Thistleton, Fl/Sgt W.J. MyGind, and Sgt F.C.H. Hampton - also patrolled a convoy in the Bizerte area without incident.
18 & 19 July	The remaining few of our ground crew detachment which proceeded to an advance Landing Ground at Cap Bon in the early part of last month (mainly for dusk and dawn operations) returned this afternoon to base.

20:15-22:15	6 - Spitfires piloted by F/O H.C. Charlesworth, F/O B. Bretherton, F/O M.W. Smyth, Sgt F.J. Bailey, Fl/Sgt F. Davies, and Sgt T.H. Ross - this evening at dusk, patrolled North of Bizerte without incident.
21:15-21:50	Also taking off at the same time, 6 other Spitfires piloted by F/O H.W. Coussens, P/O E.T. Bennett, W/O N.F. Hewitt, Fl/Sgt D.J. Green, Fl/Sgt J. Rawson, and Sgt A. Cenitch - patrolled a convoy near Zemera Island.
04:25-07:20	6 - Spitfires this morning piloted by Fl/Lt J.P. Wills, F/O R.D. Marsh, P/O F.C Bremner, P/O G.A. Martin, Fl/Sgt W.J. MyGind, and Sgt D.H. Thomas - patrolled a convoy West of Bizerte without incident.
19 & 20 July La Sebala (No. 2)	***It was today learned that Fl/Sgt C.J.A. Edwards who disappeared near Malta on the night of the 9th inst., had been picked up in his dinghy on the 18th. He was in a very weak condition but otherwise unharmed and was taken to the 45th General Hospital, Malta, where he was making satisfactory progress. He had spent 9 nights in his dinghy and as his supply of drinking water had given out, he began to lose hope of survival. He had rationed himself to 3 sips water and 2 Horlicks milk tablets per day and had drifted to within 50 miles of the Tunisian Coast before being sighted by a Baltimore, flying over Malta at 15,000 feet. A speedy rescue followed, and all ended happily.***
20:20-2:10	6 - Spitfires piloted by Fl/Lt G. P. Leggett, P/O R.H. Phillips, P/O D. Gadd, Fl/Sgt E.M. Karatau, Sgt J.L. Horn, and Sgt T.C. Stonehouse - patrolled a convoy near Bizerte. No incident.
04:15-06:35	4 - Spitfires piloted by F.O. Bretherton, F.O. Smyth, Sgt H. Wilkinson, and Sgt F.C.H. Hampton - patrolled over Bizerte without incident but on returning to base Sgt H. Wilkinson forced landed his machine about 12 miles short of base owing to shortage of petrol, pilot OK aircraft Cat. II.
04:30-06:35	4 - Spitfires piloted by F/O J. McGill, F/O D. Draper, P/O S.D. Thistleton, and P/O P.D. Jones - patrolled a convoy off Cap Serrat.
20 & 21 July 20:05-22:15	6 - Spitfires piloted by Sq/Ldr E.L. Joyce DFM, P/O E.C. Charlesworth, P/O R.D. Marsh, P/O G.A. Martin, Sgt D.H. Thomas, and Sgt F.J. Bailey - patrolled an East bound convoy which was located just North of Bizerte. The weather was rather hazy.

20:05-22:05	6 other Spitfires piloted by F/O H.W. Coussens, P/O S.D. Thistleton, P/O R. Plenderleith, W/O N.F. Hewitt, Fl/Sgt D.J. Green, and Sgt A. Cenitch - also patrolled a convoy North of Bizerte without incident.
04:20-06:35	6 - Spitfires piloted by Fl/Lt J.P. Mills, P/O F.C. Bremner, Fl/Sgt F. Davies, Fl/Sgt W.J. MyGind, and Sgt T. Ross - patrolled North of Bizerte at 15/20,000 feet observing a little shipping.
21 & 22 July 20:10	12 - Spitfires piloted by Fl/Lt G.P. Leggett, F/O B. Bretherton, P/O J. McGill DFC, F/O D. Draper, P/O R.H. Phillips, P/O D. Gadd, P/O P.D. Jones, Fl/Sgt J. Rawson, Fl/Sgt E.M. Karatau, Sgt T.C. Stonehouse, Sgt F.C. H. Hampton, and Sgt T.H. Ross - patrolled two convoys, one between Zemera Island and Cap Bon and the other which was about 5 miles East of Porto Farina. No incident.
04:30-06:50	6 - Spitfires piloted by Fl/Lt W.T.H. Gill DFC, Fl/Lt J.F. Mills, P/O E.T. Bennett, W/O N.F. Hewitt, Fl/Sgt D.J. Green, and Fl/Sgt J. Rawson - patrolled a West bound convoy located Northwest of Cap Serrat weather was good.
04:50-06:35	6 - Spitfires piloted by Sq/Ldr E.L. Joyce DFM, F/O H.C Charlesworth, P/O G.A. Martin, P/O F.C. Bremner, Sgt D.H. Thomas, and Sgt F.J. Bailey - patrolled a convoy 15 miles West of Bizerte.
22 & 23 July 19:55-22:15	6 - Spitfires piloted by F/O H.W. Coussens, P/O D. Draper, P/O F.D. Jones, P/O S.D. Thistleton, Sgt A Cenitch, and Sgt J.L. Horn - patrolled a large East bound convoy North of Zemera Island. No incident.
20:05-22:20	6 - Spitfires piloted by Fl/Lt G.P. Leggett, F/O B. Bretherton, P/O R.D. Marsh, Sgt F.C.R. Hampton, Sgt T.C. Stonehouse, and Sgt T.H. Ross - patrolled a convoy entering Bizerte harbour. While on patrol the leader was informed of unidentified aircraft above at 25,000 feet but on investigation, contact was not made with the bogey.
04:40-06:35	6 - Spitfires piloted by P/O R.H. Phillips, P/O R. Plenderleith, P/O F.C. Bremner, P/O D. Gadd, Fl/Sgt E.M. Karatau, and Sgt F.J. Bailey - Patrolled North of Bizerte at various heights. Weather good 3/10 cloud at 15,000 feet.
23 & 24 July 20:10-20:50	Fl/Lt J.P. Mills, P/O E.T. Bennett, F/O M.W. Smyth, P/O G.A. Martin, Fl/Sgt J. Rawson, and Sgt D.H. Thomas this evening again with Spitfires, patrolled a convoy Southeast of Cap Bon but returned early to base as weather was u/s. Cloud was 10/10 at 800 feet and rain.

23 & 24 July [continued] 04:45-06:45	6 - Spitfires piloted by Sq/Ldr E.L. Joyce DFM, Fl/Lt J.P. Mills, F/O D. Draper, Fl/Sgt F. Davies, Sgt F.J. Bailey, and Sgt A. Cenitch - patrolled a convoy near Bizerte.
24 & 25 July 20:00-21:55 04:30-06:30	4 - Spitfires piloted by F/O M.W. Smyth, P/O F.C. Bremner, P/O E.T. Bennett, and Fl/Sgt J. Rawson - patrolled North of Bizerte. Leader was informed of three e/a in the area and had various vectors to intercept. The hostiles were not intercepted so our aircraft returned and continued patrol. 4 - Spitfires piloted by Fl/Lt C.F. Ambrose DFC, Fl/Lt P.H.V. Wells, Fl/Sgt D.J. Green, and Fl/Sgt W.J. MyGind - patrolled North of Bizerte at 15,000 feet. No incident,
25 & 26 July 20:10-21:50 20:15-21:45 04:20-06:40	4 - Spitfires piloted by P/O R.H. Phillips, P/O R.D. Marsh, Sgt D.H. Thomas, and Sgt T.C. Stonehouse - patrolled a convoy near Cap Bon. No incident, weather was 10/10 cloud 5,000 feet. 4 - Spitfires piloted by F/O H.W. Coussens, F/O D. Draper, P/O D. Gadd, and Sgt J.L. Horn - patrolled another convoy which was in the Bizerte area. No incident. 4 - more Spitfires this morning patrolled North of Bizerte again without incident. The pilots were F/O M.W. Smyth, P/O G.A. Martin, Fl/Sgt E.M. Karatau, and Sgt A. Cenitch
26 & 27 July 20:15-21:55 La Seballa (No.2) 04:40-06:55 04:45-07:05	4 - Spitfires piloted by P/O F.C Bremner, P/O P.D. Jones, W/O N.F. Hewitt, and Sgt T.H. Ross - patrolled a small convoy 5 miles North of Bizerte at 9,200 feet without incident. 6 - Spitfires piloted by F/O J/ McGill DFC, P/O D, Gadd, Fl/Sgt D.J. Green, Fl/Sgt J. Rawson, Sgt W.J. MyGind, and Sgt A. Cenitch - patrolled North of Bizerte. No incident. 6 other Spitfires this morning piloted by Fl/Lt G.P. Leggett, F/O M.W. Smyth, F/O B. Bretherton, Fl/Sgt G.J.E. Hiltz, Fl/Sgt W. Ritchie, and Fl/Sgt F.C.N. Hampton - patrolled a West bound convoy North of Cap Serrat. This evening, we had 6 Spitfires at readiness but were not called upon.
27 & 28 July La Sebala (No.1)	This morning the squadron made another move - the second since the fall of TUNIS. This time it was only a short one, which was over to the neighbouring drome at La Sebala No. 1.' Henceforth the Squadron will operate as a day Squadron. Today also, owing to moving etc, the Squadron did not carry out any operations, but we had six Spitfires at readiness from 20:00 - 21:00 hours.

29 July La Sebala (No.1)	This morning started off with the usual readiness aircraft and convoy patrols were also continued which were maintained throughout the day.
06:30-07:40	2 - Spitfires piloted by P/O P/D. Jones, and Fl/Sgt D.J. Green - set out to patrol a small convoy North of Cap Bon but returned early owing to bad weather.
09:15-11:30	2 - Spitfires piloted by P/O R.D. Marsh, and Sgt D.H. Thomas - continued the patrol of the above convoy, which was located 20 miles North of Cap Bon, the weather on this occasion being much improved.
10:55-13:00	2 - Spitfires piloted by F/O J. McGill DFC, and Sgt J.L. Horn - on the same convoy patrol, the position this time being 40 miles North of Cap Bon.
12:20-13:40	2 - Spitfires piloted by P/O R.H. Phillips and Sgt T.H. Ross - were airborne to patrol a convoy off Cap Negro but did not locate.
12:50-15:15	2 - Spitfires piloted by W/O N.F. Hewitt and F/Sgt J.C. McCall - continued the patrol of convoy North of Cap Bon where visibility was poor.
13:45-15:45	2 - Spitfires piloted by P/O F.C. Bremner and Fl/Sgt W. Ritchie - searched for the same convoy but failed to find it. At this period the weather was becoming worse with cloud 6/10 at 2,000 feet.
14:30-16:35	2 - Spitfires piloted by Fl/Lt J.P. Mills and P/O P.D. Jones - set out to continue the patrol of the same convoy and this time they were fortunate. The convoy was located 30 miles North of Cap Bon.
15:45-17:55	2 - Spitfires piloted by F/O B. Bretherton and Fl/Sgt F. Davies - also patrolled the convoy.
16:30-18:30	Two more Spitfires were also on convoy patrol. This particular convoy which was a large one was about 20 miles East of Rass Sidi Ali-El Mekki.
16:50-18:45	2 - Spitfires piloted by P/O D. Gadd and Fl/Sgt E.M. Karatau - kept up the patrol of the convoy North of Cap Bon.
17:40:19:35	2 - Spitfires piloted by Fl/Ly C.P. Leggett and Sgt T.C. Stonehouse - also were up to patrol the convoy North of Cap Bon but failed to find it. The weather was hazy with cloud 10/10 at 500 feet.

29 July [continued] 18:05-20:10 18:30-20:20	Two more Spitfires piloted by Fl/Lt W.T.H. Gill DFC ("B" Flight Commander) and Sgt A. Cenitch patrolled the convoy in the Zemera Island area. Two more Spitfires piloted by F/O H.W. Coussens and Fl/Sgt J. Rawson were the last two pilots to operate today. They also patrolled the convoy in the Zemera Island area. This brings today's shipping escorts up to 26 sorties with a total of 51 operational hours. All patrols were without incident.
30 July	Today opened with the Squadron at 30 minutes available which stood throughout the 24 hours, and no operations were carried out, but the Squadron managed to get rid of their three remaining Hurricanes which were flown to Setif this morning.
31 July	Today also was a blank day as far as operations were concerned. The only activity was a 6 - Spitfire practice scramble. So, ends the month of July with the outstanding points being the change of Squadron Commanders, also the switching over from night fighter to a day fighter Squadron. Many convoys have been patrolled, this last month which included the largest ever to pass through the Mediterranean. **i.e., The invasion of SICILY. Operation Husky.**

Notes:
For daily pilot records of flight operations carried out by 'A' Flight of 73 Squadron refer to AIR 27/632/14. These records detail the a/c number, the pilot's name and the sortie carried out.

- The Assault on **Sicily** began on the **9 July 1943** and continued until the **17 August 1943;** for more details of **Operation Husky,** refer to Chapter 16 of this book.
- The Invasion of Italy began and took place during **September 1943** and continued through **October 1943;** for more details of **Operation Avalanche,** refer to Chapter 16 of this book.

AIR 27/632/15 & AIR 27/632/16 Pilot Ops Report August 1943	
1 August 08:15 10:15 La Sebala (No. 1) 09:55-11:30	The month of August opened by Fl/Lt C.F. Ambrose and Sgt T.H. Ross again on convoy patrol. Flying Spitfires, the convoy was located North of Cap Bon. The convoy which consisted of 18 ships, including 6 destroyers. 2 - Spitfires piloted by F/O B. Bretherton and Sgt F.J. Bailey - patrolled the same convoy as above. No incident.

10:50-12:35	2 - Spitfires piloted by Fl/Lt J.P. Mills and Sgt A. Cenitch - patrolled the same convoy in the Cap Bon area.
11:45-14:10	2 - Spitfires piloted by F/O D. Gadd and Fl/Sgt D.J. Green - patrolled same convoy.
12:45-14:40	2 - Spitfires piloted by F/O H.C. Charlesworth and Sgt D.H. Thomas - patrolled same convoy still without incident.
13:50-15:40	2 - Spitfires piloted by Fl/Lt G.P. Leggett and P/O G.A. Martin - patrolled same convoy as above. No incident.
18:20-20:10	2 - Spitfires piloted by F/O H.W. Coussens and P/O S.D Thistleton - patrolled 5 miles North of Galite Island at 20,000 feet. During the patrol they were given various vectors which took them also to 24,000 feet to intercept an e/a approaching from the North but did not intercept. Visibility was very poor.
20:00-20:50	2 - Spitfires piloted by R.H. Phillips and Sgt T.C. Stonehouse - were scrambled to intercept e/a. After receiving various vectors and heights, they eventually got to 27,500 feet without incident, so were ordered to land.
2 August 06:00-07:55 La Seballa (No. 1)	2 - Spitfires piloted by Sq/Ldr E.L. Joyce DFM and P/O G.A. Martin were scrambled to 5,000 feet over Bizerte, then 10 miles West of Bizerte at 15,000 feet, then reaching 18,000 feet and after a few more vectors were ordered to land as the hostiles had faded.
07:45-10:10	2 - Spitfires piloted by P/O R. Plenderleith and F/Sgt E.M. Karatau - were up on an air-sea rescue patrol about 10 miles of Marettimo Island but after searching for a considerable time they saw nothing.
09:35-11:25	2 - Spitfires piloted by W/O N.F. Hewitt and Sgt J.C. McCall - were also up on an air-sea rescue to the same area. They observed a couple of boxes 2 feet by 2 feet in size and there was much fish activity around the boxes but nothing else was seen.
09:55-11:10	2 - Spitfires piloted by F/O J. McGill DFC and F/O D. Draper were scrambled to 27,000 feet 30 miles West of Galite Island, but after orbiting a while nothing was seen so returned to base.
11:25	2 - Spitfires piloted by P/O F. Bremner and Fl/Sgt J. Richie were scrambled to 10,000 feet over Bizerte but after 20 minutes were ordered to land as aircraft had proved to be friendly.

2 August [continued] 14:20	2 - Spitfires piloted by P/O E.L. Bennett and Fl/Sgt J. Rawson were up on a search for a Catalina flying boat was in distress and was likely to be jumped by e/a but our Spitfires were recalled as a P.38 Squadron had arrived on the scene.
10:25-12:05	2 - Spitfires piloted by Sq/Ldr E.L. Joyce DFM and P/O G.A. Martin patrolled a convoy 15 miles North of Palermo without incident. Both a/c landed at Palermo as previously arranged and returned to base later.
18:25-20:25	2 - Spitfires piloted by Fl/Lt P.H.V. Wells and Fl/Sgt F. Davies were on an interception patrol at 15,000 feet North of Galite Island but nothing seen. These last few days a couple of FW190's reconnaissance machines have appeared in the area of Galite Island at various heights around dusk time and in the early morning but unfortunately for them both FW.190's, one day last week were caught by an American Squadron (No.5) and destroyed.
19:50	2 - Spitfires piloted by P/O R.D. Marsh and Sgt J. Bailey patrolled a convoy Northwest of Bizerte. No incident.
3 August 05:45 La Seballa (No.1)	2 - Spitfires piloted by F/O B. Bretherton and Fl/Sgt G.J.E. Hiltz patrolled a convoy 10 miles North of Cap Bon. A tanker was seen to blow up at the rear of the convoy.
07:50-08:00	2 - Spitfires piloted by P/O R.D. Marsh and Sgt D.H. Thomas were off to patrol a high-speed which was about 20 miles from Cap Zebib. After 10 minutes they were ordered to land. Early this morning, 11 N.C.Os. and airmen who have been a considerable time over-seas (some over three and half years) and who had been through all the campaign in the Middle East left the Squadron on posting to South Africa.
06:30-08:20	2 - Spitfires piloted by Fl/Lt C.F. Ambrose and Sgt D. Ross patrolled a high-speed launch which was about 70 miles North of Cap Zebib.
14:20-15:50	2 - Spitfires piloted by Fl/Lt G.P. Leggett and Sgt T.C. Stonehouse - patrolled a convoy 10 miles East of Rass Sidi El-Mekki proceeding East.
15:15-17:05	2 - Spitfires piloted by P/O M.W. Smyth and Fl/ Sgt W. Richie - patrolled the same convoy as above.
16:30-18:05	2 - Spitfires piloted by W/O N.F. Hewitt and Fl/Sgt J.L. Horn - also patrolled the above convoy, all without incident.
17:40-19:40	2 - Spitfires piloted by P/O B. Plenderleith and Fl/Sgt E.M. Karatau - patrolled a convoy off Cap Bon proceeding East.

18:35-20:20 19:55-21:25	2 - Spitfires piloted by F/O J. McGill and F/O D. Draper - patrolled a convoy near Bizerte proceeding West. 4 - Spitfires piloted by P/O P.D. Jones, W/O N.F. Hewitt, Sgt J.L. Horn and Sgt A. Cenitch - patrolled a convoy 20 miles East of Cap Bon. All these convoy patrols were carried out without incident.
4 August 14:40-16:25 La Seballa (No.1) 17:25-19:40 18:40-20:00	2 - Spitfires piloted by Fl/Lt W.T.H. Gill and P/O S.D. Thistleton - were up on-air sea rescue work searching for a dinghy which was reported 100 miles Northeast of base but returned failing to find it. 2 - Spitfires piloted by F/O H.C. Charlesworth and Fl/Sgt G.J.E. Hiltz - were airborne to patrol a Wellington and a Walrus which were on an air sea rescue (A.S.R.) job. After various courses the Spitfires found themselves North of Sicily but failed to find the A.S.R. craft. 2 - Spitfires piloted by P/O P.D. Jones and Fl/Sgt J.C. McCall were up on the interception patrol North of Galite Island. E/a were in the area but the vectors the Spitfires received failed to find them.
5 August La Sebala (No.1) 13:45-14:25 18:40-20:20	F/O J. McGill who recently was transferred from "A" Flight to "B" Flight as a Flight Commander was today promoted to Fl/Lt. 2 - Spitfires piloted by F/O D. Gadd and Sgt A. Cenitch were scrambled to 20 miles North of base to 20,000 feet but when reaching 10,000 feet were informed that the e/a had disappeared. The Spitfires orbited for a while and returned to base. 2 - Spitfires piloted by Fl/Lt G.P. Leggett and P/O G.A. Martin - were up on a dusk interception patrol North of Galite Island. The two-reconnaissance e/a were in the vicinity as usual but disappeared West. But a little later two more appeared in the area flying at 30,000 feet. The Spitfires were ordered up but at 25,000 feet ran out of oxygen and at the same time the e/a were plotted 30 miles North of Galite Island at 21,000 feet making their way back. In the meantime, No.2 Spitfire returned early with a Glycol leak.
6 August 05:55-07:15 16:25-18:15	2 - Spitfires piloted by P/O F.C. Bremner and Fl/Sgt W. Richie - patrolled a convoy entering Bizerte harbour. No incident. 2 - Spitfires piloted by Fl/Sgt F. Davies and Sgt D.H. Thomas - searched for a dinghy in the water which was reported 35 miles Northeast of Cap Bon. The dinghy was found but was empty so one of the pilots sank it with MG fire.

6 August [continued] 18:10-19:25	2 - Spitfires piloted by W/O N.F. Hewitt and Fl/Sgt J.C. McCall - were on the interception patrol off Galite Island at 25,000 feet. The pilots had various vectors and orbited at various points, but no e/a were encountered.
7 August	Today the Squadron was released for training and quite a lot of formation and practice scrambles were carried out during the morning and afternoon.
	2 - Spitfires piloted by P/O G.A. Martin and Sgt F.C.H. Hampton - while on a practice interception over base, were vectored on to an /a approaching Bizerte but the e/a disappeared before the Spitfires reached the area.
8 August	Today we have returned to readiness as from first light.
05:55-06:55	2 - Spitfires piloted by Fl/Lt J. McGill and F/O D. Draper - patrolled a convoy between Cap Serrat and Bizerte. No incident.
20:00-20:55	2 - Spitfires piloted by Fl/Lt J.P. Mills and Fl/Sgt D.J. Green - were scrambled this evening to 20,000 feet over Bizerte, then they were sent to 30 miles North Northwest of Galite Island at 18,000 feet where they orbited for a while then were ordered back to base as the e/a had disappeared.
19:45-21:15	2 - Spitfires piloted by Sq/Ldr E.L. Joyce and Sgt T.H. Ross - patrolled a convoy 30 Miles East of Cap Bon where it was taking a Northerly direction. There was no incident.
9 August 15:50-17:45	The first patrol of the day did not take place until well into the late afternoon when, 2 - Spitfires piloted by Fl/Lt G.P. Leggett and P/O G.A. Martin - patrolled a convoy between Cap Negro and Cap Serrat without incident.
16:40-18:45	2 - Spitfires piloted by F/O M.W. Smyth and Sgt T.C. Stonehouse - patrolled same convoy as above, now about 15 miles East of Cap Serrat and 5 miles offshore.
18:00-19:35	2 - Spitfires piloted by P/O B. Plenderleith and Fl/Sgt E.M. Karatau - patrolled same convoy as above, now about 20 miles Northeast of Cap Serrat. Weather becoming 7/10 cloud at 2,000 feet.
18:40-20:10	2 - Spitfires piloted by WO N.F. Hewitt and Fl/Sgt J.L. Horn - were also up to patrol the same convoy but after searching for a while were unable to find it. The weather was again poor.

20:25-20:35	2 - Spitfires piloted by P/O R.D Marsh and P/O G.A. Martin - were scrambled to North of Bizerte but when at 3,000 feet were ordered to return to base.
19:35-20:50	P/O F.C. Bremner and Fl/Lt Sgt W. Richie were the last two Spitfire pilots to operate today. They also set out to patrol the above-mentioned convoy but after a long search between Bizerte and Cap Serrat areas had to return, failing to locate.
10 August	Today the 10th was a non-operational day for the Squadron, the only flying being two communication flights with a total of 1 hour 25 minutes.
11 August	There were no operations today, but much time was devoted to shadow-firing, 20 pilots taking part Fl/Sgt C.J.A. Edwards returned from hospital.
12 August	There were again no operations today; in the afternoon, flying practice was carried out by both flights. P/O S.D. Thistleton flew on an army co-operation course.
13 August 17:00-17:40	2 - Spitfires VC flown by Sq/Ldr P.H.V. Wells and Sgt D.H. Thomas were scrambled to 17,000 feet over Bizerte but were recalled as bogey was friendly.
17:45-19:00	P/O R.D. Marsh and Sgt F.J. Bailey in Spitfires, scrambled to 20,000 feet 40 miles North of Bizerte but did not see any e/a.
19:25-20:55	P/O P.D. Jones and Fl/Sgt W.J. MyGind patrolled convoy "BONDAGE" 25 miles East pf Cap Bon. P/O P.D. Jones returned early with engine trouble and was replaced by Fl/Lt W.T.H. Gill DFC. No incident occurred. In the afternoon Sq/Ldr E.L. Joyce DFM and Fl/Lt J. McGill DFC flew to Maison Blanche to attend a party given by the A.C.C., N.A.C.A.F. the following night.
14 August	There were no operations today and the only flying done was two engine tests.
15 August 06:50-08:30	Sq/Ldr P.H.V. Wells, P/O R.D. Marsh, Sgt T.H. Ross, F/O B. Bretherton and Sgt F.J. Bailey searched for a dinghy reported to be 30 miles East of Cap Bon but could not find it. There was no more operational flying today, but practice scrambles were carried out by 6 a/c and in the evening the CC returned from Maison Blanche after a very enjoyable party.

16 August 06:40-08:20 La Sebala (No.1)	F/O H.W Coussens and Fl/Sgt W.J. MyGind searched for a dinghy reported 15 miles East of Bizerte but could not be found.
06:40-08:30	Fl/Lt J.P Mills and Fl/Sgt D.J. Green set off to patrol a convoy said to be near Cap Serrat sailing East but could not find it.
07:55-09:10	P/O G.A. Martin and Sgt T.C. Stonehouse eventually located the above convoy composed of 3 cargo boats and 4 escort vessels just offshore from Rass Zehib going East. The patrol was uneventful.
10:45-11:35	P/O E.T. Bennett and Sgt A. Cenitch patrolled two cruisers and two destroyers from 10 miles North of Rass Zehib to 15 miles East of Rass Sidi El-Mekki. No incident took place, and the patrol was continued by Fl/Lt J.P. Mills and Fl/Sgt D.J. Green until the ships were about 70 miles North of Bizerte.
13:45-14:10	Fl/Lt W.T.H. Gill DFC and Fl/Sgt J.C. McCall were scrambled to 20,000 feet over Bizerte but were recalled when they had reached 10,000 feet as the bogey turned out to be friendly.
18:25-19:05	2 - Spitfires piloted by Fl/Lt C.F. Ambrose and Sgt F.J. Bailey - were scrambled to 20,000 feet Northeast of Bizerte but when at 18,000 feet RED I experienced oxygen trouble and returned to base and RED II was recalled a few minutes later. No e/a were seen.
18:20-19:20	2 - Spitfires piloted by F/O R. Bretherton and Fl/Sgt F. Davies - were scrambled to 20,000 feet over Bizerte. They received various vectors but unfortunately the bogey plots faded. In the meantime, Fl/Sgt F. Davies returned early with engine trouble.
19:40-20:45	P/O R.D. Marsh and Sgt T.H. Ross patrolled convoy **"WASTING"** which was located about 8 miles North of Cap Serrat. The shipping was covered at 10,000 feet. Later the spitfires were ordered to 20,000 feet as there were some e/a approaching the area. 3 e/a appeared in the vicinity, the first coming from the North at 15,000 feet and the other 2 e/a from the same direction at 18,000 feet, our spitfires were ordered to investigate but very shortly afterwards the e/a turned North then Eastwards and disappeared. The weather was good.
19:40-21:00	2 other Spitfires piloted by P/O P.D. Jones and P/O S.D. Thistleton also patrolled **"WASTING"** at the same time as the above 2 pilots. They covered the convoy at 5,000 feet without incident. The convoy was about 40 units strong plus escort.

19:50-21:00	Today's good work ended with a scramble. Fl/Lt W.T.H. Gill DFC and Fl/Sgt J.C. McCall scrambled their spits to 20,000 feet due North of base. They were then given various vectors by **"Whipsnade"** which finally brought them to a point just East of Bizerte where they orbited for a while. Nothing was seen so they returned to base.
17 August La Sebala (No.1) 11:20-11:40	Five of our best and all well-known pilots were today taken off operational strength pending posting to the Delta area. They have all completed their present tour of duty in day and night operations in both Hurricanes and Spitfires. "A" Flight will be losing three officers, namely Fl/Lt G.P Leggett, F/O H.C. Charlesworth, and F/O M.W. Smyth the latter having just been recently promoted to his present rank, and "B" Flight will be losing F/O D. Gadd also just recently promoted and Fl/Sgt J. Rawson. These five pilots have done very good work with the Squadron in the past, which includes operating every night during the Eighth Army's advance from Egypt. 2 - short range Spitfires were scrambled on a vector of 360° to 20,000 feet after 2 - bogey e/a but when over Bizerte at 10,000 feet they were informed that a/c were friendly. The spitfires still continued their vector till they reached 15,000 feet where F/O D. Draper and his BLUE II Fl/Sgt E.M. Karatau orbited for a while before returning to base.

Assault on **SICILY** - **Operation Husky** continued until the **17 August 1943**.

17 August [continued]	The above was the only operational flight of the day but there was the usual non-operational flying which included air tests, cannon tests, shadow-firing and formation flying training. Also flying today was G/Cpt J.R. Hallings-Pott, Commanding Officer of the Wing, whose a/c is kept in our Squadron.
18 August 07:45-08:20 18:15-19:20	Today was an easy day for the Squadron, 3 scrambles being our total operations. 2 - long range Spitfires piloted by Sq/Ldr E.L. Joyce DFM and Sgt T.C. Stonehouse - scrambled 010° to 15,000 feet after 2 bogey e/a but on reaching a point 20miles Northeast of Bizerte, the spitfires were ordered to return to base as the lots had faded. The weather this morning was ideal for flying. The rest of the day was again taken up by formation flying and shadow firing, the shadow firing taking place out to sea just North of Bizerte.

18 August [continued]	We had our second scramble when F/O D. Draper and Fl/Sgt J.L. Horn were scrambled on 320°, angels 25, which took them to Galite Island. They got other vectors which brought them to Bizerte and to Northeast of Bizerte, but no e/a were encountered.
19:55-20:15	BLUE section again was scrambled - F/O D. Draper and Fl/Sgt J.L. Horn - on a course of 360°, angels 20 miles but F/O D. Draper had a misfortune to crash on take-off through a burst tyre. The Spitfire was badly damaged, but the pilot was unhurt. Meanwhile BLUE II was airborne and was ordered to orbit base at 20,000 feet but a little later was ordered to land.
19 August 05:50-07:40 La Sebala (No.1)	4 - Spitfires piloted by Fl/Lt J.P. Mills, P/O E.T. Bennett, Fl/Sgt D.J. Green and Sgt A. Cenitch took off to patrol convoy **"BEDSPREAD"** to a point West of Bizerte but failed to find it.
06:55-08:30	4 other Spitfires piloted by P/O G.A. Martin, P/O F.C. Bremner, Fl/Sgt F. Davies and Fl/Sgt W. Richie also took off to patrol **"BEDSPREAD".** The convoy was located about 20 miles offshore due North of Cap Negro, cloud was 5/10 at 1,000 feet.
05:50-08:05	2 - long range Spitfires piloted by Sq/Ldr P.E.V. Wells and Fl/Sgt G.J.E. Hiltz took off to patrol convoy **"SOLVENT"** which was said to be near Cap Bon. After a wide and successful search, they returned to base and were then informed by controller that the convoy had not yet left Algiers.
09:00	3 - Spitfires flown by P/O S.D. Thistleton, Fl/Sgt E.M. Karatau and Fl/Sgt W. Richie maintained a continuous patrol over Bizerte at 25,000 feet until 13:00 in anticipation of possible enemy reconnaissance aircraft but none approached.
20 August La Sebala (No.1)	Fl/Lt G.P. Leggett, F/O H.C. Charlesworth, F/O M.W. Smyth F/O D. Gadd and Fl/Sgt J. Rawson left the Squadron early this morning on their way to ALMAZA on posting.
12:40-20:40	These five pilots left with the best wishes of all ranks, and it is hoped they will get their well-earned rest before they go on their next operational tour. Today also it was learned that F/O H.W. Coussens received his certificate of membership of the "Late Arrival Club" in recognition of his return to base in June last after being shot down behind enemy lines in the Mareth area. F.O H.W. Coussens is on his second tour of duty with this Squadron

	14 - Spitfires this afternoon, operating in pairs, maintained a standing patrol over Bizerte at 25,000 feet. One or two sections had various vectors from the controller during their patrols, but all went off without incident. The pilots were: - P/O E.T. Leggett, Sgt A. Cenitch, P/O R.D. Marsh, Sgt T.C. Stonehouse, Fl/Lt J.P. Mills, Fl/Sgt D.J. Green Sq/Ldr E.L. Joyce DFM, Fl/Sgt W. Richie, Fl/Lt J. McGill DFC, F/O D. Draper, Sq/Ldr P.E.V. Wells, Fl/Sgt F. Davies, F/O R. Plenderleith and F/Sgt E.M. Karatau.
21 August 07:30-08:05 La Sebala (No.1)	2 - Spitfires piloted by P/O S.D. Thistleton and Fl/Sgt W.J. MyGind - this morning was scrambled over Bizerte at 'Angels' 20 to intercept two possible e/a but when at 11,000 feet the Spitfires were informed that bogeys were friendly. The rest of the operational flying for the day was carried out by 14 Spitfires at 25,000 feet. The a/c operated in sections of twos with RED section first off at 06:15. The patrol was carried on until 13:45 hours, all without incident. The pilots were: - Sq/Ldr P.H.V. Wells, Fl/Sgt F. Davies, P/O P.D. Jones, Fl/Sgt J.VC. McCall, P/O R.D. Marsh, Sgt T.C. Stonehouse, W/O N.F. Hewitt, Fl/Sgt J.L. Horn, P/O G.A. Martin, Sgt T.H. Ross, Fl/Lt W.T.H. Gill DFC, P/O S.D. Thistleton, F/O B. Bretherton and Fl/Sgt W. Richie. The Squadron was released for the rest of the day.
22 August La Sebala (N0.1)	P/O R.D. Marsh and Fl/Sgt F. Davies today flew to Maison Blanche near Algiers on a communication flight. Other flying this morning was confined to local formation over Bizerte when four of our Spitfires flew over the area at various heights.
12:50-14:30	2 - short-range spitfires piloted by F/O R. Plenderleith and Fl/Sgt E.M. Karatau - patrolled Bizerte at 25,00 feet. No incident.
14:00-15:10	2 - more short-range Spitfires piloted by F/O R.H. Phillips and Sgt F.C. Hampton - were also up on the standing patrol of Bizerte at 25,000 feet.
14:30-15:30	The above pilots were relieved by P/O F.C. Bremner and Sgt D.H. Thomas flying long range Spitfires.
15:00-16:30	The above was followed by F/O D. Draper and Sgt A. Cenitch. One or two bogey plots appeared in the patrol area, but it is very rarely that standing patrol pilots are vectored on to them.
16:00-17:40	Fl/Sgt G.J.E. Hiltz and Sgt F.J. Bailey were the fifth section to patrol Bizerte with nothing to report.

22 August [continued] 17:00-18:35	They were relieved by two short range Spitfires piloted by Fl/Lt J.P Mills and Fl/Sgt D.J. Green.
18:00-19:25	F/O R.H. Phillips and Sgt F.C.H. Hampton were up on patrol for the second time this afternoon.
18:40-19:40	P/O F.C. Bremner and Sgt D.H Thomas were scrambled over Bizerte at 25,000 feet. They received various vectors and were quite near to the e/a at one time Sgt D.H. Thomas (YELLOW II) jettisoned his long-range tank but unfortunately the spitfire did not see the e/a, which a little while later disappeared. The cloud at 15,000 feet was 10/10.
19:00-20:25	P/O E.T. Bennett and Fl/Sgt E.M. Karatau of "B" Flight were the last section to patrol Bizerte also without incident.
23 August La Sebala (No.1)	Today also passed with standing patrols over the town and harbour of Bizerte although we managed to get three scrambles in between. The standing patrol sections usually take off at one-hour intervals to relieve each other over the target. These last few days the Bizerte standing Patrol at 25,000 feet has been carried out on alternate days with 32 Squadron.
06:00-13:55	7 sections of two spitfires each carried out this morning's patrol over Bizerte - all without incident. The pilots being in the following order of take-off: - Sq/Ldr P.H.V. Wells, Fl/Lt J.P. Mills, F/O H.W Coussens, P/o S.D. Thistleton, F/O B. Bretherton, Sgt T.C. Stonehouse, W/O N.F. Hewitt, Fl/Sgt W.J. MyGind, P/O G.A. Martin, Sgt F.J. Bailey, Fl/Sgt J.C. McCall, Fl/Sgt J.L. Horn, Fl/Lt J.F. Mills and Sgt T.H. Ross.
07:40-08:15	Two long-range spitfires piloted by P/O P.D. Jones and Fl/Sgt W.J. MyGind - were scrambled on 360°, angels, 25 but the latter pilot was unable to take off. On being airborne BLACK I, was vectored on 330°. When at 23,000 feet just North of Bizerte he orbited for a while. No e/a were seen and a little later he was ordered to land.
09:30-10:25	2 - more Spitfires piloted by Fl/Sgt J.C. McCall and Fl/Sgt J.L. Horn - were scrambled on a course of 350° to 20.000 feet for two minutes, then again were vectored 330°. E/A wee reported 12 miles ahead coming towards our spitfires at 21,000 feet. The spitfires by then were at 17,000 feet and at

13:05-13:55	that moment the bandits turned away and the spitfires were vectored to 230°. The bandits were now reported 22,000 feet still 12 miles ahead when GREEN II's R/T faded out. The spitfires were again vectored this time 010° which took them almost to the coast of Sardinia where the e/a disappeared. W/O N.F. Hewitt and Fl/Sgt E.J. MyGind were scrambled 330°, angels 20. Later to 25,000 feet on 190° which took them a little to the North of Bizerte two bandits were reported about one mile away from the spitfire's present position but after orbiting for about 10 minutes, the a/c were ordered to land and reporting nothing seen. The visibility was about 40 miles at 20,000 feet.
24 August 13:00-20:25 La Sebala (No.1) 15:25-16:35	14 - Spitfires, operating in pairs, patrolled Bizerte at 35,000 feet again without incident. The pilots were: - Fl/Lt J.P. Mills, Fl/Sgt G.J.E. Hiltz, P/O E.T. Bennett, Sgt A. Cenitch, Sq/Ldr E.L. Joyce DFM, Sgt D.H. Thomas, F/O D. Draper, Fl/Sgt D.J. Green, Sq/Ldr P.H.V. Wells, Sgt T.H. Ross, F/O R. Plenderleith, Fl/Sgt E.M. Karatau, F/O B. Bretherton, Sgt T.C. Stonehouse. F/O R. Plenderleith and Fl/Sgt E.M. Karatau flying two long range Spitfires, were out searching for a dinghy on a course of 015° from base where it was found about 15 miles from the coast. The Spitfires patrolled the dinghy until a high-speed launch arrived and picked up the survivors.
25 August La Sebala (No.1) 05:40-12:50	Today Fl/Lt C.F, Ambrose DFC (and his dog "William") left to join 89 Squadron (Beaufighters) at Bu Amed. Fl/Lt Ambrose who was "A" Flight Commander had his share in the Battle of Britain and was awarded his DFC in the Norway campaign. Also, today two more pilots left the squadron on posting: - P/O R.D. Marsh and Fl/Sgt F. Davies. Both these pilots also belonged to Fl/Lt Ambrose's "A" Flight. This morning again 8 sections of Spitfires operating over Bizerte at 25,000 feet. Sq/Ldr E.L. Joyce DFM, and Sgt T.H. Ross patrolled 30 miles North of Bizerte for 45 minutes at 10,000 feet prior to going on the standing patrol. The other pilots were W/O N.F. Hewitt, Fl/Sgt J.L. Horn, P/O S.D Thistleton, Fl/Sgt J.C. McCall, F/O R.H. Phillips, Sgt D.H. Thomas, P/O P.D. Jones, Fl/Sgt W.J. MyGind, Sq/Ldr P.H.V. Wells, P/O F.C. Bremner, F/O G.A. Martin, and Sgt F.J. Bailey.

26 August 12:50-14:15 La Sebala (No.1) 16:00-18:00 20:10-21:45	This afternoon again the squadron patrolled Bizerte at 25,000 feet with 16 Spitfires operating in sections of twos. The first section off: - F/O D. Draper and Fl/Sgt D.J. Green had just gained their patrol height over the target area when they had a vector of 360°, angels 13 and a little later vectored 340°to intercept e/a that were approaching the patrol area. The Spitfires reached a point about, 20 miles due East of Bizerte and were then ordered to 25,000 feet again. Another e/a appeared from the North flying at 8,000 feet. The Spitfires again received various vectors to intercept and when down at 8,000 feet they got a visual on an unidentified aircraft, but the bogey disappeared over land about 15 miles West of Bizerte. 2 - long range Spitfires piloted by F/O G.A. Martin and Sgt F.J. Bailey patrolled convoy **"DECADE"** which consisted of 2 cruisers and 2 destroyers between 40 North of Cap Bon and Cap Bizerte travelling Southwest. The other pilots on the standing patrol over Bizerte were F/O B. Bretherton, Sgt T.C. Stonehouse, F/O R. Plenderleith, Fl/Sgt E.M. Karatau, Sq/Ldr P.H.V. Wells, Fl/Sgt W. Richie, P/O E.T. Bennett, Sgt A. Cenitch, Fl/Sgt G.J.E. Hiltz, Sgt D.H. Thomas, P/O D. Draper and Fl/Sgt D.J. Green. 4 - Spitfires piloted by Fl/Lt J.P. Mills, P/O F.C. Bremner, Sgt T.H. Ross and Sgt F.C.H. Hampton were up on dusk patrol 30 miles North of Bizerte. Each aircraft patrolled different heights, 7, 8, 9 and 10,000 feet but no e/a were seen. The lights of two hospital ships were seen about 70 miles offshore.
27 August 06:25-07:55 La Sebala (No.1) 07:05-08:40 08:20-09:45 09:15-10:25	2 - Spitfires piloted by F/O H.W. Coussens and P/O P.D. Jones - patrolled Bizerte at 25,000 feet. No incident. 2 - long range Spitfires were scrambled on 010° to 13,000 feet. They received various vectors to intercept e/a but the e/a kept too wide of our area. The Spitfires then went on the standing patrol of Bizerte where again they had nothing to report. The above two pilots were relieved on the standing patrol by W/O N.F. Hewitt and Fl/Sgt J.C. McCall. Fl/Sgt McCall returned early through being short of petrol. The third and last patrol of Bizerte was carried out by Fl/Lt J.P. Mills and Sgt T.H. Ross. At this stage of the standing patrol, the patrol was cancelled by Wing and the Squadron was put to readiness and 30 minutes states.

15:50-16:45	2 - Spitfires were brought to standby from readiness and immediately after were scrambled on 350°, angels 30. They got other vectors during their climb to 30,000 feet but the e/a had turned tail and fled before the Spitfires had reached their height. The controller ordered the pilots F/O H.W. Coussens and P/O S.D. Thistleton, to return to base.
28 August La Sebala (No.1)	Today was a free day as Wing decided that 73 should have a rest. But nevertheless, the pilots put in quite a few hours on shadow firing, formation flying, communication flying and engine tests.
29 August La Sebala (No.1) 17:45-19:15 18:45-20:00	The Squadron were at readiness and 30 minutes available states today from first light but only 4 sorties were carried out. 2 - Spitfires piloted by Fl/Sgt G.J.E. Hiltz and Sgt D.H. Thomas patrolled 20 miles North of Bizerte at 20,000 feet where the Hun was expected to show up. The e/a appeared in the area and the Spitfires were ordered on various vectors, but no contact was made. Fl/Lt J.P. Mills and Sgt T.H. Ross relieved the above two pilots on the same patrol. They also got a number of vectors to intercept e/a but the enemy kept rather wide of the patrol area.
30 August 13:55-15:40 La Sebala (No.1) 14:50-16:55	F/O R.H. Phillips and Sgt F.C.H. Hampton patrolled the convoy **"LIEGE"** which was off Cap Bon travelling East. The convoy was covered for an hour without incident. P/O F.C. Bremner and Fl/Sgt W. Richie flying two long range Spitfires, relieved the previous two pilots on convoy **"LIEGE"** where they also covered the shipping for an hour and were relieved by another Squadron.
31 August 06:55-08:15 La Sebala (No.1) 11:25-12:10 12:20-13:45 18:00-20:05	2 - Spitfires piloted by F/O G.A. Martin and SGT F.J. Bailey patrolled North of Bizerte. The 'spits' had a few vectors, but the e/a were not seen. F/O H.W. Coussens and P/O P.D. Jones were scrambled to 20 miles North of Bizerte, angels 20 but e/a plots faded so were ordered to land. Fl/Sgt J.C. McCall and Fl/Sgt W.J. MyGind patrolled the line 20 miles North of Bizerte but again nothing was seen. 4 - Spitfires piloted by F/O D. Draper, P/O E.T. Bennett, Fl/Sgt E.M. Karatau and Sgt A. Cenitch patrolled a line 20 miles North of Bizerte to 40 miles East of Bizerte. The Spitfires were vectored on to two hostile aircraft which were plotted in from the North but returned Northwards again before interception could be made.

31 August [continued] 16:05-17:35	The last operational sorties of the month took place while F/O B. Bretherton and Sgt T.C, Stonehouse were on practice interceptions over base. One bogey was plotted making for Bizerte. The spitfires were vectored but bogey aircraft turned out to be friendly. This brings us to the end of **AUGUST 1943** with a total of 416 operational hours which is actually less than half of **JULY's** total owing to the fact that Wing have had two more Squadrons allocated to them. The aircraft serviceability for the month stood at 95%.

Note: For daily pilot records of flight operations carried out by 'A' Flight of RAF - 73 Squadron refer to AIR 27/632/16. These records detail the a/c number, the pilot's name and the sortie carried out.

The RAF 73 Squadron's remaining months of September/October 1943 were ones where they moved to Italy under Operation Avalanche. Then from November/ December 1943, the squadron consolidated their position in Italy, being stationed at Foggia Main.

Chapter 15

Items Discovered, Hobbies, Etc.

This chapter details and shows some of the memorabilia collected during LAC Lamb's service in the RAF whilst stationed in North Africa 1940 to 1943, and Italy 1943 to 1944.

Whilst stationed in the Middle East during the Second World War it was customary to be paid in what was called Allied military currency. A sample of the typical Italian money issued to the Allied forces at the time is shown below. Unfortunately, it is a little faded with time, but still legible.

From the limited yet extremely useful information contained within the diaries of LAC Lamb it can quite easily be felt as to the type of life being experienced during the North African and Italy campaign, and how best they overcame the boredom and sometimes tediousness of the job.

Some remarkably interesting items of discovery at the time were some Russian and German bank notes. From the investigation carried out, these bank notes, along with some German, Netherlands, Belgium, and French coins, were all found in one of the deserted derelict buildings that had recently been captured from the Germans.

Above left: 1 Lira Italian Second World War Bank Note

Above right: 10 Lira Italian Second World War Bank Note

The Russian bank notes that were discovered are to the value of 500 roubles (issued by the Russian State Bank, date 1912) and 1000 roubles (issued under the name CREDIT MONEY, by the Provisional State Government of Russia, date 1917).

The German, Netherlands, Belgium, and French coins are all typical of the coins in circulation at the time. It would be fair to say that these were obviously brought to North Africa by one or more of the invading forces and lost during the ensuing battles.

In addition to the bank notes and coins found, some coins were found in the desert area whilst digging trenches for protection. The coins discovered are of a much earlier period, and it was not until December 1993, to be precise, that their actual date in history was established.

The Ashmolean Museum in Oxford were instrumental in giving precise dates to these coins, and from the information and data collated, it has been confirmed that these are genuine coins from the **Carthage** and **Ottoman** periods.

500 Rouble Bank Note.

1000 Rouble Bank Note.

There can be no doubt, that like all service men fighting abroad, if the opportunity presented itself by way of collecting souvenirs to bring back home, then my father was certainly no exception from anyone else. I would like to think that in bringing these articles back with him it was a way of keeping in touch with the reality that they all faced; just small fragments of a much larger jigsaw that had been part of their lives during the duration of the war.

German - 1000 Reichsbautnote.

However, devastated by the act of warfare and its inevitable destruction of man and his world, these items were a constant reminder to them of not only the bad times but more importantly the good times.

There were times when the Allied forces captured previously held German positions. My father would recall the fact that the first place of call, once they had been made safe from any booby traps, was to inspect the discarded and wrecked planes that the Germans had left behind, to see if any parts were salvageable: items like guns, ammunition, Perspex from the cockpit canopies and any item that they

Above left: Collection of Coins & Bank Notes Set in Sand.

Above right: Snake 3′ 3″ long Sidi Amoud, March 1941.

could best make use of. Spares of any description were hard to come by, especially if the following supply convoys were detained for one reason or another.

From the photographic evidence taken at the time, you can get a feeling for the type of life that they all led, and the conditions in which they had to live and hopefully survive.

The Allied troops, whilst stationed in the Middle East, would keep themselves occupied in the quieter moments by taking up a hobby. Some of the hobbies that were employed by the troops were making rings and cap badges out of Perspex from crashed enemy aircraft, trick photography and catching desert snakes and skinning them.

Once the snake was skinned, the skin would then be placed in oils to preserve it. (Refer to the photograph below, which is a photograph of LAC Lamb with one of his killed/skinned snakes.)

Chapter 16

Future Planned Operations: Sicily (Husky) and Italy (Avalanche), 1943

Sicilian Campaign 9 July–17 August 1943

- **Operation Husky**

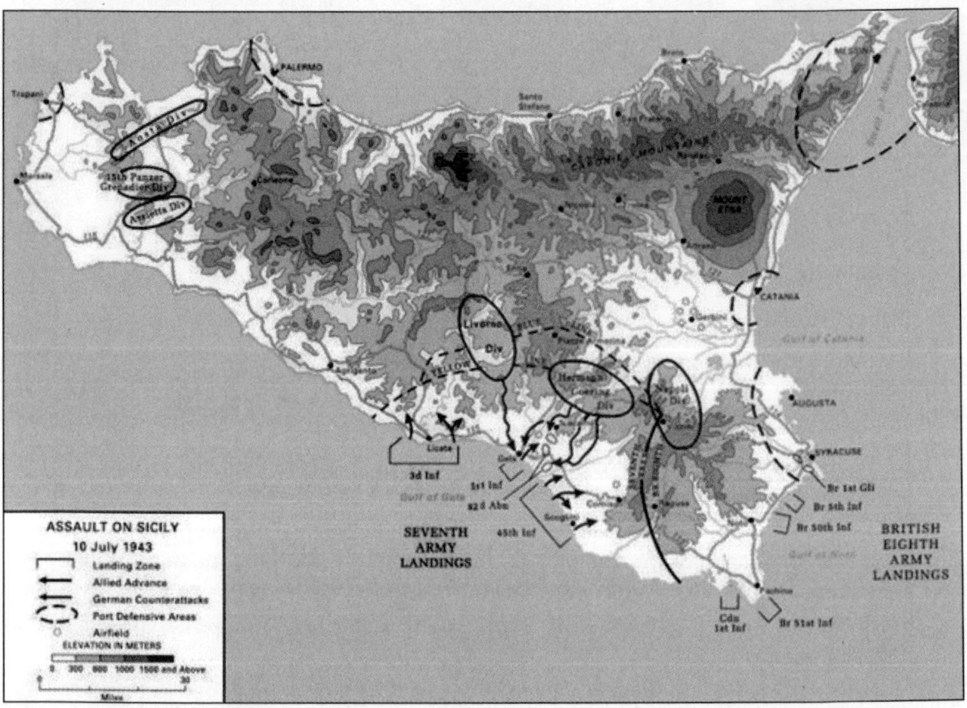

Map of the Assault Plan on Sicily.
(This is a map of the Allied army amphibious landing in Sicily, 10 July, 1943, as part of Operation Husky. It shows the deployments of the landing forces and the German and Italian formations defending the island. This image is in the public domain because it contains materials that originally came from the United States Army Center of Military History. Source: http://www.history.army.mil/brochures/72-16/map1. Email dated 20/09/2023: "Map(s) courtesy of the United States Military Academy Department of History.")

The Allied Invasion of Sicily, also known as the Battle of Sicily and Operation Husky, was a major campaign of the Second World War in which the Allied forces invaded the island of Sicily in July 1943 and took it from the Axis powers (Fascist Italy and Nazi Germany).

The battle for Sicily was one that followed on from the battles in North Africa, which saw the Axis forces defeated and prevented from evacuating from Northwest Africa to Sicily and Italy, thus preventing a great number of troops and equipment needed in the battles that followed. The final toll in captured personnel after the Tunisian campaign totalled in excess of some 267,000 German and Italian (Axis) troops.

It began with a large amphibious and airborne operation, followed by a six-week land campaign, and initiated the Italian campaign – Operation Avalanche.

To divert some of the Axis forces to other areas, the Allies engaged in several deception operations, and the most famous and successful was Operation Mincemeat. Operation Husky began on the night of 9–10 July 1943 and ended on 17 August 1943. Strategically, Operation Husky achieved the goals set out for it by the Allied planners; the Allies drove Axis air, land and naval forces from the island and the Mediterranean Sea lanes were opened for Allied merchant ships for the first time since 1941. These events led to the Italian leader, Benito Mussolini, being toppled from power in Italy on 25 July 1943, and to the Allied invasion of Italy on 3 September 1943, Operation Avalanche.

Background

Allies

The plan for Operation Husky called for the amphibious assault of Sicily by two Allied armies, one landing on the south-eastern and one on the central southern coast. The amphibious assaults were to be supported by naval gunfire, as well as tactical bombing, interdiction and close air support by the combined air forces. As such, the operation required a complex command structure, incorporating land, naval and air forces. The overall commander was the American General Dwight D. Eisenhower, as commander-in-chief (C-in-C) of all the Allied forces in North Africa. British General Sir Harold Alexander acted as his second-in-command and as the 15th Army Group commander. The American Major General Walter Bedell Smith was appointed Eisenhower's chief of staff. The overall naval force commander was the British Admiral Sir Andrew Cunningham.

The Allied forces would be made up from the American, British and Canadian armies, and were structured as two task forces. The Eastern Task Force (also known as Task Force 545) was led by General Sir Bernard Montgomery and consisted of the British Eighth Army (which included the 1st Canadian Infantry Division). The Western Task Force (was known as Task Force 543) and commanded by Lieutenant General George S. Patton and consisted of the American Seventh Army. The two task force commanders reported to Alexander as commander of the 15th Army Group.

Operation Avalanche: Invasion of Italy, September–October 1943

The Allied forces had now driven the Axis forces (Germany and Italy) from North Africa and Sicily; their next task was to push them out of Italy, and in September 1943 the Allied forces implemented Operation Avalanche. The following map shows how this plan was to be implemented, which included the

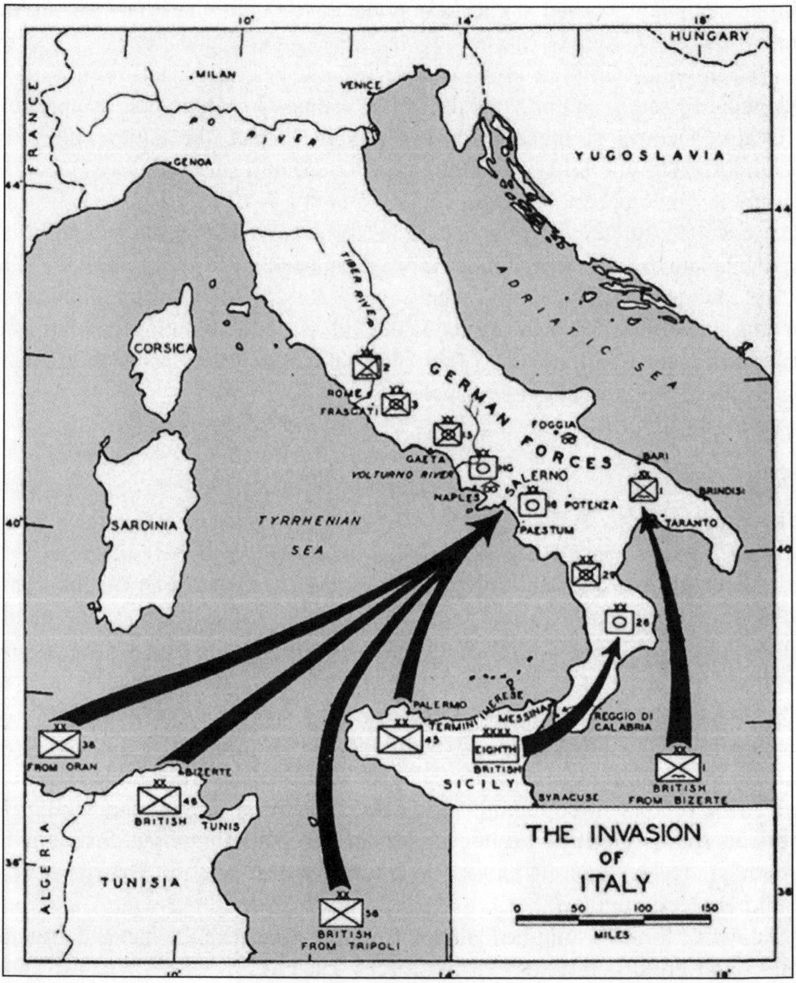

Operation Avalanche.
(*The above image is in the Public Domain in the United States–No Copyright in the USA. Source: http://army.mil/cmh-pg/books/wwii/salerno/sal-prep.htm File: Invasionofitaly 1943.jpg. Email received from susannezoumbaris@nara.gov on the 5 April 2022 at 10:44 hours. Providing the credits are set out then consent is approved.* Email dated 20/09/2023: "Map(s) courtesy of the United States Military Academy Department of History.")

relocation of the RAF squadrons from North Africa to the area around Foggia, where there were a good number of Italian airbases that, once captured, could soon be put into use.

Operation Avalanche

Operation Avalanche was the codename used by the Allies for the beach landings near the Port of Salerno. The battle for Italy was implemented to start on the 9 September 1943 as part of the Allied invasion of Italy. It is worth noting that after the Axis defeat in North Africa and the advance of the Allied forces across North Africa, the Italians withdrew from the war the day before the Allied invasion started. Unfortunately for the Allies, they landed in an area defended by the Germans.

Under the command of the American General Mark W. Clark, the landings were carried out by the US Fifth Army, which comprised of the US VI Corps, the British X Corps, and the US 82nd Airborne Division, a total of nine divisions. The landings were supported by the newly formed RAF 68 and 69 Beach unit squadrons whose prime role was of 'reconnaissance'. The main goal of the Allies was to capture the Port of Naples to ensure that supply routes for the allies would be maintained (something the Axis forces in North Africa found extremely difficult to maintain) and to cut across to the east coast, trapping the German troops further south.

As the Allies continued their assault on the Germans at Salerno, it was essential that the Allies drew the German troops away from the landing ground, and Operation Baytown was put into operation. Operation Baytown is where the British Eighth Army, after their victory in North Africa, was to land in Calabria in the 'toe' of Italy, on the 3 September 1943. At the same time, simultaneous landings were to take place by the British 1st Airborne Division at the Port of Taranto (Operation Slapstick). British General Bernard Montgomery predicted that Baytown would be a waste of effort, as he assumed the Germans would give battle in Calabria. If this failed, then the diversion would not work. (Montgomery was proved right.) The Eighth Army, after Operation Baytown's failure, marched 300 miles (483 km) north to the Salerno area without meeting any opposition other than engineering obstacles.

As the Salerno landings continued, without Allied naval or aerial bombardment so as to achieve maximum surprise, the surprise was not achieved. With the first wave of troops approaching the shore at Paestum, a German voice via a loudspeaker located somewhere on the landing area proclaimed in English, 'Come on in and give up. We have you covered.' However, the troops attacked anyway.

Prior to the Italians withdrawing from the war, they had established artillery and machine gun posts as well as scattering tanks throughout the landing zones, which made progress difficult, but the beach areas were captured. A counterattack by the 16th Panzer Division took place, causing heavy casualties were inflicted as the beachhead could not resist the concentrated attacks, but the attack was beaten off. The British and American forces' progress was slow with still a 10-mile (16 km) gap between them at the end of day one. On day two, they had linked up and now occupied 35–45 miles (56–72 km) of coastline to a depth of 6–7 miles (10–11 km).

Over the 12–14 September 1943, there were concerted counterattacks by six German divisions of motorized troops, hoping to stem the attacks by the Allies and thus throw the Salerno beachhead into the sea before it could link up with the British Eighth Army. With the Allied troops spread out too thinly, heavy casualties were inflicted as the beachhead could not resist the concentrated attacks. Outmost troops were withdrawn to reduce the perimeter, and the new perimeter was able to hold with the assistance of naval and aerial support, even though the German attacks had reached almost to the beaches in places. During this period of the fighting the Allied fighter pilots would sleep under the wings of their planes just in case they had to beat a hasty retreat to Sicily.

Allied Strategy

Following on from the defeat of the Italian forces and the Afrika Korps in North Africa and Sicily, there were disagreements in the Allied camp as to the next best step of the war. Winston Churchill was of the strong opinion that Italy should be invaded, which he called the **'underbelly of Europe'**. Popular support in Italy was on the decline, and he believed an invasion would remove Italy and the influence of the Italian navy (Regia Marina) in the Mediterranean, which would open the sea up to Allied traffic and their supply routes.

In addition, it would tie down the German forces, keeping them away from the planned invasion of Normandy – Operation Overlord.

Mount Etna: Eruptions During the Second World War

Here are some useful yet widely unknown facts about Mount Etna – Sicily's Active Volcano eruptions during the Second World War.

16 March 1940–late June 1942: Central and northeast craters: growth of cinder cones and lava effusion within central crater; at the end of this eruptive period, central crater is filled with lava.

30 June–5 July 1942: Eruption from south-west flank (2780–2250 m).

19 September 1942–15 September 1944: Northeast crater active.

Chapter 17

Special Air Services

The Second World War 1941 to 1943

When writing about the Second World War's North Africa campaigns from 1941 to 1943, no book would be complete without a chapter that relates to the Special Air Services (SAS): 'Who Dares Wins'. Many historians and other authors have written about these intrepid men and none more famous than Damien Lewis with his books about the SAS and their exploits, one which is titled *Brothers in Arms.*

From their original conception in July 1941 by David Stirling, the SAS have been active in many conflicts over the years, and I for one am a firm believer that without special forces such as the SAS, the outcome of such conflicts fought may well have had a different outcome.

This chapter is dedicated to those brave men who took up the call and fought deep behind enemy lines, during which time they caused untold damage and created havoc and mayhem. The bravery shown by these men cannot be overemphasized: heroes one and all.

SAS: 'Who Dares Wins'

A Brief History

The SAS began life in July 1941 from an unorthodox idea and plan by Scots Guards Lieutenant David Stirling, who was serving with No. 8 (Guards) Commando, for small teams of parachute-trained soldiers to operate behind enemy lines to gain intelligence, destroy enemy aircraft and attack supply and reinforcement routes.

Following an impromptu meeting to air views with Major General Ritchie, the deputy chief of staff, he was able to

The SAS in North Africa During the Second World War. Lt Colonel David Stirling DSO.
(This is photograph, E 021340 from the collections of the Imperial War Museums. Approved for use under IWM Licence Number LIC-30663-V3V8L4.)

The Special Air Services During the Second World War. (Portrait of Lt Col Robert Blair 'Paddy' Mayne, SAS, in the desert near Kabrit, 1942. This is photograph, MH 24415 from the collections of the Imperial War Museums. Approved for use under IWM Licence Number LIC-30663-V3V8L4.)

meet the new C-in-C Middle East, General Auchinleck, who liked the plan, and it was endorsed by the army high command.

At the time, there was a deception organization already in place in the Middle East area, which wished to create a phantom airborne brigade to act as a threat to enemy planning of operations. At the time this deception unit was known as K Detachment SAS Brigade; of which David Stirling's was to be the 'offensive arm' and known as L Detachment SAS Brigade.

1941: SAS Action

After locating and completing the recruitment of the men selected for the assignment, extensive training was set up at **Kabrit** camp, which was located by the Nile. Training included the preparation for the men to parachute out of an aeroplane at altitude, plus fighting behind enemy lines and all that that entailed, including how to survive and get back to base.

During the training period, both Lieutenant Colonel Robert Blair "Paddy" Mayne and Lieutenant Colonel David Stirling DSO met with C-in-C Middle East General Auchenleck at the training ground at **Kabrit** for him to witness at firsthand the progress being made in readiness for the planned operation. The planes to be used in getting the troops to their drop zone were Bristol Bombay transport and bomber aircraft, which were adapted by the SAS for parachute training in the Middle East in 1941. (The Bristol Bombay could carry twenty-four fully equipped troops. The aircraft were powered by two 1,010 HP Bristol Pegasus engines, giving a maximum speed of 192 mph [309 kph] at 6,500 feet [1,981 m].) After completion of their training, L Detachment undertook its first parachute operation on enemy airfields on 16 and 17 November 1941. The operation undertaken used five Bristol Bombay aircraft to take the SAS on their first and only mission in the Western Desert. The operation was an attack on five main enemy forward airfields at **Timini** and **Gazala**, all prior to General Auchenleck's planned offensive. In extremely bad weather (dust storms and high winds), the airborne parties were dropped in the wrong place and the operation itself was a complete failure. Although the operation was not a success, David Stirling's enthusiasm and endeavour paid off and the detachment was allowed to expand. Recruiting took place using the Layforce Commando, which was in the process of being disbanded. Thereafter, all SAS operations were made with penetration raids by vehicle.

As to the new force being supplied with equipment needed for their operations, it was very much the case that in the early days of its conception, the recruits to the SAS would beg, steal and borrow the equipment needed. After hearing of the plight of the newly formed L Detachment, Winston Churchill agreed and signed a letter approving the supply of much-needed equipment, 'without delay if we are to win this, win this war'.

Using the transport gleaned from the LRDG and then later their very own purpose-built jeeps, the detachment achieved great success attacking the enemy airfields and convoys. Following on from its successes, it was again expanded in September 1942 and officially designated 1 SAS Regiment, with Lieutenant Colonel David Stirling The Most Excellent Order of the British Empire in command. The regiment comprised of three squadrons, plus a Free French Detachment under George Bergé and a further fine unit, the Greek Sacred Squadron under Christodoulas Tigantes, as part of the command.

During their operations in 1941 to 1943, the SAS destroyed and put out of action over 400 enemy aircraft.

Unfortunately, David Stirling was captured by the Italians in January 1943 during SAS operations in southern Tunisia. As the North Africa campaign ended, his depleted 1 SAS Regiment was formed into the Special Raiding Squadron under the command of Major R B (Paddy) Mayne, and then Special Boat Squadron under the command of the Major the Earl Jellicoe. As to the outcome of David Stirling, now a prisoner of war (PoW), he ended up in Colditz Castle until the end of the war. For his distinguished actions he was made The Most Excellent Order of the British Empire.

As to its remaining years in North Africa, in May 1943, the founder's brother Lieutenant Colonel William Stirling raised 2 SAS Regiment in Philippeville, Algeria.

At the end of the North African campaign in 1943, both the Special Raiding Squadron and the 2 SAS Regiment served in Sicily and Italy. The Special Boat Squadron comprising of three squadrons went on to have great success in the Aegean and the Balkans for the remainder of the war, finally disbanded in 1945.

The SAS motto and insignia "WHO DARES WINS" came about when in October 1941, David Stirling had asked the men to come up with ideas for an insignia design for the new unit. Bob Tait, who had accompanied Stirling on the first raid produced the winning entry: the flaming sword of *Excalibur*, the legendary weapon of *King Arthur*. This motif in later years would be misinterpreted as a 'winged dagger'. As to mottoes, 'Strike and Destroy' was rejected as being too blunt. 'Descend to Ascend' seemed inappropriate since parachuting was no longer the primary methos of transport. Finally, Stirling settled on 'Who Dares Wins', which seemed to strike the right balance of valour and confidence.

SAS pattern parachute wings were designed by Lieutenant Jock Lewes and depict the wings of a scarab beetle with a parachute. The wings were to be worn on the right shoulder upon completion of parachute training. Then after three missions, they were to be worn on the left breast above medal ribbons. Stirling noted that the wings were worn and treated by the men 'as medals in their own right'.

1942: SAS Action

The SAS's first mission in 1942 was an attack on Bouerat. The squadron was transported by the LRDG, and caused severe damage to the harbour, petrol tanks and storage facilities. This was followed up in March 1942 by a raid on Benghazi harbour with limited success, although the raiding party did damage fifteen aircraft at Al-Berka. The June 1942 Crete airfield raids at Heraklion, Kasteli, Tympaki and Maleme saw significant damage caused but of the attacking force at Heraklion only Major George Jellicoe returned. In July 1942, Stirling commanded a joint SAS/LRDG patrol that carried out raids at Fuka and Mersa Matruh airfields, destroying thirty aircraft.

September 1942 was a busy month for the SAS. They were renamed 1 SAS Regiment and consisted of four British squadrons, one Free French squadron, one Greek squadron and the Special Boat Section (SBS).

Operations that the SAS took part in included Operation Agreement and the diversionary raid Operation Bigamy. Bigamy, which was led by Stirling and supported by LRDG, was an attempt at a large-scale raid on Benghazi to destroy the harbour and storage facilities and to attack the airfields at Benina and Barce.

However, they were discovered after a clash at a roadblock and with the element of surprise lost, Stirling decided not to press on with the attack and ordered a withdrawal. Operation Agreement was a joint operation by SAS and the LRDG who had to seize an inlet at Mersa Sciausc for the main force to land by sea. The SAS successfully evaded enemy defences assisted by German-speaking members of the Special Interrogation Group and captured Mersa Sciausc. The main landing failed, being met by heavy machine gun fire which forced the landing force and the SAS/LRDG force to surrender. Operation Anglo was a raid on two airfields on the island of Rhodes, from which only two men returned, that destroyed three aircraft, a fuel dump, and numerous buildings. The surviving SBS men had to hide in the countryside for four days before they could reach the waiting submarine.

SAS founder Major David Stirling (right) greets a patrol on its return from a mission, 1942. (This is photograph, E 21338 from the collections of the Imperial War Museums. Approved for use under IWM Licence Number LIC-30663-V3V8L4.)

1943: SAS Action

David Stirling, who was by that time sometimes referred to as the **'Phantom Major'** by the Germans, was captured in January 1943 in the Gabès area by a special anti-SAS unit set up by the Germans. He spent the rest of the war a s a prisoner of war, escaping numerous times before being moved to the supposedly 'escape proof' Colditz Castle.

With David Stirling now being a PoW, he was replaced as commander 1 SAS by Paddy Mayne. In April 1943, the 1 SAS was reorganized into the Special Raiding Squadron under the command of George Jellicoe. The Special Boat Squadron operated in the Aegean and the Balkans for the remainder of the war and was later disbanded in 1945.

The Special Raiding Squadron went on to spearhead the invasion of Sicily, Operation Husky, and played more of a commando role raiding the Italian coastline, from which they suffered heavy losses at Termoli. After Sicily they went on to serve in Italy with the newly formed 2 SAS, a unit which had been formed in Algeria in May 1943 by Stirling's older brother Lieutenant Colonel Bill Stirling.

The 2 SAS had already taken part in operations in support of the Allied landings in Sicily. Operation Narcissus was a raid by 40 members of the 2 SAS on a lighthouse on the southeast coast of Sicily. The team landed on 10 July with the mission of capturing the lighthouse and the surrounding high ground. Operation Chestnut involved two teams of ten men each, parachuted into northern Sicily on the night of 12 July, to disrupt communications, transport, and the enemy in general.

On mainland Italy they were involved in Operation Begonia, which was the airborne counterpart to the amphibious Operation Jonquil. From 2 to 6 October 1943, sixty-one men were parachuted in between Ancona and Pescara. The object was to locate escaped PoWs in the interior and muster them on beach locations for extraction. Operation Begonia involved the interior parachute drop by

The SAS IN North Africa: *A close-up of a heavily armed patrol of L Detachment SAS in their Jeeps, just back from a three-month patrol. The crews of the Jeeps are all wearing 'Arab style' headdress, as copied from the Long-Range Desert Group.*
(This is photograph, E 21337 from the collections of the Imperial War Museums. Approved for use under IWM Licence Number LIC-30663-V3V8L4.)

2 SAS. Operation Jonquil entailed four seaborne beach parties from 2 SAS with the Free French SAS Squadron as protection. Operation Candytuft was a raid by 2 SAS on 27 October 1943. Inserted by boat on Italy's East Coast between Ancona and Pescara, they were to destroy rail bridges and disrupt rear areas.

Near the end of the year, the Special Raiding Squadron reverted to their former title 1 SAS and together with the 2 SAS were withdrawn from Italy and placed under the command of the 1st Airborne Division.

Aftermath

During the North African campaign and later conflicts of the Second World War the Germans and in particular Adolf Hitler had been frustrated and exasperated by the work carried out by the SAS, the outcome of which was an order with an immediate effect was given by Adolf Hitler, the content of which stated, **'that should any SAS be captured they are to be shot immediately and are NOT to be taken prisoner'.**

It would be fair to say that many lives of the SAS squadrons were lost in this way, and the total number during the Second World War will never be known or in fact where they are even buried. One thing we can say is that their names will be recorded at war memorial cenotaphs around the country and were known to be buried in Commonwealth war graves.

We must all recognize the staunch work they undertook, and in extreme conditions during the conflicts fought in the Second World War.

On days of remembrance, we should all take time to **'remember them'** and pay due respect as without their duty and service we most certainly would not have our todays as we know them.

Their names and their heroics will always be remembered. God bless you one and all. RIP.

Chapter 18

6th (Royal Welch) Parachute Battalion

This chapter of the book is dedicated to the 6th (Royal Welch) Parachute Regiment who were formed by the conversion of the 10th Battalion, Welsh Fusiliers in August 1942 and became part of the 2 Parachute Brigade. They saw action in North Africa, Italy, the South of France, Greece and Palestine.

Background

Impressed by the success of German airborne operations during the Battle of France, the then-British prime minister, Winston Churchill, directed the war office to investigate the possibility of creating a corps of 5,000 parachute troops. The standards set for British airborne troops were extremely high, and from the first group of 3,500 volunteers only 500 men were accepted to go forward to parachute training.

Additionally, on 22 June 1940, a Commando unit, No. 2 Commando, was converted to parachute duties. On 21 November, it was re-designated the 11th SAS Battalion (later becoming the 1st Parachute Battalion), with a parachute and glider wing. These men took part in the first British airborne operation, Operation Colossus, on 10 February 1941. Under the command of Lieutenant Colonel Charles Hilary Vaughan Pritchard, the 10th (Merionethshire and Montgomeryshire) Battalion, Royal Welch Fusiliers was converted to the 6th (Royal Welch) Parachute Battalion in August 1942. It was then assigned to the newly raised 2 Parachute Brigade, alongside the 4th and 5th Parachute Battalions. On formation, the battalion had an establishment of 556 men in three rifle companies. The companies were divided into a small headquarters and three platoons. The platoons had three Bren machine guns and three 2-inch (5 cm) mortars, one of each per section. The only heavy weapons in the battalion were a 3-inch (8 cm) mortar platoon and a Vickers machine gun platoon. By 1944 a headquarters, or support company, was added to the battalion. This consisted of five platoons: motor transport, signals, mortar (with 3-inch [8 cm] mortars), machine gun (with four Vickers machine guns) and anti-tank (with ten PIAT anti-tank projectors).

All members of the battalion had to undergo a twelve-day parachute training course carried out at 1st Parachute Training School, RAF Ringway. The course began with parachute jumps from a converted barrage balloon and finished off with five parachute jumps from aircraft. Anyone failing to complete a descent was returned to his old unit. Those men who successfully completed the parachute course were presented with their maroon beret and parachute wings.

Airborne soldiers were expected to fight against superior numbers of the enemy armed with heavy weapons including artillery and tanks, so training was designed to encourage a spirit of self-discipline, self-resilience and aggressiveness. In addition to these qualities emphasis was given to physical fitness, marksmanship and fieldcraft. A large part of the training regime consisted of assault courses and route marching. Military exercises included the capturing and holding of airborne bridgeheads, road or rail bridges and coastal fortifications. At the end of most exercises, the battalion would march back to their barracks. An ability to cover long distances at speed was to be expected: airborne platoons were required to cover a distance of 50 miles (80 km) in 24 hours, and battalions to cover 32 miles (51 km).

When we look back and discover the history of such men, you then realize how awe-inspiring these brave men were, particularly when the country was under immense pressure to stem the tide of the German advance in Europe and then later the Axis forces (made up of German and Italian forces) in North Africa where Adolf Hitler was looking to capture the oil-rich fields in Egypt, Iraq and Iran to help maintain his armies with the much-needed oil and fuel. Without these valuable resources, the Germans in Europe, and the Axis forces in the Middle East, would not be able to sustain the level of fighting.

This was most notable when Adolf Hitler took the war into Russia, particularly the onset of winter. Hitler had stretched his forces too far and wide, which became his ultimate downfall. This was further enhanced with the Allied forces joining together to stop the Germans and Italians wherever possible.

6th (Royal Welch) Parachute Battalion Operations

The historical archived documents from the time detail the battalion fighting record and show that they fought in many theatres of war during their years as the 2 Parachute Brigade, formerly the 6th (Royal Welch) Parachute Battalion. The operations undertaken through 1942 through to 1947 were spread far and wide. Countries such as North Africa (Tunisia), Sicily, Italy, Greece, France and latterly Palestine.

On the completion of the Tunisian campaign in April 1943, the battalion prepared to take part in the amphibious landings into Italy in September 1943, under Operation Avalanche. Their part under Operation Avalanche was to sail from Bizerta to Taranto to capture the harbour and set up a foothold in the heel of Italy.

Although the landing was unopposed, the transport ship HMS *Abdiel* carrying the 6th Parachute Battalion struck a landmine in Taranto Harbour on 10 September, killing over fifty members of the battalion. (Fifty-seven officers and men are commemorated on the memorial in the Free Church of Taranto.) Refer to Chapter 16, which details the map of Operation Avalanche; Taranto is in the heel of Italy.

The battalion remained behind in Italy with the re-designation 2 Independent Parachute Brigade. In May 1944, the brigade was withdrawn to a rest area near Salerno, and three officers and fifty-seven men were selected to carry out Operation Hasty.

The 6th Parachute Battalion formed the nucleus of a small task force sixty strong under command of Captain LA Fitzroy-Smith, which parachuted behind German lines during **Operation Hasty on 1–7 June 1944** in the Abruzzo region near Trasacco to harass supply lines of communication and German troop movements. However, the operation had mixed fortunes; the Germans responded in force, using a brigade of troops to hunt down the parachutists and a division was held in reserve instead of moving to the front. However, the British parachutists were attacked almost immediately upon landing and had to evade the German searchers. Little over a week later, when the mission had ended, only two officers and twenty-five men successfully returned safely to Allied lines. There were thirty-three casualties/ losses. By the end of the year most of the division had been withdrawn to England, for operations in Northern Europe, leaving the 2 Parachute Brigade behind as an independent formation. Without a dedicated air force transport aircraft formation, opportunities for parachute operations were limited and the brigade was used in a ground attack role as normal infantry, taking part in fighting in the Moro River campaign and the Battle of Monte Cassino.

Although Operation Hasty was one of only two British airborne operations on mainland Italy during the Second World War, the 2 Parachute Brigade went on to carry out bigger airborne operations, involving the whole brigade later that same year. In August they participated in **Operation Dragoon**, the invasion of South of France and in October, **Operation Manna** in Greece.

The 2 Parachute Brigade, including the 6th Battalion, came under the command of 6th Airborne Division in Palestine from September 1945 where it served until 24 January 1947. The battalion sailed for Haifa, as part of the 2nd Parachute Brigade Group for the United Kingdom, where it amalgamated with the 4th Parachute Battalion in December 1947.

The 4/6th Parachute Battalion was posted to Germany in February 1948 and redesignated as 1 PARA in 1948.

Commanding Officers of the 6th (Royal Welch) Parachute Battalion:

1942–3 Lieutenant Colonel C.H.V. Pritchard
1943 Lieutenant Colonel J.R. Goodwin
1943–5 Lieutenant Colonel V.W. Barlow
1945–6 Lieutenant Colonel A. Tilly
1946–7 Lieutenant Colonel J.H. Cubbon, DSO**

Major General J.H. Cubbon, DSO, CB & CBE: **
During the research for this chapter information related to the 6th (Royal Welch) Parachute Battalion came to light through the son (Timothy Ibbetson) of **SN: 14031835–Fusilier: Peter D. Ibbetson**. It is quite fascinating to read and get

to understand the relationship that had been built up between the Major General and the fusilier, which is no more evident than in the **Testimonial Letter dated 4 Feb '48**, a copy of which is displayed below.

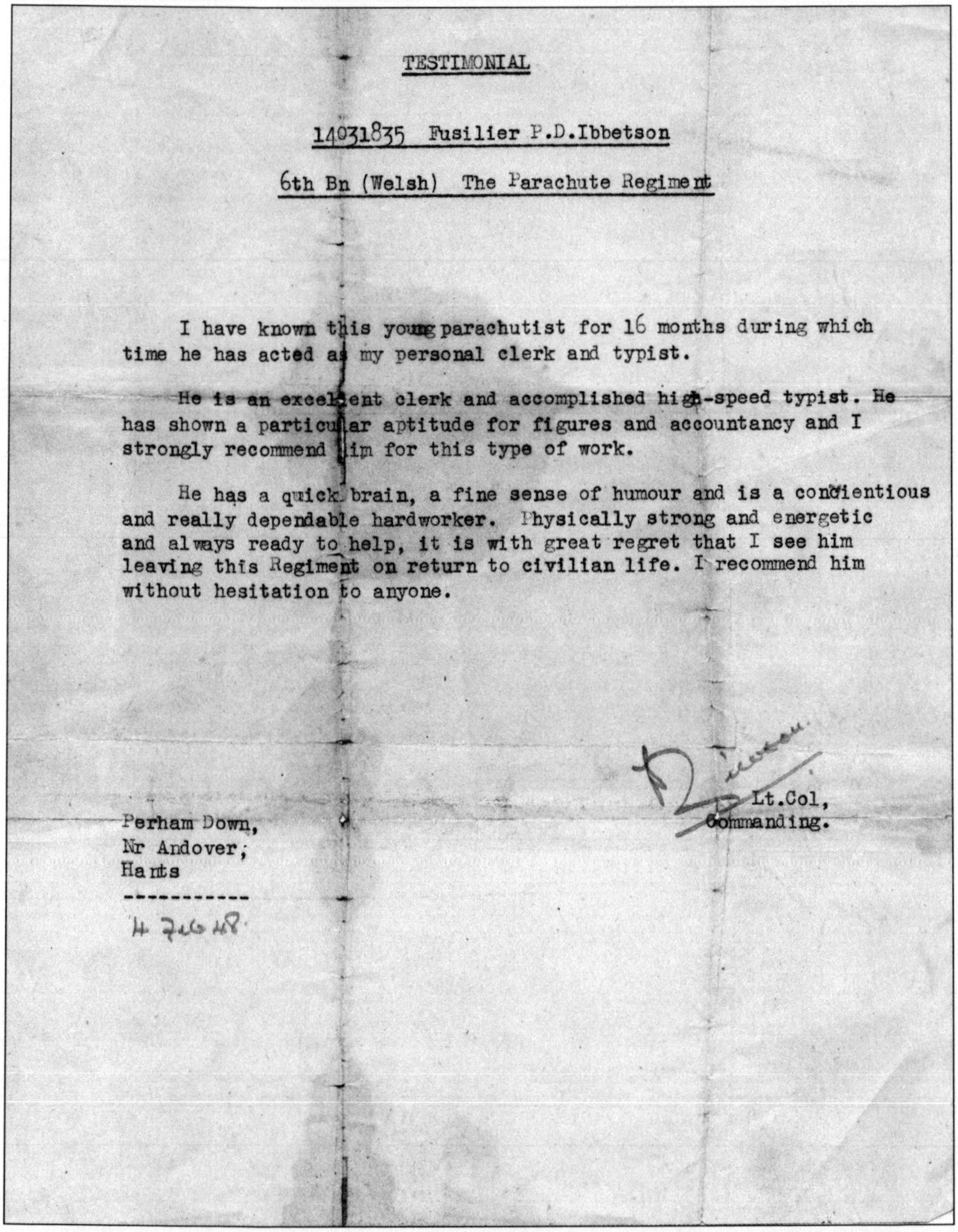

TESTIMONIAL

14031835 Fusilier P.D.Ibbetson

6th Bn (Welsh) The Parachute Regiment

I have known this young parachutist for 16 months during which time he has acted as my personal clerk and typist.

He is an excellent clerk and accomplished high-speed typist. He has shown a particular aptitude for figures and accountancy and I strongly recommend him for this type of work.

He has a quick brain, a fine sense of humour and is a conscientious and really dependable hardworker. Physically strong and energetic and always ready to help, it is with great regret that I see him leaving this Regiment on return to civilian life. I recommend him without hesitation to anyone.

Lt.Col,
Commanding.

Perham Down,
Nr Andover,
Hants
----
4 Feb 48.

Letter dated 6 November 2024 from Mr Timothy Ibbetson [son of Fusilier: Peter D. Ibbetson], giving approval/consent to use his father's memorabilia in this book.

John Cubbon letter to Peter Ibbetson–7 May 1951

The letter displayed below and written by John Cubbon to Peter Ibbetson outlines the friendship they both held with each other: a friendship that endured not only during their service career, but a friendship which continued long after their service career had finished.

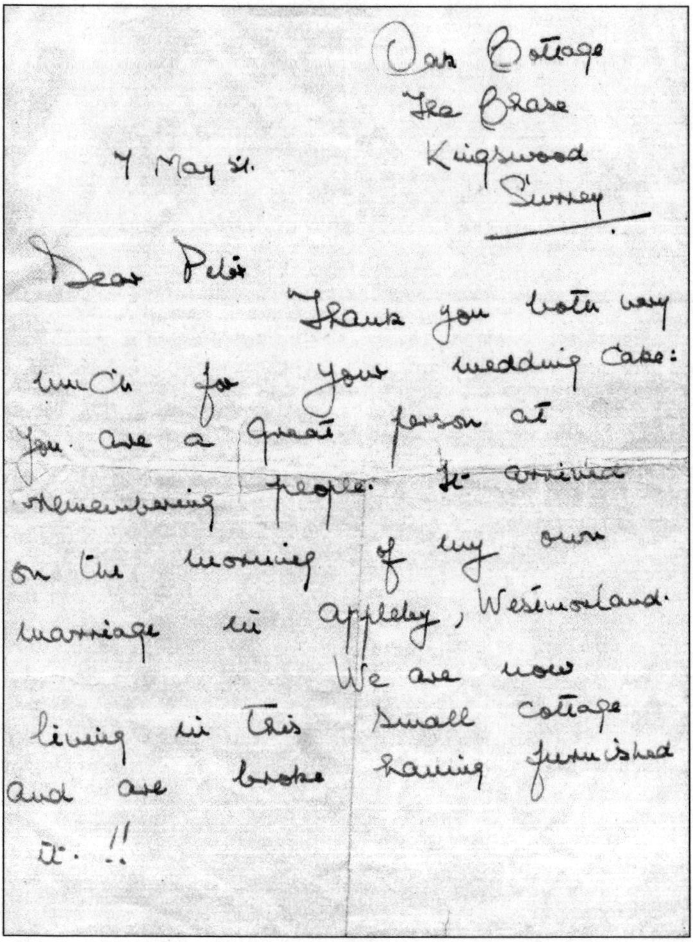

Oak Cottage
The Brase
Kingswood
Surrey

7 May 51.

Dear Peter

Thank you both very much for your wedding cake: You are a great person at remembering people. It arrived on the morning of my own marriage in Appleby, Westmoreland. We are now living in this small cottage and are broke having furnished it. !!

Transcript reads:

Oak Cottage
The Brase
Kingswood
Surrey
7 May 51

Dear Peter,

Thank you both very much for your wedding cake. You are a great person at remembering people. It arrived on the morning of my own marriage in Appleby, Westmoreland. We are now living in this small cottage and are broke having furnished it.!!

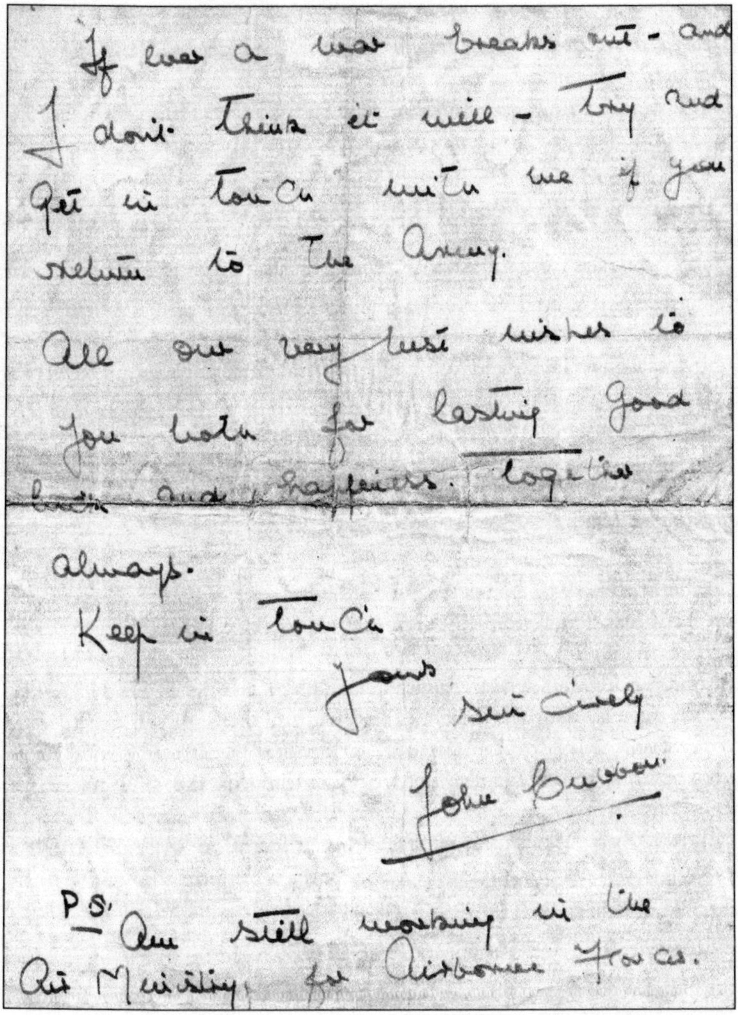

If ever a war breaks out - and I don't think it will - Try and get in touch with me if you return to the Army.

All our very best wishes to you both for lasting Good luck and happiness. together always.

Keep in touch

Yours sincerely

John Cubbon

PS. Am still working in the Air Ministry for Airborne Forces.

Transcript reads:

If ever a war breaks out–and I don't think it will. Try and get in touch with me if you return to the Army.

All our very best wishes to you both for lasting. Good luck and happiness together always.

Keep in touch.

Yours sincerely,

John Cubbon

PS: Am still working in the Air Ministry for Airborne Forces.

Opposite and above: Letter dated 6 November 2024 from Mr Timothy Ibbetson [son of Fusilier: Peter D. Ibbetson], giving approval/consent to use his father's memorabilia in this book.

The following historical details have been compiled by Harvey Grenville–Airborne Assault PARADATA and downloaded from their site as well as Wikipediae. Full accreditation will be provided to the use of the information collated.

National Portrait Gallery Company Ltd.–Consent & approval given under Invoice/Licence No. 69944. Dated 17/11/2024 Items 001 and 002

Major General J.H. Cubbon, DSO, CB & CBE: **

Major General John Hamilton Cubbon was born in 1911 and commissioned into the Cheshire Regiment in 1931. He served as adjutant of the 7th Battalion, the Cheshire Regiment with the British Expeditionary Force in September 1939 at the start of the Second World War. He then commanded the 2/5th Battalion of the Leicestershire Regiment from October 1944 to April 1945 during the Italian campaign.

After the war, in 1946, he became CO of the 6th (Royal Welch) Parachute Battalion and, in 1948, he became the CO of the 4/6th Parachute Battalion, which was redesignated as the 1st Battalion, Parachute Regiment later that year. He went on to be Commander of the 18 Infantry Brigade in Malaya in 1956 during the Malayan Emergency.

In 1958 Cubbon received a 'Citation–to be completed by the initiating officer', in Malaya, for the date of action or period covered by the citation May 1956 to December 1957 by commander 1 Infantry Brigade and later brigadier in charge, Administration 17 Gurkha Division/Corp, Companion of the British Empire (CBE); general officer commanding 43rd (Wessex) Infantry Division in February 1960; and general officer commanding Middle East land forces in Aden in May 1963 during the Aden Emergency before retiring in June 1965.

In the birthday honours of 1962, Cubbon was appointed a Companion of the Order of the Bath.

On the completion of his duty as commanding officer (CO) of the battalion, Major General J H Cubbon DSO, CB, CBE hand wrote his leaving speech **'Special Order of the Day'**, which was handed to his personal secretary (Fusilier: Peter D Ibbetson) for typing up. A copy of his letter is set out below.

***Opposite*:**
Transcript reads:

Special Order of the Day

On the termination of my period of command of this battalion I wish to tell you all how much I am going to miss you. We have been through some difficult times together and always your loyalty and good friendship has been an inspiration to me. It is impossible for me to tell you how my deep I admire the wonderful spirit of cheerfulness, tolerance and good steady common sense that animates you and how much I have valued your support & friendship. I can truly say that as a Battalion you are second to none & I am proud of you. In the future what ever

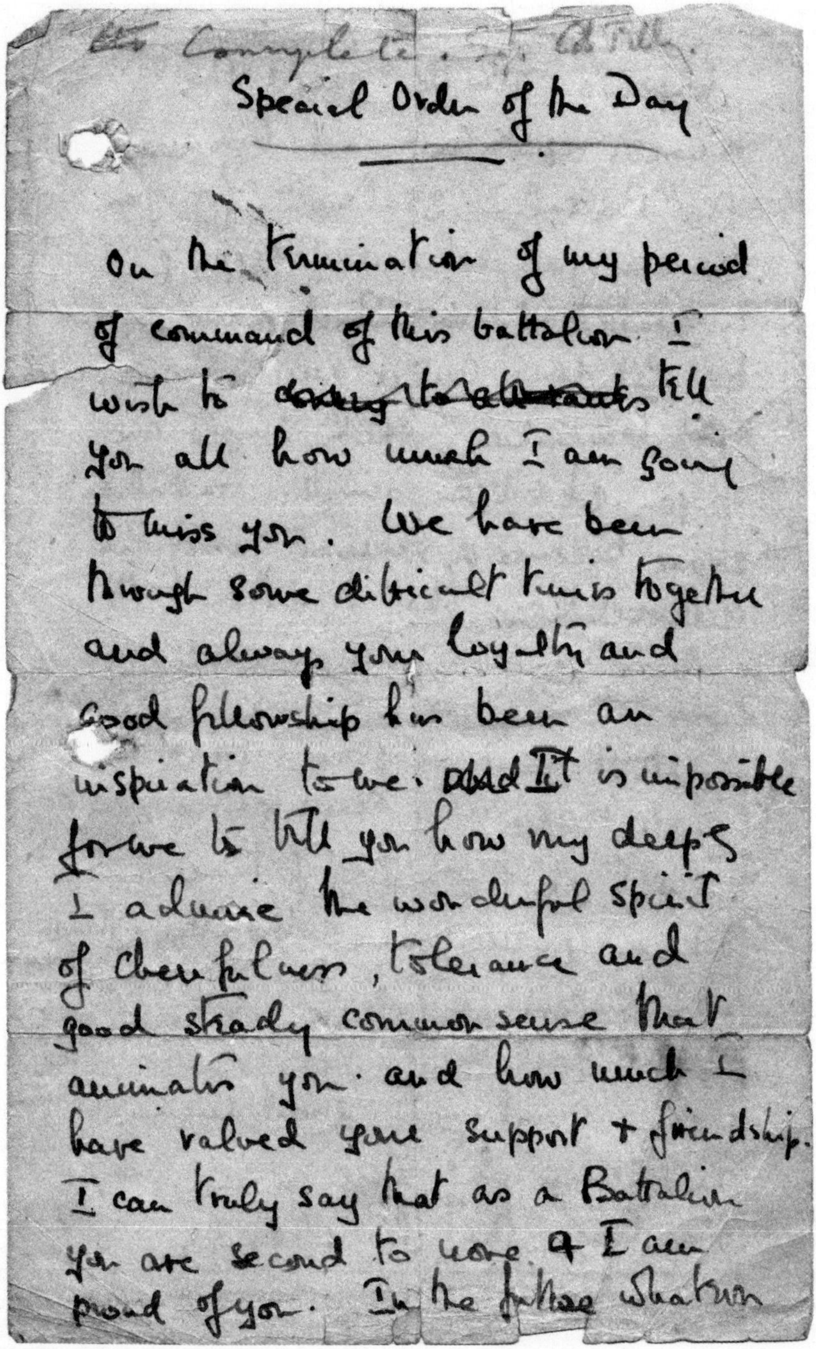

~~to~~ Complete. Sgt. [illegible]

Special Order of the Day

On the termination of my period of command of this battalion I wish to ~~convey to all ranks~~ tell you all how much I am going to miss you. We have been through some difficult times together and always your loyalty and good fellowship has been an inspiration to me. ~~And~~ It is impossible for me to tell you how very deeply I admire the wonderful spirit of cheerfulness, tolerance and good steady common sense that animates you and how much I have valued your support + friendship. I can truly say that as a Battalion you are second to none & I am proud of you. In the future whatever

Above and overleaf: Letter dated 6 November 2024 from Mr Timothy Ibbetson [son of Fusilier Peter D. Ibbetson], giving approval/consent to use his father's memorabilia in this book.

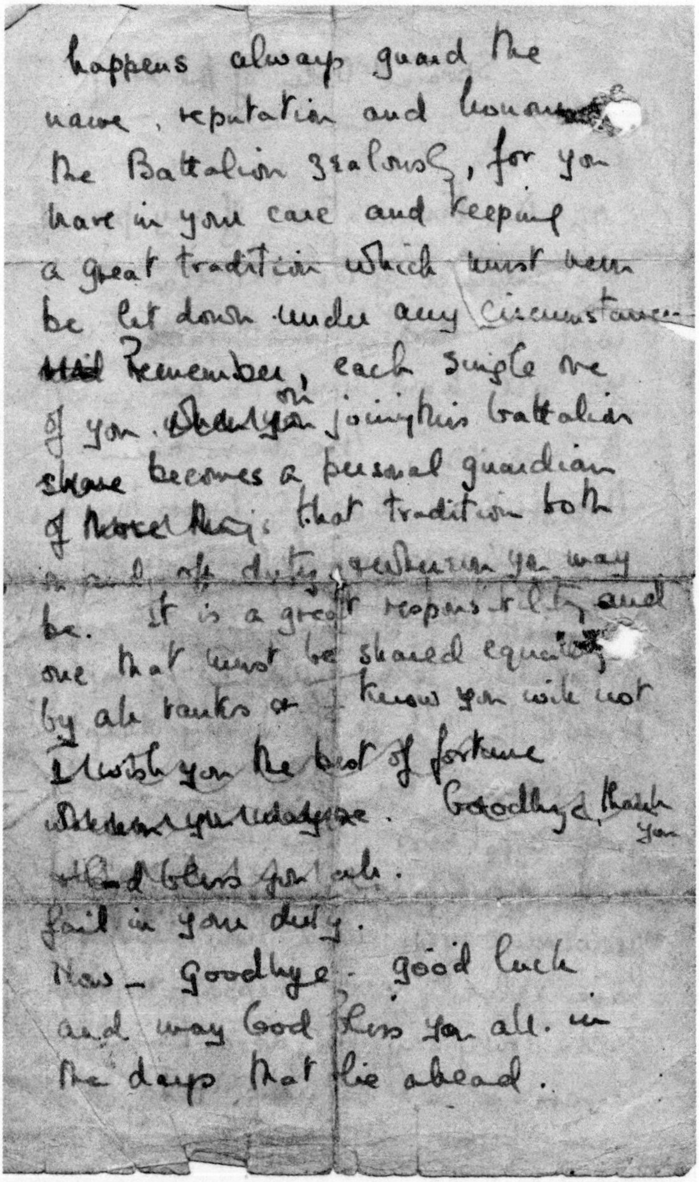

happens always guard the
name, reputation and honour
the Battalion zealously, for you
have in your care and keeping
a great tradition which must never
be let down under any circumstances.
Remember, each single one
of you, on joining this battalion
becomes a personal guardian
of that tradition both
on and off duty, wherever you may
be. It is a great responsibility and
one that must be shared equally
by all ranks & I know you will not
I wish you the best of fortune
Goodbye & thank you
God bless you all.
fail in your duty.
Now – Goodbye – good luck
and may God Bless you all. in
the days that lie ahead.

Transcript reads:

Continued

happens always guard the name, reputation and honour of the Battalion zealously, for you have in you care and keeping a great tradition which must never be let down under any circumstances. Remember, each single one of you, on joining this battalion becomes a personal guardian of that tradition both on and off duty & wherever you may be. It is a great responsibility and one that must be shared equally by all ranks & I know you will not fail in your duty.

Now, Goodbye, good luck and may God Bless you all, in the days that lie ahead.

From the personal letter to Fusilier Peter D. Ibbetson and the draft copy of Brigadier Cubbon's **'Special Order of the Day'** he held his men in great esteem and when his command of the battalion came to an end, it is quite clear that he will certainly miss them, not just for their friendship, but for their inspiration and camaraderie.

Historical Facts about Major General John H. Cubbon DSO, CB, CBE

Born:	1911
Died:	1997 (aged 85–86)
Allegiance:	United Kingdom
Service/Branch:	British Army
Years of Service:	1931–1965
Rank:	Major General
Service number:	52600
Commands:	2/5th Battalion, Royal Leicestershire Regiment 6th (Royal Welch) Parachute Battalion 1st Battalion, Parachute Regiment 18 Infantry Brigade 43rd (Wessex) Infantry Division Middle East Land forces
Battles/Wars:	The Second World War Malayan Emergency Aden Emergency
Awards:	Companion of the Order of the Bath (CB) - 1962 Commander of the Order of the British Empire (CBE) - 1958 Distinguished Service Order (DSO)

As to parachute training and battles fought in far off places, the following photographs give you a taste of what the battalion went through, both during and on conclusion of the Second World War. The battalion served in Palestine from September 1945, where it served until 24 January 1947.

Author's Note:
In writing this chapter it was never intended to rewrite their history other than to compliment the battalion for their service through the Second World War and beyond and with Major General J. H. Cubbon as their commanding officer during some extremely worrying times.

During the research work for this chapter, an essential read was that of *Men of the Red Beret* by Max Arthur, which Timothy Ibbetson handed over to me for my own library and safe keeping, and it is not intended to expand on this incredible book any further, other than make due reference where deemed necessary. Chapter Four of the book covers in greater detail the operations carried by the 1 Parachute Brigade during the Tunisian campaign.

The following two photographs were taken whilst visiting The Jet Age Museum at Staverton Airport, Gloucester, where the museum has a display of the Airborne

Parachute Battalion which is included in the museum's display, and story of the 'Horsa', the glider in which many airborne troops were transported to the point of battle. Operation Market Garden was one such battle. An Allied military operation during the Second World War, fought in German-occupied Netherlands from 17 to 25 September 1944, consisting of paratroopers and glider-borne troops numbering more than 41,000 being dropped at sites where they could capture key bridges and hold terrain until the land forces arrived. It was the largest airborne operation of the war up to that point. The battle has been well covered, and it is not intended to expand further into its story within this book.

Airborne Parachute Battalion/Regiment

Above left: The Flag of the Airborne Parachute Battalion. (*Photograph supplied by the Author, which was taken at the 'Horsa' display - Jet Age Museum, Gloucester)*

Above right: Photograph supplied by the author depicting typical uniform display. (*Photograph supplied by the Author, which was taken at the Jet Age Museum, Gloucester)*

left: Cap Badge and Uniform Insignias worn by SN: 14031835–Fusilier: Peter D. Ibbetson. (*Letter dated 6 November 2024 from Mr Timothy Ibbetson [son of Fusilier: Peter D. Ibbetson], giving approval/consent to use his father's memorabilia in this book.*)

Battalion/Regiment Photographs

Operation / Exercise Longstop

Longstop–Parachute Drop was carried out at Netheravon Airfield, Wiltshire in 1947.

Operation Longstop.
(Dmg Media Licensing–Associated Newspapers Ltd. No Copyright applies under the 70-year rule 'FREE TO USE'. Archive Projects Manager - Morag McFarland, Email dated 23/01/2025)

Netheravon Airfield: 1912–Present Day

Airfield History
Netheravon Airfield is a Ministry of Defence grass strip airfield on Salisbury Plain, Wiltshire, England. Established by the Royal Flying Corps in April 1912, it became RAF Netheravon from 1918 until 1963, then **AAC Netheravon** (Army Air Corps) until 2012. Buildings from 1913 and 1914 survive on part of the site. The site forms part of the Tidworth, Netheravon and Bulford (TidNBul) Garrison. The Ministry of Defence land which surrounds the site is part of the Salisbury Pain Training Area.

The airfield lies on Salisbury Plain, mostly in Fittleton Parish, extending south into Figheldean. It is close to Netheravon village and about 5 miles (8km) north of the town Amesbury.

Today

The airfield is used by the **Joint Services Parachute Centre**, part of the army's 'Adventurous Training' programme for serving and injured personnel, and is home to the Army Parachute Association, a charity which supports parachuting for serving and retired personnel.

Above: 6th (Royal Welch) Parachute Battalion.
(*Letter dated 6 November 2024 from Mr Timothy Ibbetson [son of Fusilier: Peter D. Ibbetson], giving approval/consent to use his father's memorabilia in this book.*)

Right: Dakota Kit Bag Drop.
(*Daily Mirror & Reach Publishing Services Ltd– Consent, Approval and Licence provided as dated 13/12/2024; Account No. A0127673. Reach PSL Sales Invoice No. SGEIV015665 dated 30/01/2025.*)

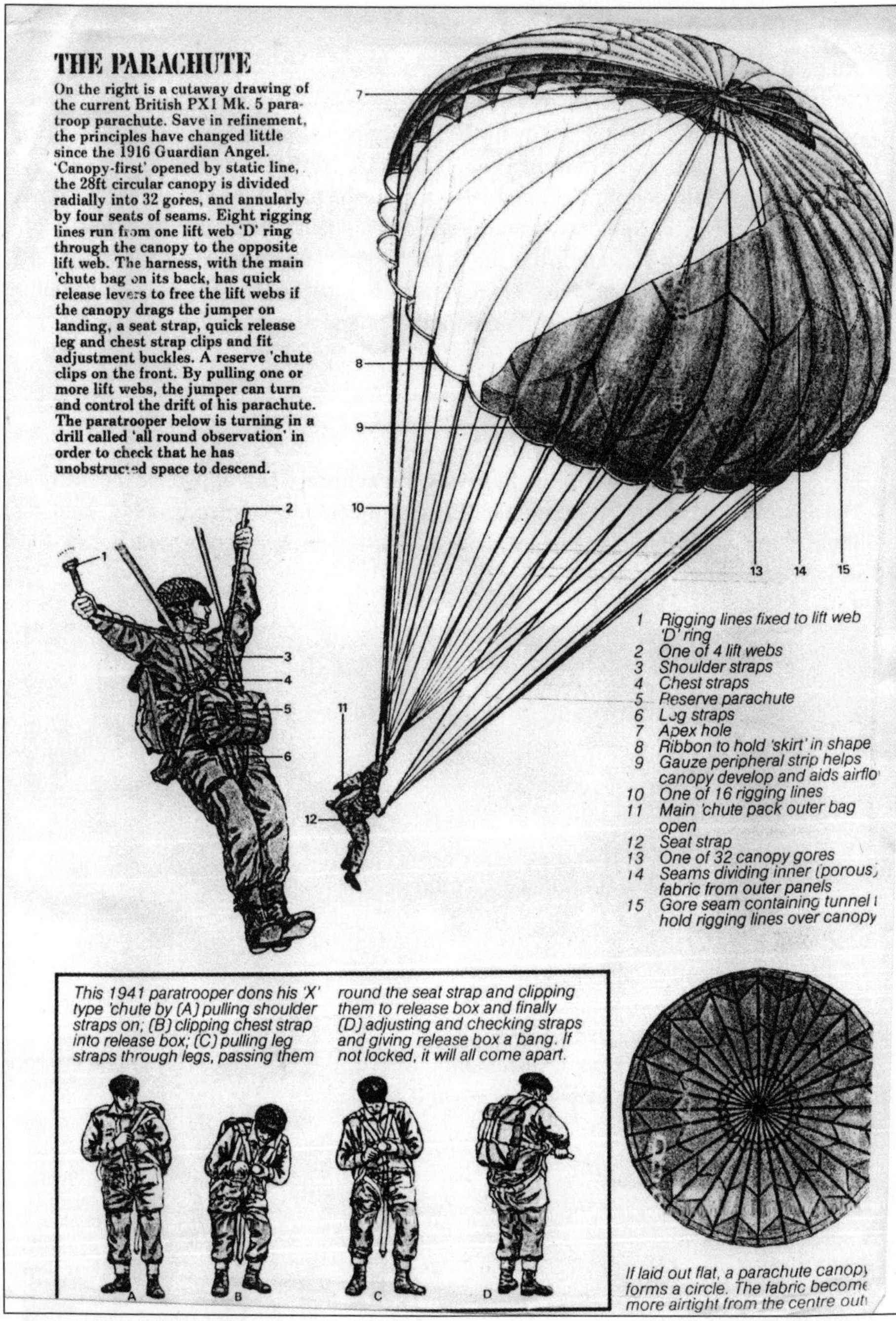

The Parachute.
(Letter dated 6 November 2024 from Mr Timothy Ibbetson [son of Fusilier: Peter D. Ibbetson], giving approval/consent to use his father's memorabilia in this book.)

Above: SN: 14031835–Fusilier: Peter D Ibbetson back row–2nd from left.

Right: 12 Platoon–2nd Parachute Regiment. Written on the back: The 'Erks' or 'Jocks' of the Inglorious 12 Platoon No 2 Parachute Regt. Fusilier Peter D Ibbetson back row–2nd from left.

(Letter dated 6 November 2024 from Mr Timothy Ibbetson [son of Fusilier: Peter D. Ibbetson], giving approval/consent to use his father's memorabilia in this book.)

Palestine 1946 to 1948

On the back, Fusilier Peter D Ibbetson writes – JAFFA but no Oranges, British trucks–Jewish Mines.
(Letter dated 6 November 2024 from Mr Timothy Ibbetson [son of Fusilier: Peter D. Ibbetson], giving approval/consent to use his father's memorabilia in this book)

Chapter 19

Entertainments National Service Association (E.N.S.A.)

No book relating to the Second World War would be complete about any conflict during 1939–1945 without the inclusion of a chapter about the Entertainments National Service Association, commonly known during the Second World War as E.N.S.A.

The inclusion of this chapter in the book is because during the Tunisian campaign of November 1942 and June 1943, **E.N.S.A. came to perform "Hello Happiness" in Tunis on 26 June 1943**. The performance was being staged managed by Mr Reg Lever; the event as written about in the **AIR 27/632/11 (1)** (refer to Chapter 14). In addition to this record, and checking a personal handwritten diary record for Saturday, 26 June 1943 by LAC - Leo Bernard Lamb S/N 1012281 (my father), and he writes on this day, **'Going into Tunis'**. This can only mean that he was going to watch (on this day) the performance being put on by **E.N.S.A.** in Tunis.

Below is an extract from the AIR 27/632/11 (1) daily record sheet:

It reads as follows:

> ***Last night an E.N.S.A. concert party, which has been touring the Middle East during the last three and half years under the direction of Mr Reg Lever and are now presenting "Hello Happiness" in TUNIS, were entertained to dinner in the Pilot's Mess. Special efforts were made to provide this veteran troupe with the sort of fare to which neither they nor we were accustomed to in the Western Desert and a most enjoyable evening followed.***
>
> E.N.S.A. was an organization established in 1939 by Basil Dean and Leslie Henson to provide entertainment for British armed forces personnel during the Second World War. E.N.S.A. operated as part of the Navy, Army and Air Force Institutes. In 1946 it was renamed to Combined Services Entertainment (CSE) operating under the Services Sound and Vision Corporation (SSVC), until 2 March 2020, when the SSVC re-branded to the British Forces Broadcasting Service (BFBS), with the CSE likewise re-branding as BSBF Live Events.

The first big wartime variety concert organized by E.N.S.A. was broadcast by the BBC to the Empire and local networks from RAF Hendon in North London on 17 October 1939.

Among the entertainers appearing on the bill were Adelaide Hall, The Western Brothers and Mantovani. A newsreel of this concert showing Adelaide Hall singing 'We're Going to Hang Out the Washing on the Siegfried Line' accompanied by Mantovani and his orchestra still exists.

Many members of E.N.S.A. later had careers in the entertainment industry after the war was over, including actors Terry Thomas, Peter Sellers and Kenneth Connor.

Tap and acrobatic dancer Vivienne Hole, stage name Vivienne Fayre, a civilian aged 19, was the only E.N.S.A. member killed in the war. Vivienne died following a performance in France. She was travelling in a truck, containing stage scenery, to her next concert engagement. The driver, taking a wrong turn, entered a minefield, hit a mine, and both he and Vivienne were killed instantly. Initially Vivienne was buried in Normandy in a symbolic white coffin. After the war, her body was disinterred and buried with full military honours at Sittard War Cemetery in Limburg, in the south of the Netherlands.

Despite many extremely talented entertainers working for E.N.S.A., the organization was necessarily spread thin over the vast area it had to cover. Thus, many entertainments were substandard, and the popular translation of the acronym E.N.S.A. was **'Every Night Something Awful'**.

E.N.S.A. plays a modest role in the motion picture *Love Story 1944*, in which Margaret Lockwood stars as a concert pianist who makes an E.N.S.A. tour to North Africa and the Mediterranean region. The film *Desert Mice 1959* follows the fictional escapades of an E.N.S.A. troop with *Sid James* assigned to the Afrika Korps.

The only known E.N.S.A. theatre to have survived in its original condition is the Garrison Theatre at Hurst Castle in the New Forest National Park. Created by servicemen in 1939, the proscenium arch still bears the badge and grenades of the RA, and the curtains still hang from an original galvanized gas pipe. Shows are presented from time to time by the friends of Hurst Castle.

Partial List of Performers

Avril Angers	Sonnie	Mantovani
Helen Clare	Adelaide Hall	Lennard Pearce
Kenneth Connor	Stanley Holloway	Bob and Alf Pearson
Noël Coward	Frankie Howard	Arthur Riscoe

Gracie Fields	Mary Lee	Thelma Ruby
George Formby	Vera Lynn	Peter Sellers
Beryl Grey	Jessie Matthews	Terry-Thomas
Geraldo	Laurence Olivier	The Western Brothers

The above list is in no way a full comprehensive list of the performers who travelled around the world to provide the troops with some much-needed R&R.

On further investigation, and between 1941 to 1947, more than 400,000 performances had taken place, and included within this list some famous entertainers such as Bing Crosby, Judy Garland, Bette Davis, Humphrey Bogart, Lauren Bacall, Frank Sinatra, Marlene Dietrich, and Glen Miller and his band gave of their time and risked their lives to ensure that those fighting for our freedom were treated to some good concerts.

Glen Miller is considered to be the father of the modern US military bands, and in 1942, he volunteered to join the US military to entertain troops during the Second World War and ended up in the US Army Air Forces and his big band became the forerunner of many US military big bands. Unfortunately, Glen Miller went missing in action (MIA) on 15 December 1944 whilst on a flight over the English Channel and his body and those flying with him were never found, and in keeping with standard operating procedures for the US military services, Glen Miller was officially declared dead a year and a day later. Glen Miller and the officers who died on the same flight (Lt Col Norman F. Baessell and F/O John R.S. Morgan) are all listed on the Tablets of the Missing at Cambridge American Cemetery and Memorial in Cambridge, England.

Since his body was not recoverable, Miller was allowed to have a memorial headstone placed at the US Army-operated Arlington National Cemetery in Arlington, Virginia.

In February 1945, Glen Miller was posthumously awarded the **Bronze Star Medal**.

Appendix 1

Souvenir Postcards of Tripoli

North Africa 1940 to 1943 Second World War Campaign

The following copies of postcards were collected by LAC Lamb L. B. 1012281 during his deployment in North Africa during the Second World War.

The postcards, whilst being 80+ years old, give a true reflection and indication of the places visited during the conflicts, and how these places looked prior to the war.

Tripoli

BANCO DI ROMA

Appendix 2

Other Related Phrase Books, Poems, Letters and the Like

French-English Phrase Book: To Learn French–Pour Apprendre L'Anglais

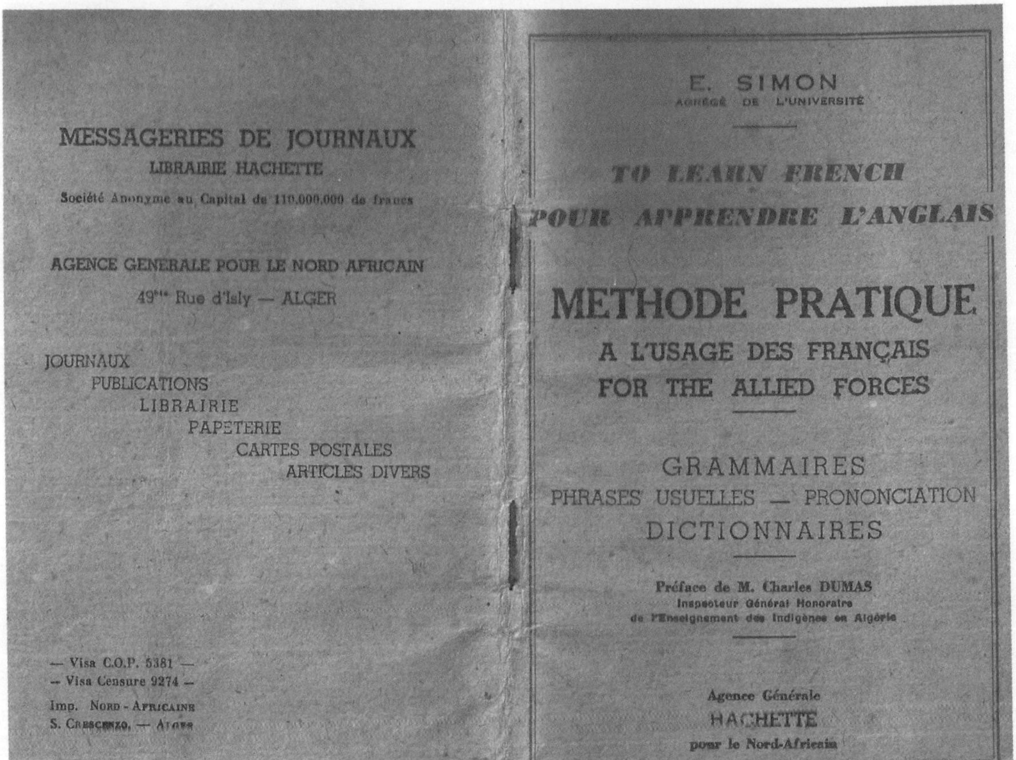

TO ENGLISH SPEAKING READERS

VERY IMPORTANT REMARK

[illegible] THIS BOOK, THE READER SHOULD [illegible] OUR LIST OF *FRENCH* [illegible]

[illegible] VERY SIMPLE : ITS [illegible] EACH PHO[illegible] IN THE SAME MANNER [illegible] AND THE [illegible]

[illegible] WILL PROVE [illegible] LANGUAGE SPOKEN [illegible] FRENCH PEOPLE.

AUX LECTEURS FRANÇAIS

AVIS TRES IMPORTANT

AVANT D'UTILISER CE MANUEL, IL EST RECOMMANDE D'ETUDIER TRES ATTENTIVEMENT NOTRE TABLEAU DES *SONS ANGLAIS ET DES SIGNES* QUI LES REPRESENTENT PAGES 7 ET 8.

NOTRE SYSTEME PHONETIQUE EST TRES SIMPLE. LES MEMES SONS SONT TOUJOURS REPRESENTES PAR LES MEMES SIGNES. GRACE A UN LEGER EFFORT PRELIMINAIRE, DONT IL SERA RECOMPENSE, LE LECTEUR LES RETIENDRA FACILEMENT.

IL SE PERFECTIONNERA RAPIDEMENT PAR LA CONVERSATION, AUSSI FREQUENTE QUE POSSIBLE, AVEC DES PERSONNES POUR QUI L'ANGLAIS EST LA LANGUE MATERNELLE.

NORTH AFRICA

North Africa is a very old country which, since French occupation, has gradually awakened, and now (to some extent) assumes the features of a new country.

Without mentioning prehistoric times which have left such curious remains in many regions, the beginnings of the historic period show that the Land of the Atlas — Djezirat el Maghrib — the Western Isle of the Arabs — already held intercourse not only with the East through Cyrenaica and Egypt, but also with Europe through Sicily and Gibraltar. From these two directions all through the centuries its civilisation has been moulded by the succession of powers with their various influences.

« The history of North Africa », said Renan, « is hardly anything more than the history of the invasions which the country has suffered» Before the arrival of the French, the Phœnicians, the Romans, the Vandals, the Byzantines, then the Arabs, and the Turks had more or less completely imposed their rule upon the native populations.

The stock of thóse people is formed by the Berbers, who also used to be called Lybians. They have survived all invasions. Nowadays they are still to be found in Aurès, in Kabylie, in Mzab, in the Sahara (Tuareg) and above all in the mountains of Morocco. In those fastnesses, they still live in closely united communities which have preserved their customs and dialects, but in the remaining parts of the country the majority of the natives who speak Arabic and call themselves Arabs are in fact more or less « Arabified » Berbers. Most of them profess the Moslem religion.

From the political point of view, North Africa now includes three divisions : Algeria, a large colony of settlement conquered between 1830 and 1857, besides, Tunisia and Morocco, two protectorates which have been reorganised by France in conformity with the Treaties of 1881 with the Bey of Tunis and of 1912 with the Sultan of Morocco. Moreover Spain maintains a protectorate over the Rif, and the Tangier area has

— 2 —

been placed under an international statute. Those recent and conventional political divisions should not make us forget that all the parts of North Africa are very strikingly alike, and that we have to deal with a well-defined natural region.

Morocco, Algeria and Tunisia, along a general line running from the South West to the North East, are commanded by a range of mountains, the Atlas, which, with great variety in its geological formations and physical features, reaches its highest summits (about 13500 ft) in Morocco, then becomes lower in Algeria and finally dwindles to a series of hills under [illegible] ft in Tunisia.

The Atlas mountains run more or less east and west and on one side slope towards the Mediterranean and Atlantic and on the other towards the Sahara. The northern slopes benefit by their proximity to the sea and the humidity derived therefrom in promoting a high degree of agriculture. Hence the rich plains of Western Morocco and the Sebou, the Riff, the Algerian Tell with its coastal plain and plateau, North Tunisia with its Eastern Sahel.

The Southern slopes however receive the influence of the Sahara with its scorching wind called the Sirocco.

The Sahara forms no impassable barrier but its vastness is an obstacle to communications, and vegetation and human existence are confined to a few wells in oases. Yet, it is through these oases that land communications with the Sudan, West Africa and the rest of Africa are carried out, and great importance is attached to a quick crossing of the Sahara, specially from the Mediterranean to the Niger.

∴

France found these countries in a state of lethargy maintained through the centuries. The people were divided among themselves and disturbed by constant anarchy. The people were inclined to isolate themselves from the outer world and led a precarious life unworthy of the part they should assume in the world's activities.

They had to be awakened and initiated in the methods of modern civilization so that they could assume the role which should be theirs. With method and perseverance France has successfully achieved her task, improving the condition of the natives and revitalizing the country.

North Africa is separated from the mother country only by a sea which can be crossed in less than 24 hours by boat and in a few hours by air. On the African coast of the Mediter-

— 3 —

ranean, the French settlers have found a climate which differs very little from that of Southern Europe, and they have come over as [illegible] families in Morocco and Tunisia, as well as in Algeria. In 1936, among a population of 17.000.000 inhabitants, there were 1.000.000 Europeans, almost 1.000.000 living in Algeria alone. They are a youthful race impregnated by French influence and possess to a remarkable degree the qualities of initiative, audacity and endurance which are indispensable in a land where so much was to be done.

The economic life of the country has been completely revived. North Africa still fundamentally remains an agricultural country, but farming processes have been transformed. The cultivation of cereals has been improved by the widespread [illegible] farming; big dams have been built for the irrigation of large tracts of land. Vineyards have been extended, especially since 1880 after the ravages caused in France by the phylloxera. In Algeria, they cover 1.000.000 acres, and their output has amounted to 22 million hectolitres (485 million gallons). The traditional cultivations, such as olive-trees, have been developed. About 10 million olive-trees have been [illegible] in Algeria, 5 million in Morocco, and the magnificent olive groves in the Tunisian Sahel are a creation of the French. — The cultivation of fruit, specially oranges, vegetables and early vegetables is a very thriving industry. Those of tobacco, cotton, and plants used in perfumery should be added to the resources of the country.

The mineral wealth too is very important. Phosphates have been worked in Algeria and Tunisia since 1885, in Morocco, since 1912; exports amount to 3 million tons in Tunisia, [illegible] tons in Morocco, and 1 million tons in Algeria. There are plentiful beds of iron, lead and zinc.

Commercial intercourse is reflected in North Africa by its good roads of which there are 36.000 kilometers, and about 7.800 kilometers of railroad, as well as efficiently equipped ports. — Moreover, it happens to lie along the great sea routes which, through Gibraltar, run to Suez, the East, the Far East, and, along the Atlantic coast, either to West, Equatorial and South Africa, or to South America. Four fifths of its commerce were carried on with the mother country. Owing to this, the African economy is at present in a critical situation.

The natives have derived great benefit from that prosperity. In Algeria, where the French have been at work for some time their number has trebled between 1872 and 1936, passing from 2 to 6 million. Order and security prevail everywhere; epidemics are becoming scarce : strong action has been taken against such diseases as trachroma, malaria, tuberculosis; a

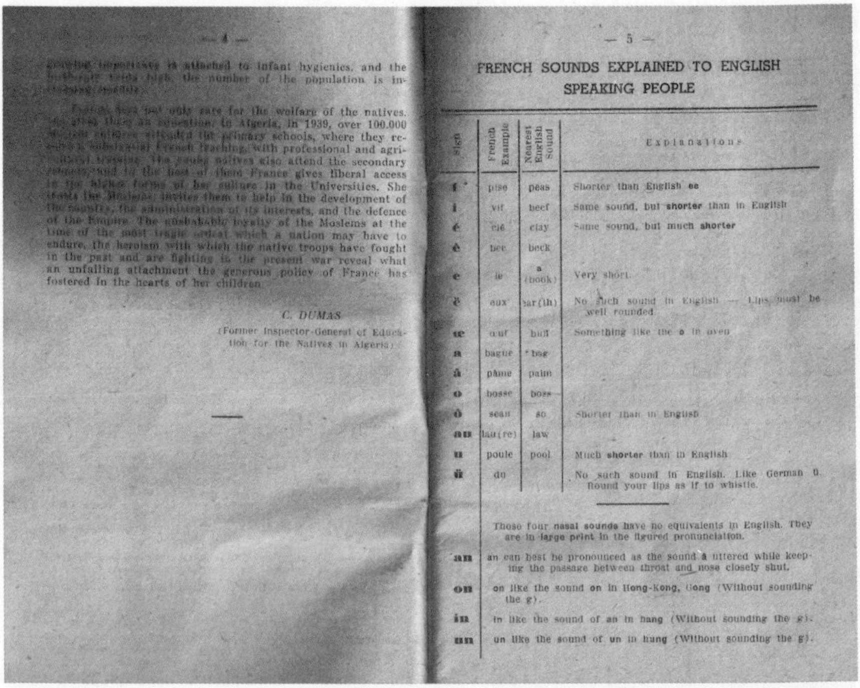

— 4 —

[illegible] is attached to infant hygienics, and the [illegible] high, the number of the population is in[illegible].

[illegible] care for the welfare of the natives. [illegible] in Algeria, in 1939, over 100.000 [illegible] attended the primary schools, where they re[illegible] French teaching, with professional and agri[illegible]. [illegible] also attend the secondary [illegible] France gives liberal access [illegible] in the Universities. She [illegible] invites them to help in the development of the [illegible], the administration of its interests, and the defence of the Empire. The unshakable loyalty of the Moslems at the time of the most tragic ordeal which a nation may have to endure, the heroism with which the native troops have fought in the past and are fighting in the present war reveal what an unfailing attachment the generous policy of France has fostered in the hearts of her children.

C. DUMAS

(Former Inspector-General of Education for the Natives in Algeria)

— 5 —

FRENCH SOUNDS EXPLAINED TO ENGLISH SPEAKING PEOPLE

Sign	French Example	Nearest English Sound	Explanations
i	pise	peas	Shorter than English **ee**
i	vif	beef	Same sound, but **shorter** than in English
é	été	clay	Same sound, but much **shorter**
è	bec	beck	
e	le	a (book)	Very short.
ë	eux	ear(th)	No such sound in English — Lips must be well rounded.
œ	œuf	bull	Something like the **o** in oven
a	bague	bag	
â	pâme	palm	
o	bosse	boss	
ô	seau	so	Shorter than in English
au	lau(re)	law	
u	poule	pool	Much **shorter** than in English
ü	du		No such sound in English. Like German ü. Round your lips as if to whistle.

Those four **nasal sounds** have no equivalents in English. They are in **large print** in the figured pronunciation.

an	an can best be pronounced as the sound **a** uttered while keeping the passage between throat and nose closely shut.
on	on like the sound **on** in **Hong-Kong, Gong** (Without sounding the g).
in	in like the sound of **an** in **hang** (Without sounding the g).
un	un like the sound of **un** in **hung** (Without sounding the g).

A Poem Compendium: ˆ138/744 'Authors unknown'

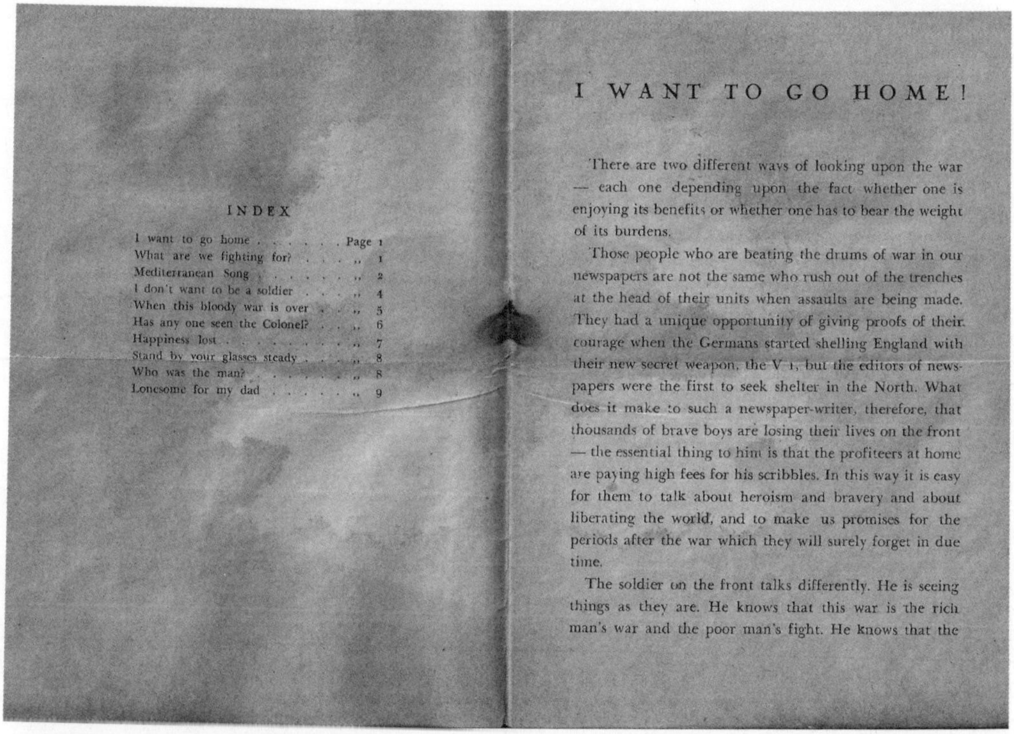

INDEX

I WANT TO GO HOME!

There are two different ways of looking upon the war — each one depending upon the fact whether one is enjoying its benefits or whether one has to bear the weight of its burdens.

Those people who are beating the drums of war in our newspapers are not the same who rush out of the trenches at the head of their units when assaults are being made. They had a unique opportunity of giving proofs of their courage when the Germans started shelling England with their new secret weapon, the V 1, but the editors of newspapers were the first to seek shelter in the North. What does it make to such a newspaper-writer, therefore, that thousands of brave boys are losing their lives on the front — the essential thing to him is that the profiteers at home are paying high fees for his scribbles. In this way it is easy for them to talk about heroism and bravery and about liberating the world, and to make us promises for the periods after the war which they will surely forget in due time.

The soldier on the front talks differently. He is seeing things as they are. He knows that this war is the rich man's war and the poor man's fight. He knows that the

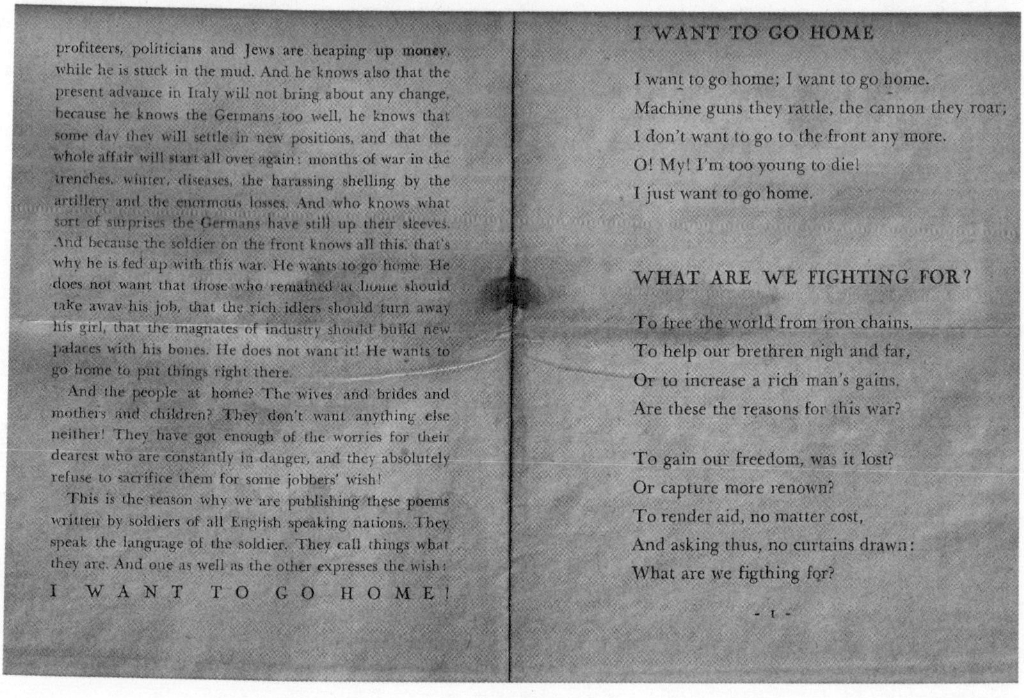

profiteers, politicians and Jews are heaping up money, while he is stuck in the mud. And he knows also that the present advance in Italy will not bring about any change, because he knows the Germans too well, he knows that some day they will settle in new positions, and that the whole affair will start all over again: months of war in the trenches, winter, diseases, the harassing shelling by the artillery and the enormous losses. And who knows what sort of surprises the Germans have still up their sleeves. And because the soldier on the front knows all this, that's why he is fed up with this war. He wants to go home. He does not want that those who remained at home should take away his job, that the rich idlers should turn away his girl, that the magnates of industry should build new palaces with his bones. He does not want it! He wants to go home to put things right there.

And the people at home? The wives and brides and mothers and children? They don't want anything else neither! They have got enough of the worries for their dearest who are constantly in danger, and they absolutely refuse to sacrifice them for some jobbers' wish!

This is the reason why we are publishing these poems written by soldiers of all English speaking nations. They speak the language of the soldier. They call things what they are. And one as well as the other expresses the wish:

I WANT TO GO HOME!

I WANT TO GO HOME

I want to go home; I want to go home.
Machine guns they rattle, the cannon they roar;
I don't want to go to the front any more.
O! My! I'm too young to die!
I just want to go home.

WHAT ARE WE FIGHTING FOR?

To free the world from iron chains,
To help our brethren nigh and far,
Or to increase a rich man's gains,
Are these the reasons for this war?

To gain our freedom, was it lost?
Or capture more renown?
To render aid, no matter cost,
And asking thus, no curtains drawn:
What are we figthing for?

- 1 -

Was England's freedom blighted?
Or did we stand alone?
Or were we too far sighted,
With an eye to every throne?

We know now what a war can do,
To make up for years of peace;
And knowing this, the chosen few
provoked a fight that will not cease,
What did they do it for?

No answer can the fighter give,
Just a tool, no more, no less,
To die or, perchance, to live;
There's only God can guess
What we are fighting for.

MEDITERRANEAN SONG

There's some who say the Medi-
Terranean air is heady;
While others, who have stayed there

- 2 -

Are very much afraid there's
A lot more to be said
About the highly vaunted Med.

For instance there's malaria
In the Mare Nostrum area;
And pox in many a guise
Small and cow and otherwise
Can easily be caught
Doing things you didn't ought.

Then there's flies and fleas and
Lice and crabs, that tease and
Make themselves a pest
Always hanging around the test-
Icles; playing hide and seek
In the ballroom, so to speak.

And many more afflictions
That cause a lot of restrictions;
The brothers »dyer« and »gunner«
Are active winter and summer.

- 3 -

And dysentry's a damned in-
Convenience notwithstanding.

So I think that you'll agree,
That those who say the sea
Is nearly always blue,
(Which is nearly always true)
Are deliberately misleading
The folks who judge by reading
That the Med for sure and certain
Is the place to do some flirting.
But you and I know better,
And you can bet an old French letter-
Box, that when this war is over
I'll count myself in clover
As long as I've a bed,
And am nowhere near the Med.

I DON'T WANT TO BE A SOLDIER

I don't want to be a soldier,
I don't want to go to war.
I would sooner hang around

- 4 -

Picadilly Underground.
And live off my earnings as I did before;
I don't want a bayonet through my coat tails
I don't want my buttons shot away.
For I would rather stay in England,
In Merrie, Merrie England
And frolic all the rest of my life away,
Gor' Blimey!
And frolic all the rest of my life away.

WHEN THIS BLOODY WAR IS OVER

When this bloody war is over
O! How happy I should be
When this bloody war is over,
no more soldiering for me.
No more church-parades on Sunday.
No more asking for a pass
Tell the bloody Sergeant-Major
to stick the passes up his . . .

- 5 -

HAS ANY ONE *SEEN* THE COLONEL?

O! Has any one seen the Colonel?
I know where he is! I know where he is!
I know where he is!
Has any one seen the Colonel?
I know where he is!
He's dining with the Brigadier.

Chorus
I saw him! I saw him!
Dining with the Brigadier,
I saw him dining with the Brigadier.

Has any one seen the Major?
He's down in the deep dug-out.

Has any one seen the Captain?
He's away on six weeks' leave.

Has any one seen the Subaltern?
He's out on a night patrol.

- 6 -

Has any one seen the Sergeant?
He's drinking up the Privates' Rum.

Has any one seen the Corporal?
He's hanging on the old barbed wire.

Has any one seen the Private?
He's holding up the whole damn line.

HAPPINESS LOST

Whenever I think of happiness
Appears your face, in it I see
A host of love and gentleness
And fond, sweet thoughts of me.
I look towards a future black
Darkened by some jobbers' wish,
But happy memories take me back
To you, your smile, your kiss.
Ever in my thoughts will be
The happiness we've known,
Enjoyed in perfect harmony,
They call it home, sweet home.

- 7 -

STAND BY YOUR GLASSES *STEADY*

O! Stand by your glasses steady
Though this world be a world full of lies,
And we'll drink to the dead already,
And hurrah for the next man who dies.

Betrayed by the country that bore us;
Betrayed by the land that we love,
Now so many have gone before us,
And they live in the skies up above.

Beneath these low hung rafters
Lie the ghosts of the lads that we love.
And at home live the bloody old bastards
Responsible for this war that we loathe.

WHO WAS THE MAN?

Who was the man who invented the War?
Why did he do it and what was it for?
Ships on the ocean and ships in the air;
Silly old blighter, he ought to be there.

- 8 -

Who was the man who said, "Parade stand at ease,
Carry on with the inspection, Gentlemen, please"
Why should our buttons be shiny and bright,
Can any one tell us what for we should fight?

LONESOME FOR MY DAD

I'm lonesome for my daddy,
Since he has gone to war,
To fight for some men's fancy
Like others, gone before.

We used to be so happy,
And could never wish for more,
Now our only link with Daddy
Is the postman at our door.

I see no great-coat hanging
With shiny buttons on,
I hear no dear voice calling
»Son, turn the radio on.«

- 9 -

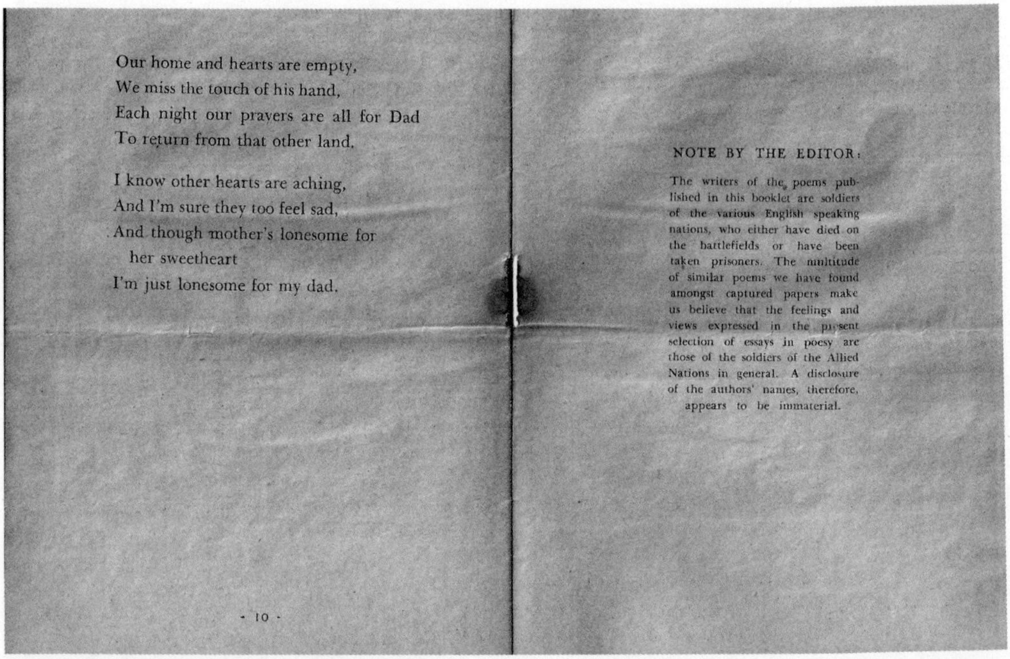

Our home and hearts are empty,
We miss the touch of his hand,
Each night our prayers are all for Dad
To return from that other land.

I know other hearts are aching,
And I'm sure they too feel sad,
And though mother's lonesome for
her sweetheart
I'm just lonesome for my dad.

- 10 -

NOTE BY THE EDITOR:

The writers of the poems published in this booklet are soldiers of the various English speaking nations, who either have died on the battlefields or have been taken prisoners. The multitude of similar poems we have found amongst captured papers make us believe that the feelings and views expressed in the present selection of essays in poesy are those of the soldiers of the Allied Nations in general. A disclosure of the authors' names, therefore, appears to be immaterial.

DE VITA COSIMO

MANUAL
of
conversation
ITALIAN - ENGLISH
With the italian
figured pronunciation
for english in Italy

STAB. TIP. A. LODESERTO - TARANTO

Manual of Conversation - Italian - English
Issued: 1943 to Allied Troops

Booklet of Poems from 1944

I originally was hoping to get this booklet published but felt a need to further research its origins, particularly regarding Copyright. Lo and behold: It had already been published by ANOTHER.

Below is what I found. The booklet hadn't been prepared and distributed by the Allies during the Second World War, it had actually been prepared by the Germans in 1944 (the poems are real and were found on dead bodies, etc.) and was used as Nazi Propaganda. Its distribution through Italy in 1944 was by using air drops over the country and my dad obviously picked up a copy to keep for himself whilst serving with the RAF in Italy 1943 to 1944.

Below is the evidence to back up the above.

I Want To Go Home - 1944

Pictorial wrappers, stapled. [2] + 10pp. A booklet of poems with a preface, the poems supposedly written by captured or killed soldiers of "all English-speaking nations".

The preface contains anti-semitic sentiments, and like the poems is clearly intended to demoralize the Allied troops. Some poem titles: "I Want to Go Home", "What Are We Fighting For?", "I Don't Want to Be A Soldier", "Lonesome For My Dad".

Tear in rear cover, inscription in pen on inner front cover, some chipping of edges and discoloration of wrappers, staple rusty, but generally a very good copy. The back cover has a printed (date?): 138/7 44. A fragile and cheaply produced item

See: Klaus Kirchner, Flugblatter aus Deutschland fur Amerikanische und Britische Soldaten in Italien, 1944/45. Second Edition, 2009, pg. 144-47. This is an original piece of German Nazi Propaganda distributed to Allied troops in Italy – 1943 to 1944. Very scarce. Seller Inventory # 55916

Bibliographic Details

Title: **I Want To Go Home**. Publisher: **[np], 1944**.
Binding: **Soft cover**

Appendix 3

LAC Lamb L.B. Service No. 1012281: His Written 1943 Diary and Transcript

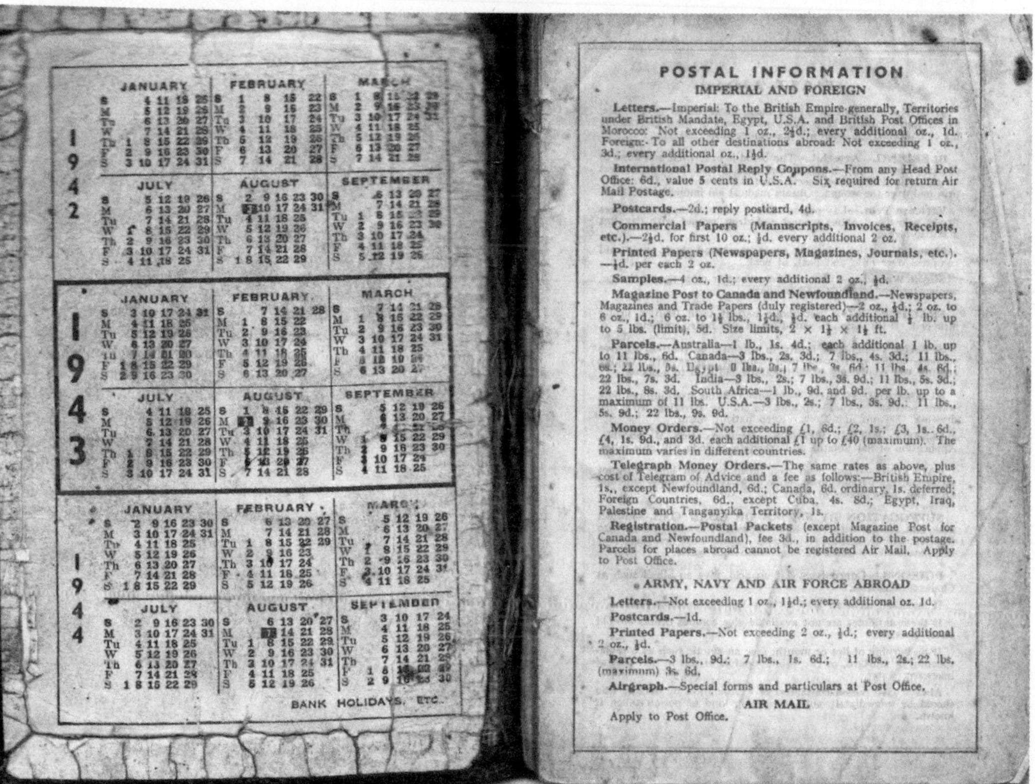

POSTAL INFORMATION

IMPERIAL AND FOREIGN

Letters.—Imperial: To the British Empire generally, Territories under British Mandate, Egypt, U.S.A. and British Post Offices in Morocco: Not exceeding 1 oz., 2½d.; every additional oz., 1d. Foreign:- To all other destinations abroad: Not exceeding 1 oz., 3d.; every additional oz., 1½d.

International Postal Reply Coupons.—From any Head Post Office: 6d., value 5 cents in U.S.A. Six required for return Air Mail Postage.

Postcards.—2d.; reply postcard, 4d.

Commercial Papers (Manuscripts, Invoices, Receipts, etc.).—2½d. for first 10 oz.; ½d. every additional 2 oz.

Printed Papers (Newspapers, Magazines, Journals, etc.).—½d. per each 2 oz.

Samples.—4 oz., 1d.; every additional 2 oz., ½d.

Magazine Post to Canada and Newfoundland.—Newspapers, Magazines and Trade Papers (duly registered)—2 oz., ½d.; 2 oz. to 6 oz., 1d.; 6 oz. to 1½ lbs., 1½d., ½d. each additional ½ lb. up to 5 lbs. (limit), 5d. Size limits, 2 × 1½ × 1½ ft.

Parcels.—Australia—1 lb., 1s. 4d.; each additional 1 lb. up to 11 lbs., 6d. Canada—3 lbs., 2s. 3d.; 7 lbs., 4s. 3d.; 11 lbs., [illegible]; 22 lbs., [illegible] Egypt [illegible] 4s. 6d.; 22 lbs., 7s. 3d. India—3 lbs., 2s.; 7 lbs., 3s. 9d.; 11 lbs., 5s. 3d.; 22 lbs., 8s. 3d. South Africa—1 lb., 9d. and 9d. per lb. up to a maximum of 11 lbs. U.S.A.—3 lbs., 2s.; 7 lbs., 3s. 9d.; 11 lbs., 5s. 9d.; 22 lbs., 9s. 9d.

Money Orders.—Not exceeding £1, 6d.; £2, 1s.; £3, 1s. 6d., £4, 1s. 9d., and 3d. each additional £1 up to £40 (maximum). The maximum varies in different countries.

Telegraph Money Orders.—The same rates as above, plus cost of Telegram of Advice and a fee as follows:—British Empire, 1s., except Newfoundland, 6d.; Canada, 6d. ordinary, 1s. deferred; Foreign Countries, 6d., except Cuba, 4s. 8d.; Egypt, Iraq, Palestine and Tanganyika Territory, 1s.

Registration.—Postal Packets (except Magazine Post for Canada and Newfoundland), fee 3d., in addition to the postage. Parcels for places abroad cannot be registered Air Mail. Apply to Post Office.

ARMY, NAVY AND AIR FORCE ABROAD

Letters.—Not exceeding 1 oz., 1½d.; every additional oz. 1d.

Postcards.—1d.

Printed Papers.—Not exceeding 2 oz., ½d.; every additional 2 oz., ½d.

Parcels.—3 lbs., 9d.; 7 lbs., 1s. 6d.; 11 lbs., 2s.; 22 lbs. (maximum) 3s. 6d.

Airgraph.—Special forms and particulars at Post Office.

AIR MAIL

Apply to Post Office.

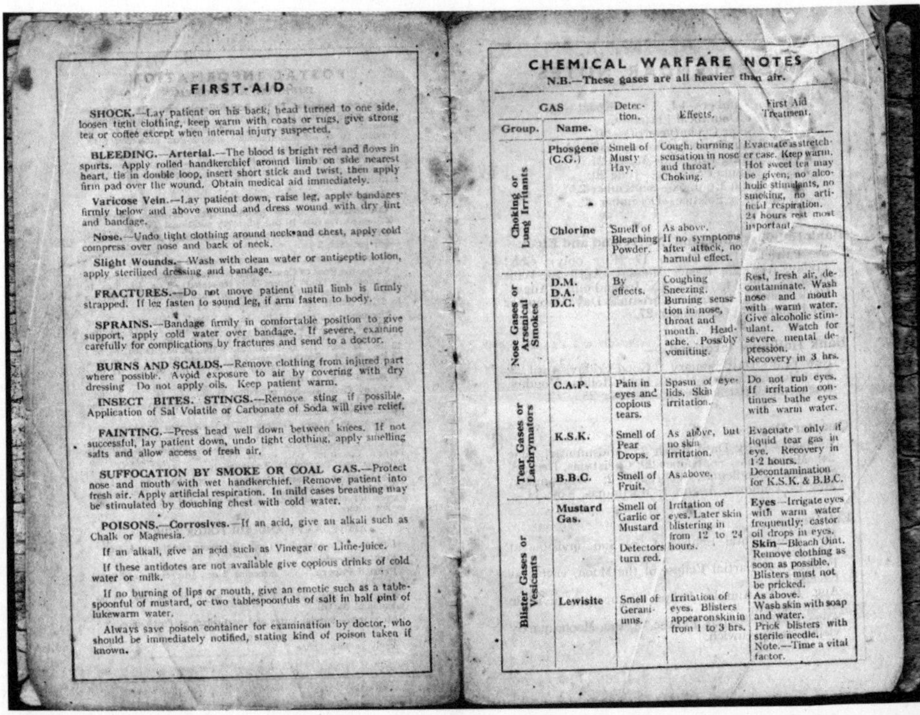

FIRST-AID

SHOCK.—Lay patient on his back, head turned to one side, loosen tight clothing, keep warm with coats or rugs, give strong tea or coffee except when internal injury suspected.

BLEEDING.—Arterial.—The blood is bright red and flows in spurts. Apply rolled handkerchief around limb on side nearest heart, tie in double loop, insert short stick and twist, then apply firm pad over the wound. Obtain medical aid immediately.

Varicose Vein.—Lay patient down, raise leg, apply bandages firmly below and above wound and dress wound with dry lint and bandage.

Nose.—Undo tight clothing around neck and chest, apply cold compress over nose and back of neck.

Slight Wounds.—Wash with clean water or antiseptic lotion, apply sterilized dressing and bandage.

FRACTURES.—Do not move patient until limb is firmly strapped. If leg fasten to sound leg, if arm fasten to body.

SPRAINS.—Bandage firmly in comfortable position to give support, apply cold water over bandage. If severe, examine carefully for complications by fractures and send to a doctor.

BURNS AND SCALDS.—Remove clothing from injured part where possible. Avoid exposure to air by covering with dry dressing. Do not apply oils. Keep patient warm.

INSECT BITES. STINGS.—Remove sting if possible. Application of Sal Volatile or Carbonate of Soda will give relief.

FAINTING.—Press head well down between knees. If not successful, lay patient down, undo tight clothing, apply smelling salts and allow access of fresh air.

SUFFOCATION BY SMOKE OR COAL GAS.—Protect nose and mouth with wet handkerchief. Remove patient into fresh air. Apply artificial respiration. In mild cases breathing may be stimulated by douching chest with cold water.

POISONS.—Corrosives.—If an acid, give an alkali such as Chalk or Magnesia.

If an alkali, give an acid such as Vinegar or Lime-juice.

If these antidotes are not available give copious drinks of cold water or milk.

If no burning of lips or mouth, give an emetic such as a tablespoonful of mustard, or two tablespoonfuls of salt in half pint of lukewarm water.

Always save poison container for examination by doctor, who should be immediately notified, stating kind of poison taken if known.

CHEMICAL WARFARE NOTES

N.B.—These gases are all heavier than air.

GAS		Detection.	Effects.	First Aid Treatment.
Group.	Name.			
Choking or Lung Irritants	Phosgene (C.G.)	Smell of Musty Hay.	Cough, burning sensation in nose and throat. Choking.	Evacuate as stretcher case. Keep warm. Hot sweet tea may be given; no alcoholic stimulants, no smoking, no artificial respiration. 24 hours rest most important.
	Chlorine	Smell of Bleaching Powder.	As above. If no symptoms after attack, no harmful effect.	
Nose Gases or Arsenical Smokes	D.M. D.A. D.C.	By effects.	Coughing Sneezing. Burning sensation in nose, throat and mouth. Headache. Possibly vomiting.	Rest, fresh air, decontaminate. Wash nose and mouth with warm water. Give alcoholic stimulant. Watch for severe mental depression. Recovery in 3 hrs.
Tear Gases or Lachrymators	C.A.P.	Pain in eyes and copious tears.	Spasm of eyelids. Skin irritation.	Do not rub eyes. If irritation continues bathe eyes with warm water.
	K.S.K.	Smell of Pear Drops.	As above, but no skin irritation.	Evacuate only if liquid tear gas in eye. Recovery in 1-2 hours.
	B.B.C.	Smell of Fruit.	As above.	Decontamination for K.S.K. & B.B.C.
Blister Gases or Vesicants	Mustard Gas.	Smell of Garlic or Mustard. Detectors turn red.	Irritation of eyes. Later skin blistering in from 12 to 24 hours.	Eyes—Irrigate eyes with warm water frequently; castor oil drops in eyes. Skin—Bleach Oint. Remove clothing as soon as possible. Blisters must not be pricked.
	Lewisite	Smell of Geraniums.	Irritation of eyes. Blisters appear on skin in from 1 to 3 hrs.	As above. Wash skin with soap and water. Prick blisters with sterile needle. Note.—Time a vital factor.

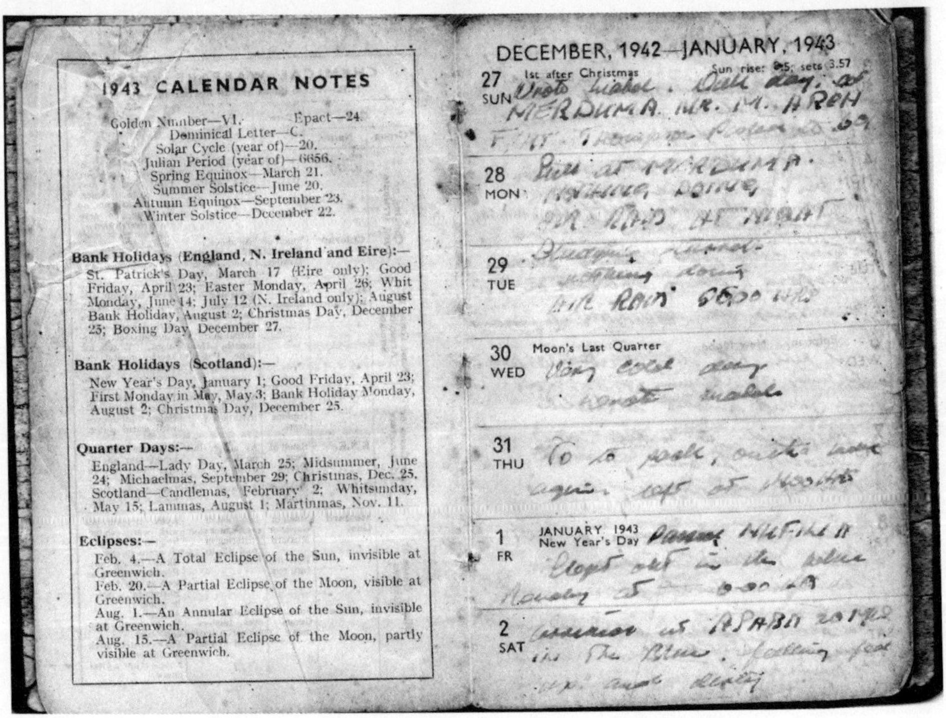

1943 CALENDAR NOTES

Golden Number—VI. Epact—24.
Dominical Letter—C.
Solar Cycle (year of)—20.
Julian Period (year of)—6656.
Spring Equinox—March 21.
Summer Solstice—June 20.
Autumn Equinox—September 23.
Winter Solstice—December 22.

Bank Holidays (England, N. Ireland and Eire):—
St. Patrick's Day, March 17 (Eire only); Good Friday, April 23; Easter Monday, April 26; Whit Monday, June 14; July 12 (N. Ireland only); August Bank Holiday, August 2; Christmas Day, December 25; Boxing Day, December 27.

Bank Holidays (Scotland):—
New Year's Day, January 1; Good Friday, April 23; First Monday in May, May 3; Bank Holiday Monday, August 2; Christmas Day, December 25.

Quarter Days:—
England—Lady Day, March 25; Midsummer, June 24; Michaelmas, September 29; Christmas, Dec. 25. Scotland—Candlemas, February 2; Whitsunday, May 15; Lammas, August 1; Martinmas, Nov. 11.

Eclipses:—
Feb. 4.—A Total Eclipse of the Sun, invisible at Greenwich.
Feb. 20.—A Partial Eclipse of the Moon, visible at Greenwich.
Aug. 1.—An Annular Eclipse of the Sun, invisible at Greenwich.
Aug. 15.—A Partial Eclipse of the Moon, partly visible at Greenwich.

DECEMBER, 1942—JANUARY, 1943

Sun rise: 8.5; sets 3.57

27 SUN 1st after Christmas — Wrote Mabel. Dull day. At MERDUMA. MR. M. AREH [illegible]

28 MON — Still at MERDUMA. Nothing doing. AIR RAID AT NIGHT

29 TUE — [illegible] nothing doing AIR RAID 0600 HRS

30 WED Moon's Last Quarter — Very cold day. Wrote Mabel.

31 THU — [illegible] again. [illegible]

1 FR JANUARY 1943 New Year's Day — [illegible] NUFILIA(?) Slept out in the blue [illegible] 0-30 HRS

2 SAT — Arrived at [illegible] in the Blue. [illegible]

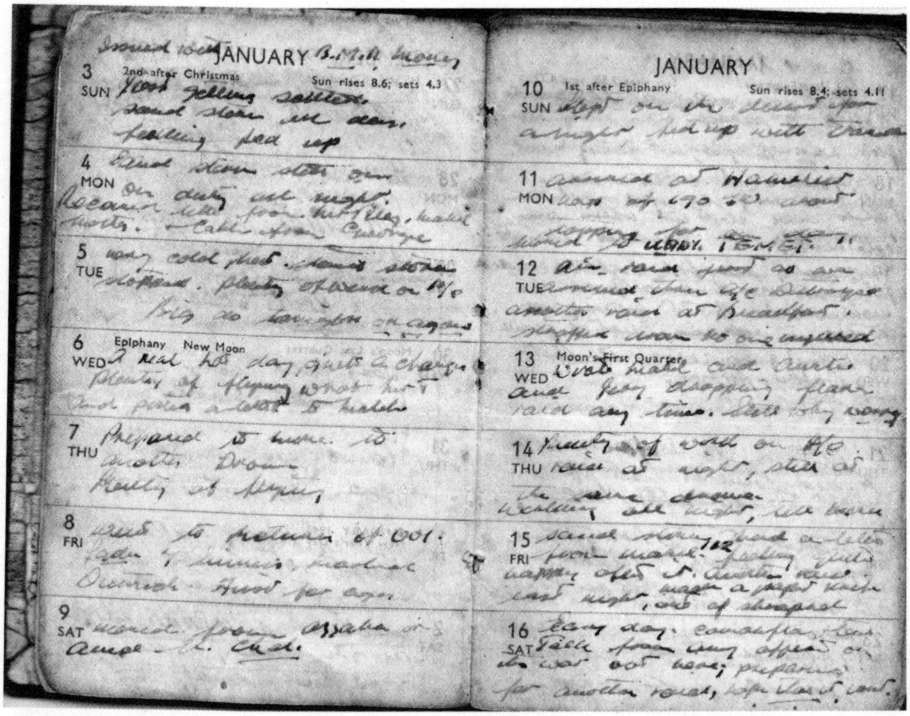
JANUARY

3 SUN 2nd after Christmas Sun rises 8.6; sets 4.3

4 MON

5 TUE

6 WED Epiphany New Moon

7 THU

8 FRI

9 SAT

JANUARY

10 SUN 1st after Epiphany Sun rises 8.4; sets 4.11

11 MON

12 TUE

13 WED Moon's First Quarter

14 THU

15 FRI

16 SAT

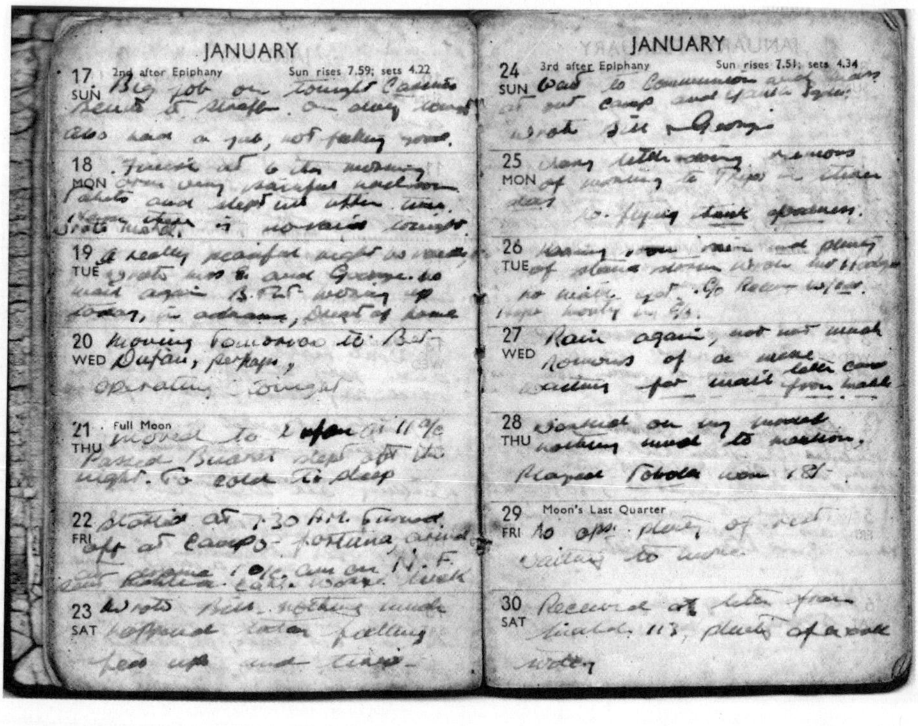
JANUARY

17 SUN 2nd after Epiphany Sun rises 7.59; sets 4.22

18 MON

19 TUE

20 WED

21 THU Full Moon

22 FRI

23 SAT

JANUARY

24 SUN 3rd after Epiphany Sun rises 7.51; sets 4.34

25 MON

26 TUE

27 WED

28 THU

29 FRI Moon's Last Quarter

30 SAT

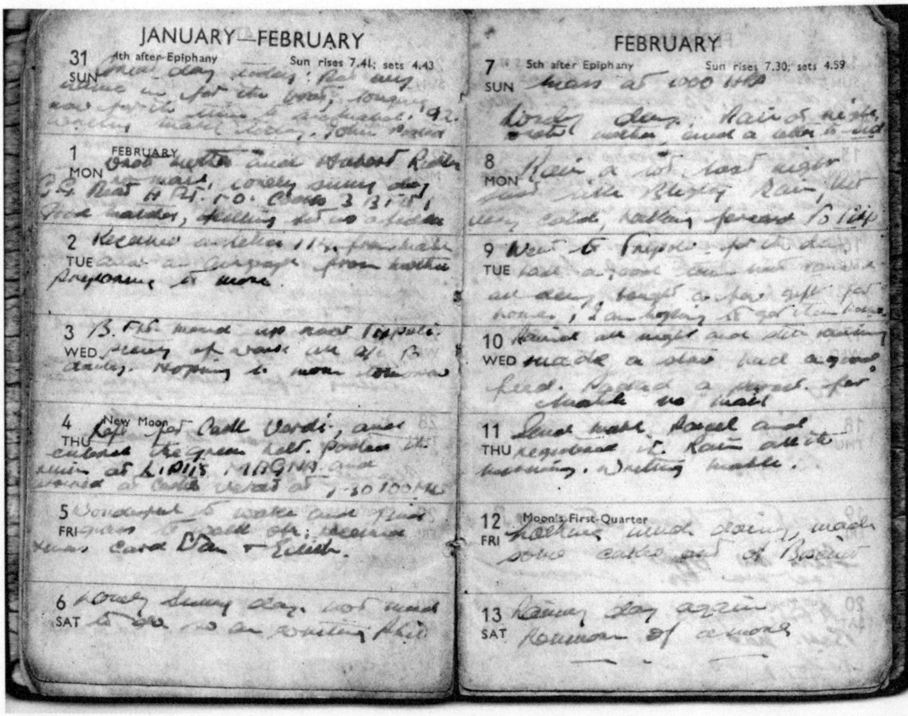
JANUARY—FEBRUARY
31 4th after Epiphany Sun rises 7.41; sets 4.43
FEBRUARY
7 5th after Epiphany Sun rises 7.30; sets 4.59
4 New Moon
12 Moon's First-Quarter

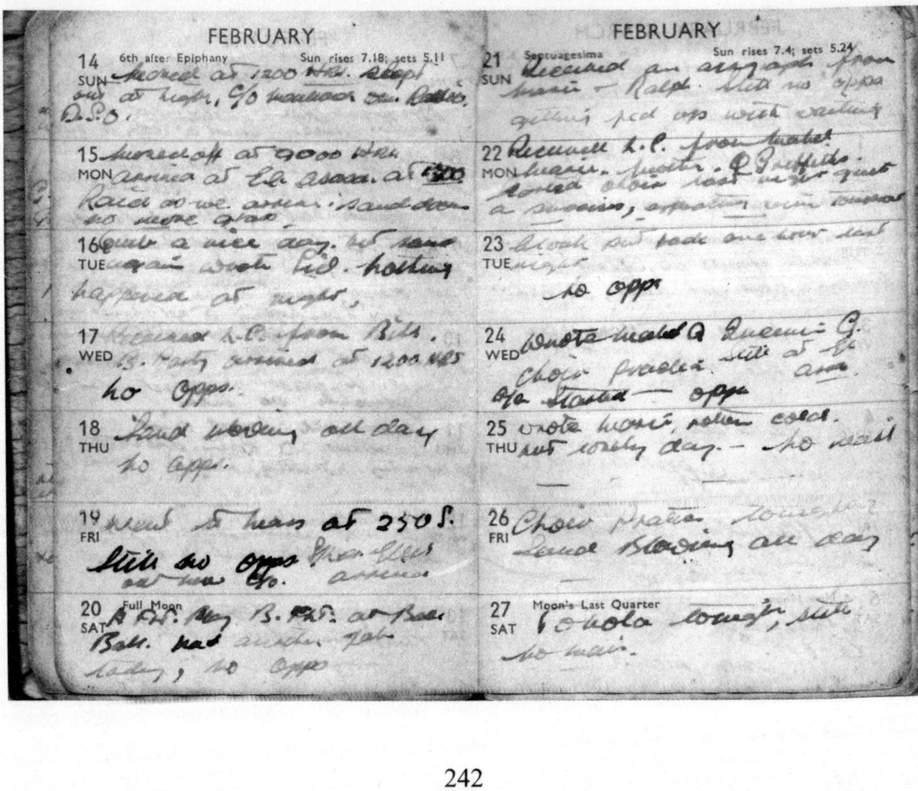
FEBRUARY
14 6th after Epiphany Sun rises 7.18; sets 5.11
FEBRUARY
21 Septuagesima Sun rises 7.4; sets 5.24
20 Full Moon
27 Moon's Last Quarter

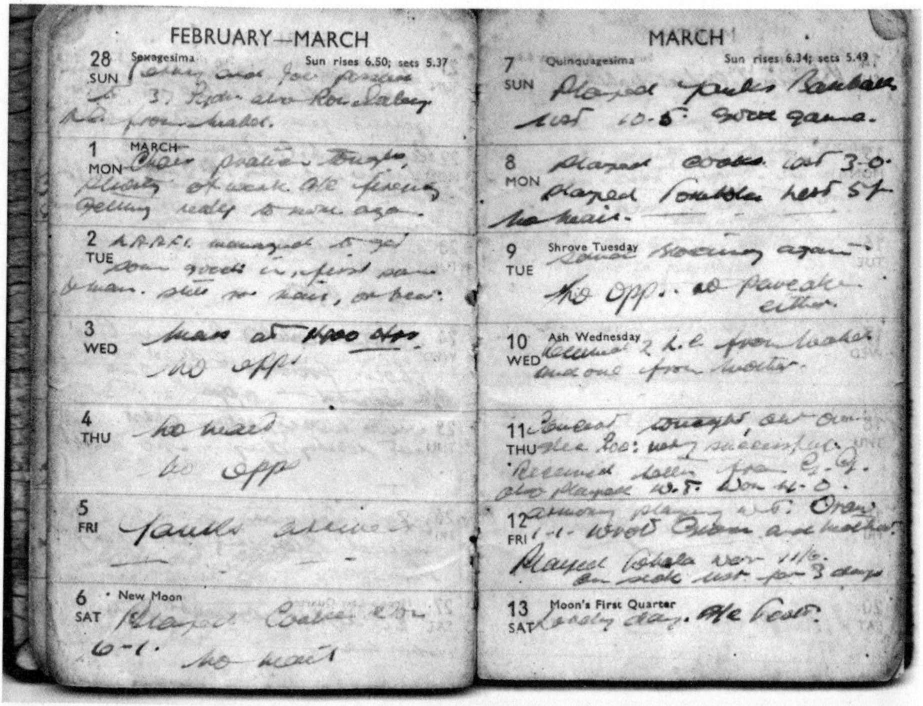
FEBRUARY—MARCH
28 Sexagesima Sun rises 6.50; sets 5.37 SUN
1 MARCH MON
2 TUE
3 WED
4 THU
5 FRI
6 New Moon SAT
MARCH
7 Quinquagesima Sun rises 6.34; sets 5.49 SUN
8 MON
9 Shrove Tuesday TUE
10 Ash Wednesday WED
11 THU
12 FRI
13 Moon's First Quarter SAT

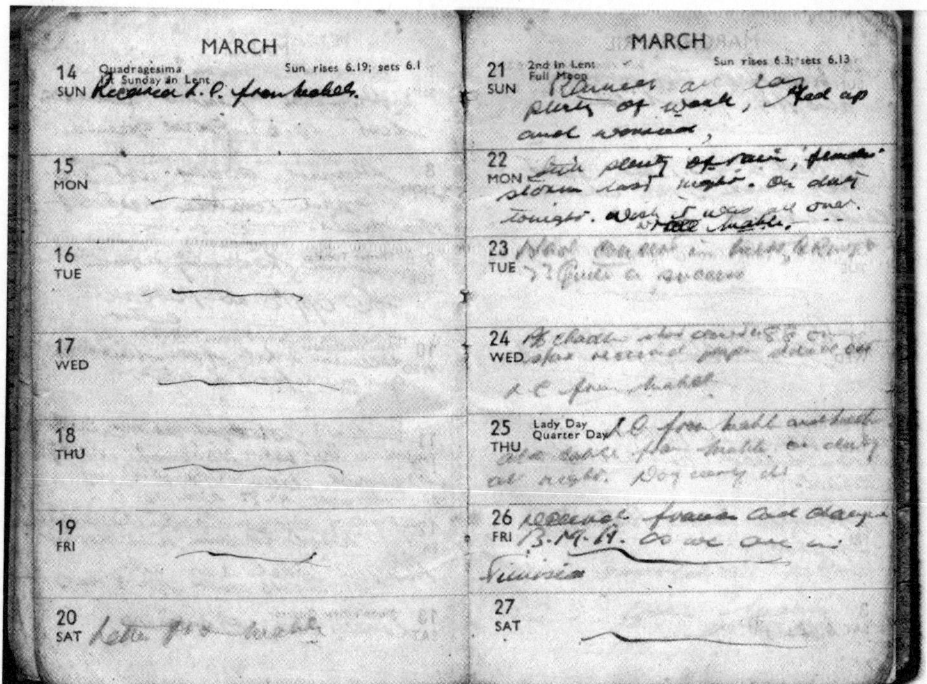
MARCH
14 Quadragesima 1st Sunday in Lent Sun rises 6.19; sets 6.1 SUN
15 MON
16 TUE
17 WED
18 THU
19 FRI
20 SAT
MARCH
21 2nd in Lent Full Moon Sun rises 6.3; sets 6.13 SUN
22 MON
23 TUE
24 WED
25 Lady Day Quarter Day THU
26 FRI
27 SAT

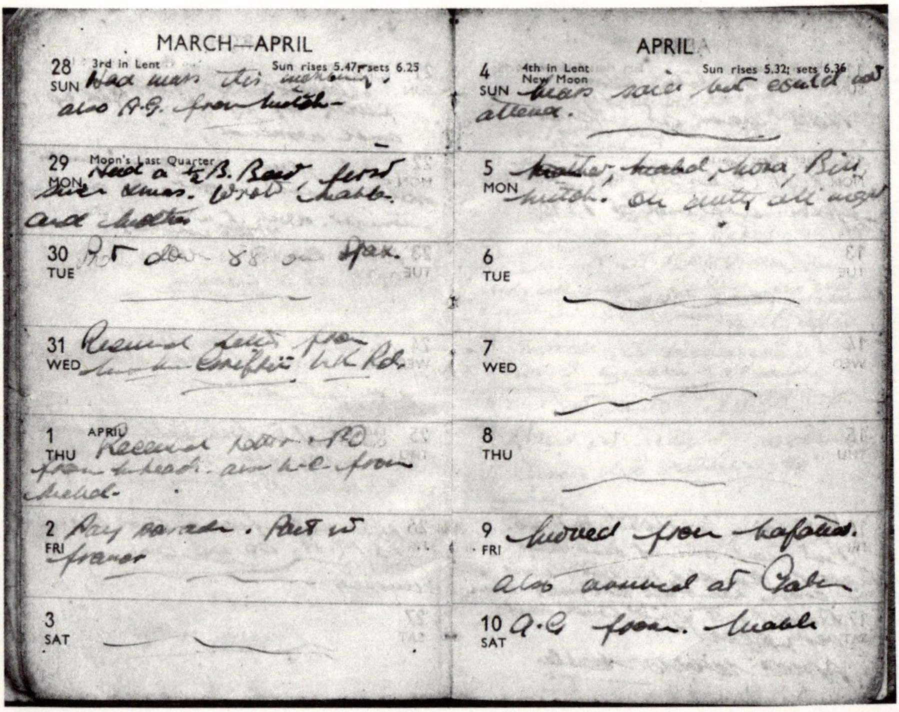
MARCH—APRIL
28 SUN 3rd in Lent Sun rises 5.47; sets 6.25
29 MON Moon's Last Quarter
30 TUE
31 WED
1 THU APRIL
2 FRI
3 SAT
APRIL
4 SUN 4th in Lent New Moon Sun rises 5.32; sets 6.36
5 MON
6 TUE
7 WED
8 THU
9 FRI
10 SAT

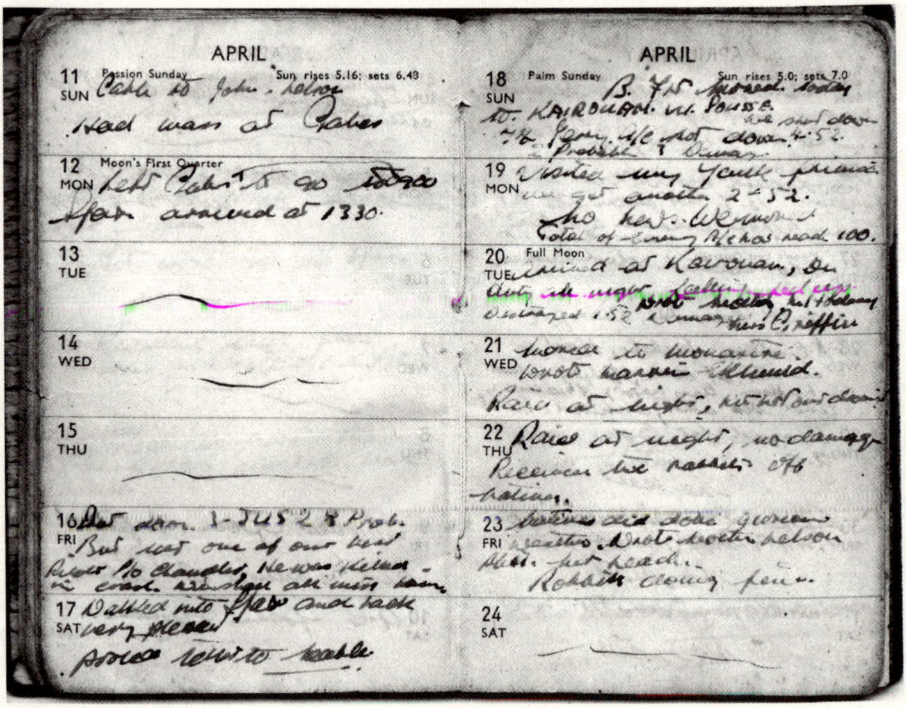
APRIL
11 SUN Passion Sunday Sun rises 5.16; sets 6.48
12 MON Moon's First Quarter
13 TUE
14 WED
15 THU
16 FRI
17 SAT
APRIL
18 SUN Palm Sunday Sun rises 5.0; sets 7.0
19 MON
20 TUE Full Moon
21 WED
22 THU
23 FRI
24 SAT

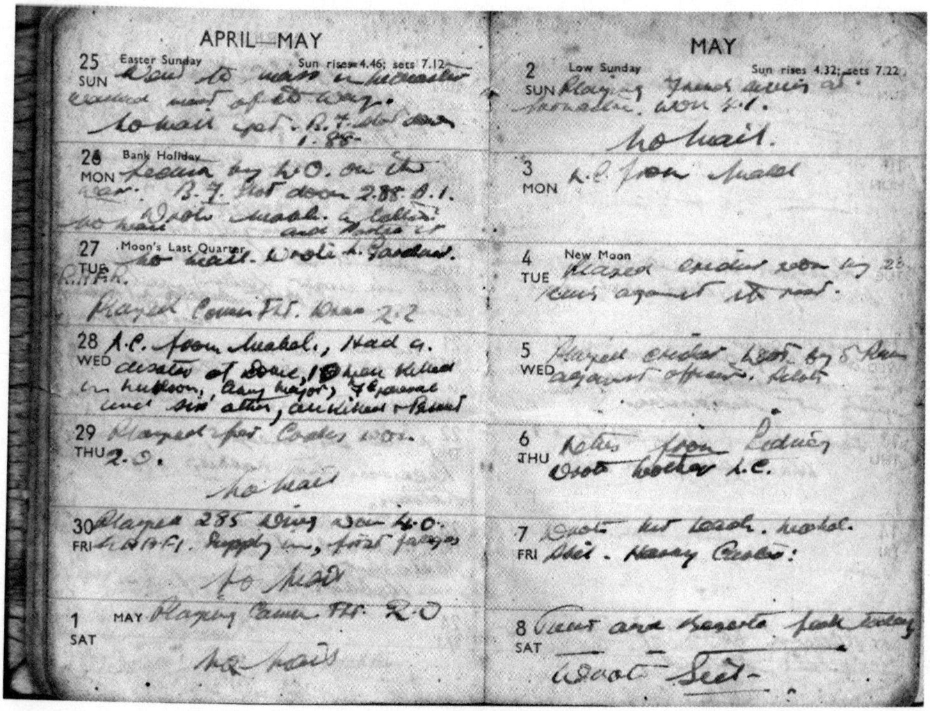

APRIL—MAY

25 SUN Easter Sunday. Sun rises 4.46; sets 7.12. Went to mass in Monastir, walked most of the way. No mail. Sat. B.7. shot down 1.88.

26 MON Bank Holiday. [illegible] by H.Q. on the [illegible]. B.7. shot down 2.88. B.1. No mail. Wrote Mabel a letter and [illegible]

27 TUE Moon's Last Quarter. No mail. Wrote L. Gardner. Played Comm Flt. Drew 2.2

28 WED L.C. from Mabel. Had a disaster of some, 10 men killed in [illegible], Army major, 7 [illegible] and six others, all killed & [illegible]

29 THU Played for Cooks won 2.0. No mail

30 FRI Played 285 Wing won 4.0. [illegible] No mail

1 SAT MAY Playing Comm Flt. 2.0. No mail

MAY

2 SUN Low Sunday. Sun rises 4.32; sets 7.22. Playing [illegible] at Monastir won 4.1. No mail.

3 MON L.C. from Mabel

4 TUE New Moon. Played cricket won by 28 runs against the [illegible].

5 WED Played cricket lost by 5 runs against officers. [illegible]

6 THU Letter from [illegible]. Wrote mother L.C.

7 FRI Wrote [illegible]. [illegible]

8 SAT [illegible] Wrote Seet.

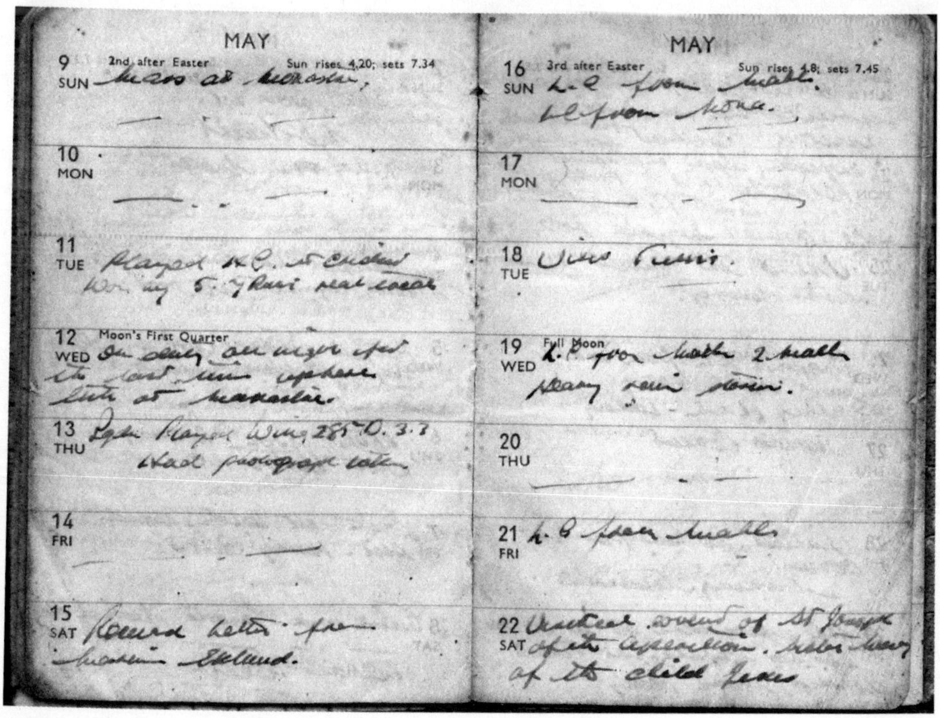

MAY

9 SUN 2nd after Easter. Sun rises 4.20; sets 7.34. Mass at Monastir.

10 MON

11 TUE Played H.Q. at cricket won by 5 [illegible]

12 WED Moon's First Quarter. On duty all night [illegible] [illegible] at Monastir.

13 THU [illegible] Played Wing 285 D. 3.3 Had photograph taken

14 FRI

15 SAT Received letter from [illegible] England.

MAY

16 SUN 3rd after Easter. Sun rises 4.8; sets 7.45. L.C. from Mabel. L.C. from Mona.

17 MON

18 TUE [illegible]

19 WED Full Moon. L.C. from Mabel 2 mail [illegible]

20 THU

21 FRI L.C. from Mabel

22 SAT [illegible] of St Joseph [illegible]

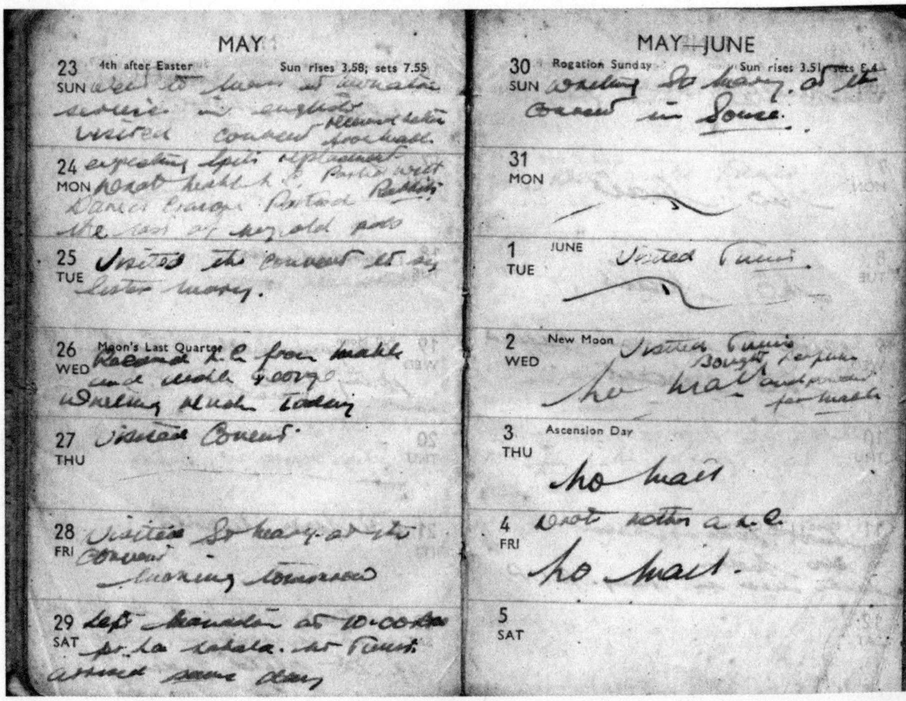

MAY

23 SUN 4th after Easter Sun rises 3.58; sets 7.55
Went to Mass at ... service in English
Visited convent. Received letter from ...

24 MON expecting Spits replacement
... Parked with
... Parked ...
the last of my old pals

25 TUE Visited the convent to see
Sister Mary.

26 WED Moon's Last Quarter Received L.C. from ...
and ... George
Waiting ... today

27 THU Visited Convent

28 FRI Visited Sr Mary at the
Convent
leaving tomorrow

29 SAT left ... at 10.00 ...
for La ... at Tunis
arrived same day

MAY—JUNE

30 SUN Rogation Sunday Sun rises 3.51; sets 8.4
Visiting Sr Mary at the
Convent in Sousse.

31 MON

1 TUE JUNE Visited Tunis.

2 WED New Moon Visited Tunis
Bought ...
No mail ...

3 THU Ascension Day
No mail

4 FRI Wrote letter ...
No mail.

5 SAT

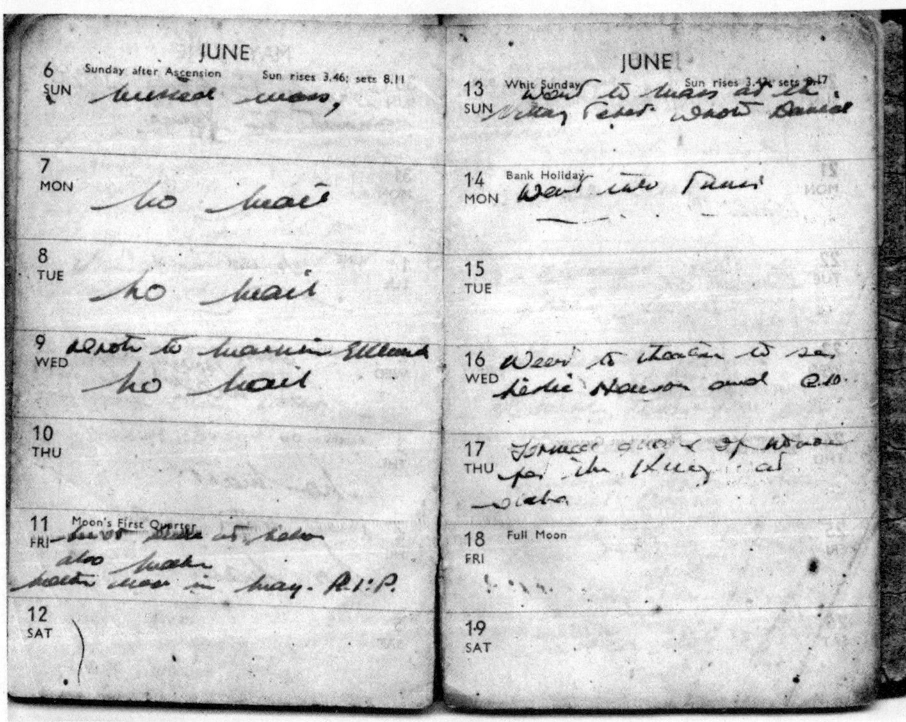

JUNE

6 SUN Sunday after Ascension Sun rises 3.46; sets 8.11
Missed mass,

7 MON No mail

8 TUE No mail

9 WED Wrote to ...
No mail

10 THU

11 FRI Moon's First Quarter ...
also ...
... in May. R.I.P.

12 SAT

JUNE

13 SUN Whit Sunday Sun rises 3.4?; sets 8.17
Went to Mass at St
... wrote ...

14 MON Bank Holiday Went into Tunis

15 TUE

16 WED Went to theatre to see
Leslie Henson and ...

17 THU ... for the King at
...

18 FRI Full Moon

19 SAT

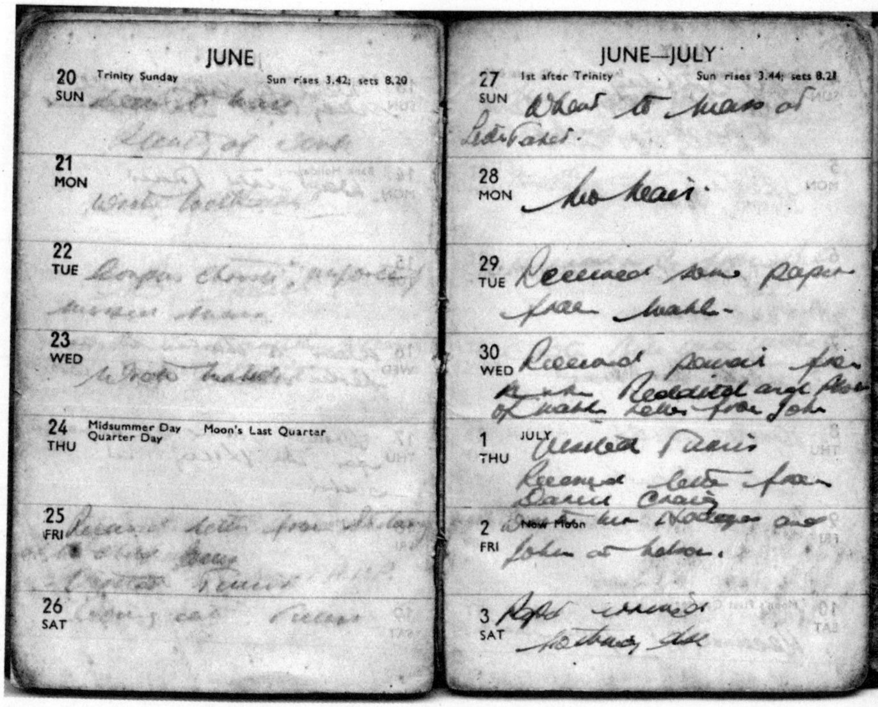

JUNE

20 SUN Trinity Sunday — Sun rises 3.42; sets 8.20

21 MON

22 TUE

23 WED

24 THU Midsummer Day, Quarter Day — Moon's Last Quarter

25 FRI

26 SAT

JUNE—JULY

27 SUN 1st after Trinity — Sun rises 3.44; sets 8.21

28 MON

29 TUE

30 WED

1 THU JULY

2 FRI New Moon

3 SAT

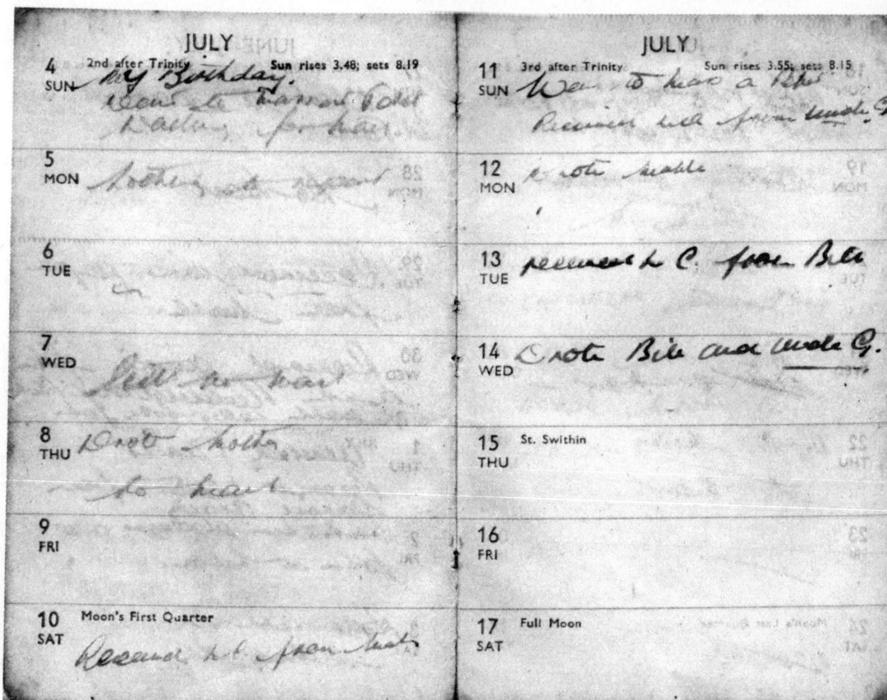

JULY

4 SUN 2nd after Trinity — Sun rises 3.48; sets 8.19 — My Birthday.

5 MON

6 TUE

7 WED

8 THU

9 FRI

10 SAT Moon's First Quarter

JULY

11 SUN 3rd after Trinity — Sun rises 3.55; sets 8.15

12 MON

13 TUE

14 WED

15 THU St. Swithin

16 FRI

17 SAT Full Moon

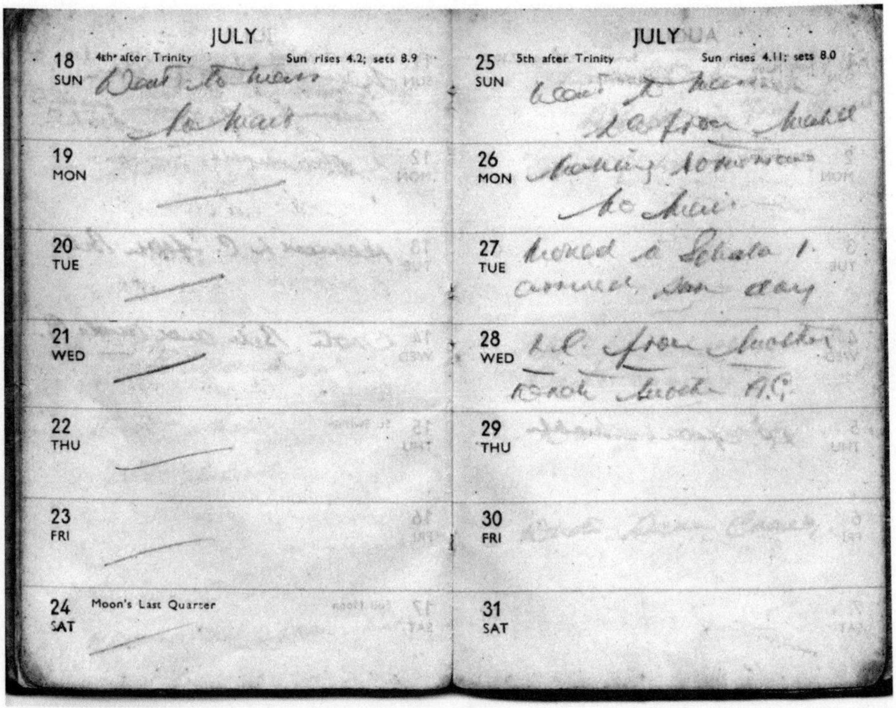

JULY

18 SUN — 4th after Trinity — Sun rises 4.2; sets 8.9
Went to mass
No mail

19 MON

20 TUE

21 WED

22 THU

23 FRI

24 SAT — Moon's Last Quarter

JULY

25 SUN — 5th after Trinity — Sun rises 4.11; sets 8.0
Went to mass
L.C. from Mabel

26 MON
Nothing tomorrow
No mail

27 TUE

28 WED
L.C. from Mabel
Wrote Mabel A.G.

29 THU

30 FRI

31 SAT

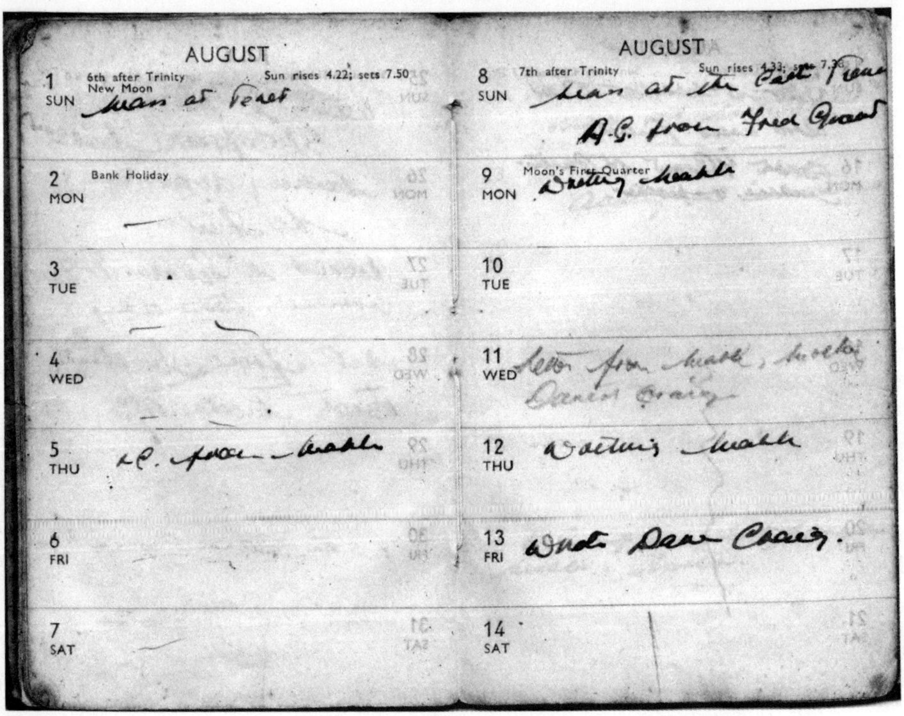

AUGUST

1 SUN — 6th after Trinity — New Moon — Sun rises 4.22; sets 7.50
Mass at Ferat

2 MON — Bank Holiday

3 TUE

4 WED

5 THU
L.C. from Mabel

6 FRI

7 SAT

AUGUST

8 SUN — 7th after Trinity — Sun rises 4.33; sets 7.36
Mass at the
A.G. from Fred

9 MON — Moon's First Quarter
Writing Mabel

10 TUE

11 WED
Letter from Mabel

12 THU
Writing Mabel

13 FRI
Wrote Dan Craig.

14 SAT

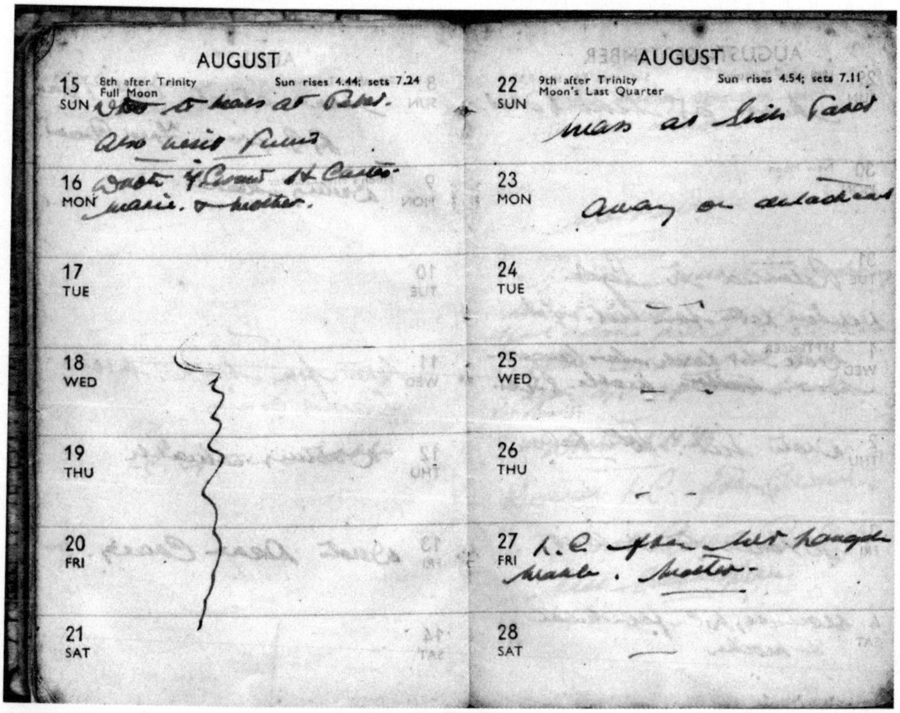

AUGUST

15 SUN 8th after Trinity, Full Moon. Sun rises 4.44; sets 7.24

16 MON

17 TUE

18 WED

19 THU

20 FRI

21 SAT

AUGUST

22 SUN 9th after Trinity, Moon's Last Quarter. Sun rises 4.54; sets 7.11

23 MON Away on detachment

24 TUE

25 WED

26 THU

27 FRI L.C. ... Mabel. Mother.

28 SAT

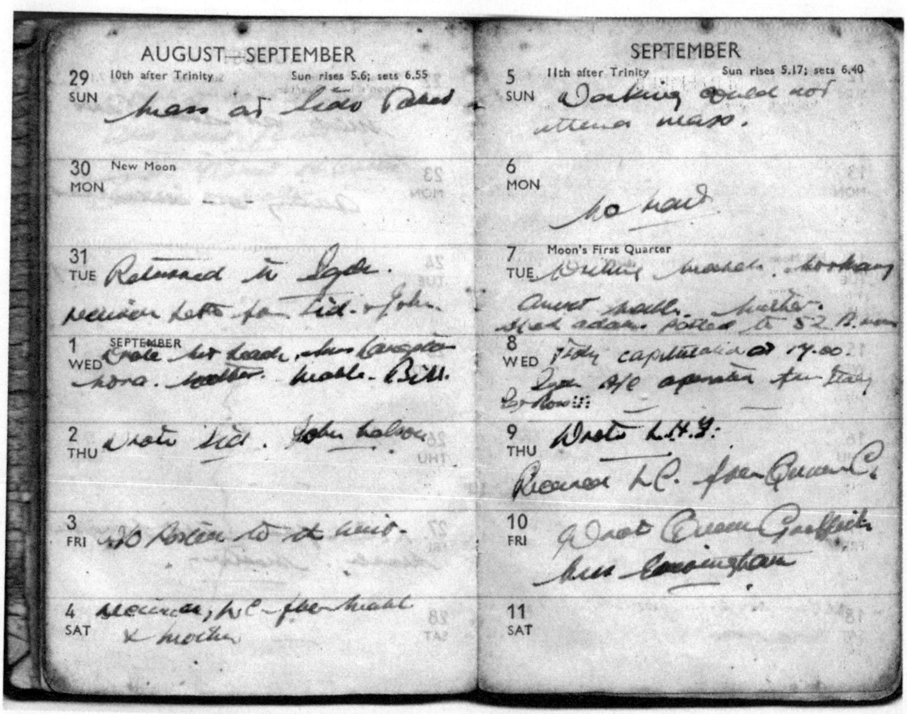

AUGUST—SEPTEMBER

29 SUN 10th after Trinity. Sun rises 5.6; sets 6.55

30 MON New Moon

31 TUE Returned to ... received letters from Sid & John.

1 SEPTEMBER WED Wrote ... Nora. Mother. Mabel. Bill.

2 THU Wrote Sid. John ...

3 FRI

4 SAT Received, L.C. from Mabel & Mother

SEPTEMBER

5 SUN 11th after Trinity. Sun rises 5.17; sets 6.40. Working could not attend mass.

6 MON No mail

7 TUE Moon's First Quarter.

8 WED Italy capitulated 17.00.

9 THU Wrote ... Received L.C. from ...

10 FRI Wrote ... Mrs Cunningham

11 SAT

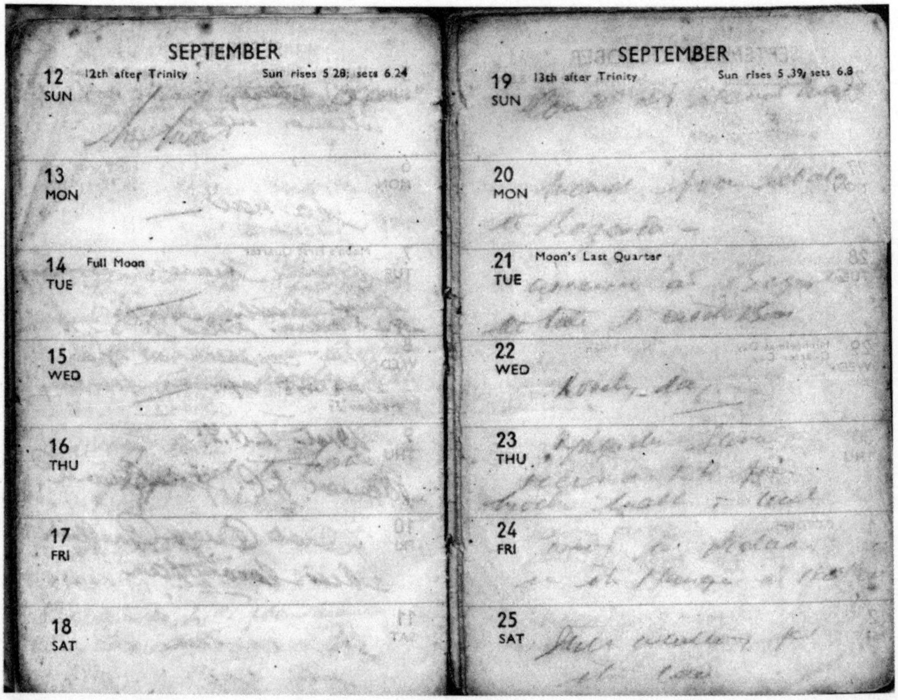
SEPTEMBER

12 SUN 12th after Trinity Sun rises 5.28; sets 6.24

13 MON

14 TUE Full Moon

15 WED

16 THU

17 FRI

18 SAT

SEPTEMBER

19 SUN 13th after Trinity Sun rises 5.39; sets 6.8

20 MON

21 TUE Moon's Last Quarter

22 WED

23 THU

24 FRI

25 SAT

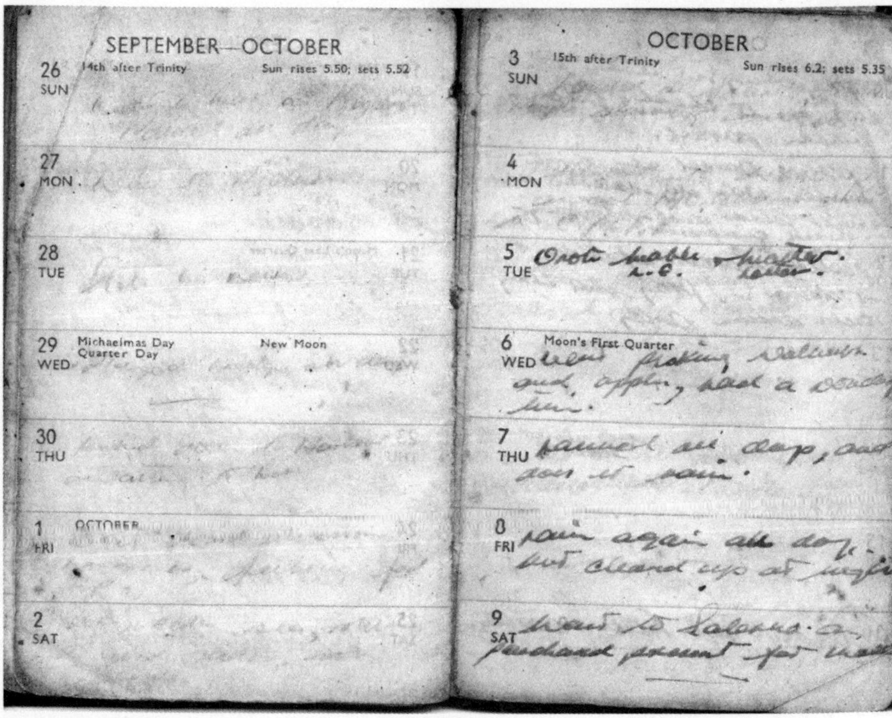
SEPTEMBER—OCTOBER

26 SUN 14th after Trinity Sun rises 5.50; sets 5.52

27 MON

28 TUE

29 WED Michaelmas Day Quarter Day New Moon

30 THU

1 FRI OCTOBER

2 SAT

OCTOBER

3 SUN 15th after Trinity Sun rises 6.2; sets 5.35

4 MON

5 TUE [illegible]

6 WED Moon's First Quarter [illegible]

7 THU [illegible] all day, and [illegible] it rain.

8 FRI rain again all day, but cleared up at night.

9 SAT Went to Salerno and purchased present for [illegible]

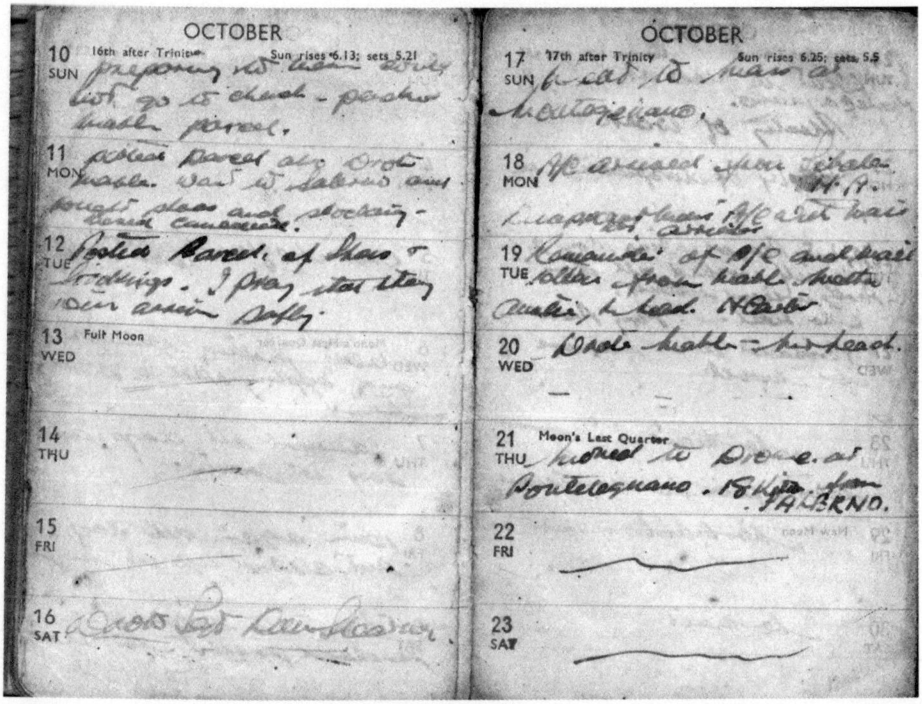
OCTOBER

10 SUN 16th after Trinity Sun rises 6.13; sets 5.21
preparing to [illegible] list. go to church – packed [illegible] parcel.

11 MON [illegible] parcel [illegible]. Went to Salerno and bought shoes and stockings – [illegible]

12 TUE Posted parcel of shoes & stockings. I pray that they [illegible] safely.

13 WED Full Moon

14 THU

15 FRI

16 SAT

OCTOBER

17 SUN 17th after Trinity Sun rises 6.25; sets 5.5
Went to mass at Montecorvino.

18 MON A/C arrived from [illegible] H.R.
[illegible] A/C [illegible]

19 TUE [illegible] of A/C and mail [illegible]

20 WED [illegible]

21 THU Moon's Last Quarter
Moved to Drome at Pontecagnano. 18 kilos from SALERNO.

22 FRI

23 SAT

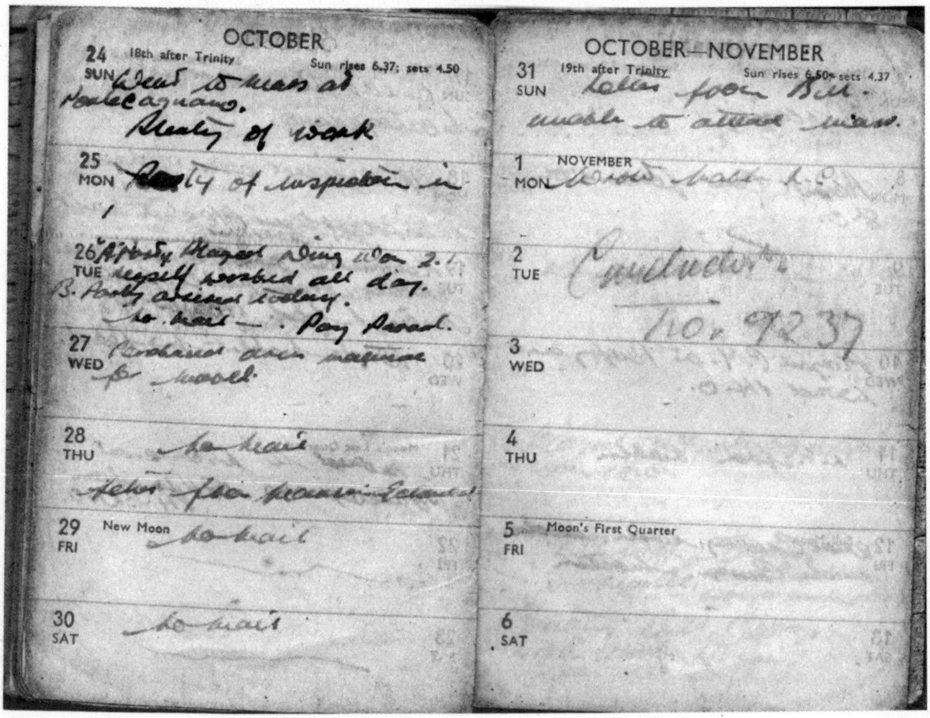
OCTOBER

24 SUN 18th after Trinity Sun rises 6.37; sets 4.50
Went to mass at Pontecagnano.
[illegible] of work

25 MON [illegible] of inspection in

26 TUE [illegible] all day. B. Party arrived today.
No mail – Pay Parade.

27 WED Purchased [illegible] for [illegible]

28 THU No mail
Letter from [illegible]

29 FRI New Moon No mail.

30 SAT No mail

OCTOBER—NOVEMBER

31 SUN 19th after Trinity Sun rises 6.50; sets 4.37
Letter from Bill. unable to attend mass.

1 MON NOVEMBER [illegible]

2 TUE Conductor
No. 9237

3 WED

4 THU

5 FRI Moon's First Quarter

6 SAT

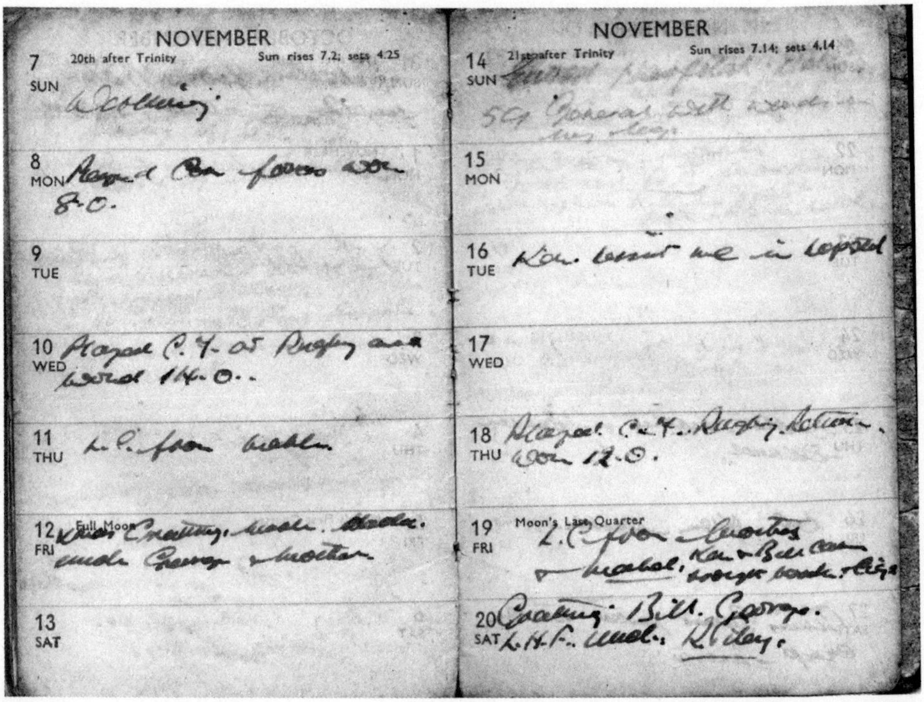
NOVEMBER
7 20th after Trinity Sun rises 7.2; sets 4.25
SUN
8
MON
9
TUE
10
WED
11
THU
12 Full Moon
FRI
13
SAT
NOVEMBER
14 21st after Trinity Sun rises 7.14; sets 4.14
SUN
15
MON
16
TUE
17
WED
18
THU
19 Moon's Last Quarter
FRI
20
SAT

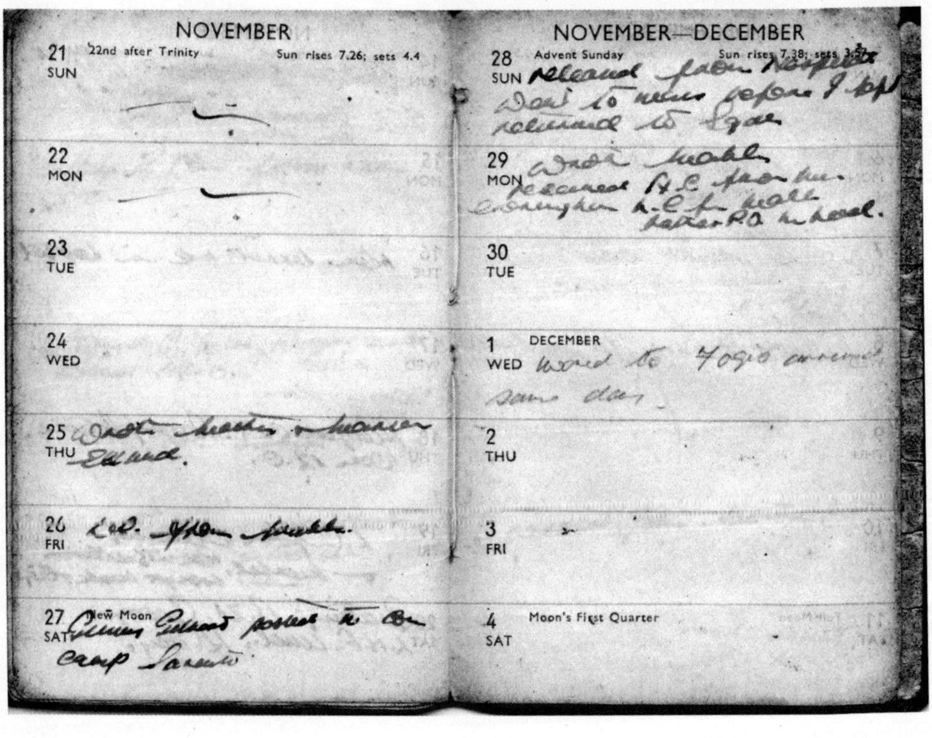
NOVEMBER
21 22nd after Trinity Sun rises 7.26; sets 4.4
SUN
22
MON
23
TUE
24
WED
25
THU
26
FRI
27 New Moon
SAT
NOVEMBER—DECEMBER
28 Advent Sunday
SUN
29
MON
30
TUE
1 DECEMBER
WED
2
THU
3
FRI
4 Moon's First Quarter
SAT

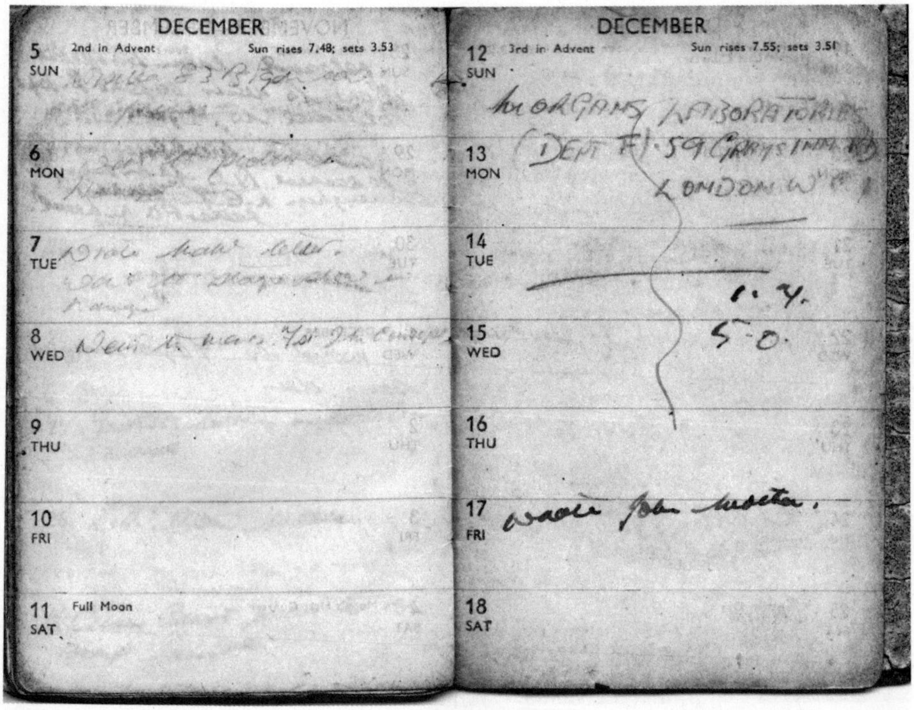
DECEMBER
5 SUN 2nd in Advent Sun rises 7.48; sets 3.53
6 MON
7 TUE
8 WED
9 THU
10 FRI
11 SAT Full Moon
DECEMBER
12 SUN 3rd in Advent Sun rises 7.55; sets 3.51
13 MON
14 TUE
15 WED
16 THU
17 FRI
18 SAT

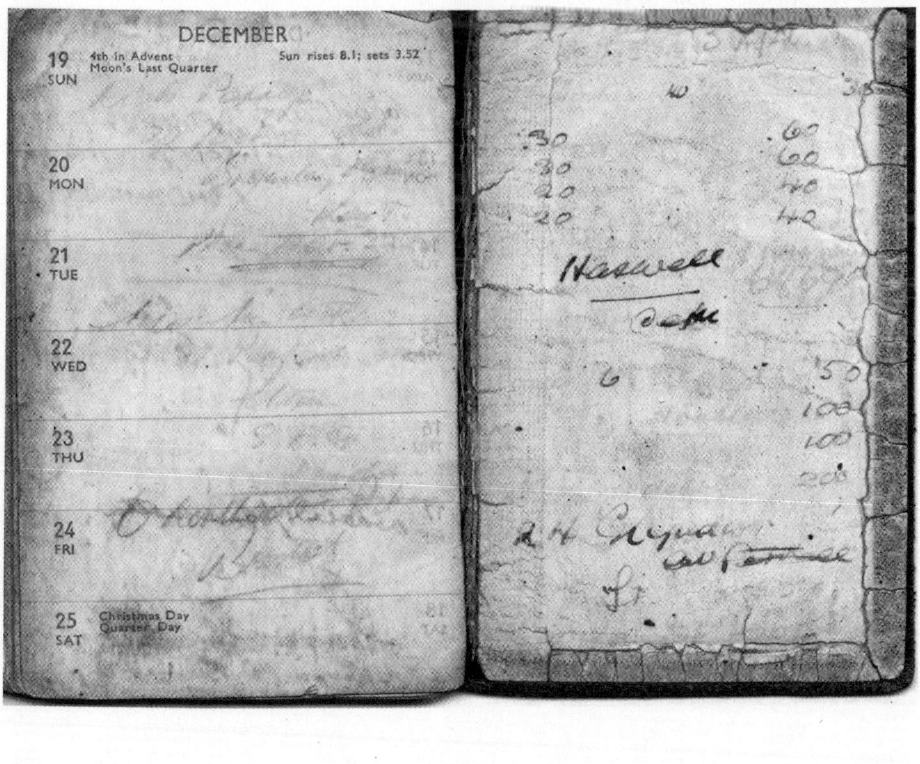
DECEMBER
19 SUN 4th in Advent Moon's Last Quarter Sun rises 8.1; sets 3.52
20 MON
21 TUE
22 WED
23 THU
24 FRI
25 SAT Christmas Day Quarter Day

Unfortunately, the final pages to complete the month of December 1943 and the start of January 1944 are missing.

When you think that the diary (in 2023) is 80 years old, it is no wonder that some pages are missing and that some writing has faded with time. The faded writing is mainly where a pencil was used to write the daily entrees, whilst writing in ink has lasted the test of time.

The following transcript identifies the written word from 27 December 1942 to 31 December 1943 by LAC Lamb L.B. Serial Nr. 1012281. All taken from his written diary.

NOTE: The recorded 73 Squadron AIRs during the Second World War in North Africa & Italy (late December 1942 to April 1944) have been referred to and cross referenced, where applicable.

AIR 27/631/23 & AIR 27/631/24 Pilot Ops Report December 1942	
Sunday, 27 December	Wrote Mabel. Dull day at Merduma. Mr M Arch F/LT Thompson posted to 601 Squadron. *Refer to the above AIR 27/631/23.*
Monday, 28 December	Still at Merduma. Nothing doing. Air raid at night. *Refer to the above AIR 27/631/23.*
Tuesday, 29 December	Sludging Tunnel. Nothing doing. Air raid 20:00 hours. *Refer to the above AIR 27/631/23.*
Wednesday, 30 December	Very cold day. Wrote Mabel. *Refer to the above AIR 27/631/23.*
Thursday, 31 December	Go to pack, on the move again. Left at 14:00 hours. *Refer to the above AIR 27/631/23.*
AIR 27/632/1 & AIR 27/632/2 Pilot Ops Report January 1943	
Friday, 1 January Merduma	Passed Nofilia II. Slept out in the blue open skies at 06:00 hours. *AIR 27/632/1 covers operations for the day.*
Saturday, 2 January Alem el Chel	Arrived at Asaba 20:00 hours in the Blue. Feeling fed up and dirty. *AIR 27/632/1 covers operations for the day.*
Sunday, 3 January	Issued with B.M.A. money. Just settled. Sandstorm all day. Feeling fed up. *AIR 27/632/1 covers operations for the day.*
Monday, 4 January	Sandstorm still on. On duty all night. Received letters from Mr Riley, Mabel & mother. Cable from George. *AIR 27/632/1 covers operations for the day.*

Tuesday, 5 January	Very cold feet. Sandstorm stopped. Plenty of work on A/C. Big do tonight on again.
Wednesday, 6 January	A nice hot day, quite a change. Plenty of flying. Wrote to Mr T and post a letter to Mabel. *AIR 27/632/1 covers operations for the day.*
Thursday, 7 January	Prepared to move to another drome. Plenty of flying. *AIR 27/632/1 covers operations for the day.*
Friday, 8 January	Went to matinee of 601 Squadron, '7 Sinners', Marlene Dietrich. First for ages. *AIR 27/632/1 covers operations for the day.*
Saturday, 9 January	Moved from Assalia on Alem El Chel. *AIR 27/632/1 covers operations for the day.*
Sunday, 10 January	Slept on the desert what a night. Fed up with travelling. *AIR 27/632/1 covers operations for the day.*
Monday, 11 January Tamet Satellite	Arrived at Hamaliar, lots of 190 710's about. Stopping for a day. Moved to Wadi Tamet. *AIR 27/632/1 covers operations for the day.*
Tuesday, 12 January	Air raid just as we arrived then A/C destroyed. Another raid at breakfast. Strafed drome no one injured. *AIR 27/632/1 covers operations for the day.*
Wednesday, 13 January	Wrote Mabel and Aunty, jerry dropping flares, raid any time. Still why worry. *AIR 27/632/1 covers operations for the day.*
Thursday, 14 January	Plenty of work on A/C. rained at night. Still at the same drome. Working all night till dusk. *AIR 27/632/1 covers operations for the day.*
Friday, 15 January	Sandstorm. Had a letter from Mabel [112], feeling quite happy after it. Another raid last night. Made a paper knife out of shrapnel. *AIR 27/632/1 covers operations for the day.*
Saturday, 16 January	Easy day. Camouflage tanks. Talk from Army Officer on the war out here. Preparing for another raid, hope that it is not. *AIR 27/632/1 covers operations for the day.*
Sunday, 17 January	Big job on tonight, Cassino, Castel Benito & strafed. On duty tonight. Also had a jab, not feeling well. *AIR 27/632/1 covers operations for the day.*
Monday, 18 January	Finish at 06:00 hours this morning. Arm very painful medication tablets and slept well after time. Hope there is no raid tonight. Wrote Mabel. *AIR 27/632/1 covers operations for the day.*
Tuesday, 19 January	A really peaceful night, no raids. Wrote to Mrs E and George. No mail again. B. Flt moving up today, in advance. Dreamt of home. *AIR 27/632/1 covers operations for the day.*

Wednesday, 20 January	Moving tomorrow to Bir Dufan, perhaps. Operating tonight. AIR 27/632/1 covers operations for the day. *AIR 27/632/1 covers operations for the day.*
Thursday, 21 January Bir Dufan	Moved to Bir Dufan at 11:00 hours. Passed Buaret, slept out the night. Too cold to sleep. *AIR 27/632/1 covers operations for the day.*
Friday, 22 January	Started at 07:30 hours. Turned off at Campo-Fortuna, arrived at 10:00 hours, am on N.F. Sent Mabel cable. Worse luck. *AIR 27/632/1 covers operations for the day.*
Saturday, 23 January	Wrote Bill, nothing much happened today. Feeling fed up and tired. *AIR 27/632/1 covers operations for the day.*
Sunday, 24 January	Went to communion and mass at our camp and yanks squadron. Wrote Bill and George. *AIR 27/632/1 covers operations for the day.*
Monday, 25 January	Very little doing, rumours of moving to Tripoli in three days. No flying, thank goodness. *AIR 27/632/1 covers operations for the day.* Mabel's birthday.
Tuesday, 26 January	Having some rain and plenty of sandstorms. Wrote Mr Hodges. No mail yet. C/O Relax W/CDR. Hope Monty is C/O. *AIR 27/632/1 covers operations for the day.*
Wednesday, 27 January	Rain again, not that much. Rumours of a move. Waiting for mail, letter came from Mother. *AIR 27/632/1 covers operations for the day.*
Thursday, 28 January	Worked on my model. Nothing much to mention. Played tombola won 18/-. *AIR 27/632/1 covers operations for the day.*
Friday, 29 January	No operations, plenty of rest. Waiting for move. *AIR 27/632/1 covers operations for the day.*
Saturday, 30 January	Received a letter from Mabel [113]. Plenty of work today. *AIR 27/632/1 covers operations for the day.*
Sunday, 31 January	Great day today, put my name in for the boat? Longing now for the time to see Mabel (192). Writing Mabel today + John, posted. *AIR 27/632/1 covers operations for the day.*
AIR 27/632/3 & AIR 27/632/4 Pilot Ops Report February 1943	
Monday, 1 February Bir Dufan Gasr Garabulli	Wrote mother and Hubert Ridler. No mail. Lovely sunny day. CG Beat A Flt 1-0; Cooks 3 B Flt 1, good matches. Feeling fit as a fiddle. *AIR 27/632/3 cover operations for the day.*
Tuesday, 2 February	Received a letter from Mabel [114] and an 'airgraph' from mother. Preparing to move. *AIR 27/632/3 cover operations for the day.*

Wednesday, 3 February	'B' Flt moved up to Tripoli. Plenty of work on A/C 13 daily. Hoping to move tomorrow. *AIR 27/632/3 cover operations for the day.*
Thursday, 4 February	Left for Castel VERDI and entered the 'green belt'. Posted the music at Liptis Magna and arrived at Castel VERDI at 07:30 hours 100 miles. *AIR 27/632/3 cover operations for the day.*
Friday, 5 February	Wonderful to wake and find grass to walk on. Received Xmas cards Stan & Edith. *AIR 27/632/3 cover operations for the day.*
Saturday, 6 February	Lovely sunny day. Not much to do so am writing Phil. *AIR 27/632/3 cover operations for the day.*
Sunday, 7 February	Mass at 10:00 hours. Lovely day. Rain at night. Wrote mother, and a letter to Sid. *AIR 27/632/3 cover operations for the day.*
Monday, 8 February	Rained a lot, last night, just like blighty rain, kit very cold. Looking forward to trip. *AIR 27/632/3 cover operations for the day.*
Tuesday, 9 February	Went to Tripoli for the day. Had a good time but rained all day. Bought a few gifts for home; I am hoping to get them home. *AIR 27/632/3 cover operations for the day.*
Wednesday, 10 February	Rained all night and still raining. Made a star. Had a good feed. Packed a parcel for Mabel. No mail. *AIR 27/632/3 cover operations for the day.*
Thursday, 11 February	Sent Mabel parcel and registered it. Rain all morning. Writing Mabel. *AIR 27/632/3 cover operations for the day.*
Friday, 12 February	Nothing much doing. Made some cakes out of biscuits. *AIR 27/632/3 cover operations for the day.*
Saturday, 13 February	Rainy day again. Rumours of a move. *AIR 27/632/3 cover operations for the day.*
Sunday, 14 February	Moved at 12:00 hours. Slept out at night. C/O mentioned on Radio DSO *AIR 27/632/3 cover operations for the day.*
Monday, 15 February El Assa Castel Benito	Moved off at 09:00 hours. Arrived at EL ASSA at 13:00 hours. Raid as we arrived. Sandstorm, no more grass. *AIR 27/632/3 cover operations for the day.*
Tuesday, 16 February	Quite a nice day. Not sand again. Wrote Sid. Nothing happened at night. *AIR 27/632/3 cover operations for the day.*
Wednesday, 17 February Castel Benito	Received L.C. from Bill. B party arrived at 12:00 hours. No ops. *AIR 27/632/3 cover operations for the day.*

Thursday, 18 February	Sand blowing all day. No ops. *AIR 27/632/3 cover operations for the day.*
Friday, 19 February	Went to mass at 250 Sqdn. Still no ops. S/Ldr Ellis out, new C/O arrived. *AIR 27/632/3 cover operations for the day.*
Saturday, 20 February	A Flt played B Flt at baseball. Had another jab today. No ops. *AIR 27/632/3 cover operations for the day.*
Sunday, 21 February	Received an air graph from Marie and Ralph. Still no ops. Getting fed up waiting. *AIR 27/632/3 cover operations for the day.*
Monday, 22 February	Received LP from Mabel, Marie and Mother. Q Griffiths sorted choir last night, quite a success, expecting rain tomorrow. *AIR 27/632/3 cover operations for the day.*
Tuesday, 23 February	Clock put back one-hour last night. No ops. *AIR 27/632/3 cover operations for the day.*
Wednesday, 24 February El Assa	Wrote Mabel. Q Queenie G choir practice. Still at El Assa. A/C started ops. *AIR 27/632/3 cover operations for the day.*
Thursday, 25 February	Wrote Marie. Rotten cold, but lovely day. No mail. *AIR 27/632/3 cover operations for the day.*
Friday, 26 February	Choir practice tonight. Sand blowing all day. *AIR 27/632/3 cover operations for the day.*
Saturday, 27 February	Tombola tonight. Still no mail. *AIR 27/632/3 cover operations for the day.*
Sunday, 28 February	Terry and Joe passed to 37 Sqdn. also Ron Daley. A/G from Mabel. *AIR 27/632/3 cover operations for the day.*
AIR 27/632/5 & AIR 27/632/6 Pilot Ops Report March 1943	
Monday, 1 March El Assa	Choir practice tonight. Plenty of work. A/C Firing. Getting ready to move again. *AIR 27/632/5 cover operations for the day.*
Tuesday, 2 March	NAAFI managed to get some goods in. First some Oman. Still no mail, or beer. *AIR 27/632/5 cover operations for the day.*
Wednesday, 3 March El Assa, Castel Benito	Mass at 14:00 hours. No ops. *AIR 27/632/5 cover operations for the day.*
Thursday, 4 March	No mail. No ops. *AIR 27/632/5 cover operations for the day.*
Friday, 5 March	Yanks arrived. *AIR 27/632/5 cover operations for the day.*

Saturday, 6 March	Played cooks, won 6-1. No mail. *AIR 27/632/5 cover operations for the day.*
Sunday, 7 March	Played yanks baseball lost 10-5. Good game. *AIR 27/632/5 cover operations for the day.*
Monday, 8 March	Played cooks lost 3-0. Played tombola lost 5/-. No mail. *AIR 27/632/5 cover operations for the day.*
Tuesday, 9 March	Sand blowing again. No ops. No pancakes either. *AIR 27/632/5 cover operations for the day.*
Wednesday, 10 March	Received 2 L.C. from Mabel and one from mother. *AIR 27/632/5 cover operations for the day.*
Thursday, 11 March	Concert tonight. Our own gala ROC, very successful. Received letter from G.G. Also played W.T. won 4-0. *AIR 27/632/5 cover operations for the day.*
Friday, 12 March	Armoury played W.T. drew 1-1. Wrote Gran and mother. Played Tombola won 11/6d. On sick list for 3 days. *AIR 27/632/5 cover operations for the day.*
Saturday, 13 March	Lovely day. A/C tests. *AIR 27/632/5 cover operations for the day.*
Sunday, 14 March El Assa	Received L.P. from Mabel. *AIR 27/632/5 cover operations for the day.*
Monday, 15 March	**No recorded details in his diary.** *AIR 27/632/5 cover operations for the* day.
Tuesday, 16 March	**No recorded details in his diary.** *AIR 27/632/5 cover operations for the day.*
Wednesday, 17 March	**No recorded details in his diary.** *AIR 27/632/5 cover operations for the day.*
Thursday, 18 March	**No recorded details in his diary.** *AIR 27/632/5 cover operations for the day.*
Friday, 19 March	**No recorded details in his diary.** *AIR 27/632/5 cover operations for the day.*
Saturday, 20 March Nefatia South	Letter from Mabel. *AIR 27/632/5 cover operations for the day.*
Sunday, 21 March	Rained all day. Plenty of work. Fed up and worried. *AIR 27/632/5 cover operations for the day.*
Monday, 22 March	Still, plenty of rain, thunderstorm last night. On duty tonight. Wish it was all over. Wrote Mabel. *AIR 27/632/5 cover operations for the day.*

Tuesday, 23 March	Had concert in Mess. Q Range 73 quite a success. *AIR 27/632/5 cover operations for the day.*
Wednesday, 24 March	P/O Chandler shot down JU88 over SFAX. Received paper dated 4th. L.C. from Mabel. *AIR 27/632/5 cover operations for the day.*
Thursday, 25 March	L.C. from Mabel and mother, air cable from Mabel. On duty all night. Dog extremely ill. *AIR 27/632/5 cover operations for the day.*
Friday, 26 March	Received Francs and changed. B.M.A. as we are in Tunisia. *AIR 27/632/5 cover operations for the day.*
Saturday, 27 March	**No recorded details in his diary.** *AIR 27/632/5 cover operations for the day.*
Sunday, 28 March	Had mass this morning. Also A.G. from Mitch. *AIR 27/632/5 cover operations for the day.*
Monday, 29 March	Need a ½ B Beer. First since Xmas. Wrote Mabel and Mother. *AIR 27/632/5 cover operations for the day.*
Tuesday, 30 March	Shot down JU88 over SFAX. *AIR 27/632/5 cover operations for the day.*
Wednesday, 31 March	Received letter from mother. Griffin UK ROC. *AIR 27/632/5 cover operations for the day.*
AIR 27/632/7 & AIR 27/632/8 Pilot Ops Report April 1943	
Thursday, 1 April Nefatia South	Received letter and PO from Mr Leach. Also L.C. from Mabel. *AIR 27/632/7 cover operations for the day.*
Friday, 2 April	Pay parade. Back to Francs. *AIR 27/632/7 cover operations for the day.*
Saturday, 3 April	**No recorded details in his diary.** *AIR 27/632/7 cover operations for the day.*
Sunday, 4 April	Mass said but could not attend. *AIR 27/632/7 cover operations for the day.*
Monday, 5 April	Mother, Mabel, Nora, Bill, Mitch. On duty all night. *AIR 27/632/7 cover operations for the day.*
Tuesday, 6 April	**No recorded details in his diary.** *AIR 27/632/7 cover operations for the day.*
Wednesday, 7 April	**No recorded details in his diary.** *AIR 27/632/7 cover operations for the day.*
Thursday, 8 April Gabes Main	**No recorded details in his diary.** *AIR 27/632/7 cover operations for the day.*

Friday, 9 April	Moved from Nefatia, also arrived at Gabes. *AIR 27/632/7 cover operations for the day.*
Saturday, 10 April	A.G. from Mabel. *AIR 27/632/7 cover operations for the day.*
Sunday, 11 April	Cable to John, Nelson. Had mass at Gabes. *AIR 27/632/7 cover operations for the day.*
Monday, 12 April Sfax el Macu	Left Gabes at 09:00 hours to go to SFAX, arrived at 13:30 hours. *AIR 27/632/7 cover operations for the day.*
Tuesday, 13 April	**No recorded details in his diary.** *AIR 27/632/7 cover operations for the day.*
Wednesday, 14 April	**No recorded details in his diary.** *AIR 27/632/7 cover operations for the day.*
Thursday, 15 April	**No recorded details in his diary.** *AIR 27/632/7 cover operations for the day.*
Friday, 16 April	Shot down 3 – JU52, 3 prob's. But lost one of our best. Pilot P/O Chandler, he was killed in crash. We shall all miss him. *AIR 27/632/7 cover operations for the day.*
Saturday, 17 April	Walked into Sfax and back, very pleasant. Posted letter to Mabel. *AIR 27/632/7 cover operations for the day.*
Sunday, 18 April	B Flt moved today to Kairouan nr Sousse. We shot down 4 – JU52. 7th Jerry A/C shot down; 2 probable's and 3 damaged. *AIR 27/632/7 cover operations for the day.*
Monday, 19 April Alem	Visited my American friends. We got another 2 – JU52. No news. We moved. Total of enemy A/C has reached 100. *AIR 27/632/7 cover operations for the day.*
Tuesday, 20 April	Arrived at Kairouan. On duty all night, feeling fed up. Wrote mother, Mrs Griffin, Mabel today. Destroyed 1–JU52, damaged 1. *AIR 27/632/7 cover operations for the day.*
Wednesday, 21 April Monastir	Moved to Monastir. Wrote Martin Ekland. Raid at night, bit hot our drome. *AIR 27/632/7 cover operations for the day.*
Thursday, 22 April	Raid at night, no damage. Received two rabbits off natives. *AIR 27/632/7 cover operations for the day.*
Friday, 23 April	Natives did my 'dobi' *[washing]*. Glorious weather. Wrote mother, nelson, Phil Mr Leach. Rabbits doing fine. *AIR 27/632/7 cover operations for the day.*
Saturday, 24 April	**No recorded details in his diary.** *AIR 27/632/7 cover operations for the day.*

Sunday, 25 April	Went to mass in Monastir. Walked most of the way. No mail. Yet B.7 shot down 1–JU88. *AIR 27/632/7 cover operations for the day.*
Monday, 26 April	Lecture by WO on the war. B.7 shot down 2–JU88 and damaged 1. Wrote to Mabel a letter and posted it. No mail. *AIR 27/632/7 cover operations for the day.*
Tuesday, 27 April	No mail. Wrote Mr Gardner. R.A.F.R. Played Cover Flt drew 2-2. *AIR 27/632/7 cover operations for the day.*
Wednesday, 28 April	A.C. from Mabel. Had a disaster at drome, 10 men killed in Hudson. Army Major, 7 personnel and six others, all killed and burnt. *AIR 27/632/7 cover operations for the day.*
Thursday, 29 April	Played for Cooks, won 2-0. No mail. *AIR 27/632/7 cover operations for the day.*
Friday, 30 April	Played 285 Wing won 4-0. NAAFI supply in, first half. *AIR 27/632/7 cover operations for the day.*
AIR 27/632/9 (1) & AIR 27/632/10 (1) Pilot Ops Report May 1943	
Saturday, 1 May Monastir	Played Cover Flt 2-0. No mail. *AIR 27/632/9 cover operations for the day.*
Sunday, 2 May	Played French Services at Monastir. Won 4-1. *AIR 27/632/9 cover operations for the day.*
Monday, 3 May	L.C. from Mabel. *AIR 27/632/9 cover operations for the day.*
Tuesday, 4 May	Played cricket, won by 20 runs against the rest. *AIR 27/632/9 cover operations for the day.*
Wednesday, 5 May	Played cricket. Lost by 5 runs against officers and pilots. *AIR 27/632/9 cover operations for the day.*
Thursday, 6 May	Letter from Sidney. Wrote mother L.C. *AIR 27/632/9 cover operations for the day.*
Friday, 7 May	Wrote Mr Leach, Mabel, Phil. Harry Curtis. *AIR 27/632/9 cover operations for the day.*
Saturday, 8 May	Flew over Bizerta and back today. Wrote Sid. *AIR 27/632/9 cover operations for the day.*
Sunday, 9 May	Mass at Monastir. *AIR 27/632/9 cover operations for the day.*
Monday, 10 May	***No recorded details in his diary.*** *AIR 27/632/9 cover operations for the day.*
Tuesday, 11 May	Played 14 C at cricket. Won by 57 runs, a real treat. *AIR 27/632/9 cover operations for the day.*
Wednesday, 12 May	On duty all night for the last time up here. Still at Monastir. *AIR 27/632/9 cover operations for the day.*

Thursday, 13 May	Sqdn. played 285 Wing, drew 3-3. Had photograph taken***[see pictures below]*** *AIR 27/632/9 cover operations for the day.*

73 (F) SDN Tunisia 13.5.43

[1012281 LAC - L B Lamb, Back Row 1st on the right. Front Row–middle is 'Johnny Johnson' with sandy the mascot]

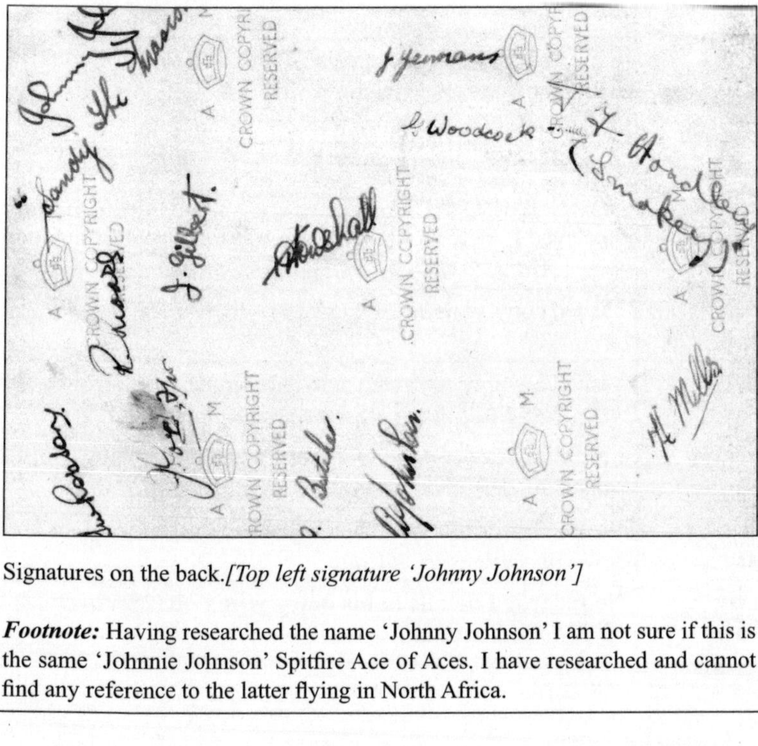

Signatures on the back.*[Top left signature 'Johnny Johnson']*

Footnote: Having researched the name 'Johnny Johnson' I am not sure if this is the same 'Johnnie Johnson' Spitfire Ace of Aces. I have researched and cannot find any reference to the latter flying in North Africa.

Friday, 14 May	**No recorded details in his diary.** *AIR 27/632/9 cover operations for the day.*
Saturday, 15 May	Received letter from Martin Eklund. *AIR 27/632/9 cover operations for the day.*
Sunday, 16 May	L.C. from Mabel, L.C. from Nora. *AIR 27/632/9 cover operations for the day.*
Monday, 17 May	**No recorded details in his diary.** *AIR 27/632/9 cover operations for the day.*
Tuesday, 18 May	Visit Tunis. *AIR 27/632/9 cover operations for the day.*
Wednesday, 19 May	LP from Mother, 2 Mabel. Heavy rainstorm. *AIR 27/632/9 cover operations for the day.*
Thursday, 20 May	**No recorded details in his diary.** *AIR 27/632/9 cover operations for the day.*
Friday, 21 May	L.C. from Mabel. *AIR 27/632/9 cover operations for the day.*
Saturday, 22 May	Visited convent of St Joseph of the L'Aparition at Sousse. Sister Mary of the Child Jesus. *AIR 27/632/9 cover operations for the day.*
Sunday, 23 May	Went to mass at Monastir. Service in English. Visited convent. Received letter from Mabel. *AIR 27/632/9 cover operations for the day.*
Monday, 24 May	Expecting Spits replacements. Wrote Mabel L.C. Parted with rabbits. Daniel Garson parted last of my old pals. *AIR 27/632/9 cover operations for the day.*
Tuesday, 25 May	Visited the convent to see Sister Mary. *AIR 27/632/9 cover operations for the day.*
Wednesday, 26 May	Received L.C. from Mabel and Uncle George. Writing mother today. *AIR 27/632/9 cover operations for the day.*
Thursday, 27 May	Visited convent. *AIR 27/632/9 cover operations for the day.*
Friday, 28 May	Visited Sister Mary at the convent. Moving tomorrow. *AIR 27/632/9 cover operations for the day.*
Saturday, 29 May	Left Monastir at 10:00 hours for La Sebala at Tunis. Arrived same day. *AIR 27/632/9 cover operations for the day.*
Sunday, 30 May	Writing Sister Mary at the convent in Sousse. *AIR 27/632/9 cover operations for the day.*
Monday, 31 May La Seballa	**No recorded details in his diary.** *AIR 27/632/9 cover operations for the day.*

AIR 27/632/11 (1) & AIR 27/632/12 Pilot Ops Report June 1943	
Tuesday, 1 June La Sebala	Visited Tunis. *AIR 27/632/11 cover operations for the day.*
Wednesday, 2 June	Visited Tunis. Bought perfume and powder for Mabel. No mail. *AIR 27/632/11 cover operations for the day.*
Thursday, 3 June	No mail. *AIR 27/632/11 cover operations for the day.*
Friday, 4 June	Wrote mother a L.C. *AIR 27/632/11 cover operations for the day.*
Saturday, 5 June	**No recorded details in his diary.** *AIR 27/632/11 cover operations for the day.*
Sunday, 6 June	Missed Mass. *AIR 27/632/11 cover operations for the day.*
Monday, 7 June	No mail. *AIR 27/632/11 cover operations for the day.*
Tuesday, 8 June	No mail. *AIR 27/632/11 cover operations for the day.*
Wednesday, 9 June	Wrote to Martin Eklund. No mail. *AIR 27/632/11 cover operations for the day.*
Thursday, 10 June	**No recorded details in his diary.** *AIR 27/632/11 cover operations for the day.*
Friday, 11 June	Wrote dad at Nelson, also mother. Mabel's mother died in May 1943; R.I.P. *AIR 27/632/11 cover operations for the day.*
Saturday, 12 June	***No recorded details in his diary.*** *AIR 27/632/11 cover operations for the day.*
Sunday, 13 June	Went to mass at the Altar, Tamet. Wrote David. *AIR 27/632/11 cover operations for the day.*
Monday, 14 June	Went to Tunis. *AIR 27/632/11 cover operations for the day.*
Tuesday, 15 June	**No recorded details in his diary.** *AIR 27/632/11 cover operations for the day.*
Wednesday, 16 June	Went to the theatre to see Cedric Neilson and Q10. *AIR 27/632/11 cover operations for the day.*
Thursday, 17 June	Formed choir. *AIR 27/632/11 cover operations for the day.*
Friday, 18 June	**No recorded details in his diary.** *AIR 27/632/11 cover operations for the day.*

Saturday, 19 June	**No recorded details in his diary.** *AIR 27/632/11 cover operations for the day.*
Sunday, 20 June	Planes to base. Plenty of work. *AIR 27/632/11 cover operations for the day.*
Monday, 21 June	Wrote Mother. *AIR 27/632/11 cover operations for the day.*
Tuesday, 22 June	Corpus Christi. Unfortunately missed mass. *AIR 27/632/11 cover operations for the day.*
Wednesday, 23 June	Wrote Mabel. *AIR 27/632/11 cover operations for the day.*
Thursday, 24 June	**No recorded details in his diary.** *AIR 27/632/11 cover operations for the day.*
Friday, 25 June	Received letter from Sister Mary at the Child Jesus, dated 20 June. Visited Tunis. ***[see envelope and letter below]*** *AIR 27/632/11 cover operations for the day.*

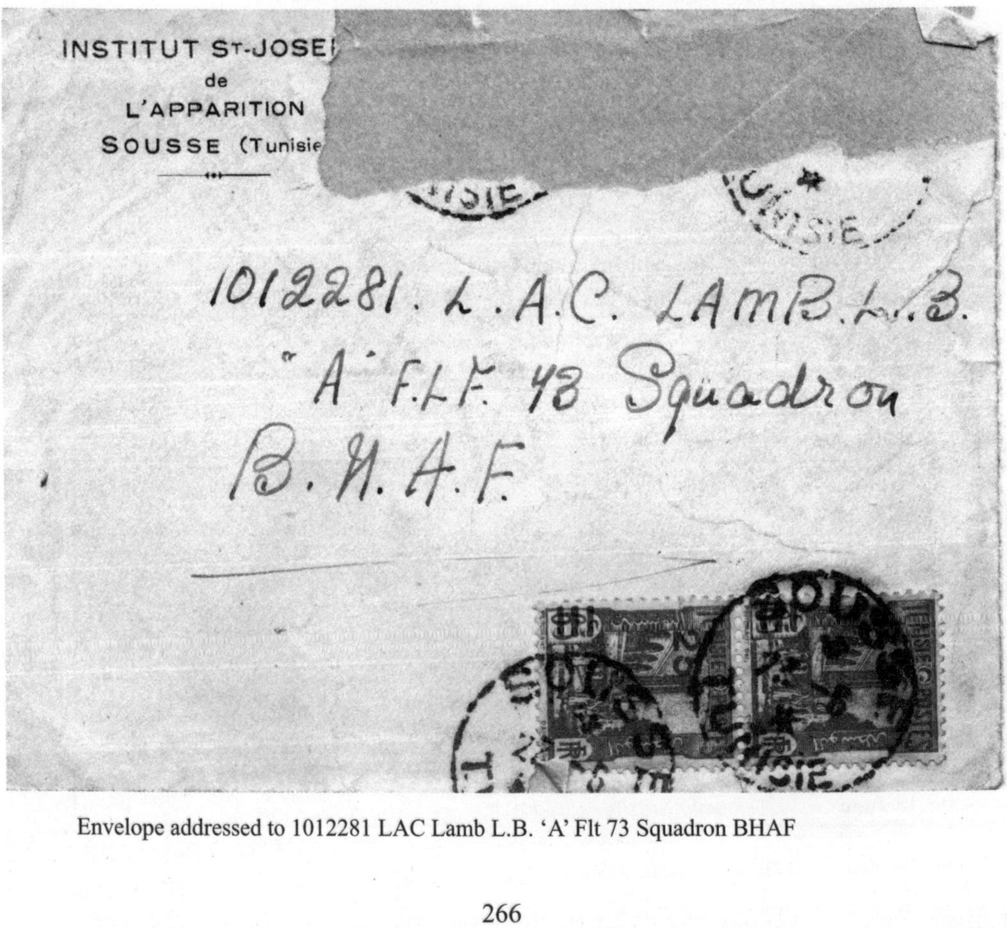

Envelope addressed to 1012281 LAC Lamb L.B. 'A' Flt 73 Squadron BHAF

How is Rex and all your pets or had you to leave them all behind you! If so I am very sorry for you. You know I meant to tell you that if ever you had to part with Rex I should be delighted to take him & at the same time I'm sure it would be a consolation to you to know that he had found a British friend. But your going away was so abrupt that I did not think of the dog.

J. M. J.

St. Joseph's C.
Monastir
Sunday 20th

Dear Bernard,

I could not sit down & call you Mr. Lamb could I? Now it was a real pleasure to get your letter. I received it last Sunday – Whit-Sunday. I was fairly busy during the week so I put off answering till to-day.

Page 1 of letter

Don't worry about the vases. They're splendid & made a rather grand effect in our little chapel in Sousse, for it was for my own Convent in Sousse that they were destined.
I am still in Monastir but shall be soon going back to Sousse.
Remember me to your friend Frank Smith. I'm glad to know that you are still together.
Now for those French sentences. The first sentence contains "heart" used in its proper meaning, the second in a figurative sense. Word for word: I never slept with such a good heart. meaning I never slept so soundly or well.
"(de) Bon cœur" also means willingly.

Here now that's enough for chatting & I've plenty of letters to write.

I promise to pray for you until the end of the war.

Yours sincerely in Christ
Sr. Mary of the Child Jesus.

Page 2 of letter

Saturday, 26 June	Going to Tunis. [E.N.S.A. are putting on a show]. *AIR 27/632/11 cover operations for the day.*
Sunday, 27 June	Went to mass at Sidi Tamet. *AIR 27/632/11 cover operations for the day.*
Monday, 28 June	No mail. *AIR 27/632/11 cover operations for the day.*
Tuesday, 29 June	Received some papers from Mabel. *AIR 27/632/11 cover operations for the day.*
Wednesday, 30 June	Received parcel from Alan Redditch and photo of Mabel. Letter from John. *AIR 27/632/11 cover operations for the day.*
AIR 27/632/13 (1) & AIR 27/632/14 Pilot Ops Report July 1943	
Thursday, 1 July La Sebala	Visited Tunis. Received letter from Darrell Craig. *AIR 27/632/13 cover operations for the day.*
Friday, 2 July	Wrote Mr Hodges and John at Nelson. *AIR 27/632/13 cover operations for the day.*
Saturday, 3 July	Paper arrived. Mending a/c. *AIR 27/632/13 cover operations for the day.*
Sunday, 4 July	My birthday. Went to Mass at Tamet. Waiting for mail. *AIR 27/632/13 cover operations for the day.*
Monday, 5 July	Nothing to report. *AIR 27/632/13 cover operations for the day.*
Tuesday, 6 July	Nothing to report. *AIR 27/632/13 cover operations for the day.*
Wednesday, 7 July	Still no mail. *AIR 27/632/13 cover operations for the day.*
Thursday, 8 July	Wrote mother. No mail. *AIR 27/632/13 cover operations for the day.*
Friday, 9 July	**No recorded details in his diary.** *AIR 27/632/13 cover operations for the day.*
Saturday, 10 July	Received L.C. from Mabel. *AIR 27/632/13 cover operations for the day.*
Sunday, 11 July	Went to Mass at Tamet. Received letter from Uncle G. *AIR 27/632/13 cover operations for the day.*
Monday, 12 July	Wrote Mabel. *AIR 27/632/13 cover operations for the day.*
Tuesday, 13 July	Received L.C. from Bill. *AIR 27/632/13 cover operations for the day.*
Wednesday, 14 July	Wrote Bill and Uncle George. *AIR 27/632/13 cover operations for the day.*

Thursday, 15 July	**No recorded details in his diary.** *AIR 27/632/13 cover operations for the day.*
Friday, 16 July	**No recorded details in his diary.** *AIR 27/632/13 cover operations for the day.*
Saturday, 17 July	**No recorded details in his diary.** *AIR 27/632/13 cover operations for the day.*
Sunday, 18 July	Went to Mass. No mail. *AIR 27/632/13 cover operations for the day.*
Monday, 19 July	**No recorded details in his diary.** *AIR 27/632/13 cover operations for the day.*
Tuesday, 20 July	**No recorded details in his diary.** *AIR 27/632/13 cover operations for the day.*
Wednesday, 21 July	**No recorded details in his diary.** *AIR 27/632/13 cover operations for the day.*
Thursday, 22 July	**No recorded details in his diary.** *AIR 27/632/13 cover operations for the day.*
Friday, 23 July	**No recorded details in his diary.** *AIR 27/632/13 cover operations for the day.*
Saturday, 24 July	**No recorded details in his diary.** *AIR 27/632/13 cover operations for the day.*
Sunday, 25 July	Went to Mass. L.C. from Mabel. *AIR 27/632/13 cover operations for the day.*
Monday, 26 July	Moving tomorrow. No mail. *AIR 27/632/13 cover operations for the day.*
Tuesday, 27 July	Moved to Sebala 1, arrived same day. *AIR 27/632/13 cover operations for the day.*
Wednesday, 28 July	L.C. from Mother. Wrote mother A.G. *AIR 27/632/13 cover operations for the day.*
Thursday, 29 July	**No recorded details in his diary.** *AIR 27/632/13 cover operations for the day.*
Friday, 30 July	**No recorded details in his diary.** *AIR 27/632/13 cover operations for the day.*
Saturday, 31 July	**No recorded details in his diary.** *AIR 27/632/13 cover operations for the day.*
AIR 27/632/15 & AIR 27/632/16 Pilot Ops Report August 1943	
Sunday, 1 August La Sebala	Mass at Tamet. *AIR 27/632/15 cover operations for the day.*
Monday, 2 August	**No recorded details in his diary.** *AIR 27/632/15 cover operations for the day.*

Tuesday, 3 August	**No recorded details in his diary.** *AIR 27/632/15 cover operations for the day.*
Wednesday, 4 August	**No recorded details in his diary.** *AIR 27/632/15 cover operations for the day.*
Thursday, 5 August	L.C. from Mabel. *AIR 27/632/15 cover operations for the day.*
Friday, 6ᵗAugust	**No recorded details in his diary.** *AIR 27/632/15 cover operations for the day.*
Saturday, 7 August	**No recorded details in his diary.** *AIR 27/632/15 cover operations for the day.*
Sunday, 8 August	Mass at the Cathedral, Tunis. A.G. from Fred Grant. *AIR 27/632/15 cover operations for the day.*
Monday, 9 August	Writing Mabel. AIR 27/632/15 cover operations for the day.
Tuesday, 10 August	**No recorded details in his diary.** *AIR 27/632/15 cover operations for the day.*
Wednesday, 11 August	Letter from Mabel, Mother and David Craig. *AIR 27/632/15 cover operations for the day.*
Thursday, 12 August	Writing Mabel. *AIR 27/632/15 cover operations for the day.*
Friday, 13 August	Wrote David Craig. *AIR 27/632/15 cover operations for the day.*
Saturday, 14 August	**No recorded details in his diary.** *AIR 27/632/15cover operations for the day.*
Sunday, 15 August	Went to Mass at Tamet. Also visit Tunis. *AIR 27/632/15 cover operations for the day.*
Monday, 16 August	Wrote F. Grant, H. Carter, Marie, and Mother. *AIR 27/632/15 cover operations for the day.*
Tuesday, 17 August	**No recorded details in his diary.** AIR 27/632/15 cover operations for the day.
Wednesday, 18 August	**No recorded details in his diary.** *AIR 27/632/15 cover operations for the day.*
Thursday, 19 August	**No recorded details in his diary.** *AIR 27/632/15 cover operations for the day.*
Friday, 20 August	***No recorded details in his diary.*** *AIR 27/632/15 cover operations for the day.*
Saturday, 21 August	***No recorded details in his diary.*** *AIR 27/632/15 cover operations for the day.*
Sunday, 22 August	Mass at Sidi Tamet. *AIR 27/632/15 cover operations for the day.*

Monday, 23 August	Away on 'Detachment'. *AIR 27/632/15 cover operations for the day.*
Tuesday, 24 August	Away on 'Detachment'. *AIR 27/632/15 cover operations for the day.*
Wednesday, 25 August	Away on 'Detachment'. *AIR 27/632/15 cover operations for the day.*
Thursday, 26 August	Away on 'Detachment'. *AIR 27/632/15 cover operations for the day.*
Friday, 27 August	Away on 'Detachment'. L.C. from Mr Langston, Mabel, Mother. *AIR 27/632/15 cover operations for the day.*
Saturday, 28 August	Away on 'Detachment'. *AIR 27/632/15 cover operations for the day.*
Sunday, 29 August	Away on 'Detachment'. Mass at Sidi Tamet. *AIR 27/632/15 cover operations for the day.*
Monday, 30 August	Away on 'Detachment'. *AIR 27/632/15 cover operations for the day.*
Tuesday, 31 August	Returned to Squadron. Received letter from Sid and John. *AIR 27/632/15 cover operations for the day.*
AIR 27/632/17 (1) & AIR 27/632/18 (1) Pilot Ops Report September 1943	
Wednesday, 1 September La Sabala	Wrote Mr Leach, Mr Langston, Nora, Mother, Mabel, and Bill. *AIR 27/632/17 cover operations for the day.*
Thursday, 2 September	Wrote Sid and John, Nelson. *AIR 27/632/17 cover operations for the day.*
Friday, 3 September	W/O posted to Wing. *AIR 27/632/17 cover operations for the day.*
Saturday, 4 September	Received L.C. from Mabel and Mother. *AIR 27/632/17 cover operations for the day.*
Sunday, 5 September	Working could not attend Mass. *AIR 27/632/17 cover operations for the day.*
Monday, 6 September	No mail. *AIR 27/632/17 cover operations for the day.*
Tuesday, 7 September	Writing Mabel, Aunt Mabel, and Mother. Working. S/LDR. Adam posted to 52B Group. *AIR 27/632/17 cover operations for the day.*
Wednesday, 8 September	Italy capitulated at 17:00 hrs. Sqdn. A/C operated from Italy, Par Roso. *AIR 27/632/17 cover operations for the day.*
Thursday, 9 September	Wrote L.H. 7, received L.C. from Derek Griffith. *AIR 27/632/17 cover operations for the day.*

Friday, 10 September	Wrote Derek Griffith, Mrs Earningshaw. *AIR 27/632/17 cover operations for the day.*
Saturday, 11 September	No recorded details in his diary. *AIR 27/632/17 cover operations for the day.*
Sunday, 12 September	No Mail. *AIR 27/632/17 cover operations for the day.*
Monday, 13 September	**No recorded details in his diary.** *AIR 27/632/17 cover operations for the day.*
Tuesday, 14 September	**No recorded details in his diary.** *AIR 27/632/17 cover operations for the day.*
Wednesday, 15 September	**No recorded details in his diary.** *AIR 27/632/17 cover operations for the day.*
Thursday, 16 September	Prepared to move. *AIR 27/632/17 cover operations for the day.*
Friday, 17 September	**No recorded details in his diary.** *AIR 27/632/17 cover operations for the day.*
Saturday, 18 September	**No recorded details in his diary.** *AIR 27/632/17 cover operations for the day.*
Sunday, 19 September	Could not attend Mass. *AIR 27/632/17 cover operations for the day.*
Monday, 20 September	Moved from Sebala to Bizerta. *AIR 27/632/17 cover operations for the day.*
Tuesday, 21 September	Arrived at Bizerta too late to catch boat. *AIR 27/632/17 cover operations for the day.*
Wednesday, 22 September	Lovely day. *AIR 27/632/17 cover operations for the day.*
Thursday, 23 September	Moving today. Received letter from Mother, Mabel, and Cecil. *AIR 27/632/17 cover operations for the day.*
Friday, 24 September	Went to pictures in the hanger at harbour. *AIR 27/632/17 cover operations for the day.*
Saturday, 25 September	Still awaiting boat. *AIR 27/632/17 cover operations for the day.*
Sunday, 26 September	Went to Mass at Bizerta. Rained all day. *AIR 27/632/17 cover operations for the day.*
Monday, 27 September	Went to pictures. *AIR 27/632/17 cover operations for the day.*
Tuesday, 28 September	Still no news. *AIR 27/632/17 cover operations for the day.*
Wednesday, 29 September	Played bridge all day. *AIR 27/632/17 cover operations for the day.*
Thursday, 30 September	Moved down to harbour, awaiting to board. *AIR 27/632/17 cover operations for the day.*

73 Squadron – LAC Lamb 1012281 diary continued

AIR 27/632/19 & AIR 27/632/20 (1) Pilot Ops Report October 1943	
Friday, 1 October La Sebala	Will board, **invasion has started**. Feeling fed up. *AIR 27/632/19 covers operations for the day.*
Saturday, 2 October	Very calm sea. Still a good sailor, not seasick. *AIR 27/632/19 covers operations for the day.*
Sunday, 3 October	**Landed at Salerno** and moved in land, strange time. *AIR 27/632/19 covers operations for the day.*
Monday, 4 October	**Moved to Foggia Main**, awaiting A/C to fly in. Onto C.M.F. *AIR 27/632/19 covers operations for the day.*
Tuesday, 5 October	Wrote L.C. letters to Mabel and Mother. *AIR 27/632/19 covers operations for the day.*
Wednesday, 6 October	Went picking walnuts and apples, had a wonderful time. *AIR 27/632/19 covers operations for the day.*
Thursday, 7 October	Rained all day and what rain. *AIR 27/632/19 covers operations for the day.*
Friday, 8 October	Rain again all day but cleared up at night. *AIR 27/632/19 covers operations for the day.*
Saturday, 9 October	Went to Salerno and purchased present for Mabel. *AIR 27/632/19 covers operations for the day.*
Sunday, 10 October	Preparing to move. Could not get to church. Packed Mabel parcel. *AIR 27/632/19 covers operations for the day.*
Monday, 11 October	Posted parcel also wrote Mabel. Went to Salerno and bought shoes and stockings. Move cancelled. *AIR 27/632/19 covers operations for the day.*
Tuesday, 12 October	Posted parcel of shoes and stockings. I pray that they arrive safely. *AIR 27/632/19 covers operations for the day.*
Wednesday, 13 October	**No recorded details in his diary.** *AIR 27/632/19 covers operations for the day.*
Thursday, 14 October **Wedding Anniversary**	**No recorded details in his diary.** *AIR 27/632/19 covers operations for the day.*
Friday, 15 October	**No recorded details in his diary.** *AIR 27/632/19 covers operations for the day.*
Saturday, 16 October	Wrote Sgt Dan Stevens. *AIR 27/632/19 covers operations for the day.*
Sunday, 17 October	Went to Mass at Montecorvino. *AIR 27/632/19 covers operations for the day.*

Monday, 18 October Bizerte	A/C arrived from Sebala. H.A. disappointment, A/C with mail not arrived. *AIR 27/632/19 covers operations for the day.*
Tuesday, 19 October	Remainder of A/C and mail. Letters from Mabel, Mother, Auntie, Mr Leach, H. Carter. *AIR 27/632/19 covers operations for the day.*
Wednesday, 20 October Montecorvino	Wrote Mabel and Mr Leach. *AIR 27/632/19 covers operations for the day.*
Thursday, 21 October	Moved to drome at Pontelequano. 18 kites from Salerno. *AIR 27/632/19 covers operations for the day.*
Friday, 22 October	**No recorded details in his diary.** *AIR 27/632/19 covers operations for the day.*
Saturday, 23 October	**No recorded details in his diary.** *AIR 27/632/19 covers operations for the day.*
Sunday, 24 October	Went to Mass at Pontelequano. Plenty of work. *AIR 27/632/19 covers operations for the day.*
Monday, 25 October	Plenty of Inspections In. *AIR 27/632/19 covers operations for the day.*
Tuesday, 26 October	'A' Party Played Wing won 2–1. I worked all day. 'B' party arrived today. No mail, Pay Parade. *AIR 27/632/19 covers operations for the day.*
Wednesday, 27 October	Purchased dress material for Mabel. *AIR 27/632/19 covers operations for the day.*
Thursday, 28 October	No mail. Letter from Mariann Ekland. *AIR 27/632/19 covers operations for the day.*
Friday, 29 October	No mail. *AIR 27/632/19 covers operations for the day.*
Saturday, 30 October	No mail. *AIR 27/632/19 covers operations for the day.*
Sunday, 31 October	Letter from Bill. Unable to attend Mass. *AIR 27/632/19 covers operations for the day.*
AIR 27/632/21 & AIR 27/632/22 Pilot Ops Report November 1943	
Monday, 1 November Montecorvino	Wrote Mabel L.C. *AIR 27/632/21 covers operations for the day.*
Tuesday, 2 November	Conductor Tior 9237. *AIR 27/632/21 covers operations for the day.*

Wednesday, 3 November	**No recorded details in his diary.** *AIR 27/632/21 covers operations for the day.*
Thursday, 4 November	**No recorded details in his diary.** *AIR 27/632/21 covers operations for the day.*
Friday, 5 November	**No recorded details in his diary.** *AIR 27/632/21 covers operations for the day.*
Saturday, 6 November	**No recorded details in his diary.** *AIR 27/632/21 Squadron released from camp, no operations for the day.*
Sunday, 7 November	Working. *AIR 27/632/21 covers operations for the day.*
Monday, 8 November	Played Com Forces won 8 – 0. *AIR 27/632/21 covers operations for the day.*
Tuesday, 9 November	**No recorded details in his diary.** *AIR 27/632/21 covers operations for the day.*
Wednesday, 10 November	Played C.7 at Rugby and won 14 – 0. *AIR 27/632/21 covers operations for the day.*
Thursday, 11 November	LP from Mabel. *AIR 27/632/21 covers operations for the day.*
Friday, 12 November	Xmas Greeting, Mabel Cards, Uncle George, and Mother. *AIR 27/632/21 covers operations for the day.*
Saturday, 13 November	**No recorded details in his diary.** *AIR 27/632/21 covers operations for the day.*
Sunday, 14 November	**Entered Hospital today. 59 General with wounds in my leg.** *AIR 27/632/21 covers operations for the day.*
Monday, 15 November	**No recorded details, in his diary.** *AIR 27/632/21 covers operations for the day.*
Tuesday, 16 November	Ken visited me in hospital. *AIR 27/632/21 covers operations for the day.*
Wednesday, 17 November	**No recorded details in his diary.** *AIR 27/632/21 covers operations for the day also states that operations were cancelled due to poor weather.*
Thursday, 18 November	Played C.7 at Rugby Sqdn. Won 12 – 0. *AIR 27/632/21 covers operational flying for the day.*
Friday, 19 November	L.C. from Mother and Mabel. Ken and Bill came, bought book, at Foggia Main. *AIR 27/632/21 covers operational flying for the day.*
Saturday, 20 November	Greetings, Bill, George. L.H.F. - R. Tiler. *AIR 27/632/21 confirms the arrival of the new CO, S/Ldr. Chase. Operations carried out.*

Sunday, 21 November	**No recorded details in his diary.** *AIR 27/632/21 confirms the Squadrons operations for the day.*
Monday, 22 November	**No recorded details in his diary.** *AIR 27/632/21 confirms the Squadrons operations for the day.*
Tuesday, 23 November	**No recorded details in his diary.** *AIR 27/632/21 states heavy rain, and no flying operations all cancelled. Rumours of move to Foggia.*
Wednesday, 24 November	**No recorded details in his diary.** *AIR 27/632/21 states heavy rain, and no flying operations all cancelled.*
Thursday, 25 November	Wrote Mabel and Mariann Ekland. *AIR 27/632/21 states heavy rain, and no flying operations all cancelled.*
Friday, 26 November	L.C. from Mabel. *AIR 27/632/21 states that the rain stopped in the night and some flying took place.*
Saturday, 27 November	Graham Gilbert posted to new base camp, Sorento. *AIR 27/6323/21 states that no flying could take place due to the waterlogged aerodrome.*
Sunday, 28 November	**Released from hospital.** Went to Mass before I left, returned to 73 Squadron. *AIR 27/6323/21 states that no flying could take place due to the waterlogged aerodrome.*
Monday, 29 November	Wrote Mabel, received H.C. from Mr Etherington, L.C. for Mabel. Letter P.O. Mr Leach. *AIR 27/632/21 confirms that a flying operation's took place today.*
Tuesday, 30 November	**No recorded details in his diary.** *AIR 27/632/21 covers the daily happenings with the CO returning from Foggia.*
AIR 27/632/23 & AIR 27/632/24 Pilot Ops Report December 1943	
Wednesday, 1 December Montecorvino	Moved to Foggia, arrived the same day. *AIR 27/632/23 covers the Squadrons move from Montecorvino to Foggia Main.*
Thursday, 2 December Foggia Main	**No recorded details in his diary.** *AIR 27/632/23 confirms that the Squadrons aircraft arrived today.*
Friday, 3 December	**No recorded details in his diary.** *AIR 27/632/23 confirms that 73 Squadrons remaining party arrived. The personnel have billets and not tents.*
Saturday, 4 December	**No recorded details in his diary.** *AIR 27/632/23 confirms that the Squadrons dispersal tents and other equipment was installed.*
Sunday, 5 December	Visited 83 B Sqdn, saw some films. *AIR 27/632/23 confirms that sector flying was carried out.*

Monday, 6 December	Went to pictures in hanger. *AIR 27/632/23 states that a section of Spitfires was at readiness all day.*
Tuesday, 7 December	Wrote Mabel letter. Went to stage show in hanger. *AIR 27/632/23 some operations undertaken.*
Wednesday, 8 December	Went to Mass and F/Sqt John Courage. *AIR 27/632/23 some operations undertaken.*
Thursday, 9 December	**No recorded details in his diary.** *AIR 27/632/23 confirms that 2 Spitfire IX carried out flying operations.*
Friday, 10 December	**No recorded details in his diary.** *AIR 27/632/23 confirms that 2 Spitfire IX carried out flying operations.*
Saturday, 11 December	**No recorded details in his diary.** *AIR 27/632/23 confirms that 2 Spitfire IX carried out flying operations.*
Sunday, 12 December	**No recorded details in his diary.** *AIR 27/632/23 confirms that no flying operations were carried out.*
Monday, 13 December	**No recorded details in his diary.** *AIR 27/632/23 confirms that no flying operations were carried out.*
Tuesday, 14 December	**No recorded details in his diary.** *AIR 27/632/23 records that a number of operations were carried out and one DC3 landed with some VIPs on board.*
(Reference made to ***Morgan Laboratories****, (Dept F) 59, Gray's Inn Road. London WC1)* ***Could this be the place where tests were submitted for the allergic reaction he had had to penicillin?***	
Wednesday, 15 December	**No recorded details in his diary.** *AIR 27/632/23 some operations carried out along with some local flying practice and recces.*
Thursday, 16 December	**No recorded details in his diary.** *AIR 27/632/23 some operations undertaken.*
Friday, 17 December	Wrote John and Mother. *AIR 27/632/23 confirms a good number of operations were carried out.*
Saturday, 18 December	**No recorded details in his diary.** *AIR 27/632/23 confirms a good number of operations took place.*
Sunday, 19 December	**No recorded details in his diary.** *AIR 27/632/23 confirms that 'scrambles' took place plus practice flying.*
Monday, 20 December	**No recorded details in his diary. AIR 27/632/23 confirms only calibration tests undertaken today.**
Tuesday, 21 December	**No recorded details in his diary.** *AIR 27/632/23 refers to a good number of long-range operations undertaken by Spitfires.*

Wednesday, 22 December	**No recorded details in his diary.** *AIR 27/632/23 records No operational flying done.*
Thursday, 23 December	**No recorded details in his diary.** *AIR 27/632/23 records No operational flying done.*
Friday, 24 December	**No recorded details in his diary.** *AIR 27/632/23 – Squadron at Foggia Main South Italy equipped with the latest Spitfires.*
Saturday, 25 December.	**No recorded details in his diary.** *AIR 27/632/23 Christmas day was celebrated as a non-working day and the airmen served a hearty meal by the CO.*
Sunday, 26 December	**Final page missing of diary.** *AIR 27/632/23 – Squadron at Foggia Main South Italy equipped with the latest Spitfires.*
Monday, 27 December	**Final page missing of diary.** *AIR 27/632/23 – Squadron at Foggia Main South Italy equipped with the latest Spitfires.*
Tuesday, 28 December	**Final page missing of diary.** *AIR 27/632/23 – Squadron at Foggia Main South Italy equipped with the latest Spitfires.*
Wednesday, 29 December	**Final page missing of diary.** *AIR 27/632/23 – Squadron at Foggia Main South Italy equipped with the latest Spitfires.*
Thursday, 30 December	**Final page missing of diary.** *AIR 27/632/23 – Squadron at Foggia Main South Italy equipped with the latest Spitfires.*
Friday, 31 December	**Final page missing of diary.** *AIR 27/632/23 – Squadron at Foggia Main South Italy equipped with the latest Spitfires.*

Acknowledgements

This book would not have been possible without the help of the following people, and please forgive me if I may have inadvertently forgotten anyone. I wish to thank you all for your continued support, advice, mentoring and assistance.

The RAF Disclosures, Ministry of Defence–Air Historical Branch; Frank Haslam, editor of 207 Squadron Royal Air Force History Website; Malcolm Barrass, RAF Historical Society, RAF Museum, Hendon; Damien Lewis, a world-renowned author of the SAS stories who provided the book endorsement; and Lieutenant Colonel Roger S Metcalfe (retired) who provided the book review.

All the staff at various archives and museums deserve a special mention, including those at National Archives (Kew), Ashmolean Museum (Oxford), Imperial War Museum plus many others, you know who you are.

Also, I would also take this opportunity to thank Damien Lewis, author, for his mentoring and support in getting the job done. All very much appreciated.

My Family

Jane (my ever-supportive wife), my son Mark, and my daughter Emma-Jane, all of whom have ensured that this the Second World War story is told.

There is one other person who needs to be thanked: Timothy Ibbetson, whose father had signed up to serve his country and joined the 6th (Royal Welch) Parachute Battalion, and a man who served in several conflicts and finally completing his service in Palestine. When given the opportunity of looking through the records and memorabilia of Fusilier Private Peter D Ibbetson, it became apparent that this should be documented. Henceforth Chapter 18 became an addition to the book and as an author I was only too pleased to hold back and get this story told, all as part of the book's title, *The Tunisian Campaign.*

My heartfelt gratitude to you all.

Bibliography

- Operation Torch
  - Operation Terminal
  - Naval Battle of Casablanca
- Tunisia Campaign
  - Battle of the Kasserine Pass
  - Battle of Sidi Bou Zid
  - Battle of Médenine
  - Battle of the Mareth Line
  - Battle of El Guettar
  - Operation Flax
  - Battle of Longstop Hill
  - Battle of Hill 609
  - Operation Vulcan & Strike
  - Operation Retribution

All the above operations researched at the National Archives in Kew, along with research carried out on the internet via Wikipedia, in close association with the US Army when obtaining consent/approval to use maps from that period and their Archives **(Email dated 20/09/2023: "Map(s) courtesy of the United States Military Academy Department of History.") Approved for use.** Along with *Encyclopaedia Brittanica* and listed books written by renowned war historians, which make incredible reading along with imperative research material.

Archives, Museums, and Research Organizations

The one prime place for looking at and undertaking research on the Second World War is the National Archives at Kew, which is rich in information when understanding and establishing the build-up to war in North Africa and Italy, as well as the movements of army battalions, RAF squadrons, naval fleets and their personnel.

The Ashmolean Museum in Oxford did work on establishing the period and age of the coins found in the Western Desert.

Other sources of information are the Imperial War Museums, RAF museums, Public Record Office, Census Records, RAF Disclosures, Royal Air Force History website, Ministry of Defence Air Historical Branch (RAF) and the Gloucestershire Heritage Hub.

Unpublished Sources

- Diary and notebooks written by LAC–Lamb L.B. 1012281
- Purchased postcards
- RAF War Records, held at National Archives Kew Gardens
- RAF Records Cranwell
- RAF Northolt
- RAF Historical Society
- Royal Air Forces Association
- Special Air Services (SAS)
- E.N.S.A.

National Archives Squadron Operational Reports

73 Squadron

AIR 27/631/21	AIR 27/632/9 (1)
AIR 27/631/22	AIR 27/632/10 (1)

AIR 27/631/23	AIR 27/632/11 (1)
AIR 27/631/24	AIR 27/632/12
AIR 27/632/1	AIR 27/632/13 (1)
AIR 27/632/2	AIR 27/632/14
AIR 27/632/3	AIR 27/632/15
AIR 27/632/4	AIR 27/632/16
AIR 27/632/5	AIR 27/633
AIR 27/632/6 (1)	AIR 27/638-1 (1)
AIR 27/632/7	AIR 27/638-2 (1)
AIR 27/632/8	AIR 27/639 (1)

Other Related AIRs

AIR 23/7069 operations Accolade, Husky, Avalanche and Tidal Wave dated 1943.

Other Researched Documents

Catalogue ref: HW 1/672
CAB 121/620
WOP 169/9298
PREM 3/311
CAB 122/1192
Operation Avalanche: WO 234/46
El Adem; WO 234/48
Tobruk: WO 234/49 Tobruk: WO 106/2273; ADM 199/862.
Battle of Kasserine Pass: HW1/1370; HW1/1380.
Tunisian Campaign: AIR 20/2567, WO 204/10334, WO 204/1579, WO 204/1580, WO 204/282, HW 12/287/1, WO 204/939; WO 204/5430; WO 244/115; WO 204/1653; WO 201/449.

Accreditations to Author and Image Providers

This book has been compiled using documents found and related to historical content of the battles fought and their outcome. The documents used have further enhanced and gives the book a greater historical meaning. It would be remiss of me to not say that if only those that fought in conflicts throughout 1939 to 1945 could have expressed their true feelings of what they endured would only speak about their experiences, only in the company of others that fought in the various battles. In writing and compiling this book I recognize the great value of those authors and image providers for their work that can be found in National Archives, IWM, Wikipedia, and I credit their work, which has helped me in completing the book.

Accreditations as follows

MOD, DDC Brand & Licensing Manager: Pauline Aquiline email 09/02/2022 Approval to use Squadron Insignia/Badges (only inside the book NOT on Front & Rear Covers)

RAF 73 Squadron: No restrictions all 'Public Domain'

National Archives: Contains public sector information licensed under the Open Government License v3.0.

Wikipedia

wiki@wikimedia.org Stephen Kirrage @ 15:58 on 2 May 2023 *[I think you are FREE to use providing CC BY-SA3.0 license rules apply.* ***Source:*** *Own Work by Author- S. Kirrage File: Tunisia 1942-1945, svg*

Source: www.dean.usma.edu *'The War at Sea 1939-1945, Chapter XII by S.W. Roskill*

Source: https://www.ibiblio.org/hyperwar/USA/USA-MTO-NWA/maps/USA-MTO-NWA-IX.jpg

Source: http://www.ibiblio.org/hyperwar/USA/USA-MTO-NWA/USA-MTO-NWA-26.html

Source: US Army Center of Military History Online Bookshelves

wiki@wikimedia.org Author: Stephen Kirrage, MarethMap1943.png: Memnon335bcderivative work.

Source: MarethMap1943.png: Creative Commons–CC BY-SA 3.0

wiki@wikimedia.org Author: Norman Einstein–own work

Source: File; Strait of Sicily map.png Creative Commons BY-SA 3.0

wiki@wikimedia.org

[Written consent via Wikipedia (82.39.186.68) (talk) 14:58 hours - 24 August 2023 (UTC)]

This covers all maps and articles covered by the Creative Commons BY-SA 3.0, provided that due accreditations are provided and adhered to.

This image is in the public domain because it contains materials that originally came from the United States Army Center of Military History. Source: http://www.history.army.mil/brochures/72-16/map1

Email dated 20/09/2023: "Map(s) courtesy of the United States Military Academy Department of History."

Imperial War Museum [London]: 4 images used in Chapter 16. Images E21337, E21338, E21340 and MH24415. All approved for use under IMW License LIC-30663-V3V8L4 Dated: 09/10/2023.

15th Army Group letter issued to all army personnel by General USA Commanding - Mark W. Clark. No restrictions all 'Public Domain'

Crown Copyright: Email received on 5 September 2023 from **Defence Intellectual Property Rights [DIPR-Crown Copyright] - Mr Richard Hieron** Copyright expiry set at 50 to 125 years after publication. The 50-year expiry period applies. Produced by The National Archives, Kew.

Timothy Ibbetson (son of the late Peter D. Ibbetson–Fusilier with the 6th (Royal Welch) Parachute Battalion). Original hardcopy photographs (outside 70 years expiry period).

Letter dated 6th November 2024 from Mr Timothy Ibbetson [son of Fusilier: Peter D. Ibbetson], giving approval/consent to use his father's memorabilia in this book. Documents and photographs used in Chapter 18 of this book.

Other Copyright Accreditations

Grich el Oued: *[Chapter 9]*
The following extract is taken from the Panzer Grenadier Headquarters (https://pg-hq.com)

The Army At War: Tunisia - dated 1944 *[prepared by the War Office for the Ministry of Information]. Part of the Army at War, Trilogy.*

(Crown copyright reserved. 50 years Rule Applies–Copyright expires 50 years after publication.)

National Portrait Gallery Company Ltd. *(John Hamilton Cubbon by Hay Wrightson Ltd)*

National Portrait Gallery Company Ltd–Invoice/Licence No. 69944 dated 17 November 2024 consent/approval to use image.

Daily Mirror / Reach PLC Accreditation *(Dakota Kit Bag Drop)*

REACH Publishing Services Limited - Pro Forma Invoice & Licence dated 13 December 2024, Account No. A0127673 giving consent/approval. ***Reach Purchasing Services Limited, Sales Invoice No. SGEIV015665 dated 30/01/2025.***

Major General J.H. Cubbon, DSO, CB & CBE: Details compiled by Harvey Grenville–Airborne Assault PARADATA and downloaded from their site as well as from Wikipedia. Full accreditation provided to the use of the information collated.

Dmg Media Licensing–Associated Newspapers Ltd. *(Operation Exercise/ Longstop)* No Copyright applies under the 70-year rule 'FREE TO USE'. Archive Projects Manager - Morag McFarland, Email dated 23/01/2025

iStock.com–Getty Images (UK) Limited. *(Invoice No. 2577673, Customer No. 36053127, date 01-March-2025, Sales Order No. 2102470271)* Image used in the preparation of the Front & Back Cover of Book

Published Books and Media

Reference to and extracts taken from the following reference books:

- *The Squadrons of the Royal Air Force & Commonwealth 1918–88* by James J. Halley.
- *The Squadrons of the Royal Air Force* by James J. Halley
- *The Desert Air War 1939–1945* by Richard Townshend Bickers
- *African Trilogy* by Alan Moorehead
- *Middle East 1940–1942, A Study in Air Power* by Philip Guedall
- *Rommel and the Defeat of the Allies–Tobruk 1942* by David Mitchell Hill-Green
- *The Second World War* by Antony Beevoir
- *All Hell Let Loose: The World at War 1939–1945* by Max Hastings
- *Finest Hours: Churchill as Warlord 1940–45* by Max Hastings
- *Tobruk: The Birth of a Legend* by Frank Harrison
- *Hurricane: The Last Witnesses* by Brian Milton
- *The Sky Suspended: A Fighter Pilot's Story* by Jim Bailey
- *Spitfire Ace of Aces: The Wartime Story of Johnnie Johnson* by Dilip Sarkar
- *They Flew Hurricane*s by Adrian Stewart
- *The History of 73 Squadron Volumes 1, 2 & 3* by Don Minterne
- *A Spitfire Named Connie* by Air Marshal 'Black' Robertson
- *From Spitfires to Vampires and Beyond: A Kiwi Ace's RAF Journey* by Owen Hardy
- *SAS Brothers in Arms* by Damien Lewis
- *Men of the Red Beret* by Max Arthur (Chapter 4, North Africa Operation Torch 1942–3)
- *The Army at War: The Eighth Army September 1941 to January 1943* Prepared for the War Office by the Ministry of Information (First published in 1944 S.O. Code 70-437*) Price 1s net
- The "TWO TYPES" by Jon–Produced by British Army Newspaper Unit, C.M.F. for the fighting men of all ranks and services in this theatre. DISTRIBUTED by the Directorate of Army Welfare Services AFHQ PRICE twenty-five lire a coy (see Forward)
- *My Middle East Campaigns* by Brian Robb, First published in 1944
- *Enter Trubshaw* by Major Ian Fenwick

- *Eighth Army 'Service of Thanksgiving'* (The Second World War Eighth Army Service of Thanksgiving was a ceremony held by the British Eighth Army in Egypt in 1942, to celebrate their victory over the Axis forces in the Western Desert Campaign[1]. The program of the service included hymns, prayers, readings and a message from King George VI.)
- *Headquarters 15th Army Group - To the Soldiers 'OF THE 15TH ARMY GROUP' May 1945* by Mark W. Clark General, USA Commanding
- *The Second World War North Africa & Italy 1940–1945 'One Man's Story'* by Philip Lamb, published in October 2022.
- *Operation Biting* by Max Hastings
- *The Army at War: Tunisia* dated 1944, prepared by the War Office for the Ministry of Information
- *Army at Dawn: The War in North Africa, 1942–1943* by Rick Atkinson
- A series of books written about the SAS - WWII and beyond by Damien Lewis
- *Winston S. Churchill: The Second World War: Volumes I to VI: The Gathering Storm, Their Finest Hour, The Grand Alliance, The Hinge of Fate, Closing the Ring and Triumph and Tragedy* by The Reprint Society, London

Letter Distributed and Issued to the 15th Army Group in 1945

The following letter was instigated by General Mark W. Clark, USA Commanding 15th Army Group and is one that epitomizes his thoughts and feelings for all the soldiers, airmen, sailors and the like under his command.

The letter itself makes fascinating reading and one that every service man at the time of the ongoing conflicts no doubt would have read, given the opportunity, and would have helped bolster their morale and helped them to overcome adversity whilst in the midst of battle when it was needed most, and those battles still to be fought to liberate the people and their country of the Nazi oppressors. The letter embodies the period that is inclusive of North Africa, Sicily, Italy and Europe campaigns each equally important when fighting the combined forces of Germany and Italy.

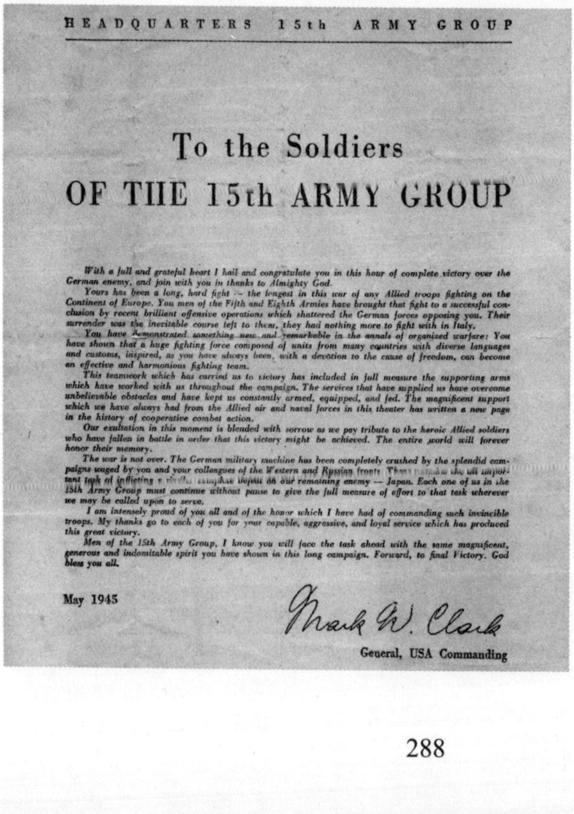

HEADQUARTERS 15th ARMY GROUP

To the Soldiers

OF THE 15th ARMY GROUP

With a full and grateful heart I hail and congratulate you in this hour of complete victory over the German enemy, and join with you in thanks to Almighty God.

Yours has been a long, hard fight — the longest in this war of any Allied troops fighting on the Continent of Europe. You men of the Fifth and Eighth Armies have brought that fight to a successful conclusion by recent brilliant offensive operations which shattered the German forces opposing you. Their surrender was the inevitable course left to them, they had nothing more to fight with in Italy.

You have demonstrated something new and remarkable in the annals of organized warfare: You have shown that a huge fighting force composed of units from many countries with diverse languages and customs, inspired, as you have always been, with a devotion to the cause of freedom, can become an effective and harmonious fighting team.

This teamwork which has carried us to victory has included in full measure the supporting arms which have worked with us throughout the campaign. The services that have supplied us have overcome unbelievable obstacles and have kept us constantly armed, equipped, and fed. The magnificent support which we have always had from the Allied air and naval forces in this theater has written a new page in the history of cooperative combat action.

Our exultation in this moment is blended with sorrow as we pay tribute to the heroic Allied soldiers who have fallen in battle in order that this victory might be achieved. The entire world will forever honor their memory.

The war is not over. The German military machine has been completely crushed by the splendid campaigns waged by you and your colleagues of the Western and Russian fronts. There remains the all important task of inflicting a similar complete defeat on our remaining enemy — Japan. Each one of us in the 15th Army Group must continue without pause to give the full measure of effort to that task wherever we may be called upon to serve.

I am intensely proud of you all and of the honor which I have had of commanding such invincible troops. My thanks go to each of you for your capable, aggressive, and loyal service which has produced this great victory.

Men of the 15th Army Group, I know you will face the task ahead with the same magnificent, generous and indomitable spirit you have shown in this long campaign. Forward, to final Victory. God bless you all.

May 1945

Mark W. Clark

General, USA Commanding

Index

Royal Air Force - Squadrons

About the Author

I was born in Pontypridd, Glamorgan, South Wales, on 24 September 1949 in Church Village Hospital (Top Floor). At the time, my mum and my sister lived with my grandfather and aunty in Nelson, 10 Wern Crescent, to be precise, then I came along and eventually lived there too. My father worked away in Gloucester and would visit us every two weeks, travelling down on what was then the 'Red & White' bus service. My childhood, which I can honestly say was incredible, was one in which I had some wonderful moments with my grandfather, otherwise known as Grandon, on a farm in the Welsh hills above Nelson.

When old enough I would ask my dad about his wartime experiences. Never did get the answers I was searching for; he would always say 'best left where they are'. We eventually moved to Gloucester in 1957, when I was 8 years old.

As the author of this book (the second of my Second World War books) – having little or no previous experience in writing other than the English essays we had to do at school – after my first attempt at writing and putting words together about the heroes from the Second World War, it is an honour to get their story told. As for myself, I am a retired engineer who over the years has been fortunate to work across many industries. In those years I have always had an interest in the RAF and other military services, which spurred me on to put down in words the experiences and exploits that made up my first published book *One Man's Story* (namely, my dad) and the writing of this book that tells of the battles fought.

I love reading historical military books and reading about those who gave their service for king and country, and in some cases, their lives, so that we could live in freedom.

This book is a follow on from my first introduction to becoming an author. Having got the writing bug, I felt that this book was my next step in relating the war operations undertaken during the North African campaigns and, in particular, those fought in Tunisia.

Finally, I dedicate this book to all the men and women who took part in the various conflicts of the Second World War, the greater majority of which are no longer with us. But through their fortitude and perseverance, **'They gave of their tomorrows, so that we can have our todays'**. God bless you all; thank you for your service and duty to king and country. May you all rest in peace.

I hope you have enjoyed the telling of their story during the reading of 'The Tunisian Campaign'.

Philip Lamb, Author